Introducing C To Pascal Programmers

Related Titles of Interest

Turbo Pascal® DOS Utilities, *Alonso*

Programming with Macintosh Turbo Pascal®, *Swan*

Turbo C® Survival Guide, *Miller and Quilici*

Advanced Turbo C® Programmer's Guide, *Mosich, Shammas, Flamig*

Turbo C® DOS Utilities, *Alonso*

Turbo C® and Quick C® Functions: Building Blocks for Efficient Code, *Barden*

The Turbo Programmer's Reference: Language Essentials, *Weiskamp*

Quick C® DOS Utilities, *Alonso*

C Programming Reference: An Applied Prospective, *Miller and Quilici*

C Wizard's Programming Reference, *Schwaderer*

Introducing C to Pascal Programmers, *Shammas*

DOS Productivity Tips and Tricks, *Held*

Introducing C To Pascal Programmers

NAMIR SHAMMAS

John Wiley & Sons, Inc.
New York • Chichester • Brisbane • Toronto • Singapore

Publisher: Stephen Kippur
Editor: Therese A. Zak
Managing Editor: Corinne McCormick
Electronic Book Production: Publishers Network, Morrisville, PA

This publication is designed to provide accurate and authoritative information in regard to the subject matter covered. It is sold with the understanding that the publisher is not engaged in rendering legal, accounting, or other professional services. If legal advice or other expert assistance is required, the services of a competent proffesional person should be sought. FROM A DECLARATION OF PRINCIPLES JOINTLY ADOPTED BY A COMMITTEE OF THE AMERICAN BAR ASSOCIATION AND A COMMITTEE OF PUBLISHERS.

Copyright © 1988 by John Wiley & Sons, Inc.

All rights reserved. Published simultaneously in Canada.

Reproduction or translation of any part of this work beyond that permitted by section 107 or 108 of the 1976 United States Copyright Act without the permission of the copyright owner is unlawful. Requests for permission or further information should be addressed to the Permission Department, John Wiley & Sons, Inc.

Librry of Congress Cataloging in Publication Data:

Shammas, Namir Clement, 1954–
  Introducing C to pascal programmers / Namir Clement Shammas.
     p. cm.

  ISBN 0-471-609080 (pbk.)
  1. C (Computer program language)   I. Title.
QA76.73.C1547   1988
005.13'3—dc19

Printed in the United States of America

88 89 10 9 8 7 6 5 4 3 2 1

*To my former colleague Riadh Al-Sabti,
wherever he may be, who taught me
that learning FORTRAN, and any other
programming language is fun.*

TRADEMARKS

Ada is a registered trademark of the U.S. Government, Ada Joint Program Office.

DEC PDP-11 is a trademark of Digital Equipment Corporation.

MS-DOS is a trademark of Microsoft Corporation.

PC-DOS is a trademark of International Business Machines.

Turbo C is a registered trademark of Borland International.

Turbo Pascal if a registered trademark of Borland International.

UCSD-Pascal is a trademark of the regions of the University of California, San Diego.

UNIX is a trademark of AT&T.

WordStar is a registered trademark of MicroPro International Corporation.

CONTENTS

Chapter 1: Why Learn C? — 1
The Origin of C — 1

Chapter 2: A Quick Tour of C — 4
General C Program Components — 4
Basic Data Types and Variables — 5
Operators — 6
Constants — 7
Basic Console I/O — 7
Decision-Making — 8
Loops — 10
Arrays — 11
Strings — 12
User-Defined Data Types — 13
Functions — 14
File I/O — 15

Chapter 3: Getting Started — 18
A Simple C Program — 18
Simple Data Types in C — 20
Constants In C — 24
Basic Console I/O in C — 26
Chapter Summary — 35

Chapter 4: C Operators — 36
Using Various Operators to Create Expressions — 36
Arithmetic Operators — 36
Increment and Assignment Operators — 39

Character Operators	43
Sizing Data Objects	45
Type Casting	47
Relational Operators and Conditional Expressions	51
Bit-Manipulation Operators	55
Comma Operator	58
Chapter Summary	60

Chapter 5: The C Preprocessor and Compiler Directives   62

The C Preprocessor	62
Predefined Macros	71
Compiler Directives	71
Chapter Summary	73

Chapter 6: Decision-Making   75

The if Statement	75
The switch Statement	85
Chapter Summary	93

Chapter 7: Loops   95

Loops: An Overview	95
The for Loop	96
Exiting Loops	104
The do-while Loop	105
The While Loop	111
Chapter Summary	119

Chapter 8: Simple Functions   120

Overview	120
C Functions	120
Making a C Function Work as a Procedure	131
Recursive Functions	135
Exiting Functions	137
Chapter Summary	137

Chapter 9: Pointers, Arrays, and Strings   139

Storage Classes	139
Scope of Variables	144
Pointers to Simple Data Types	148
Arrays in C: An Overview	153
One-Dimensional Arrays	153
MultiDimensional Arrays	157
Accessing Arrays with Pointers	161
Strings in C	169
Chapter Summary	182

Chapter 10: Enumerated and Structured Data Types   185

Type Redefinition in C	185
Enumerated Data Types	187
Structured Data Types	193
Accessing Arrays of Structures	196
Bitfields in C	203

Using Pointers to Structures	205
Unions and Pointers to Unions	211
Far Pointers	218
Chapter Summary	220

Chapter 11: Advanced Functions — 223

Using Arrays as Arguments	223
Using Strings as Arguments	227
Using Structures as Arguments	229
Passing Arguments by Reference Using Pointers	231
Passing Simple Variables and Simple Arrays	232
Passing Strings	236
Passing Structures	237
Passing Numeric Matrices	240
Passing Pointers to Dynamic Structures	244
More Array Sorting	251
Accessing the Command Line Arguments	259
Pointers to Functions	262
Functions with a Variable Number of Arguments	275
Chapter Summary	277

Chapter 12: Basic File I/O — 279

Modes of File I/O in C	279
Character I/O	282
String I/O	286
Writing and Reading Numeric Data Using Sequential Files	295
Binary Stream I/O	306
Using Structures to Write and Read Numeric Data in Binary Streams	306
Using Unions with Random Access Binary Streams	316
Stream I/O Error	328
Basic Low-Level File I/O	331
Chapter Summary	335

Appendix A: C Escape Sequences — 339

Appendix B: Formatted I/O String Control — 340

Appendix C: Predefined Data Types in Turbo C — 341

Appendix D: Operators in C — 342

Appendix E: Memory Models for Turbo C — 344

LISTINGS

Demonstration	Pascal Listing number	page	C Listing number	page
Greetings	3.1	18	3.2	19
Greetings			3.3	20
Simple data type	3.4	21	3.5	22
Constants	3.6	24	3.7	25
Constants			3.8	26
Formatted output			3.9	30
Character I/O	3.10	32		
Character I/O	3.11	33	3.12	33
Character I/O	3.13	34	3.14	34
Arithmetic operators	4.1	37	4.2	38
Arithmetic operators	4.3	41	4.4	42
Arithmetic operators			4.5	43
Character operators	4.6	44	4.7	44
sizeof operator	4.8	45	4.9	46
Type casting	4.10	48	4.11	49
Relational operators	4.12	52	4.13	54
Bit-manipulation operators	4.14	56	4.15	56
Bit-manipulation operators			4.16	57
Using #define			5.1	63
Using #define			5.2	69
Conditional compilation			5.3	72

xi

xii   INTRODUCING C TO PASCAL PROGRAMMERS

Demonstration	Pascal Listing		C Listing	
	number	page	number	page
if statement	6.1	77	6.2	77
if-else statement	6.3	79	6.4	80
nested if-else statements	6.5	81	6.6	82
Nested if-else statements	6.7	83	6.8	84
switch statement	6.9	87	6.10	88
switch statement			6.11	89
switch statement	6.12	90	6.13	91
switch statement	6.14	92		
for loop	7.1	96	7.2	97
for loop	7.3	98	7.4	98
Nested for loops	7.5	99	7.6	101
Open loop	7.7	103	7.8	103
Exiting for loops			7.9	105
do-while loop	7.10	106	7.11	106
do-while loop	7.12	108	7.13	109
while loop	7.14	111	7.15	112
while loop	7.16	114		
while loop	7.17	115	7.18	116
Word count	7.19	117	7.20	118
Square function	8.1	122	8.2	122
Solve root pf math function	8.3	124	8.4	125
Functions replacing macros			8.5	127
void functions			8.6	132
Recursive function	8.7	136	8.8	136
Static variables	9.1	140	9.2	141
Scope of variables	9.3	145	9.4	145
Scope of variables			9.5	146
Pointers to simple data types	9.6	151	9.7	152
Simple array	9.8	154	9.9	155
Simple array	9.10	156	9.11	157
Two-dimensional array	9.12	159	9.13	159
Initializing a C matrix			9.14	161
Accessing an array with a pointer			9.15	163
Accessing an array with a pointer			9.16	164
Sieve benchmark	9.17	165	9.18	166
Sieve benchmark			9.19	166
Accessing a matrix with a pointer			9.20	168
Translate characters of a string	9.21	170	9.22	170

CONTENTS xiii

Demonstration	Pascal Listing number	page	C Listing number	page
Translate characters of a string	9.23	171		
String manipulation	9.24	172	9.25	173
Enumerated types	10.1	189	10.2	190
Enumerated types			10.3	192
Sorting with structures	10.4	196	10.5	197
Sorting with nested structures	10.6	201	10.7	202
Bitfields			10.8	204
Sorting with pointers to structures	10.9	206	10.10	208
Sorting with pointers to structures			10.11	209
Complex math with unions	10.12	213	10.13	214
Complex math with unions			10.14	216
Far pointers and direct video output			10.15	219
Far pointers and direct video output			10.16	219
Passing arrays to functions	11.1	224	11.2	225
Passing arrays to functions	11.3	226		
Passing strings to functions	11.4	227	11.5	228
Passing structures to functions	11.6	230	11.7	231
Passing arrays by reference	11.8	232	11.9	233
Passing strings to functions	11.10	236	11.11	237
Passing structures	11.12	238	11.13	239
Matrix inversion benchmark	11.14	241	11.15	242
Binary tree benchmark	11.16	245	11.17	246
Binary tree benchmark	11.18	248	11.19	249
Quick sort	11.20	251	11.21	252
Interactive Shell sort	11.22	254	11.23	256
Accessing command line arguments	11.24	260	11.25	261
Pointer to a function			11.26	263
Pointer to a function			11.27	268
Pointer to a function			11.28	272
Variable number of arguments			11.29	276
WordStar to ASCII converter (character I/O)	12.1	283	12.2	285
File printer (string I/O)	12.3	289	12.4	290
File Lister (string I/O)	12.5	292	12.6	293
Write strings to sequential file	12.7	296	12.8	298
Read strings from sequential file	12.9	302	12.10	303

Demonstration	Pascal Listing		C Listing	
	number	page	number	page
Write structure to sequential file	12.11	308	12.12	310
Read structure from sequential file	12.13	314	12.14	315
Write union to sequential file	12.15	318	12.16	320
Read union from sequential file	12.17	324	12.18	326
Stream I/O error			12.19	328
Copy file	12.20	333	12.21	334

INTRODUCTION

This introductory book is written for the Pascal programmer who wants to learn C using microcomputer implementations. While the material caters to these two languages in general, specifics and examples are presented based on two popular Pascal and C implementations: Turbo Pascal (version 4) and Turbo C (version 1.5 and up).

The reader is assumed to be at least moderately familiar with programming in Pascal. The basic presentation strategy employs listings in Pascal and their equivalent versions in C. Learning by comparing similar listings of the two languages enables the reader to draw on his or her experience as a Pascal programmer. This permits the reader to learn about the similarities and differences between the two languages and gradually develop a working knowledge of C. To accomplish this goal, simple (but not too trivial), short, and easy-to-read Pascal programs are generally used. The Pascal source code allows the reader to understand in more depth the task of the equivalent C listing. Throughout the chapters there are special notes for programming in C, as well as Pascal-to-C translation hints.

CHAPTER

1

Why Learn C?

THE ORIGIN OF C

C is a language that has come of age. Its roots go back to the BCPL language, developed by Martin Richards, and the B language, developed by Kenneth Thompson in 1970. C itself was developed for and implemented under UNIX™, by Dennis Ritchie, at Bell Laboratories, and first ran on a DEC PDP-11™ in the early 1970s. C was the first high-level assembler (that is, a cross between an assembler and a high-level language) that was successfully used to port UNIX over to different machines.

The ANSI Standard for C

In 1978, Prentice-Hall published *The C Programming Language* by, Brian Kernighan and Dennis Ritchie. This book described the C version accompanying the UNIX version 5. Dubbed the K&R definition, the book provided a de facto language reference, despite the fact that no ANSI standard existed for C in the seventies. In 1983, an ANSI standard committee was formed to look into the issue of defining a standard for C. In 1987, the committee completed its work, introducing a number of modifications over the K&R definition. This book looks at the ANSI standard and not the K&R definition.

The Dual Nature of C

Using C to write operating systems (like UNIX and MS-DOS®, to name a few) draws from its powerful features as a high-level assembler. Essentially, C is a small-core language with no predefined I/O routines whose compilers are notorious for producing fast and tight code. As a structured high-level assembler, C enjoys two natures, depending on the type of application for which it is used.

C as a High-Level Structured Language

You can use C as a high-level language and take advantage of its support for extended numeric precision, user-definable record structures, powerful operators, loops, and decision-making constructs. Consequently, high-level applications can be developed in various fields, such as statistics, engineering design, accounting, and database management. As a high-level language, C is compared with other similar, well-known languages, such as Pascal, Modula-2, and Ada.

C: The High-Level Assembler

On the other hand, you can employ the power of C to perform advanced data manipulation and low-level access and to implement some unusual programming tricks. C gives you the freedom to perform these tasks, assuming that you know what you are doing. Compared to Pascal, C removes programming guard rails and puts more responsibility on the programmer's shoulders. Thus, C can be used to develop many low-level applications, such as operating systems, compilers, interpreters, and word processors.

The Journey From Pascal To C

Why migrate from Pascal to C? Why change from one structured language to another? Is it worth it? These are some of the questions that Pascal programmers might ask in contemplating learning C.

As a Pascal programmer, you developed the skill of crafting your programs in a structured, modular manner. The more a software developer programs in a language, the more programming tricks he or she discovers. However, there is usually an asymptotic limit that is reached, beyond which any language cannot be pushed. You can rewrite Pascal programs to run faster or compile into smaller code, until further refinement is either not possible or not feasible. The above reason points to one of the major reasons why high-level programmers migrate to C: to develop programs that have more speed and/or smaller code.

The good news for you as a Pascal programmer is that you already have the experience of using a structured language. This makes learning C easier than, say, if you migrated from BASIC. Keep in mind that C has its own peculiar way of handling a number of program aspects, such as strings, nested expressions, and terse expression, to name a few. It is important to pick up these new notions in C. Practice is the best method suggested. Therefore, practice as much as you can!

CHAPTER

2

A Quick Tour of C

CHAPTER GOALS

This chapter gives an overview of the C language. It is aimed at the reader who wants to start learning C by first gaining a general view of the language, before going into the details. You may move directly to the next chapter if this does not apply to you.

GENERAL C PROGRAM COMPONENTS

C programs are composed of global declarations and single-level functions. The general form of a C program is

```
/* This is a comment */
<global declarations>
main()
{
  <local declarations>
  <function statements>
}
<other functions declared here>
```

Each C program must contain the function **main**. The runtime system starts executing the program beginning with **main**. C comments are enclosed in pairs of /* and */. Single C statements and declarations always end with a semicolon, and blocks of statements are enclosed within the open and close braces. In addition, identifiers in C are case-sensitive, as in Modula-2, unlike BASIC and Pascal.

BASIC DATA TYPES AND VARIABLES

Basic data types in C include the following:

Data Type Identifier	Category
char	character
int	integer
float	floating point
double	double-precision floating point

In addition, C employs type modifiers to manipulate the signed representation and precision of the above basic data types. They are as follows:

Data Type Modifier	Effect
signed	High bit is used for a +/- sign
unsigned	High bit is used to contribute to number
long	Extend precision
short	Reduce precision

For historical reasons, the **long** modifier may be used as a shorthand for **long int**.

Declaring variables (and functions) involves stating the data type first, followed by the identifier name. Examples are

```
short int i;
double x = 3.24;
long n = 70000;
long int m;
char c = 'a';
```

The above declarative statements also reveal that C allows the initialization of variables when they are declared.

Pointers are special variables in C. They specialize in storing the addresses of other variables. To make them more versatile, C requires that you associate them with a data type. This enables your program to perform special pointer arithmetic: altering the value of a pointer by **n** changes the address it is pointing to by (n * size of data type it points to). Pointers are declared by placing an * before the pointer name, as in:

```
/* declare a pointer to int and an int variable */
int *ptr1, i;
/* declare two pointers to int, int* is a pointer type   */
int* ptr1, j;
```

The first statement declares both a pointer to **int** and an integer variable. The second statement declares two integer-pointers, since the **int*** is a pointer-to-integer type.

Pointers must be initialized by making reference to existing data objects or through dynamic allocation. The ampersand is the operator used to obtain the address of a data object. Once a pointer is assigned an address, you can access it using the asterisk operator. An example is as follows:

```
main()
{
  int i, j, *int_ptr;
  double x = 23.2, y = 78.9;
  double* dbl_ptr = &x; /* assign address of x to pointer */
  i = 3;
  j = 5;
  int_ptr = &i; /* assign address of i to pointer */
  /* access integer pointer */
  *int_ptr = 2 * j + *int_ptr; /* same as i = 2 * j + i */
  /* access double pointer */
  *dbl_ptr = *dbl_ptr * x * y; /* same as x = x * x * y */
}
```

OPERATORS

C is a language that comes with a rich and powerful set of operators. They fall into the following categories:

1. Arithmetic operators. They include +, -, /, *, and % (the modulus).
2. Relational and bitwise operators. These include the following sets:

Relational Operator	Bitwise Operator	Function
&&	&	AND
||	|	OR
	^	XOR
	~	NOT
	>>	Shift right
	<<	Shift left
>		greater than
<		less than
>=		greater or equal
<=		less or equal
==		equal to
!=		not equal to

3. Pointer operators. These include the & to obtain the address of an object, and * to access its contents.
4. Increment and decrement operators. C uses the ++ and -- operators to, respectively, increment and decrement the value of a simple variable by 1. Applying these operators to a pointer causes the address used by the pointer to alter by the byte-size of the referenced data type.
5. Assignment operators. They include the basic assignment operator (the equal sign) as well as arithmetic and bitwise assignment operators. The last two enable you to write shorter statements using the general form:

    <variable> <assignment operator> <expression>

    which is equivalent to the the longer form:

    <variable> = <variable> <operator> <expression>

For example,
x += 10

is equivalent to long form,
x = x + 10

CONSTANTS

Under the new ANSI standard, C provides two routines to define constants. The first and older way employs the **#define** preprocessor to define macros.

```
#define ARRAY_SIZE 100
#define MESSAGE "Prototype version 1.0"
```

When the compiler runs, it first invokes the preprocessor to substitute the defined macros with their values.

The second and newer routine employs the **const** keyword to define a fixed data object. Such constants are declared in a manner similar to declaring initialized variables. An example is as follows:

```
const char DELIMITER = '|';
const int  SIZE = 100;
const double GRAVITY = 98.1;
```

BASIC CONSOLE I/O

The C language relies on a number of libraries to supply all I/O routines. The "stdio.h" is the standard I/O header file that should be included in C programs. The **printf** function provides flexible formatted-output. The **printf** accepts a variable number of arguments: the first must be a string constant or variable. The following example illustrates **printf** at work:

```
#include <stdio.h>
main()
{
    int i = 77;
    printf("Hello world");
    printf("\n i = %d \n", i);
}
```

The first **printf** is used to display a message. The second one illustrates the formatting power of **printf**. The **\n** is interpreted as a request to send a carriage return. As a matter of fact, C supports a number of other control characters in the form "\<character>". The "%d" is another format control command that informs **printf** to display an integer. The **printf** function accepts a set of % format commands that specify the exact form of display, including numeric representation (that is, hexadecimal or octal) and width used to display a variable.

The "stdio.h" offers the formatted input function, **scanf**. It uses a format control string, similar to that of **printf**, to define the exact form of the console input. The **scanf** accepts a variable number of arguments: the first must be a string constant or variable. The other arguments must be addresses of the variables receiving the data. An example of console I/O using **printf** and **scanf** is as follows:

```
#include <stdio.h>
main()
{
   int i, j;
   long k;
   printf("Enter two integers delimited ");
   printf("by a single space : ");
   scanf("%d %d", &i, &j);
   k = i + j;
   printf("\n %d + %d = %ld \n", i, j, k);
}
```

The "conio.h" offers other routines to perform character I/O. While **printf** and **scanf** can be used for the same purpose, many C programmers prefer the specialized routines, since they compile into tighter code. Single characters can be read from the keyboard using the **getch** and **getche** functions. Similarly, the **putch** and **putchar** are used to display characters. An example of simple character I/O is as follows:

```
#include <stdio.h>
#include "conio.h"
main()
{
   char c, d;
   printf("Enter a character : ");
   c = getche(); /* input with echo */
   printf("\nYou typed ");
   putchar(c);
   printf("\nEnter a character : ");
   d = getch(); /* input with no echo */
   printf("\nYou typed ");
   putchar(d);
}
```

DECISION-MAKING

Logical expressions in C must always be enclosed in parentheses. If the value of a logical expression is 0, it is interpreted as a false boolean value, otherwise it is true.

C supports the **if** and **if-else** constructs with the ability to nest them. There is no **then** keyword. An example of a simple if statement is as follows:

```
#include <stdio.h>
#include "conio.h"
main()
{
   char c;
   printf("Enter a character : ");
   c = getche(); /* input with echo */
   if (c >= 'a' && c <= 'z') {
```

```
        c += 'A' - 'a'; /* convert to uppercase */
        printf("\nThe uppercase equivalent is %c", c);
    }
}
```

The **if-else** adds the **else** clause to offer an alternate course of action when the tested expression is false. The following program toggles the case of a letter:

```
#include <stdio.h>
#include "conio.h"
main()
{
    char c;
    int shift = 'a' - 'A';
    printf("Enter a character : ");
    c = getche(); /* input with echo */
    if (c >= 'A' && c <= 'z') {
    /* make sure that you typed a character */
        if (c >= 'a' && c <= 'z') {
            c -= shift; /* convert to uppercase */
            printf("\nThe uppercase equivalent is %c \n", c);
        }
        else {
            c += shift; /* convert to lowercase */
            printf("\nThe lowercase equivalent is %c \n", c);
        }
    }
}
```

In addition to the **if** construct, C implements the **switch** construct that replaces a battery of **if-else** statements. The **switch** statement uses case labels with constant values to select the course of action. The **break** statement is employed to exit from a case label once its statements are all executed. An example of using the **switch** statement is shown below:

```
#include <stdio.h>
#include "conio.h"
main()
{
    char c;
    printf("Enter a digit : ");
    c = getche(); /* input with echo */
     switch (c) {
       case '1':
       case '3':
       case '5':
       case '7':
       case '9':
          printf("\nYou typed an odd digit");
          break;
       case '0':
       case '2':
       case '4':
       case '6':
       case '8':
```

```
            printf("\nYou typed an even digit");
            break;
         default:
            printf("\nYou did not enter a digit");
      }
}
```

As the above example shows, C does not provide a mechanism to consolidate case labels into a shorter form.

LOOPS

There are three loop constructs in C: **for**, **do-while**, and **while**. The **for** loop in C is very different than loops with similar names in other languages. The **for** loop can act as a fixed, conditional, or open loop. The **for** loop has three control parts: initialization, loop-termination test, and loop increment. A normal usage of the **for** loop is shown in the next program that displays the square of integers between 1 and 20:

```
#include <stdio.h>
main()
{
   int i;
   for (i = 1; i <= 20; i++)
   /*       —    —     —
            ^    ^     ^
            |    |     |
            |    |     +— increment loop counter by 1
            |    |
            |    +— loop-continuation test
            |
            initialize loop counter
   */
      printf("%d squared = %d \n", i, i*i);
}
```

The three parts of the **for** loop are optional. If all of them are omitted, the **for** loop behaves like an infinite loop.

The **do-while** loop continues to iterate as long as the expression tested in the while clause is not 0. The **for** loop example is translated into the following **do-while** loop:

```
#include <stdio.h>
main()
{
   int i = 1;
   do {
      printf("%d squared = %d \n", i, i*i);
      i++;
   } while (i <= 20);
}
```

The **while** conditional loop iterates as long as the logical expression tested is not 0. Rewriting the above example using the **while** loop, you have the following:

```
#include <stdio.h>
main()
{
   int i = 1;
   while (i <= 20) {
      printf("%d squared = %d \n", i, i*i);
      i++;
   }
}
```

ARRAYS

When arrays in C are declared, their size is specified. C has the lower bound of every array dimension fixed at 0. Each dimension is enclosed in its own set of brackets. The following example declares and accesses a 20-element array of integers:

```
#include <stdio.h>
#define MAX 20
main()
{
   int i;
   int x[MAX]; /* declare x[0],x[1],...,x[19] */
   for (i = 0; i < MAX; i++) {
      x[i] = i * i - 10;
      printf("x[%d] = %d \n", i, x[i]);
   }
}
```

Multidimensional arrays are declared and accessed in a similar fashion. Keep in mind that each dimension employs a separate set of brackets. The following example illustrates the declaration and access of a matrix:

```
#include <stdio.h>
#define MAX_ROW 20
#define MAX_COL 3
main()
{
   int row, col;
   int x[MAX_ROW][MAX_COL]; /* declare x[0][0] to x[19][2] */
   /* use nested for loop to access the matrix */
   for (j = 0; j < MAX_COL; j++) {
      for (i = 0; i < MAX_ROW; i++) {
         x[i][j] = i * i + j * i - 10;
         printf("x[%d][%d] = %d \n", i, j, x[i][j]);
      }
   }
}
```

STRINGS

C regards strings as arrays of characters that always terminate with an ASCII 0 (that is, the null character). This permits strings in C to go well beyond the 255 character of Turbo Pascal strings. When dimensioning a string as an array of characters, you must take into consideration the space required to store the null character.

String I/O from the console may be performed using **printf** and **scanf**. However, the **gets** and **puts** functions are specialized in string I/O. The following example shows string I/O and character-by-character case conversion:

```
#include <stdio.h>
#define MAX 81
main()
{
   int i;
   char string[MAX];
   printf("Enter a string : ");
   gets(string);
   for (i = 0; string[i] != '\0'; i++);
      if (string[i] >= 'a' && string[i] <= 'z')
         string[i] += 'A' - 'a';

   printf("\nThe uppercase version is: ");
   puts(string);
}
```

Notice that the **gets** and **puts** functions take the bare string name. This is very significant and special for C. The bare name of an array is a pointer to its first element. Thus, the identifier **string** is the same as **&string[0]**. Pointers are used in C to manipulate arrays and strings more efficiently than array indexing. Consequently, the array reference **string[i]** is replaced by ***(ptr + i)**, where **ptr** is a pointer to the first string character **string[0]**. The above example can be rewritten as follows:

```
#include <stdio.h>
#define MAX 81
main()
{
   int i;
   char string[MAX], *ptr;
   printf("Enter a string : ");
   gets(string);
   ptr = string; /* or ptr = &string[0] */
   for (i = 0; *(ptr+i) != '\0'; i++);
      if (*(ptr + i) >= 'a' && *(ptr + i) <= 'z')
         *(ptr + i) += 'A' - 'a';
   printf("\nThe uppercase version is: ");
   puts(string);
}
```

USER-DEFINED DATA TYPES

Under the new ANSI standard, C enables your programs to define enumerated data types. Enumerated types assign integer values to sets of unique identifiers to enhance the readability of you program. Thus, explicit numeric coding for sets of objects, such as weekdays, colors, and program status, is replaced with unique and highly readable words. Examples of enumerated types are

```
enum booleans { FALSE, TRUE };
enum colors { red, blue, green };
enum days { Sun, Mon, Tue, Wed, Thu, Fri, Sat };
```

By default, the first element of an enumerated type is assigned 0, the second one is assigned 1, and so on. An example of using the **booleans** enumerated type is

```
#include <stdio.h>
#include "conio.h"
enum booleans { FALSE, TRUE };
main()
{
   double a, b, c;
   char ch;
   enum boolean flag;
   do {
      printf("\nEnter first number : "); scanf("%lf", &a);
      printf("Enter second number : "); scanf("%lf", &b);
      c = a + b;
      printf("c = %lf\n", c);
      printf("Add more numbers ? (Y/N) ");
      ch = getche();
      if (ch == 'Y' || ch == 'y')
         flag = TRUE;
      else
         flag = FALSE;
   } while (flag == TRUE);
}
```

C also permits your applications to define structures that connect logically related fields of various data types. For example, the following structure enables you to define a mailing address record:

```
/* structure name is 'mail_rec' */
struct mail_rec {
            char last_Name[31];      /* field 1 */
            char middle;             /* field 2 */
            char first_Name[31];     /* field 3 */
            char address[31];        /* field 4 */
            char city[21];           /* field 5 */
            char state[3];           /* field 6 */
            char zip[11];            /* field 7 */
            int age;                 /* field 8 */
            double weight;           /* field 9 */
   };
```

Declaring a structure-type variable involves the keyword **struct**, the structure name, and the declared variable name. Using the **mail_rec** as an

example, a C program is able to declare the variable **mail** using:
```
struct mail_rec mail;
```
To access the fields of structured variables you state its name and the sought field, delimited by a dot. For example, a reference to the **last_Name** and **age** fields employs
```
mail.last_name[0]  <-- the first character of the array field
mail.age
```
Pointers to structures are popular in accessing C structures. They are declared by combining the rules of declaring pointers and structures. For example, to declare a pointer to the **mail_rec** data type, use
```
    struct mail_rec mail, *mail_ptr = &mail;
```
To access the fields of structured variables using a pointer, replace the dot with the **->** operator. For example, to make a reference to the **last_Name** and **age** fields using the **mail_ptr** pointer, you write
```
mail_ptr->last_name[0]
mail_ptr->age
```
C implements another structure type with its fields overlaid in memory. This data structure is called the union. It enables you to examine the same data in different ways. An example of a union is
```
union four {
      int i[2];
      long j;
      };
```
Union-type variables and pointers are declared in a manner very similar to C structures. The difference is that the union fields offer alternate ways to store information instead of a complementary framework.

FUNCTIONS

C is a small-core language that thrives on functions to extend it. It supports nonnested functions that are declared using the following general syntax:
```
<type> <function_name>(<parameter list>)
{
   <local declaration of data types, constants and variables>
   <statements for the function body>
   return <expression for the function value>;
}
```
Under the new ANSI standard, the parameter list consists of a comma-delimited list containing the type and the name of each parameter. Functions can declare their own constants, data types, and variables that are not accessible by other functions. The **return** statement is utilized to supply the function value to the calling routine. The ANSI standard has formally recognized functions that perform a specific task, with no **return** statements (and hence emit no value).

The ANSI standard provides the typeless **void** to be used as the returned typed for such functions.

An example of a simple function is shown in the following program that calculates the square root of a number:

```
#include <stdio.h>
main()
{
   double x;
   /* declare prototype of function */
   double sqrt(double, double);
   printf("Enter a number : ");
   scanf("%lf", &x);
   printf("\nsqrt(%lf) = %lf\n", x, sqrt(x, 0.00001));
}
double sqrt(double guess, double accr)
{
   double t, q = accr * accr, s = guess / 2.0;
   if (guess >= 0.0) {
      do {
         s = (guess/s + s) / 2;
         t = s*s - guess;
      } while (t*t > q);
      return s;
   }
   else
      return -1;
}
```

The above program also reveals another ANSI rule for declaring functions in **main**, called function prototyping. It informs the compiler of the function form and enables it to trap illegal function calls (that is, those with the wrong type and/or number of arguments). Function prototyping is required for all functions that do not return a result of the **int** type. Functions with no parameters use **void** to indicate that no arguments are involved in the function call.

FILE I/O

The standard library "stdio.h" provides C applications with file and device I/O. To unify the treatment of these different I/O devices, the C library supports the abstract concept of character or byte streams. This notion or abstraction exists in the high-level I/O that involves text and binary streams, as well as the low-level system I/O.

Text streams are different from binary streams in the fact that the text I/O routines translate certain characters during the I/O operations.

Text and binary streams are opened and closed using the **fopen** and **fclose** functions, respectively. The "stdio.h" library defines the type FILE which is used to declare the file pointers required in the stream I/O. Text stream input is carried out using the **fgets** and **fscanf** functions, and the output mode utilizes the **fputs** and **fprintf** functions. The following example illustrates the use of text stream I/O to copy the contents of one file to the printer (itself treated as a file):

```
#include <stdio.h>
#define SIZE 81
```

```
main()
{
    FILE *inptr, *outptr;
    char infile[65], outfile[65] = "prn";
    char line[SIZE];
    do {
        printf("Enter input filename : ");
        gets(infile);
        /* open to read in text mode */
        inptr = fopen(infile, "rt");
        if (inptr == NULL)
            printf("\nCannot open file %s\n",infile);
    } while (infile == NULL);
    do {
        printf("Enter output filename : ");
        gets(outfile);
        /* open to write in text mode */
        outptr = fopen(outfile, "wt");
        if (outptr == NULL)
            printf("\nCannot open file %s\n",outfile);
    } while (outfile == NULL);
    while(! feof(inptr) ) {
        fgets(line, SIZE-1, inptr); /* read line from infile */
        fputs(line, outptr);    /* write line to outfile */
    }
    /* close text streams */
    fclose(inptr);
    fclose(outptr);
}
```

The above program reads one text file and writes it to another. Not apparent in the code is the string delimiter conversion that occurs behind the scene when a text line is read and written.

Binary stream I/O employs the **fread** and **fwrite** functions to read and write bytes, respectively. The above program can be adapted to copy any file by using binary streams, as shown below:

```
#include <stdio.h>
#define BUFFER 1024
main()
{
    FILE *inptr, *outptr;
    char infile[65], outfile[65];
    char line[BUFFER];
    int num_read;
    do {
        printf("Enter input filename : ");
        gets(infile);
        /* open to read in binary mode */
        inptr = fopen(infile, "rb");
        if (inptr == NULL)
            printf("\nCannot open file %s\n",infile);
    } while (infile == NULL);
    do {
```

```
        printf("Enter output filename : ");
        gets(outfile);
        /* open to write in binary mode */
        outptr = fopen(outfile, "wb");
        if (outptr == NULL)
            printf("\nCannot open file %s\n",outfile);
    } while (outfile == NULL);
    do {
        /* read buffer from infile */
        num_read = fread(line, sizeof(char), BUFFER, inptr);
        /* write buffer to outfile */
        fwrite(line, sizeof(char), num_read, outptr);
    } while (num_read == BUFFER);
    /* close binary streams */
    fclose(inptr);
    fclose(outptr);
}
```

The above program uses a large memory buffer to carry out stream I/O.

Using stream I/O, an application is able to read and write data structures, such as arrays, structures, and unions. In addition, binary streams enable you to use the **fseek** function to alter the location of the file pointer. This gives a powerful random-access capability.

Low-level system I/O is somewhat similar to binary streams. It uses its own set of functions and delegates the responsibility of buffer management to your applications.

CHAPTER

3

Getting Started

CHAPTER GOALS

- Getting started with simple C programs.
- Introducing data types supported by C.
- Using constants in C.
- Basic console I/O in C.

A SIMPLE C PROGRAM

The first C program I present follows in the footsteps of many language introduction books. This trivial program merely displays a greeting message and may be useful in familiarizing you with the process of compiling a C program. The Pascal version is shown below:

Listing 3.1

```
PROGRAM Greetings1;
{ simple Pascal program that greets you }
BEGIN
    WRITE('Hello World!')
END.
```

The C version, shown below, does not appear to be very complex either:

Listing 3.2

```
/* simple C program that greets you */
main()
{
   printf("Hello World!");
}
```

In comparing the two listings, let me point out the following features of the C language:

1. Comments in C are enclosed in **/*** and ***/**. The braces used for comments in Pascal are employed for entirely different purposes in C. Certain compilers may allow nested comments. In Turbo C you can enable or disable nested comments.

2. C has no formal keywords that parallel the Pascal PROGRAM and "END.", which declare the start and finish of a program, respectively. In addition, a C program has only two levels of coding: global and single-level function bodies. In C, the **main()** function is very unique in the fact that, at run-time, it is the function that is executed first. In Pascal, the main function body follows all of the other data and routine declarations. In C the main function can be anywhere. However, I will adopt the convention of placing the main function as the first one, following global declarations. There is also another important difference between the **main()** function of C and the main code segment of a Pascal program. Function **main()** can have its own local data objects and still access any global data objects. No similar local scope exists for the main program code in Pascal.

3. In C you enclose string constants in double quotes, while character constants are placed within single quotes.

4. The open and close braces in C are equivalent to the BEGIN and END block-containing keywords in Pascal.

5. All C statements require the semicolon as a statement delimiter. If you remove the semicolon from the C program and attempt to recompile, you will get a compile-time error. In this respect, C is more systematic in requiring the semicolon at the end of statements than Pascal. Using semicolons in Pascal is context sensitive.

6. The **printf** function (it really IS a function whose result is ignored) in C is similar to the predefined Pascal WRITE procedure. Both **printf** and WRITE accept a list of arguments that varies in size. As I will demonstrate later, **printf** is actually more powerful and versatile than WRITE. If you are familiar with the FORTRAN language, then think of **printf** as somewhat similar to the combination of the WRITE and FORMAT statements in FORTRAN.

An important difference between the **printf** function (and all other I/O functions in C) and the Pascal WRITE procedure is that the C language does not define I/O operations as part of the core language. Instead, C is a small-core language that relies on various libraries to supply programs with I/O functions, and **printf** is one of them. The **printf** function is defined in the standard I/O library, "stdio.h". A more correct version of the C greeting program should literally include the "stdio.h" file, as shown below:

Listing 3.3

```
/* simple C program that greets you */
/* the following compiler directive
   works like {$I stdio.h} in Pascal */
#include <stdio.h>
main()
{
   printf("Hello World!");
}
```

What is the difference between the two C versions? In the first version, you relied on the intelligence of the compiler to implicitly include "stdio.h". In the second version, I have added a compiler directive to include "stdio.h" explicitly, a better practice. Compiler directives are discussed in the next chapter.

SIMPLE DATA TYPES IN C

In general, the data types and structures of C and Pascal are fairly similar. C supports the following simple data types: **char, int, float, double,** and **void.** The first four types parallel the CHAR, INTEGER, REAL, and EXTENDED in Turbo Pascal 4. The **void** type is a valueless data type whose use will be explained later, when I discuss functions. Unlike Pascal, C also supports type modifiers to enable you, so to speak, to fine-tune the value ranges of the above simple data types. The type modifiers are: **signed, unsigned, short,** and **long.** Table 3.1 shows the different data type combinations resulting from applying the type modifiers, their ranges, sizes, and the closest corresponding Pascal data type. Notice that the boolean and string types are missing from the table, since C does not formally support them. Boolean types in C are emulated using integers, and strings are considered to be arrays of characters.

You may have noticed that a number of different data type declarations have the same range, such as **double** and **long double.** The duplication depends on the C implementation and most likely differs from one compiler to another, especially those implemented on different processors. It is also interesting to note that Turbo Pascal 4 is able to match almost all of the C data types, with the exception of the **unsigned long int.** Earlier Turbo Pascal versions lacked the SHORTINT, WORD, and LONGINT data types.

Table 3.1   The different simple data types in C

Simple Data Type	Byte Size	Value Range	Pascal Type
char	1	-128 to 127	CHAR and SHORTINT
signed char	1	-128 to 127	SHORTINT
unsigned char	1	0 to 255	BYTE
int	2	-32768 to 32767	INTEGER
signed int	2	-32768 to 32767	INTEGER
unsigned int	2	0 to 65535	WORD
short int	2	-32768 to 32767	INTEGER
signed short int	2	-32768 to 32767	INTEGER
unsigned short int	2	0 to 65535	WORD
long int	4	-2147483648 to 2147483647	LONGINT
signed long int	4	-2147483648 to 2147483647	LONGINT
unsigned long int	4	0 to 4294967295	none
float	4	3.4E-38 to 3.4E+38 and -3.4E-38 to -3.4E+38	SINGLE
long float	8	1.7E-308 to 1.7E+308 and -1.7E-308 to -1.7E+308	DOUBLE
double	8	1.7E-308 to 1.7E+308 and -1.7E-308 to -1.7E+308	DOUBLE
long double	8	1.7E-308 to 1.7E+308 and -1.7E-308 to -1.7E+308	EXTENDED

To demonstrate the declarations and use of various simple data types, I present the following simple program in its Pascal and C versions. The program declares a number of variables, assigns values to them, and displays a few values and results. The Pascal version is

Listing 3.4

```
PROGRAM Simple_Data;
{$N+}
{ program to demo simple use of basic
  data types of Turbo Pascal 4         }
VAR k : SHORTINT;
    i : INTEGER;
    j : BYTE;
    n : WORD;
    m : LONGINT;
    c : CHAR;
    x : SINGLE;
    y : DOUBLE;
BEGIN
```

22   INTRODUCING C TO PASCAL PROGRAMMERS

```
      { assign values }
      k := 1;
      i := 10;
      j := 2;
      n := 40000;
      m := 1000000;
      c := 'X';
      x := 10.5;
      y := 2.5;
      { display a few expressions }
      WRITELN(j:1,' + ',i:2,' = ',(i+j):2);
      WRITELN('Character c stores ',c);
      WRITELN(x:3:1,' / ',y:3:1,' = ',(x/y):3:1)
END.
```

The C version is shown below:

Listing 3.5

```
/* C program to demo simple use of basic data types */
/* NOTE:
   no 80x87 directive is needed to use double precision reals */
#include <stdio.h>
main()
{
  /* declare variables and assign initial values to i and j */
  char k; /* same range of values as Pascal's SHORTINT */
  int i = 10;
  unsigned char j = 2;/* same range of values as Pascal's BYTE */
  unsigned int n = 40000;
  long int m;
  char  c;
  float x;
  long float y = 2.5L; /* or use "double y = 2.5L;" */
  /* assign values to uninitialized variables */
  k = 1;
  c = 'X';
  m = 1000000L;
  x = 10.5;
  /* display a few expressions */
  /* the \n is inserted in printf to make it send
     a carriage return */
  printf("%1d + %2d = %2d \n", i, j, i+j);
  printf("Character c stores %c \n", c);
  printf("%3.1f / %3.1f = %3.1f \n", x, y, x/y);
}
```

Comparing the Pascal and C versions, notice the following characteristics of C:

1. C declares variables by stating first the data type and then the list of identifiers. No colons are used between the data type identifier and the variable names. Instead, spaces are the separators used. Like Pascal, each group of declared variables must be followed by a semicolon. Unlike

Pascal, the names of variables in C are case-sensitive. Thus, for example, the identifiers **first**, **FIRST**, and **First** refer to different variables.
2. The C language enables you to initialize variables when you declare them. The above C program version initializes some of the variables to demonstrate this feature. In Turbo Pascal you employ typed constants to obtain a similar effect. Other implementations, such as MS_Pascal, resort to a VALUE section to perform the sought initialization of variables. However, most other Pascal implementations do not support the above feature.
3. C enables you to distinguish between ordinary numeric constants and long numeric constants by appending the letter **L** at the end of the latter. The C program uses the long float 2.5L and the long integer 1000000L to declare long numeric constants explicitly. Omitting the **L** makes these constants ordinary, and, consequently, the C compiler resorts to automatic data type conversion. Hence, the omission of **L** is not fatal.
4. C assignments employ the equal sign and do not need the colon character.
5. The Pascal WRITELN statements are translated into **printf** function calls. This example reveals more about the nature and functionality of **printf**. It clearly illustrates the capability of **printf** to perform formatted output. The first argument of **printf** is the formatting string that contains both output text and output format instructions. This resembles BASIC's PRINT USING more than the Pascal WRITELN. The rest of the arguments of **printf** is the list of output constants, variables, and expressions. The **printf** employs the % character to detect output format instructions. The % character is followed by optional output width numbers and one or two letters that indicate the type of data output. The format string also contains special character combinations to issue tabs, carriage returns, etc. These start with the '****' character followed by a special lower-case letter. In this example I use the '**\n**' to request **printf** to send a carriage return, making it work like WRITELN and not WRITE. I will discuss the formatted output of **printf** in detail later. For now, however, I will explain the format strings used in the program to give you a basic idea.

Consider the first **printf** statement:
```
printf("%1d + %2ld = %2ld  \n", i, j, i+j);
```
In the above, **%1d** requests that variable **i** be displayed as an integer using a single column width. The variable **j** and the expression **i+j** should be displayed as long integers occupying two columns, as instructed by the **%2ld**.

The second **printf** statements outputs a character using the **%c** format:
```
printf("Character c stores %c  \n", c);
```
The third **printf** statement displays floating-point variables and expressions:
```
printf("%3.1f / %3.1lf = %3.1lf \n", x, y, x/y);
```
The **%3.1f** requests that variable **x** be displayed as a **float** type using a three-column width and one decimal place. The variable **y** and expression **x/y** are displayed as **long float** using a three-column width and a single decimal place.

The screen output of the C program is show below:

```
10 + 786434 = -1673526783
Character c stores X
10.5 / 2.5 = 4.2
```

CONSTANTS IN C

Constants are very important data objects that are available in both Pascal and C. Turbo Pascal supports both typed and untyped constants (the former being a language extension unique to Turbo Pascal). C also supports two types of constants: macro-based and the new ANSI typed constants. C books that were written solely following the K&R standard only employ the first type. Interestingly, the macro-based constants parallel the untyped Pascal constants, while the new ANSI typed constants in C are similar to the Turbo Pascal typed constants.

The macro-based constants involve the **#define** C preprocessor instruction using the following general syntax:

```
#define <constant_name> <constant value>
```

The **#define** instruction causes the C preprocessor (something not available in Pascal) to substitute the constant name with its accompanying value, before program compilation begins. Thus, it is highly recommended to make macro-based constant names entirely different from each other. Debugging programs with errors related to bad macro translation is very, very tricky.

The new ANSI typed constant is employed using the following general syntax:

```
const <data type> <constant name> = <constant value>
```

The <data type>, if omitted, is taken by default as **int**. While the C-typed constants look similar to the Pascal-typed constants, there is an important functional difference. The C constants with simple data types ARE TRUE CONSTANTS, and their values cannot be altered. This contrasts typed constants in Turbo Pascal that are really initialized variables.

The following simple Pascal program uses both untyped and typed constants. The program calculates the Fahrenheit temperature that corresponds to 100°C and displays the result:

Listing 3.6

```
PROGRAM Test_Constants;
{ Simple Pascal program that uses constants }
CONST MESSAGE = 'The temperature ';
      INTERCEPT = 32;
      TEMP_C_CHAR = 'C';
      { Turbo Pascal's typed constants }
      TEMP_F_CHAR : CHAR = 'F';
      SLOPE : REAL = 1.8;
VAR temp_f, temp_c : REAL;
```

```
BEGIN
    temp_c := 100.0;
    temp_f := INTERCEPT + SLOPE * temp_c;
    { display the contents of the variables }
    WRITE(MESSAGE);
    WRITE(temp_f:3:1,' ',TEMP_F_CHAR,' is equal to ');
    WRITELN(temp_c:3:1,' ',TEMP_C_CHAR)
END.
```

The C version is shown below:

Listing 3.7

```
/* Simple C program that uses constants */
#include <stdio.h>
main()
{
        /* define constant as macro */
        #define MESSAGE "The temperature "
        #define INTERCEPT 32
        #define TEMP_C_CHAR 'C'
        /* NOTE: #define TEMP_C_CHAR C will
           not work without the single quotes */
        /* define formal constants (new ANSI C) */
        const char TEMP_F_CHAR = 'F';
        const float SLOPE = 1.8;
        /* define variables */
        float temp_f, temp_c;
        temp_c = 100.0;
        temp_f = INTERCEPT + SLOPE * temp_c;
        /* display the contents of the variables */
        printf(MESSAGE);
        printf("%3.1f %c is equal to ",temp_f, TEMP_F_CHAR);
        printf("%3.1f %c\n", temp_c, TEMP_C_CHAR);
}
```

In comparing both listings, notice the following features of C:

1. Macro-based constants DO NOT REQUIRE EQUAL SIGN ASSIGNMENTS, and they MUST NOT END WITH A SEMICOLON.
2. C allows only one defined macro per line.
3. Using upper-case names for constants is optional. However, it is a widely used programming style in C, as it is in Pascal.
4. Typed constants in C put the keyword **const** and the data type before the constant name, all of them being delimited by spaces.

All of the constants are defined inside function **main**. While this is fine for this example and for exact translation, the macro-based constants are normally placed outside **main** (or any function) to make them global. This becomes necessary when other functions use the same macro-based constants. The same can also be done with the typed constants. The above C program may be rewritten as:

Listing 3.8

```c
/* Simple C program that uses global constants */
#include <stdio.h>
/* define constant as macro */
#define MESSAGE "The temperature "
#define INTERCEPT 32
#define TEMP_C_CHAR 'C'
/* NOTE: #define TEMP_C_CHAR C will
   not work without the single quotes */
/* define formal constants (new ANSI C) */
const char TEMP_F_CHAR = 'F';
const float SLOPE = 1.8;
main()
{
      /* define variables */
      float temp_f, temp_c;
      temp_c = 100.0;
      temp_f = INTERCEPT + SLOPE * temp_c;
      /* display the contents of the variables */
      printf(MESSAGE);
      printf("%3.1f %c is equal to ",temp_f, TEMP_F_CHAR);
      printf("%3.1f %c\n", temp_c, TEMP_C_CHAR);
}
```

When either program version is run, the following line is displayed:

`The temperature 212.0 F is equal to 100.0 C`

Table 3.2 lists special character sequences in C. You will probably recognize the '\n' sequence that has been utilized in some of the **printf** calls.

Table 3.2 C Escape sequences

Sequence	As Hex Value	Decimal Value	Task of Sequence
\a	0x07	7	Bell.
\b	0x08	8	Backspace.
\f	0x0C	12	Formfeed.
\n	0x0A	10	New line.
\r	0x0D	13	Carriage return.
\t	0x09	9	Horizontal tab.
\v	0x0B	11	Vertical Tab.
\\	0x5C	92	Backslash.
\'	0x2C	44	Single quote.
\"	0x22	34	Double quote.
\?	0x3F	63	Question Mark.
\OOO			1 to 3 digits for an octal value.
\XHHH and \xHHH	0xHHH		1 to 3 digits for a hexadecimal value.

BASIC CONSOLE I/O IN C

There are a number of popular functions that perform basic console I/O. So far, you have been exposed to **printf** only, since all of the programs I have presented assign values to the variables, instead of reading data from the keyboard. Hence, it is fit to focus on this powerful **printf** function first and then examine others that perform input or output.

The **printf** function packs a lot of power and offers formatted control that surpasses the features of the Pascal WRITE and WRITELN to which you have been accustomed. The previous C examples have only touched the tip of the iceberg, so to speak, in exploiting the power of **printf**. Perhaps the most appropriate next step is to state the general form of options that may be employed with **printf**. Most of the power and flexibility of **printf** comes from its first argument, the format control string. The general syntax of each format instruction in the letter string is

```
% [flags] [width] [.precision] [ F | N | h | l ] <type character>
```

The **flags** option specifies output justification, numeric signs, decimal points, and trailing zeros, as well as octal and hexadecimal prefixes. Table 3.3 shows the various options for the flag characters and their effects.

The **width** option specifies the minimum number of characters to show. Blanks or zeros are used for padding, if required. If the width number begins with a zero, leading zeros are used for padding, instead of space characters. If the * character is used instead of a width number, the actual width is then supplied by the argument list of **printf**. The argument specifying the desired width must appear before the actual argument being formatted.

Table 3.3 The options for the flags portion in the format string of printf

Flag Character	Effect
-	Justify to the left within the designated field. The right side is padded with blanks.
+	Display the plus or minus sign of value.
blank	Display a leading blank if value is positive. If output is negative, a minus sign is used.
#	Display a leading zero for octals. Display a leading 0X or 0x for hexadecimals. Display the decimal point for reals. No effect on integers.

28 INTRODUCING C TO PASCAL PROGRAMMERS

The **precision** option indicates the maximum number of characters to display. When used with integers, the same option defines the minimum number of digits to print. If the ***** character is used instead of a precision number, the actual precision is then supplied by the argument list of **printf**. The argument specifying the desired precision must appear before the actual argument being formatted.

The **F, N, h** and **l** size options are used to override the argument's default size. The **F** and **N** are used in conjunction with far and near pointers, respectively. The **h** and **l** are utilized to indicate **short int** or **long**, respectively.

Table 3.4 Type characters used in the format string of printf

Category	Type Character	Output Format
character	c	single character
integer	d	signed decimal int
	i	signed decimal int
	o	unsigned octal int
	u	unsigned decimal int
	x	unsigned hexadecimal int. The numeric character set used is [01234567890abcdef]
	X	unsigned hexadecimal int. The numeric character set used is [01234567890ABCDEF]
pointer	p	prints only offset of near pointers as AAAA and far pointers as SSSS:OOOO
pointer to int	n	
real	f	signed value in the form [-]dddd.dddd
	e	signed scientific format using [-]d.dddd e[+|-]ddd
	E	signed scientific format using [-]d.dddd E[+|-]ddd
	g	signed value using either 'e' or 'f' formats, depending on value and specified precision.
	G	signed value using either 'E' or 'f' formats, depending on value and specified precision.
string pointer	s	emits characters until a null-terminator or precision is attained.

The mandatory data-type characters are listed in Table 3.4. It is important to point out that you can perform implicit conversion when displaying one data type using a type specifier character that belongs to another type. This is especially true between characters and integers, as well as integers of one precision displayed as being of higher precision.

Translation Hints

The following are some general rules for translating Pascal formatted WRITEs to **printf** in C:

Pascal:
```
WRITE(strng:<width>);
```
C:
```
printf("%<width>s", strng);
```
Pascal:
```
WRITE(integer_var:<width>);
```
C:
```
printf("%<width>d", integer_var);
```
Pascal:
```
WRITE(long_integer_var:<width>);
```
C:
```
printf("%<width>ld", long_integer_var);
```
Pascal:
```
WRITE(real_var:<width>:<decimals>);
```
C:
```
printf("%<width>.<decimals>f", 'real_var');
```

The second console I/O function is **scanf** which is the counterpart of **printf**. It is a formatted input function, and like **printf**, its first argument is an input format string. The main difference from **printf** is that all of the input arguments must be listed as addresses or pointers. For scalar variables, this means prepending the ampersand **&** symbol to the name of the variable. This enables the **scanf** function to assign what you type to the variables in its argument list. It is important to point out that when using **scanf** to key data into more than one variable, the spaces in the the format strings dictate the exact pattern of delimiters that must be typed. For example, if I want to read two integers and store them into variables **i** and **j**, I can use **scanf("%d %d", &i, &j)** to indicate that there should be one space delimiting the two entered integers. Compare the above with **scanf("%d %d", &i, &j)**, which requires two spaces between the integers (and DO NOT forget to use **&** characters with **scanf!**).

30 INTRODUCING C TO PASCAL PROGRAMMERS

> **Programming Note**
>
> The **scanf** function employs the address of the variables receiving data from the console. The ampersand character is the address operator used for that purpose, especially with simple variables.

The following program illustrates a few aspects of using **printf**, **scanf**, and their formatted I/O features. The program performs the following simple tasks:

1. Prompts you to enter an integer and displays it in decimal, octal, and hexadecimal forms.
2. Prompts you to enter an unsigned integer and displays it in decimal, octal, and hexadecimal forms.
3. Prompts you to enter an long integer and displays it in decimal, octal, and hexadecimal forms.
4. Prompts you to enter a real number and displays it using the **f**, **E** and **g** formats. The square of the number is also calculated and similarly displayed, using the long conversion character, **l**.
5. Prompts you to enter three consecutive characters (with no space delimiters between them) and displays them along with the ASCII code number of the first typed character. The latter demonstrates the ability of **printf** (and C) to perform data type conversions.

The program is listed below:

Listing 3.9

```
/* program to demonstrate output formatting with printf() */
/* and keyboard input using scanf()                       */
#include <stdio.h>
main()
{
  int i;
  long j;
  unsigned int k;
  char c1, c2, c3;
  float x;
  long float y;
  /* test keyboard I/O for an integer */
  printf("Enter an integer : ");
  scanf("%d", &i);
  printf("\ndecimal %d = octal %o = hexadecimal %X",i,i,i);
  /* test keyboard I/O for an unsigned integer */
  printf("\n\nEnter a positive integer : ");
  scanf("%u", &k);
  printf("\ndecimal %u = octal %o = hexadecimal %X",k,k,k);
  /* test keyboard I/O for a long integer */
  printf("\n\nEnter a long integer : ");
  scanf("%ld", &j);
```

```
    printf("\ndecimal %ld = octal %lo = hexadecimal %lX",j,j,j);
    /* test keyboard I/O for a single precision
        floating point number                            */
    printf("\n\nEnter a floating point number : ");
    scanf("%f", &x);
    printf("\nnumber = \n");
    printf("          %f  (in %%f format)\n", x);
    printf("          %E  (in %%E format)\n", x);
    printf("          %g  (in %%g format)\n", x);
    /* test keyboard I/O for a double precision
        floating point number                            */
    y = x * x;
    printf("\nnumber = \n");
    printf("          %lf (in %%lf format)\n", y);
    printf("          %lE (in %%lE format)\n", y);
    printf("          %lg (in %%lg format)\n", y);
    /* test keyboard I/O for characters */
    printf("\n\n\n\n");
    printf("Type three characters followed by [Enter] : ");
    /* if you experience a bug with the program properly */
    /* reading 3 characters, uncomment the following line */
    /* and enclose the next one in a comment.          */
    /* scanf("%c%c%c%c", &c1, &c1, &c2, &c3);  */
    scanf("%c%c%c", &c1, &c2, &c3);
    printf("\nYou typed %c%c%c\n\n", c1, c2, c3);
    printf("The ASCII code of %c is %d\n\n\n", c1, c1);
}
```

A sample session with the above C program is shown below:

```
Enter an integer : 55
decimal 55 = octal 67 = hexadecimal 37
Enter a positive integer : 155
decimal 155 = octal 233 = hexadecimal 9B
Enter a long integer : 99999
decimal 99999 = octal 303237 = hexadecimal 1869F
Enter a floating point number : 3.12456
number =
          3.124560 (in %f format)
          3.124560E+000 (in %E format)
          3.12456 (in %g format)
number =
          9.894800 (in %lf format)
          9.894800E+000 (in %lE format)
          9.8948 (in %lg format)
Type three characters followed by [Enter] : abc
You typed abc
The ASCII code of a is 97
```

The above C program should give you a better idea of the power of **printf** and the features of **scanf** that are unparalleled by Pascal's I/O routines. For example, a single **printf** can issue multiple carriage returns, while in Pascal you need to write your own procedure to imitate that capability alone!

As it turns out, **scanf** may be suitable for the input of reals and integers; it is seldom used to enter characters and strings (more about strings in another chapter). C provides a number of functions that specialize in character I/O and compile into code sizes smaller than those for **scanf**. The character I/O functions are

1. Function **getche()**: used to input a character from the console with an echo.
2. Function **getch()**: used to input a character from the console without an echo.
3. Function **getchar()**: used to input a character from the console, which is treated as a data **stream**.
4. Function **putch()**: places one character on the console.
5. Function **putchar()**: places one character on the console, which is treated as a data **stream**.

If you inquire about why some of these functions seem redundant in what they do, the answer lies in the fact that **getchar()** and **putchar()** also work with **streams** (more about this in Chapter 12). Their use in console I/O is regarded as a special case of what these functions generally do.

The character input functions need no arguments and return integer-typed results! This may seem very odd for Pascal programmers. The answer lies in the fact that C draws a very close connection between characters (always stored as their ASCII code numbers: integers) and formal integer variables. Thus, when you request the ASCII code of a character, C returns the unconverted or raw contents stored in the character-typed variable. The character output functions each take one integer-typed argument (here we go again!) and returns an integer result that is most frequently discarded.

Turbo Pascal also employs its own routines to perform similar highly specialized tasks. In the first three versions of Turbo Pascal, you may use READ(Kbd,<character-type variable>) to read a single character without echoing your input. Turbo Pascal 4 uses a character-typed function, ReadKey, imported from unit CRT. The following two Turbo Pascal programs are used to illustrate simple character input in both versions 3.0 and 4.0. The program for the earlier Pascal versions is

Listing 3.10

```
PROGRAM Char_IO;
{ simple Turbo Pascal 3.0 program to demonstrate character I/O }
VAR C1, C2, C3 : CHAR;
BEGIN
    WRITELN; WRITELN;
    WRITE('Type the first  character : ');
    READ(Kbd,C1); WRITELN(C1);
    WRITE('Type a second character   : ');
    READ(Kbd,C2); WRITELN(C2);
    WRITE('Type a third  character   : ');
    READ(Kbd,C3); WRITELN(C3);
    WRITELN; WRITELN;
    WRITE('You typed ', C1, C2, C3);
    WRITELN; WRITELN;
END.
```

The version for Pascal 4.0 (and up) is

Listing 3.11

```
PROGRAM Char_IO;
Uses CRT;
{ simple Turbo Pascal 4.0 program to demonstrate character I/O }
VAR C1, C2, C3 : CHAR;
BEGIN
    WRITELN; WRITELN;
    WRITE('Type the first  character : ');
    C1 := ReadKey; WRITELN(C1);
    WRITE('Type a second character   : ');
    C2 := ReadKey; WRITELN(C2);
    WRITE('Type a third  character   : ');
    C3 := ReadKey; WRITELN(C3);
    WRITELN; WRITELN;
    WRITE('You typed ', C1, C2, C3);
    WRITELN; WRITELN;
END.
```

The following C version uses **getche()** to input characters, with echo and **putchar** to display them:

Listing 3.12

```
/* C program to demonstrate character I/O using getche and */
/* putchar. The program demonstrates how getche is used    */
/* in character console-input with echoing.                */
#include <stdio.h>
#include "conio.h"
main()
{
   char c1, c2, c3;
   printf("\n\n");
   printf("\nType the first character  : ");  c1 = getche();
   printf("\nType a second character   : ");  c2 = getche();
   printf("\nType a third character    : ");  c3 = getche();
   printf("\n\nYou typed ");
   putchar(c1);
   putchar(c2);
   putchar(c3);
   printf("\n\n");
}
```

When running the above program, type the letters **a**, **b**, and **c**. Like the Pascal versions, you need not press the [Enter] key, as shown below:

```
Type the first character  : a
Type a second character   : b
Type a third character    : c
You typed abc
```

The next program version uses **getch()** instead of **getche()**. In addition, the output of characters is handled by **putch()** and **putchar()**:

Listing 3.13

```
/* C program to demonstrate character I/O using getch, putch */
/* and putchar. The program demonstrates the effect of       */
/* getch() in not echoing console character input            */
#include <stdio.h>
#include "conio.h"
main()
{
    char c1, c2, c3;
    printf("\n\n");
    printf("\nType the first character : ");   c1 = getch();
    printf("\nType a second character : ");   c2 = getch();
    printf("\nType a third character  : ");   c3 = getch();
    printf("\n\nYou typed ");
    putchar(c1);
    putch(c2);
    putchar(c3);
    printf("\n\n");
}
```

Run the above C program version and type the letters **a**, **b**, and **c**, one letter for each prompt. Notice how your input is not echoed on the screen, as shown below:

```
Type the first character : <you type a but char does not echo>
Type a second character : <you type b but char does not echo>
Type a third character  : <you type c but char does not echo>
You typed abc
```

The output does not seem to differ from that of the previous version, despite the use of two different character output functions. The function **putch()** always writes to the console, while **putchar()** writes to a character stream which is the console in this case.

The third C program version tests the use of **getchar()**, the stream input function:

Listing 3.14

```
/* C program to demonstrate character I/O using getchar, putch */
/* and putchar the program demonstrates the effects of using   */
/* getchar() for console input.                                */
#include <stdio.h>
#include "conio.h"
main()
{
    char c1, c2, c3;
    printf("\n\n");
    printf("\nType the first character : ");   c1 = getchar();
    printf("\nType a second character : ");   c2 = getchar();
    printf("\nType a third character  : ");   c3 = getchar();
    printf("\n\nYou typed ");
    putchar(c1);
    putch(c2);
```

```
    putchar(c3);
    printf("\n\n");
}
```

This program version behaves quite differently from the previous two. To enter the letters **a**, **b**, and **c**, type them all on one line in response to the first prompt, and press the [Enter] key. The **getchar()** function will read the character from the keyboard buffer (that is, the data stream):

```
Type the first character : abc<CR>
Type a second character  :
Type a third character   :
You typed abc
```

The above example indicates that **getchar()** may be less suitable than **getche()** or **getch()** in promptly reading single characters from the keyboard.

CHAPTER SUMMARY

- The simple data types in C are **char, int, float, double,** and **void**. The first four types may employ type modifiers to alter the range of values. The type modifiers are **signed, unsigned, short** and **long**.
- C variables are case-sensitive.
- C variables are declared using the following syntax:

  `<data type identifier> <list of variables>;`

  The list is delimited by commas and may contain variable initialization.
- C assignments are carried out using the equal sign.
- Macro-based constants are declared with the **#define** preprocessor which employs the following general syntax:

  `#define <constant_name> <constant value>`

- ANSI constants are declared using the following general syntax:

  `const <data type> <constant name> = <constant value>`

- Formatted console I/O uses the **printf** and **scanf** functions imported from the "stdio.h" library. The general syntax of **printf** is

  `printf(<format string>,<list of variables to display>);`

  where the format string is

  `"% [flags] [width] [.precision] [F|N|h|l] <type character>"`

  The general syntax for **scanf** is:

  `scanf(<format string>,<list of variables to display>);`

- Character I/O from the console involves other functions that are compiled into smaller code. The **getche()**, **getch()**, and **getchar()** are used to input a character from the console. The **putch()** and **putchar()** display single characters to the console.

CHAPTER

4

C Operators

CHAPTER GOALS

In this chapter you will learn about the various types of operators in C. C supports the following types of operators:
- Arithmetic operators (monadic and dyadic).
- Increment operators.
- Arithmetic assignment operators.
- Character operators.
- Data size operator.
- Type casting and data conversions.
- Relational operators and conditional expressions.
- Bit manipulating operators.
- Comma operator.

USING VARIOUS OPERATORS TO CREATE EXPRESSIONS

Expressions and operators are important components of any language, and C is no exception. Interestingly, C has the reputation for supporting terse expressions that are shorter than their counterparts in many other languages, including Pascal. I will discuss the various types of C operators and expressions by using the same categories listed in this chapter's goals.

ARITHMETIC OPERATORS

This set of arithmetic operators includes the four basic operations and the modulus operator. Table 4.1 shows the arithmetic operators in C and the corresponding ones in Pascal. I present below a simple Turbo Pascal program to compare arithmetic operators being used in both languages. The program exercises the arithmetic operators on integers and floating-point numbers:

Listing 4.1

```
PROGRAM Numeric_Math;
{ simple Turbo Pascal program to
  illustrate simple math operations }
VAR i, j : INTEGER;
    L1, L2, L3, L4, L5 : LONGINT;
    x, y, Z1, Z2, Z3, Z4 : REAL;
BEGIN
   WRITE('Enter first  integer : '); READLN(i);
   WRITE('Enter second integer : '); READLN(j);
   WRITELN;
   L1 := i + j;
   L2 := i - j;
   L3 := i * j;
   L4 := i div j;
   L5 := i mod j;
   WRITELN(i,' + ',j,' = ',L1);
   WRITELN(i,' - ',j,' = ',L2);
   WRITELN(i,' * ',j,' = ',L3);
   WRITELN(i,' / ',j,' = ',L4);
   WRITELN(i,' mod ',j,' = ',L5);
   WRITELN; WRITELN;
   WRITE('Enter first  real number : '); READLN(x);
   WRITE('Enter second real number : '); READLN(y);
   WRITELN;
   Z1 := x + y;
   Z2 := x - y;
   Z3 := x * y;
   Z4 := x / y;
   WRITELN(x,' + ',y,' = ',Z1);
   WRITELN(x,' - ',y,' = ',Z2);
   WRITELN(x,' * ',y,' = ',Z3);
   WRITELN(x,' / ',y,' = ',Z4);
   WRITELN; WRITELN;
END.
```

When you run the above program enter the integers 25 and 5, and enter the reals 355 and 113. The screen image is shown below:

```
Enter first  integer : 25
Enter second integer : 5
25 + 5 = 30
25 - 5 = 20
25 * 5 = 125
25 / 5 = 5
25 mod 5 = 0
Enter first  real number : 355
Enter second real number : 113
  3.55000000000E+002 +  1.13000000000E+002 =  4.68000000000E+002
```

```
3.55000000000E+002  -  1.13000000000E+002  =  2.42000000000E+002
3.55000000000E+002  *  1.13000000000E+002  =  4.01150000000E+004
3.55000000000E+002  /  1.13000000000E+002  =  3.14159292035E+000
```

The C version is shown below:

Listing 4.2

```
/* simple C program to illustrate simple math operations */
#include <stdio.h>
main()
{
    int i, j;
    long L1, L2, L3, L4, L5;
    float x, y, Z1, Z2, Z3, Z4;
    printf("\nEnter first  integer : "); scanf("%d", &i);
    printf("\nEnter second integer : "); scanf("%d", &j);
    printf("\n");
    L1 = i + j;
    L2 = i - j;
    L3 = i * j;
    L4 = i / j;
    L5 = i % j;
    printf("\n%d + %d = %ld", i, j, L1);
    printf("\n%d - %d = %ld", i, j, L2);
    printf("\n%d * %d = %ld", i, j, L3);
    printf("\n%d / %d = %ld", i, j, L4);
    printf("\n%d mod %d = %ld", i, j, L5);
    printf("\n\n");
    printf("\nEnter first  real number : "); scanf("%f", &x);
    printf("\nEnter second real number : "); scanf("%f", &y);
    printf("\n");
    Z1 = x + y;
    Z2 = x - y;
    Z3 = x * y;
    Z4 = x / y;
    printf("\n%f + %f = %lf", x, y, Z1);
    printf("\n%f - %f = %lf", x, y, Z2);
    printf("\n%f * %f = %lf", x, y, Z3);
    printf("\n%f / %f = %lf", x, y, Z4);
    printf("\n\n");
}
```

The screen image of a session with the C program, entering the same data as with the Pascal version, is as follows:

```
Enter first  integer : 25
Enter second integer : 5
25 + 5 = 30
25 - 5 = 20
25 * 5 = 125
25 / 5 = 5
25 mod 5 = 0
Enter first  real number : 355
Enter second real number : 113
355.000000 + 113.000000 = 468.000000
```

```
355.000000 - 113.000000 = 242.000000
355.000000 * 113.000000 = 40115.000000
355.000000 / 113.000000 = 3.141593
```

In comparing the Pascal and C output, notice the following features of C:
1. By using **printf** in C, you have more control over the format of the output than in Pascal.
2. C uses the / character for dividing both integers and reals.

Table 4.1 Arithmetic operators in C and their equivalent in Pascal

C Operator	Function	Data Types	Pascal Operator
+	Unary Plus	all numeric	+
-	Unary Minus	all signed numeric types	-
+	Add	all numeric	+
-	Subtract	all numeric	-
*	Multiply	all numeric	*
/	Divide	all numeric	DIV (integers) / (floats)
%	Modulus	integers	MOD

INCREMENT AND ASSIGNMENT OPERATORS

Turbo Pascal 4 brought with it two predefined procedures that increment and decrement ordinal-typed variables. The INC() and DEC() routines take one or two arguments. The first argument is always an ordinal-typed variable being altered. The second optional argument specifies the magnitude of change in the altered variable. If it is omitted, the variable is incremented or decremented by one. Neither of the previous Turbo Pascal versions nor most of the other Pascal implementations support the INC() and DEC() functions.

The designers of the C language were very conscious of the need for an easy way to increment or decrement variables. Consequently, C supports the ++ and -- operators to increment and decrement variables by one, respectively. Your next question may be where to place the ++ or -- operators, before or after the variable name? The answer, very surprisingly, is that you can do either. However, the location of the ++ or -- operators, with respect to the name of the variable, has a special significance in C that is perhaps new to you as a veteran Pascal programmer. This stems from the fact that C supports nested expressions. They are NOT subexpressions, instead they are semi-independent expressions that exist in other expressions! I will clarify this by explaining the significance of placing increment operators on either side of a variable name. When the increment operator is placed before the variable name it is called preincrementing. The effect it has is that the variable associated with the increment operator is first altered, and the new value is *possibly* used in an expression. Consider the following example: you increment an array index to access the next array member. This is first shown in a familiar form as follows:

```
i = i + 1;
x = names[i];
```

The next step is to use the increment operator to alter index i, as shown below:

```
++i;
x = names[i];
```

In the above lines, I incremented the index in a separate statement and then proceeded to access the array. I am using two separate expressions, which can be combined into one expression as shown below:

```
x = names[++i];
```

In the above C expression, the index i is first incremented, and the new value is used to access an array member.

If, instead, the increment operator is placed after the variable name it is called postincrement. This means that the *old* value of the variable is first used before it is altered. Applying postincrementing to the above simple example, I now have the following:

```
x = names[i++];
```

which means that I am accessing the member indexed by the value of i BEFORE it is incremented. It is worthwhile to point out that the version:

```
i++; /* use post-increment */
x = names[i]
```

is the same as:

```
x = names[++i];
```

since the index i is incremented in a previous and separate statement, and it does not matter whether it is preincrementing or postincrementing.

The increment operators in C change the value of a variable by only one. By comparing this feature with that of Turbo Pascal's INC() and DEC() procedures, it first appears that Pascal has an edge on the incrementing and decrementing by more than one. However, C supports another set of operators that accomplish the above purpose. They are called the assignment operators and Table 4.2 lists the arithmetic assignment operators (there are other types of similar operators that I will present later). Notice that the arithmetic assignments not only cover all of the basic arithmetic operators, but also the ones associated with the basic four arithmetic operations support floating-point numbers. The INC() and DEC() intrinsics in Turbo Pascal only allow ordinal-typed variables.

Table 4.2 Arithmetic assignment operators in C

Assignment Operator	Long Form	Equivalent Turbo Pascal Intrinsic
x += y	x = x + y	INC(x,y)
x -= y	x = x - y	DEC(x,y)
x *= y	x = x * y	
x /= y	x = x / y	
x %= y	x = x % y	

Having introduced the increment and arithmetic assignment operators, I now present the following simple Pascal example. It performs various arithmetic operations on both integer and floating-point variables:

Listing 4.3

```
PROGRAM Numeric_Math2;
{ simple Turbo Pascal program to illustrate
  more simple math operations }
VAR i, j : INTEGER;
    x, y : REAL;
BEGIN
    WRITE('Enter first  integer : '); READLN(i);
    WRITE('Enter second integer : '); READLN(j);
    WRITELN;
    INC(i, j);
    DEC(j, 5);
    i := i * 10;
    j := j div 5;
    INC(i);
    DEC(j);
    WRITELN('i = ',i); WRITELN;
    WRITELN('j = ',j); WRITELN;
    WRITELN; WRITELN;
    WRITE('Enter first  real number : '); READLN(x);
    WRITE('Enter second real number : '); READLN(y);
    WRITELN;
    x := x + y;
    y := y - 5.0;
    x := x * 10.0;
    y := y / 5.0;
```

```pascal
      x := x + 1.0;
      y := y - 1.0;
      WRITELN('x = ',x); WRITELN;
      WRITELN('y = ',y); WRITELN;
END.
```

The C version of the program is shown below:

Listing 4.4

```c
/* simple C program to illustrate simple math operations */
#include <stdio.h>
main()
{
   int i, j;
   float x, y;
   printf("Enter first  integer : "); scanf("%d", &i);
   printf("Enter second integer : "); scanf("%d", &j);
   printf("\n");
   i += j; /* same as Pascal's INC(i, j) */
   j -= 5; /* same as Pascal's DEC(j, 5) */
   i *= 10; /* same as Pascal's i := i * 10 */
   j /= 5; /* same as Pascal's j := j div 5 */
   i++;    /* same as Pascal's INC(i) */
   j--;    /* same as Pascal's DEC(j) */
   printf("\ni = %d\n",i);
   printf("\nj = %d\n\n",j);
   printf("\nEnter first  real number : "); scanf("%f", &x);
   printf("\nEnter second real number : "); scanf("%f", &y);
   printf("\n");
   /* abbreviated assignments also work with floats in C */
   x += y;    /* no similar operations are allowed for */
   y -= 5.0;  /* reals in Turbo Pascal 4.0             */
   x *= 10.0;
   y /= 5.0;
   x++; /* Cannot be matched by Turbo Pascal's INC() and */
   y--; /* DEC() since they only work on ordinal-valued  */
        /* data types                                    */
   printf("\nx = %f\n",x);
   printf("\ny = %f\n\n\n",y);
}
```

In comparing the two program versions, notice the following:
1. C has a set of arithmetic operators that work more consistently with different numeric data types. They cover a wider range of operations than Pascal and enable you to write expressions in *shorthand*.
2. The C increment and arithmetic assignment operators also support floating-point variables. This does not exist at all in Pascal.

Since Pascal does not support the features of pre- and postincrementing, I present the next example in C only to illustrate these features:

Listing 4.5

```
/* C program illustrates the feature of the increment operator.*/
/* The ++ or -- may be included in an expression. The value    */
/* of the associated variable is altered after the expression  */
/* is evaluated if the var++ (or var--) is used, or before     */
/* when ++var (or --var) is used.                              */
#include <stdio.h>
main()
{
   int i, k = 10;
   /* use post-incrementing */
   i = 5 * (k++); /* k contributes 10 to the expression */
   printf("i = %d\n\n", i); /* displays 50 (= 5 * 10) */
   k--; /* restore the value of k to 10 */
   /* use pre-incrementing */
   i = 5 * (++k); /* k contributes 11 to the expression */
   printf("i = %d\n\n", i); /* displays 55 (= 5 * 11) */
}
```

The above short program illustrates the effect of the two incrementing types. In the first assignment expression, i = 5 * (k++), the variable k first contributes its current value of 10 and is then incremented. The effect is that the variable i is assigned the value of 50. This is compared to the preincrementing of k in the second assignment expression, i = 5 * (++k). There, the variable k is first incremented from 10 to 11. The new value of 11 is contributed in evaluating the assignment expression, causing i to be assigned 55. The trivial program output is shown below.

```
i = 50
i = 55
```

CHARACTER OPERATORS

One of the unique features of C compared to other languages (such as Pascal, FORTRAN, and BASIC) is close association between characters and integers. In the last chapter, I mentioned that character-typed variables store their values as ASCII numeric values. Thus, manipulating characters can employ arithmetic operators. As a matter of fact, C keeps predefined character operators to a bare minimum. Most of the character and string manipulation routines and macros are located in included files and libraries.

I will demonstrate the two-way automatic conversion between characters and integers with the next program, presented in Pascal and C. The program prompts you for a lower-case character and converts it into an upper-case letter. The program also requests an upper-case letter and converts it into a lower-case letter. The Pascal version is shown on the following page:

Listing 4.6

```
PROGRAM ASCII_Code;
Uses CRT;
{ Turbo Pascal program to convert characters between
uppercase and lowercase.                              }
VAR ch : CHAR;
BEGIN
    { convert uppercase to lowercase }
    WRITE('Enter an uppercase character : ');
    ch := ReadKey; WRITELN(ch); WRITELN;
    ch := CHR(Ord(ch) + Ord('a') - Ord('A'));
    WRITE('The character in lowercase is : ', ch);
    WRITELN; WRITELN;
    { convert lowercase to uppercase }
    WRITE('Enter a lowercase character : ');
    ch := ReadKey; WRITELN(ch); WRITELN;
    ch := CHR(Ord(ch) + Ord('A') - Ord('a'));
    WRITE('The character in uppercase is : ', ch);
    WRITELN; WRITELN;
END.
```

When running the program enter the upper-case letter "K" and the lower-case "d":

```
Enter an uppercase character : K
The character in lowercase is : k
Enter a lowercase character : d
The character in uppercase is : D
```

The C version is listed below:

Listing 4.7

```
/* C program to convert characters between */
/* uppercase and lowercase.                 */
#include <stdio.h>
#include "conio.h"
main()
{
    char ch;
    /* convert uppercase to lowercase */
    printf("Enter an uppercase character : ");
    ch = getche();
    ch += 'a' - 'A'; /* or ch = ch + 'a' - 'A' */
    printf("\n\nThe character in lowercase is : %c\n\n", ch);
    /* convert lowercase to uppercase */
    printf("Enter a lowercase character : ");
    ch = getche();
    ch += 'A' - 'a'; /* or ch = ch + 'A' - 'a' */
    printf("\n\nThe character in uppercase is : %c\n\n", ch);
}
```

In comparing the two versions, observe the following: the Pascal code resorts to using ORD() and CHR() to carry out the conversions between characters and integers. By contrast, the C version requires no such functions, since C uses the integer-based representation of characters to perform the required operations. Using assignment operators in C makes the character-conversion expressions even shorter.

When running the program enter the upper-case letter K and the lower-case letter **d**. The screen images of the Pascal and C versions are identical:

```
Enter an uppercase character : K
The character in lowercase is : k
Enter a lowercase character : d
The character in uppercase is : D
```

SIZING DATA OBJECTS

An important C operator is **sizeof**, which returns the byte size occupied by a variable or data type. The general syntax for using **sizeof** is

```
sizeof(<variable name>|<data type>)
```

Turbo Pascal has also implemented the **SizeOf** intrinsic that fulfills the same purpose and uses the same syntax.

The following program displays the byte size of selected data types and variables associated with them. The Pascal version is shown below:

Listing 4.8

```
PROGRAM Sizing_Data;
{
   simple Turbo Pascal program that returns the data sizes
   using the SizeOf() function with variables and data types.
}
VAR i : BYTE;
    j : INTEGER;
    k : LONGINT;
    c : CHAR;
    x : REAL;
BEGIN
    WRITELN('Table 1. Data sizes using SizeOf(var) ');
    WRITELN;
    WRITELN('     Data type         Memory used (bytes)');
    WRITELN('     ---------         -------------------');
    WRITELN('        byte           ',sizeof(i));
    WRITELN('        integer        ',sizeof(j));
    WRITELN('        long integer   ',sizeof(k));
    WRITELN('        character      ',sizeof(c));
    WRITELN('        real           ',sizeof(x));
    WRITELN; WRITELN; WRITELN;
    WRITELN('Table 2. Data sizes using SizeOf(data_type) ');
    WRITELN;
    WRITELN('     Data type         Memory used (bytes)');
    WRITELN('     ---------         -------------------');
    WRITELN('        byte           ',sizeof(BYTE));
    WRITELN('        integer        ',sizeof(INTEGER));
    WRITELN('        long integer   ',sizeof(LONGINT));
    WRITELN('        character      ',sizeof(CHAR));
    WRITELN('        real           ',sizeof(REAL));
    WRITELN; WRITELN; WRITELN;
END.
```

46 INTRODUCING C TO PASCAL PROGRAMMERS

When the above program is run, the following screen image appears (no user input is required):

Table 1 Data sizes using SizeOf(var)

Data type	Memory used (bytes)
byte	1
integer	2
long integer	4
character	1
real	6

Table 2 Data sizes using SizeOf(data_type)

Data type	Memory used (bytes)
byte	1
integer	2
long integer	4
character	1
real	6

The above results are one way of letting Turbo Pascal inform you of the sizes of the different data types. The C version, which performs a very similar task, is shown below:

Listing 4.9

```
/*
   simple Turbo Pascal program that returns the data sizes
   using the SizeOf() function with variables and data types.
*/
main()
{
    short int i;
    int j;
    long k;
    char c;
    float x;
    printf("Table 1. Data sizes using SizeOf(var)\n\n");
    printf("     Data type           Memory used (bytes)\n");
    printf("    ----------           -------------------\n");
    printf("     short int               %d\n",sizeof(i));
    printf("      integer                %d\n",sizeof(j));
    printf("    long integer             %d\n",sizeof(k));
    printf("     character               %d\n",sizeof(c));
    printf("       float                 %d\n",sizeof(x));
    printf("\n\n\n");
printf("Table 2. Data sizes using SizeOf(data_type)\n\n");
```

```
    printf("      Data type        Memory used (bytes)\n");
    printf("——————————————         ——\n");
    printf("      short int        %d\n",sizeof(short int));
    printf("      integer          %d\n",sizeof(int));
    printf("      long integer     %d\n",sizeof(long));
    printf("      character        %d\n",sizeof(char));
    printf("      float            %d\n",sizeof(float));
    printf("\n\n\n");
}
```

When the C program version runs, the following screen image is displayed:

Table 1 Data sizes using SizeOf(var)

Data type	Memory used (bytes)
short int	2
integer	2
long integer	4
character	1
float	4

Table 2 Data sizes using SizeOf(data_type)

Data type	Memory used (bytes)
short int	2
integer	2
long integer	4
character	1
float	4

Notice that Turbo C stores the **short int** in two bytes, and the **float** type in four bytes. This is compared with Turbo Pascal's BYTE and REAL that occupy one and six bytes, respectively. The REAL type in Turbo Pascal 4 (and later) is equivalent to the DOUBLE precision floating-point type. The two versions illustrate how similar the use of **sizeof** is between Pascal and C.

TYPE CASTING
Many language implementations incorporate behind-the-scene conversions between data objects of similar and even not-so-similar data types. The purpose is to relieve practical programmer aggravations. This may result from having to watch like a hawk for every expression that mixes data objects of relatively similar types (integers and reals are perhaps the most popular example). Many users of different language implementations sing the praises of the automatic data conversion features supported. The Pascal and C languages are no different. However, the need arises when you wish to force

the result of an expression into a specific data type, if it is possible. This is known as type casting and is available in many languages and implementations, such as C, Turbo Pascal, Modula-2, and Ada.

Turbo Pascal supports type casting using the following general syntax:

<type casted>(<expression>)

while type casting in C employs the following general syntax:

(<type casted>) <expression>

In addition to the difference between the Turbo Pascal and C in the syntax of applying type casting, there is another difference. In Pascal, type casting works with ordinal-valued types, while in C it extends to include floating-point types.

The following Pascal and C program versions perform two kinds of operations: first without and then with type casting. The Pascal listing is presented below:

Listing 4.10

```
PROGRAM Type_Cast;
{ simple Turbo Pascal 4.0 program that demonstrates typecasting }
VAR i, j : SHORTINT;
    k : BYTE;
    m : INTEGER;
    n : LONGINT;
    c : CHAR;
    x : REAL;
BEGIN
    { assign values }
    i := 10;
    j := 6;
     { perform operations without user-specified typecasting }
    k := i + j;
    m := i - j;
    n := i * j;
    c := CHR(n + 5);
    x := i * j + 0.5;
    WRITELN('i = ',i);
    WRITELN('j = ',j);
    WRITELN('k = ',k);
    WRITELN('m = ',m);
    WRITELN('n = ',n);
    WRITELN('c is ',c);
    WRITELN('x = ',x);
    WRITELN; WRITELN;
    { perform operations with typecasting }
    k := BYTE(i + j);
    m := INTEGER(i - j);
    n := LONGINT(i * j);
    c := CHR(BYTE(n + 5));
    { x := REAL(i * j + 0.5); IS NOT A VALID TYPECAST }
    WRITELN('i = ',i);
    WRITELN('j = ',j);
    WRITELN('k = ',k);
    WRITELN('m = ',m);
```

```
    WRITELN('n = ',n);
    WRITELN('c is ',c);
    WRITELN; WRITELN;
END.
```

When the program runs the following output is displayed on the screen:

```
i = 10
j = 6
k = 16
m = 4
n = 60
c is A
x =   6.05000000000000E+0001
i = 10
j = 6
k = 16
m = 4
n = 60
c is A
```

The C version is listed below:

Listing 4.11

```
/* simple C program that demonstrates typecasting */
#include <stdio.h>
main()
{
    short i, j;
    unsigned short k;
    int m;
    long n;
    char c;
    float x;
    /* assign values */
    i = 10;
    j = 6;
    /* perform operations without typecasting */
    k = i + j;
    m = i - j;
    n = i * j;
    c = n + 5; /* conversion is automatic to character */
    x = i * j + 0.5;
    printf("i = %d\n",i);
    printf("j = %d\n",j);
    printf("k = %d\n",k);
    printf("m = %d\n",m);
    printf("n = %ld\n",n);
    printf("c is %c\n",c);
    printf("x = %f\n\n\n",x);
    /* perform operations with typecasting */
    /* note that C encloses the data type in parentheses */
    /* and not the expression, as does Turbo Pascal 4.0  */
    k = (unsigned short) (i + j);
```

```
        m = (int) (i - j);
        n = (long) (i * j);
        c = (unsigned char) (n + 5);
        /* the assignment below is valid in C, but not in Pascal */
        x = (float) (i * j + 0.5);
        printf("i = %d\n",i);
        printf("j = %d\n",j);
        printf("k = %d\n",k);
        printf("m = %d\n",m);
        printf("n = %ld\n",n);
        printf("c is %c\n",c);
        printf("x = %f\n\n\n",x);
}
```

The screen output of the C version is as follows:

```
i = 10
j = 6
k = 16
m = 4
n = 60
c is A
x = 60.500000
i = 10
j = 6
k = 16
m = 4
n = 60
c is A
x = 60.500000
```

In comparing the two listings, observe the following language differences and features of C:

1. In the automatic conversion section the two languages have almost equivalent expressions. One exception is the need to use the CHR() intrinsic in Pascal, while C sails smoothly in assigning the integer result to a character-typed variable. All other expressions are handled properly in both languages. Notably, Pascal converts (or perhaps *promotes* is a better word) integers into reals without a hitch.

2. In the type casting section the Pascal code is unable to type cast an integer expression into a floating-point one. If you uncomment the statement:

   `{ x := REAL(i * j + 0.5); }`

   and try to recompile, you will obtain a compile-time error message. The message basically informs you that you are attempting to type cast between two incompatible types. With C, no such problem arises.

   Also notice that in the C version, the assignment to the character-typed variable **c** uses the expression **(unsigned char) n + 5** to store the ASCII code number of the letter **A**.

3. The typecasting in C has a higher precedence than the +, -, /, and * operators. Therefore, the arithmetic expressions are enclosed in paren-

theses to typecast the result of the expression instead of a single operand. Removing the parentheses in the above C program yields the same answer, but through a slightly different route. The effect is that only the operands immediately following the typecast are converted. The compiler then promotes the other operands to obtain an expression with uniform types before evaluating it.

RELATIONAL OPERATORS AND CONDITIONAL EXPRESSIONS

The basic building blocks of decision-making constructs are relational operators. Table 4.3 lists these operators in C and their equivalent in Pascal. It is worth pointing to the equality test operator as a potential source of logical bugs when improperly written in C. Pascal programmers test for equality using the = operator, while C programs use ==. What happens when a = is used in a C program, by force of habit ? Turbo C compiles the program and displays a warning. When you run the program it will behave very strangely or even crash, when it reaches the part that is supposed to test for equality. Actually it is attempting to assign a value. Also keep in mind that the operators in Table 4.3 enter into logical expressions and are NOT used for bit manipulation; another set of operators is. Many relational operators utilize the same symbols in both languages. Those that do not will, in many cases, be a source of compiling errors, since old reflexes die hard. In the next chapter, I will discuss the use of macros that enable you to use the Pascal-inherited words and symbols, such as AND, OR, NOT, and <>. However, many recommend (for the sake of consistent readability) that you simply learn to use the relational operators without disguising them.

Table 4.3 Relational operators in C and their equivalent in Pascal

C Operator	Pascal Operator
&&	AND
||	OR
!	NOT
N/A	XOR
<	<
<=	<=
>	>
>=	>=
==	=
!=	<>
? :	N/A

Another important difference between Pascal and C is the precedence of the logical operators. In Pascal, logical operators have higher precedence that relational operators, while in C the reverse is true. Thus Pascal expressions like the ones shown below:

```
(x > 5) AND (y < 7)
(x <> 0) OR (y <> 0)
```

Are written in C as:

```
x > 5 && y < 7
x != 0 || y != 0
```

The C expression are equivalent to the Pascal ones, even though they do not use parentheses.

You will also notice in Table 4.3 two interesting items. First, C has no relational XOR operator (it does have a bit-wise XOR operator that is presented later). You can construct an XOR operator, as I will soon demonstrate. The second new item in the table is the "? :" operator, which is called the conditional expression. This is a miniature form of an IF statement that is invoked using the following general syntax:

```
<tested expression> ? <value 1> : <value 2>
```

The conditional expression tests an expression and returns <value 1> if the expression is not 0. Otherwise, <value 2> is returned. The <value 1> and <value 2> may be constants, variables, or expressions of any data type. In addition, the returned values need not match the data type of the tested expression.

The next program performs the following:

1. Prompts you for three integers.
2. Tests to determine if the first integer is a two-digit number.
3. Tests to determine if any of the three numbers you typed are equal.
4. Carries out a battery of logical tests to exercise various relational operators.

The Pascal version is shown below:

Listing 4.12

```
PROGRAM Logical_Expressions_1;
{ simple Turbo Pascal program that uses logical expressions }
VAR i, j, k : INTEGER;
    flag1, flag2,
    two_digit,  same_int   : BOOLEAN;
BEGIN
    WRITE('Enter first  integer : '); READLN(i); WRITELN;
    WRITE('Enter second integer : '); READLN(j); WRITELN;
    WRITE('Enter third  integer : '); READLN(k); WRITELN;
    { test for range [10..99] }
    flag1 := i >= 10;
    flag2 := i < 100;
    two_digit := flag1 AND flag2;
    WRITELN(i,' is a two-digit number : ',two_digit);
```

```
{ test if two or more entered numbers are equal }
same_int := (i = j) OR (i = k) OR (j =k);
WRITELN('at least two integers you typed are equal : ',
        same_int);
{ miscellaneous tests }
WRITELN(i,' = ',j,' : ',(i = j));
WRITELN('NOT (',i,' >= ',j,') : ',NOT(i >= j));
WRITELN(i,' > ',j,' : ',(i > j));
WRITELN(k,' <= ',j,' : ',(k <= j));
WRITELN('(',k,' = ',i,') OR (',j,' <> ',k,') : ',
        ((k = i) OR (j <> k)));
WRITELN('(',k,' <> ',i,') XOR (',j,' <> ',k,') : ',
        ((k <> i) XOR (j <> k)));
WRITELN('(',k,' < ',i,') AND (',j,' >= ',k,') : ',
        ((k < i) AND (j >= k)));
WRITELN; WRITELN;
END.
```

When you run the above program enter the integers 15, 55, and 77, as prompted. The screen image that contains the input and various logical conclusions about the numbers is shown below:

```
Enter first  integer : 15
Enter second integer : 25
Enter third  integer : 77
15 is a two-digit number : TRUE
at least two integers you typed are equal : FALSE
15 = 25 : FALSE
NOT (15 >= 25) : TRUE
15 > 25 : FALSE
77 <= 25 : FALSE
(77 = 15) OR (25 <> 77) : TRUE
(77 <> 15) XOR (25 <> 77) : FALSE
(77 < 15) AND (25 >= 77) : FALSE
```

Converting the Pascal program into C reveals some important differences between both languages. They are

1. C has no formal boolean type like Pascal. Therefore, all of the boolean types in the Pascal program are converted into **int**. C regards an expression with a zero value as false, and one with a nonzero value as true. This is important to remember. The C program uses the macros TRUE and FALSE to associate with them the values 1 and 0, respectively.

> **Programming Hint**
>
> It is safer to test a logical expression for a zero value and interpret it as false. A nonzero value, be it positive or negative, is taken as true.

2. Since C does not formally support booleans, the programmer is responsible for devising a method to display "TRUE" or "FALSE" to match Pascal's support for boolean output. The conditional expression can be

used to provide the needed solution using the following syntax:

 (((<expression>) ? "TRUE" : "FALSE"))

Such expressions are used with the **printf** to supply the sought text output.

3. Converting the Pascal XOR operator also requires working around the lack of a relational XOR operator in C. The solution comes in two steps and involves a new variable **xor_flag**. The first step is to add the numeric result from the logical tests **k != i** and **j != k** and assign the final result to **xor_flag**. The latter has a value in the range of 0 to 2. If **xor_flag** is 2, it is reset to 0. Finally, the conditional expression **((xor_flag) ? "TRUE" : "FALSE"))** is able to work properly.

Listing 4.13

```
/* simple C program that uses logical expressions     */
/* this program uses the conditional expression to display */
/* TRUE or FALSE messages, since C does not support the    */
/* BOOLEAN data type.                                  */
/* the use of conditional expression may easily be replaced */
/* by functions or macros, discussed later.            */
#include <stdio.h>
#define TRUE  1
#define FALSE 0
main()
{
    int i, j, k;
    int flag1, flag2, two_digit, same_int, xor_flag;
    printf("Enter first   integer : ");   scanf("%d", &i);
    printf("\nEnter second integer : ");  scanf("%d", &j);
    printf("\nEnter third  integer : ");  scanf("%d", &k);
    /* test for range [10..99] */
    flag1 = i >= 10;
    flag2 = i < 100;
    two_digit = flag1 && flag2;
    printf("\n%d is a two-digit number : %s", i,
              (two_digit) ? "TRUE" : "FALSE" );
    /* test if two or more entered numbers are equal */
    same_int = i == j || i == k || j == k;
    printf("\nat least two integers you typed are equal : %s",
              (same_int) ? "TRUE" : "FALSE");
    /* miscellaneous tests */
    printf("\n%d = %d : %s",i,j,(i == j) ? "TRUE" : "FALSE");
    printf("\nNOT (%d >= %d) : %s",i, j,
              ( !(i >= j) ) ? "TRUE" : "FALSE");
    printf("\n%d > %d : %s",i,j, (i > j) ? "TRUE" : "FALSE");
    printf("\n%d <= %d : %s",k,j,(k <= j) ? "TRUE" : "FALSE");
    printf("\n(%d = %d) OR (%d <> %d) : %s", k, i, j, k,
              (k == i || j != k) ? "TRUE" : "FALSE");
    /* NOTE: C does NOT support the logical XOR operator for   */
    /* boolean expressions.                                    */
    /* add numeric results of logical tests. Value is in 0..2 */
```

```
    xor_flag = (k != i) + (j != k);
    /* if xor_flag is either 0 or 2 (i.e. not = 1), it is */
    /* FALSE therefore interpret 2 as false.              */
    xor_flag = (xor_flag == 2) ? FALSE : TRUE;
    printf("\n(%d <> %d) XOR (%d <> %d) : %s", k, i, j, k,
           (xor_flag) ? "TRUE" : "FALSE");
    printf("\n(%d < %d) AND (%d >= %d) : %s", k, i, j, k,
           (k < i && j >= k) ? "TRUE" : "FALSE");
    printf("\n\n");
}
```

Run the C version and type the same integers used for the Pascal version (15, 55, and 77). The output of the C program appears to be identical to that of the Pascal version:

```
Enter first  integer : 15
Enter second integer : 55
Enter third  integer : 77
15 is a two-digit number : TRUE
at least two integers you typed are equal : FALSE
15 = 55 : FALSE
NOT (15 >= 55) : TRUE
15 > 55 : FALSE
77 <= 55 : FALSE
(77 = 15) OR (55 <> 77) : TRUE
(77 <> 15) XOR (55 <> 77) : FALSE
(77 < 15) AND (55 >= 77) : FALSE
```

BIT-MANIPULATION OPERATORS

C uses a separate set of operators for bit manipulation. Table 4.4 lists them, and some appear to resemble the relational operators. The relational AND and OR operators use **&&** and **||**, respectively, while the bitwise AND and OR operators use the single characters **&** and **|**. C goes beyond Pascal in supporting bit-manipulating operators: it also supports bit-manipulating assignments, listed in Table 4.5.

Table 4.4 Bit-manipulating operators in C and their equivalent Pascal operators

C Operator	Pascal Operator
&	AND
|	OR
^	XOR
~	NOT
<<	SHL
>>	SHR

Table 4.5 Bit-manipulating assignment operators in C

C Operator	Long Form
x &= y	x = x & y
x |= y	x = x | y
x ^= y	x = x ^ y
x <<= y	x = x << y
x >>= y	x = x >> y

The following simple program illustrates bit manipulations in Turbo Pascal:

Listing 4.14

```
PROGRAM Bit_Manipulation;
{ Turbo Pascal program that performs bit manipulations }
VAR i, j, k : INTEGER;
BEGIN
     { assign values to i and j }
     i := $F0;
     j := $AA;
     k := j AND i;
     WRITELN(j:3,' AND ',i:3,' = ',k:3);
     k := j OR i;
     WRITELN(j:3,' OR  ',i:3,' = ',k:3);
     k := j XOR $AB;
     WRITELN(j:3,' XOR ',$AB:3,' = ',k:3);
     k := i Shl 2;
     WRITELN(i:3,' shifted left 2 times = ',k:3);
     k := i Shr 2;
     WRITELN(i:3,' shifted right 2 times = ',k:3);
     WRITELN; WRITELN;
END.
```

When the above program runs, the following lines of output appear on the screen:
```
170 AND 240 = 160
170 OR  240 = 250
170 XOR 171 =   1
240 shifted left 2 times = 960
240 shifted right 2 times =  60
```

The C version of the above program is shown below:

Listing 4.15

```
/* C program to perform bit manipulations */
#include <stdio.h>
main()
{
```

C OPERATORS

```
    int i, j, k;
    /* assign values to i and j */
    i = 0xF0;
    j = 0xAA;
    k = j & i;
    printf("%3d AND %3d = %3d", j, i, k);
    k = j | i;
    printf("\n%3d OR  %3d = %3d", j, i, k);
    k = j ^ 0xAB;
    printf("\n%3d XOR %3d = %3d", j, 0xAB, k);
    k = i << 2;
    printf("\n%3d shifted left  2 times = %3d", i, k);
    k = i >> 2;
    printf("\n%3d shifted right 2 times = %3d", i, k);
    printf("\n\n");
}
```

The output of the C program is identical to that of Pascal:

```
170 AND 240 = 160
170 OR  240 = 250
170 XOR 171 =   1
240 shifted left  2 times = 960
240 shifted right 2 times =  60
```

The preceding two versions of the program illustrate that the corresponding operators function in the same fashion.

The next C program demonstrates the use of bit-manipulating assignment operators:

Listing 4.16

```
/* C program to perform bit manipulation assignments */
#include <stdio.h>
main()
{
    int i, j;
    /* assign values to i and j */
    i = 0xF0;
    j = 0xAA;
    printf("\n%3d AND %3d = ", j ,i);
    j &= i; /* same as j = j & i */
    printf("%3d", j);
    printf("\n%3d OR  %3d = ", j, i);
    j |= i; /* same as j = j | i */
    printf("%3d", j);
    printf("\n%3d XOR %3d = ", j, (i - 0xF));
    j ^= i - 0xF; /* same as j = j ^ (i - 0xF) */
    printf("%3d", j);
    printf("\n%3d shifted left  2 times = ", i);
    i <<= 2; /* same as i = i << 2 */
    printf("%3d", i);
    printf("\n%3d shifted right 2 times = ", i);
    i >>= 2; /* same as i = i >> 2 */
    printf("%3d\n\n", i);
}
```

The screen output of the above C program is as follows:
```
170 AND 240 = 160
160 OR  240 = 240
240 XOR 225 =  17
240 shifted left  2 times = 960
960 shifted right 2 times = 240
```

COMMA OPERATOR

The comma operator is one that is new to Pascal programmers. The general syntax of using the comma operator is
<expression 1>,<expression 2>

The comma forces the first expression to be completely evaluated before evaluating the second one WITHIN THE SAME STATEMENT. As a veteran Pascal programmer, you are probably wondering whether or not the designers of the C language have gone insane! You may ask, "What on earth does WITHIN THE SAME STATEMENT mean? Why use the comma operator at all?" Admittedly, the comma operator, with its rather unusual role, serves a particular and very powerful purpose in the **for** loop. Basically, by using the comma operators you are able to construct **for** loops with multiple loop control variables. Normally, in Pascal you have the main loop control variable and other variables that are initialized just outside the loop and systematically incremented within the loop. Well, C empowers you to implement the above with more style (now you realize that the designers of C really knew what they were doing!). I will discuss the use of the comma operators in the chapter on looping (Chapter 7).

Now that you have been exposed to most of the C operators (I have left out a few that deal with arrays and pointers, which I will discuss in the appropriate chapters) you may ask the following questions. First, "What is the precedence of the C operators?" Second, "What is the direction of evaluation of an expression influenced by the operators present in the expression?" Table 4.6 contains the list of operators you have encountered so far, along with the evaluation direction and precedence numbers. The evaluation direction indicates the order of evaluation for operators with the same precedence and separated by operands (for example, 4 * y * x). It it worth pointing out that lower precedence values have high priorities and vice versa.

CHAPTER SUMMARY

- C supports arithmetic operators that perform the four basic operations as well as the modulus, and the change of sign (see Table 4.1).
- The ++ and -- increment operators enable you to alter the value of any numeric-typed variable by one. Placing the ++ operator before the name of the variable is called preincrementing. Putting the ++ operator after the name of the variable is called postincrementing. Similarly, you have pre-

C OPERATORS 59

Table 4.6 Operators in C with their precedence and evaluation direction. Operators that have the precedence of 1 are not included here. The complete table is found in the appendix section.

Category	Name	Symbol	Eval. Direction	Precedence
Monadic				
	Post-increment	++	left to right	2
	Post-decrement	--	left to right	2
	Address	&	right to left	2
	Bitwise NOT	~	right to left	2
	Type cast	(type)	right to left	2
	Logical NOT	!	right to left	2
	Negation	-	right to left	2
	Plus sign	+	right to left	2
	Pre-increment	++	right to left	2
	Pre-decrement	--	right to left	2
	Type cast	(type)	right to left	2
	Size of data	sizeof	right to left	2
Multiplicative				
	Modulus	%	left to right	3
	Multiply	*	left to right	3
	Divide	/	left to right	3
Additive				
	Add	+	left to right	4
	Subtract	-	left to right	4
Bitwise Shift				
	Shift left	<<	left to right	5
	Shift right	>>	left to right	5
Relational				
	Less than	<	left to right	6
	Less or equal	<=	left to right	6
	Greater than	>	left to right	6
	Greater or equal	>=	left to right	6
	Equal to	==	left to right	7
	Not equal to	!=	left to right	7
Bitwise				
	AND	&	left to right	8
	XOR	^	left to right	9

Category	Name	Symbol	Eval. Direction	Precedence
	OR	|	left to right	10
Logical				
	AND	&&	left to right	11
	OR	||	left to right	12
Ternary				
	Cond. Express.	? :	right to left	13
Assignment				
	Arithmetic	=	right to left	14
		+=	right to left	14
		-=	right to left	14
		*=	right to left	14
		/=	right to left	14
		%=	right to left	14
	Shift	>>=	right to left	14
		<<=	right to left	14
	Bitwise	&=	right to left	14
		|=	right to left	14
		^=	right to left	14
	Comma	,	left to right	15

and postdecrementing with the -- operator. The effect is that the preoperation affects the value variable before it is used in any nested expression (for example, x = array[++i]), while the postoperation alters the value of the variable after is used in a nested expression [for example x = (y--) * z].

- C supports arithmetic assignment operators for all of the numeric types. The general syntax for using an assignment operator is

    <variable> <arithmetic operator>= <expression>

    which is equivalent to the longer form:

    <variable> = <variable> <arithmetic operator> <expression>

    C offers arithmetic assignment operators for all of the dyadic arithmetic operators.
- The **sizeof** operator returns the byte size of a data type of a variable.
- Type casting in C employs the following general syntax:

    (type casted) <expression>

    Type casting in C is able to promote integer types to floating point types.

- Relational operators in C include the && (AND), && (OR), ! (NOT), >, >=, !=, ==, <, and <= operators. An expression is false if it is 0, otherwise it is true. C has no relational XOR operator.
- The conditional expression is a miniature form of an IF statement used to return one of two values based on the result of a tested expression. The general syntax is

    (<tested expression>) ? <value if true> : <value if false>
- Bit manipulating operators in C include the & (AND), | (OR), ^ (XOR), ~ (NOT), << (shift left), and >> (shift right).

CHAPTER

5

The C Preprocessor and Compiler Directives

CHAPTER GOALS

This chapter focuses on two special aspects of C:
- The C preprocessor.
- The C compiler directives.

Compiler directives and the preprocessor play a very important role in C. Since C is meant to be a language for systems development, the ability to fine-tune the compiler's action is very important. While Turbo Pascal has added more directives, some of which seem to be inspired by C itself, it lacks an integrated preprocessor. The remedy for this situation in Turbo Pascal (as well as other Pascal implementations and other languages like Modula-2 and Ada) is to develop a separate utility that preprocesses your listings before you compile them. However, this still deprives the programmer of the convenience of having a preprocessor incorporated with the compiler, as is the case with C compilers.

THE C PREPROCESSOR

The C preprocessor works by examining your C source code for the **#define** directive. You have been exposed to this directive earlier while discussing constants in Chapter 3. The general syntax for using the macro-definition directive is

```
#define <macro> <macro text or value>
#define <macro>(<list of argument>) <macro expression>
```

C allows for one macro per line. The power of the macro definition is that you may include arguments. This enables you to create pseudofunctions using macros with arguments. Compared with formal functions, these macro-based functions are faster but occupy more code space because the preprocessor replaces every occurrence of macros with expressions.

Macros can be used for various purposes:
1. Defining constants.
2. Substituting reserved words or symbols with others.
3. Creating pseudodata type identifiers from standard ones. This is performed when a data type is used to emulate another type not available in C.
4. Creating shorthand commands.
5. Defining macro-based functions.

Macro definitions can be undone by utilizing the **#undef** directive followed by the macro name, as shown below:
#undef <macro name>

You need not undefine a macro to redefine it. The new macro definition automatically overwrites any previous one (a warning message to that effect is displayed).

The following example illustrates the above different applications for the C preprocessor:

Listing 5.1

```
/* C program that demonstrates the many uses of the #define   */
/* preprocessor directives to create pseudo types, functions */
/* and keywords.                                              */
#include <stdio.h>
#include "conio.h"
/* define a keyword macro */
#define MAIN_PROGRAM main()
#define BEGIN {
#define begin {
#define END_PROGRAM }
#define END }
#define end }
/* define data type macros */
#define BOOLEAN char
#define BYTE unsigned char
#define REAL double
#define INTEGER int
#define PRINT printf
#define WRITE printf
#define INPUT scanf
#define READ scanf
#define ReadKey getch()
#define ReadChar getche()
```

INTRODUCING C TO PASCAL PROGRAMMERS

```c
#define WRITELN printf("\n")
#define WRITELN2 printf("\n\n")
#define WRITELN3 printf("\n\n\n")
/* macros for popular shorthand command sequences */
#define readvar(msg,frmt,var) printf(msg); scanf(frmt,&var)
#define read2var(msg,frmt,x,y) printf(msg); scanf(frmt,&x,&y)
#define readchar(msg,var) printf(msg); var = getche()
#define wait_for_key akey = getch()
/* define screen macros. The ANSI.SYS driver MUST be installed  */
#define clrscr printf("\x1b[2J")
#define gotoxy(col,row)  printf("\x1b[%d;%dH",col,row)
#define clreol printf("\x1b[K")
/* define boolean constants */
#define FALSE 0
#define TRUE 1
/* boolean pseudo-functions */
#define boolean(x) ((x) ? "TRUE" : "FALSE")
#define yesno(x) ((x) ? "Yes" : "No")
/* macros that define pseudo one-line functions */
#define abs(x) (((x) >= 0) ? (x) : -(x))
#define max(x,y) (((x) > (y)) ? (x) : (y))
#define min(x,y) (((x) > (y)) ? (y) : (x))
#define sqr(x) ((x) * (x))
#define cube(x) ((x) * (x) * (x))
#define reciprocal(x) (1 / (x))
#define XOR(t1,t2) (((t1 + t2) == TRUE) ? TRUE : FALSE)
/* macros useful in translating Turbo Pascal programs */
#define inc(x) x++
#define dec(x) x--
#define dinc(x,y) x += (y)
#define ddec(x,y) x -= (y)
/* macros used for character testing */
#define islower(c) (c >= 'a' && c <= 'z')
#define isupper(c) (c >= 'A' && c <= 'Z')
#define isdigit(c) (c >= '0' && c <= '9')
#define isletter(c) ((c >= 'A' && c <= 'Z') || (c >= 'a' && c <= 'z'))
/* macros used in character case conversions */
#define tolowercase(c) (c - 'A' + 'a')
#define touppercase(c) (c - 'a' + 'A')
MAIN_PROGRAM
BEGIN
BOOLEAN bool;
BYTE i, j;
INTEGER k, m;
char ch, akey;
REAL x = 0.10;
readvar("Enter an integer : ","%d",k);
WRITELN;
WRITE("You entered %d", k);
WRITELN2;
WRITE("Enter another integer : "); READ("%d", &k);
WRITELN;
WRITE("%d squared = %d ", k, sqr(k));
WRITELN2;
```

THE C PREPROCESSOR AND COMPILER DIRECTIVES 65

```
WRITE("1 / %f = %f", x, reciprocal(x));
WRITELN2;
ch = 'A';
WRITE("The lowercase of %c is %c", ch, tolowercase(ch));
WRITELN2;
ch = 'g';
WRITE("The uppercase of %c is %c", ch, touppercase(ch));
printf("\n\npress any key to continue");
wait_for_key;
clrscr;
WRITE("\n\nType a letter or a digit : "); ch = ReadChar;
WRITELN2;
bool = isupper(ch);
gotoxy(5,10);
WRITE("character is uppercase : %s\n",boolean(bool));
bool = islower(ch);
gotoxy(6,10);
WRITE("character is lowercase : %s\n",boolean(bool));
bool = isletter(ch);
gotoxy(7,10);
WRITE("character is a letter   : %s\n",boolean(bool));
bool = isdigit(ch);
gotoxy(8,10);
WRITE("character is a digit    : %s\n",boolean(bool));
WRITELN;
read2var("Enter two integers (separated by a space) : ",
         "%d %d",k,m);
WRITELN2;
WRITE("The largest  of the two numbers is %d\n\n",max(k,m));
WRITE("The smallest of the two numbers is %d\n\n",min(k,m));
WRITE("ABS(%d) = %d\n\n", k, abs(k));
WRITE("%d + 1 = ", k);
inc(k);
WRITE("%d\n\n", k);
WRITE("%d - 1 = ", m);
dec(m);
WRITE("%d\n\n", m);
END_PROGRAM
```

I will now analyze each set of macros presented in the above program:

1. The first set of macros simply redefine C keywords, as shown below:
   ```
   #define MAIN_PROGRAM main()
   #define BEGIN {
   #define begin {
   #define END_PROGRAM }
   #define END }
   #define end }
   ```
   I have deliberately selected most of the macro names to be Pascal keywords. By using enough of such macros, you can disguise your C program to look like a Pascal program. While you can technically get away with such a code make-up job, other C programmers would find it less amusing. Such use of macros hurts the readability of your code and really

should be avoided. I have included the above set of macros to illustrate the extent of their use, which can include abusing them!

2. The second macro set is similar to the first, except is it used for a much sounder purpose. Recall that C does not have a predefined boolean data type. Thus, programmers resort to using integers, associating 0 with the logical false, and either 1 or -1 with the logical true. While the C type **int** is suitable, it occupies two bytes, whereas the character type occupies one byte and handles short integers. Consequently, I create the following macro:

```
#define BOOLEAN char
```

In addition, C does not explicitly have a one-word type identifier for bytes. The C type that matches Turbo Pascal's BYTE is the **unsigned char**. The following macro defines BYTE as the unsigned character type:

```
#define BYTE unsigned char
```

The next two macros are really optional conveniences for a novice C programmer:

```
#define REAL double
#define INTEGER int
```

3. The next set of macros create shorthand commands. The macro names are taken from Pascal keywords or derived from them:

```
#define PRINT printf
#define WRITE printf
#define INPUT scanf
#define READ scanf
#define ReadKey getch()
#define ReadChar getche()
#define WRITELN printf("\n")
#define WRITELN2 printf("\n\n")
#define WRITELN3 printf("\n\n\n")
```

4. The following set of macros also represents shorthand command sequences; the difference from the one above is that macro arguments are used. This adds much versatility to the macros and makes them behave like procedures. Notice that most of these macros are expanded into multiple C statements:

```
#define readvar(msg,frmt,var) printf(msg); scanf(frmt, &var)
#define read2var(msg,frmt,x,y) printf(msg); scanf(frmt, &x, &y)
#define readchar(msg,var) printf(msg); var = getche()
#define wait_for_key akey = getch()
```

5. The next set of macros is from the same category as the last one. I have deliberately grouped these macros since they provide commonly used cursor control and screen management operations. They require the ANSI.SYS screen driver. Turbo C 1.5 and later include libraries of functions that perform the same screen management tasks. Nevertheless, they are included to illustrate how easy it is to write macros for screen/cursor management, in case you program with a C compiler that lacks such functions:

```
#define clrscr printf("\x1b[2J")
#define gotoxy(col,row) printf("\x1b[%d;%dH",col,row)
#define clreol printf("\x1b[K")
```

6. The next two macros should look familiar, since they appeared in an earlier example. Despite their simplicity, these macros are important and are used rather extensively in C programs:

```
#define FALSE 0
#define TRUE 1
```

7. The following set of macros defines one-line math functions. Notice that the macro expressions are enclosed in parentheses. This is important to make sure that you get the correct result when the macro is used in a mathematical expression. Similarly, observe how the arguments of the macros are enclosed in parentheses. This insures that the macros yield the correct results if expressions are used as arguments:

```
#define abs(x) (((x) >= 0) ? (x) : -(x))
#define max(x,y) (((x) > (y)) ? (x) : (y))
#define min(x,y) (((x) > (y)) ? (y) : (x))
#define sqr(x) ((x) * (x))
#define cube(x) ((x) * (x) * (x))
#define reciprocal(x) (1 / (x))
#define XOR(t1,t2) (((t1+t2)==TRUE) ? TRUE : FALSE)
```

Programming Hint

When declaring a mathematical macro with arguments, enclose each argument, as well as the entire macro expression, in parentheses in the macro expression.

8. The next set of macros mimics the Turbo Pascal intrinsics INC() and DEC(). The **dinc** and **ddec** macros mimic the INC() and DEC() intrinsics with two arguments:

```
#define inc(x) x++
#define dec(x) x--
#define dinc(x,y) x += (y)
#define ddec(x,y) x -= (y)
```

Remember that these macros also work with floating-point data types, something that Turbo Pascal is unable to support with its INC() and DEC() intrinsics.

9. The following collection of macros perform character classification tests. These include lower-case, upper-case, digit, and alphabet letters:

```
#define islower(c) (c >= 'a' && c <= 'z')
#define isupper(c) (c >= 'A' && c <= 'Z')
#define isdigit(c) (c >= '0' && c <= '9')
#define isletter(c)  \
            ((c >= 'A' && c <= 'Z') || (c >= 'a' && c <= 'z'))
```

10. The last set of macros defines pseudofunctions that convert the case of characters:
    ```
    #define tolowercase(c)  (c - 'A' + 'a')
    #define touppercase(c)  (c - 'a' + 'A')
    ```
    When you run the program, follow these steps:
1. Type the integer 55 in response to the first prompt. The program displays the number you typed. The **readvar** macro is involved in the input step, while the **WRITE** macro is used to display the output.
2. In response to the second prompt, enter 67. The program displays the square of the number you typed. The **WRITE** and **sqr** macros are employed in displaying the square of the number you typed.
3. The program proceeds to display the reciprocal of 0.1, the lower-case equivalent of the letter **A**, and the upper-case equivalent of the upper-case letter **G**. The **reciprocal, tolowercase**, and **touppercase** macros are involved in displaying the above information.
4. You are prompted to press any key to proceed. The **wait_for_key** macro is used in this prompt. After you press any key, the screen is cleared using the **clrscr** macro.
5. You are then prompted to type a letter or a digit. Type the letter **h**. The macros **islower, isupper, isdigit,** and **isletter** are engaged in classifying your input.
6. The program prompts you to enter two integers delimited by a space. In response, enter 11 and 100. The **max** and **min** macros are applied to obtain the larger and smaller of the two numbers you typed.
7. The program displays the absolute value of the first number you typed in the last prompt, using the **abs** macro.
8. The macro **inc** and **dec** are applied to the last two numbers you typed.

The screen image for the session described above is shown here:

```
Enter an integer : 55
You entered 55
Enter another integer : 67
67 squared = 4489
1 / 0.100000 = 10.000000
The lowercase of A is a
The uppercase of g is G
press any key to continue <cr>
Type a letter or a digit : h
character is uppercase : FALSE
character is lowercase : TRUE
character is a letter  : TRUE
character is a digit   : FALSE
Enter two integers (separated by a space) : 11 100
The largest  of the two numbers is 100
The smallest of the two numbers is 11
ABS(11) = 11
11 + 1 = 12
100 - 1 = 99
```

THE C PREPROCESSOR AND COMPILER DIRECTIVES   **69**

Despite the fact that the above program is perfectly functional, some of the macros are considered undesirable. Not wanting to leave you with an odd-looking program, I present a toned-down version of the program. In addition, this new version includes the file SCRNCURS.H that contains the screen-handling macros. The new version is shown below:

Listing 5.2

```
/* C program that demonstrates the many uses of the #define */
/* preprocessor directives to create pseudo types and       */
/* functions.                                               */
/* this version avoids macros that 'redefine'               */
/* important C keywords and symbols.                        */
#include <stdio.h>
#include "conio.h"
#include "scrncurs.h"
/* define data type macros */
#define BOOLEAN char
#define BYTE unsigned char
/* define boolean constants */
#define FALSE 0
#define TRUE 1
/* define macro used in waiting for a key to be pressed */
#define wait_for_key  akey = getch()
/* boolean pseudo-functions */
#define boolean(x) (x) ? "TRUE" : "FALSE"
#define yesno(x) (x) ? "Yes" : "No"
/* macros that define pseudo one-line functions */
#define abs(x) (((x) >= 0) ? (x) : -(x))
#define max(x,y) (((x) > (y)) ? (x) : (y))
#define min(x,y) (((x) > (y)) ? (y) : (x))
#define sqr(x) ((x) * (x))
#define cube(x) ((x) * (x) * (x))
#define reciprocal(x) (1 / (x))
#define XOR(t1,t2) (((t1+t2) != 1) ? 0 : 1)
/* macros useful in translating Turbo Pascal programs */
#define inc(x) x++
#define dec(x) x--
#define dinc(x,y) x += (y)
#define ddec(x,y) x -= (y)
/* marcos used for character testing */
#define islower(c) (c >= 'a' && c <= 'z')
#define isupper(c) (c >= 'A' && c <= 'Z')
#define isdigit(c) (c >= '0' && c <= '9')
#define isletter(c) \
             ((c >= 'A' && c <= 'Z') || (c >= 'a' && c <= 'z'))
/* macros used in character case conversions */
#define tolowercase(c) (c - 'A' + 'a')
#define touppercase(c) (c - 'a' + 'A')
main()
{
    BOOLEAN bool;
    BYTE i, j;
    int k, m;
```

```
    char ch, akey;
    double x = 0.10;
    printf("Enter an integer : "); scanf("%d", &k);
    printf("\n");
    printf("You entered %d", k);
    printf("\n\n");
    printf("Enter another integer : "); scanf("%d", &k);
    printf("\n");
    printf("%d squared = %d ", k, sqr(k));
    printf("\n\n");
    printf("1 / %f = %f", x, reciprocal(x));
    printf("\n\n");
    ch = 'A';
    printf("The lowercase of %c is %c", ch, tolowercase(ch));
    printf("\n\n");
    ch = 'g';
    printf("The uppercase of %c is %c", ch, touppercase(ch));
    printf("\n\npress any key to continue");
    wait_for_key;
    clrscr;
    printf("\n\nType a letter or a digit : "); ch = getche();
    bool = isupper(ch);
    gotoxy(10,5);
    printf("character is uppercase : %s\n",boolean(bool));
    bool = islower(ch);
    gotoxy(10,6);
    printf("character is lowercase : %s\n",boolean(bool));
    bool = isletter(ch);
    gotoxy(10,7);
    printf("character is a letter  : %s\n",boolean(bool));
    bool = isdigit(ch);
    gotoxy(10,8);
    printf("character is a digit   : %s\n",boolean(bool));
    printf("\n");
    printf("Enter two integers (delimted by a space) : ");
    scanf("%d %d", &k, &m);
    printf("\n\n");
    printf("The largest  of the two numbers is %d\n\n",max(k,m));
    printf("The smallest of the two numbers is %d\n\n",min(k,m));
    printf("ABS(%d) = %d\n\n", k, abs(k));
    printf("%d + 1 = ", k);
    inc(k);
    printf("%d\n\n", k);
    printf("%d - 1 = ", m);
    dec(m);
    printf("%d\n\n", m);
}
```

The new version works the same way as the previous one. The contents of file "scrncurs.h" are

```
/* contents of file scrncrs.h */
#define clrscr printf("\x1b[2J")
#define gotoxy(col,row) printf("\x1b[%d;%dH",col,row)
#define clreol printf("\x1b[K")
```

PREDEFINED MACROS

There are five predefined macros specified by the ANSI standard. They are
1. __LINE__ returns the line number assigned by the **#line** directive (see the discussion on the directive later in this chapter).
2. __FILE__ returns the filename assigned by the **#line** directive (see the discussion on the directive later in this chapter).
3. __DATE__ is the macro that contains the date of compiling the source code into object form. The <month>/<day>/<year> date form is returned.
4. __TIME__ is the macro that contains the time of compiling the source code into object form. The time format used is HH:MM:SS.
5. __STDC__ is a macro that returns a value of 1 to indicate that the C implementation conforms to the ANSI standard.

Turbo C predefines additional macros. Consult the Turbo C manuals for more information.

COMPILER DIRECTIVES

C compilers support a number of compiler directives. They are
1. The **#include** directive. This directive enables you to include the text of another file as though you had typed it. The contents of the included file are merged at the location of the directive. The general syntax for this directive takes two forms:
   ```
   #include <filename>
   ```
   or
   ```
   #include "filename"
   ```
   The two forms differ in the way the included file is sought. Using the angle brackets, the search takes place only in the special directory for included files. To extend the search into the default directory employ the quoted form.

   This directive has been used in many of the programs presented in this and earlier chapters.
2. The **#error** error message directive. This directive halts program compilation when encountered and displays an accompanying error message. The general syntax is
   ```
   #error <error message text>
   ```
3. The **#if, #else, #elif,** and **#endif** conditional compilation directives. These directives act in a fashion similar to IF statements, except the outcome involves the decision of whether or not to compile certain code portions.

   The following example illustrates the use of the above directives. Given a function (defined using a macro), the program gives you three choices for evaluating its first derivative: (1) using another macro-based pseudofunction, (2) using a more accurate numerical method, (3) or using a less accurate but faster numerical method. The macros USE_MACRO and MORE_ACCURATE are used to select one of the three alternative methods. The version presented below will compile the statement in the #elif clause and discard the other two options. The C listing is shown below:

Listing 5.3

```
/* C program to demonstrate conditional directives */
#include <stdio.h>
#define myfunc(x) ((x) * (x) * (x) - 5.0L)
#define frst_drv(x) (3.0L * (x) * (x))
#define INCREMENT 0.01L
/*
    the following macro switches causes the numerical evaluation of
    of the first derivative to be used.
*/
#define USE_MACRO 0
/*
    the following macro causes more accurate numerical
    evaluation to be used.
*/
#define MORE_ACCURATE 1
main()
{
       double x, derivative;
        printf("Enter nonzero value : "); scanf("%lf", &x);
       printf("\n\n");
       #if USE_MACRO == 1
           derivative = frst_drv(x);
       #elif MORE_ACCURATE == 1
               derivative = (myfunc(x+INCREMENT)-myfunc(x-INCREMENT))
                                    /(2.0L * INCREMENT);
       #else
               derivative = (myfunc(x+INCREMENT)-myfunc(x))/INCREMENT;
       #endif
          printf("df/dx = %lf at %lf\n\n", derivative, x);
}
```

4. The **#line** directive. This directive enables you to assign a value to the predefined macro __LINE__ and a filename to the macro __FILE__. The general syntax for using this directive is

    ```
    #line <line number> ["filename"]
    ```

    The combination of the __LINE__ and __FILE__ macros with the **#line** directive is used in debugging.

5. The **#pragma** directive. The ANSI standard loosely defines a set of general-purpose **#pragma** directives in the following form:

    ```
    #pragma <directive name>
    ```

The pragma directives may vary in the C implementations that support them. The rule that is used is "if the directive is not recognized, ignore the pragma directive altogether."

There are two pragma directives supported by Turbo C:

5.1. The **#pragma inline** directive informs the compiler that your source code contains in-line assembly language code.

5.2. The **#pragma warn** causes the Turbo C to override warning messages. You can include settings to turn on, turn off, or restore warning values (to those same values as when file compilation started). The above settings are shown below:

Directive	Meaning
#pragma warn +<wrn1>	Warning <wrn1> is turned on.
#pragma warn -<wrn2>	Warning <wrn2> is turned off.
#pragma warn .<wrn3>	Warning <wrn3> is restored.

CHAPTER SUMMARY

C has the following directives:

- **#define** defines numeric or text-based macros with optional arguments. The general syntax is

  ```
  #define <macro> <macro text or value>
  #define <macro>(<list of argument>) <macro expression>
  ```

- Macros created by **#define** are undefined using the **#undef** directive. The general syntax is

  ```
  #undef <macro name>
  ```

- The **#include** directive is used to include the source code from another file.

  ```
  #include <filename>
  ```

  or

  ```
  #include "filename"
  ```

  The two forms differ in the way the included file is sought. Using the angle brackets, the search takes place only in the special directory for included files. To extend the search into the default directory employ the quoted form.

  This directive has been used in many of the programs presented in this and earlier chapters.

- The **#error** error message directive is used to halt program compilation when encountered and displays an accompanying error message. The general syntax is

  ```
  #error <error message text>
  ```

- The **#if**, **#else**, **#elif**, and **#endif** conditional compilation directives. These directives act in a fashion similar to IF statements, except the outcome involves the decision of whether or not to compile certain code portions.
- The **#line** directive. This directive enables you to assign a value to the predefined macro __LINE__ and a filename to the macro __FILE__. The general syntax for using this directive is

    #line <line number> ["filename"]

- The **#pragma** directive. The ANSI standard loosely defines a collection of general-purpose **#pragma** directives in the following form:

    #pragma <directive name>

    Turbo C supports two pragma directives, namely, **inline** and **warn**.

CHAPTER

6

Decision-Making

CHAPTER GOALS

This chapter looks at the two main decision-making constructs in C:
- The various forms of the if statement.
- The switch construct.

While this aspect of a programming language is vital, the type and features of decision-making constructs varies from one language to another. This chapter looks at the decision-making constructs in C and how they differ from those used in Pascal.

THE if STATEMENT

Like many languages, such as BASIC, Pascal, and Modula-2, C supports the **if** statement in the various forms you expect. However, C uses a syntax that is slightly different from these other languages.

The Simple if Statement

Notice that I did not say, as you might have expected, the **if-then** statement. This is because C does not use the keyword **then**. Your next question is, most likely, "How does C delimit between the tested expression and the statements executed?" The answer lies in the fact that the tested expression is always enclosed in parentheses for all forms of the **if** statements in C. The general syntax for an **if** statement that executes a single statement, when the tested

75

expression is true, (that is, nonzero) is
```
if (<tested expression is not zero>)
      <C statement>;
```
When the **if** statement needs to execute multiple statements, they are enclosed in braces, much like the BEGIN-END block of Pascal. The general syntax is then
```
if (<tested expression is not zero>) {
      <sequence of C statements>;
}
```
The location of the braces need not adhere to the above representation, as long as the open brace is found between the close parenthesis and the first statement in the block. Every statement in the **if** block MUST end with a semicolon. The closed brace MUST NOT be followed by a semicolon. This is an aspect where C and Pascal differ, and it is important to remember.

Program Translation

To translate a simple IF statement in Pascal to C, use the following general format:
```
Pascal:
          IF <boolean expression> THEN <statement>
C:
          if (<boolean expression>) <statement>
```
For THEN clauses that contain a statement block, use:
```
Pascal:
          IF <boolean expression> THEN BEGIN
             <sequence of statements>
          END;
C:
          if (<boolean expression>) {
             <sequence of statements>
          }
```

The following program in both its Pascal and C versions solve for the real root of a quadratic equation in the form:

A X^2 + B X + C = 0

The program sequentially prompts you to enter values for the coefficients **A, B,** and **C**. The program calculates the value of the discriminant. If it is found to be negative, then the roots are imaginary and a warning message is displayed. By contrast, if the discriminant is not negative, the roots are calculated and displayed. I am using two separate IF statements for the sake of illustration. The first IF statement has only one statement in its THEN clause, while the second one has a block of statements. The Pascal version is shown below:

Listing 6.1

```pascal
PROGRAM Decision_Making_1;
{ Turbo Pascal program that solves the real roots of
  a quadratic equation                                 }
VAR a, b, c,
    discriminant,
    root1, root2 : REAL;
BEGIN
    WRITE('SOLVE FOR THE REAL ROOTS OF A QUADRATIC EQUATION':60);
    WRITELN; WRITELN; WRITELN;
    WRITELN('The equation is Y = A X^2 + B X + C');
    WRITELN; WRITELN;
    WRITE('Enter A : '); READLN(a); WRITELN;
    WRITE('Enter B : '); READLN(b); WRITELN;
    WRITE('Enter C : '); READLN(c); WRITELN;
    discriminant := b * b - 4.0 * a * c;
    IF discriminant < 0 THEN
       WRITELN('Imaginary roots');
    IF (discriminant >= 0) AND (a <> 0.0) THEN BEGIN
       root1 := (-b + SQRT(discriminant)) / (2 * a);
       root2 := (-b - SQRT(discriminant)) / (2 * a);

       WRITELN('Root1 = ',root1); WRITELN;
       WRITELN('Root2 = ',root2); WRITELN;

    END; { IF }
END.
```

The C version is presented below. Notice that I have defined the macros **THEN** and **then** as dummy macros (that is, they are simply removed by the preprocessor). They are for the die-hard Pascal programmer who is just beginning to learn C. However, their prolonged use is not recommended.

Listing 6.2

```c
/* C program that solves the real roots
   of a quadratic equation                              */
/* These macros make THEN and then harmless.            */
/* They are provided for the die-hard Pascal programmer. */
/* NOT recommended by veteran C programmers!!           */
#define THEN
#define then
#include <stdio.h>
#include "math.h"
main()
{
    float a, b, c;
    float discriminant;
    float root1, root2;
    printf("\t\t"); /* tab twice */
    printf("SOLVE FOR THE REAL ROOTS OF A QUADRATIC EQUATION");
```

```
    printf("\n\n");
    printf("The equation is Y = A X^2 + B X + C\n");
    printf("\nEnter A : "); scanf("%f", &a);
    printf("\nEnter B : "); scanf("%f", &b);
    printf("\nEnter C : "); scanf("%f", &c);
    printf("\n\n");
    discriminant = b * b - 4.0 * a * c;
    /* note logical expression MUST be enclosed in
       parentheses in C                              */
    if (discriminant < 0) THEN
       printf("Imaginary roots\n");
    if (discriminant >= 0 && a != 0.0) {
       root1 = (-b + sqrt(discriminant)) / (2 * a);
       root2 = (-b - sqrt(discriminant)) / (2 * a);
       printf("Root1 = %f\n\n",root1);
       printf("Root2 = %f\n\n",root2);

    } /* if */

}
```

In comparing the Pascal and C listings, notice how different the second Pascal IF statement becomes when translated into C:

Pascal:
```
    IF (discriminant >= 0) AND (a <> 0.0) THEN BEGIN
```
C:
```
    if (discriminant >= 0 && a != 0.0) {
```
Observe the following differences:

1. The Pascal operators AND and <> are translated into && and !=.
2. The entire tested C expression is enclosed in parentheses.
3. The Pascal THEN keyword is removed from that particular **if** statement in the C version.
4. The BEGIN and END keywords are replaced by the open and close braces.

While these differences have been pointed out in various places earlier, it is beneficial for many readers to be reminded of them again. Using Pascal keywords for relational operators in your C program causes compile-time errors.

The if-else Statement

This form offers two alternative action routes based on the outcome of the tested experession, and is equivalent to the IF-THEN-ELSE statement in Pascal. The **else** keyword is used to delimit the two alternate courses of action. The general syntax for an **if-else** statement with a single statement in each clause is

```
if (<tested expression is not zero>)
      <C statement>;
else
      <C statement>;
```

If the **if** statement needs to execute multiple statements, they are enclosed in braces. The general syntax is then

```
if (<tested expression is not zero>) {
      <sequence of C statements>;
}
else {
      <sequence of C statements>;
}
```

> **Program Translation**
>
> To translate a simple IF-THEN-ELSE statement in Pascal to C, use the following general format:
>
> Pascal:
>
>   IF <boolean expression> THEN
>   <single statement> | BEGIN <statement block> END
>   ELSE
>   <single statement> | BEGIN <statement block> END
>
> C:
>
>   if (<boolean expression>)
>   <single statement> | { <statement block> }
>   else
>   <single statement> | { <statement block> }

To illustrate the use of the **if-else** statement, I now enhance the above example, enabling the program to yield both real and complex roots for the quadratic equation. The discriminant is calculated and its value is tested in a Pascal IF-THEN-ELSE and C if-else statements. The Pascal version is listed below:

Listing 6.3

```
PROGRAM Decision_Making_2;
{ Turbo Pascal program that solves the roots of a quadratic }
{ equation this version uses IF-THEN-ELSE clauses.          }
VAR a, b, c,
    discriminant,
    real_part, imag_part,
    root1, root2          : REAL;
BEGIN
    WRITELN('SOLVE FOR THE ROOTS OF A QUADRATIC EQUATION':60);
    WRITELN; WRITELN;
    WRITELN('The equation is Y = A X^2 + B X + C');
    WRITELN; WRITELN;
    WRITE('Enter A : '); READLN(a); WRITELN;
    WRITE('Enter B : '); READLN(b); WRITELN;
    WRITE('Enter C : '); READLN(c); WRITELN;
    discriminant := b * b - 4.0 * a * c;
    IF discriminant >= 0.0  THEN BEGIN
        root1 := (-b + SQRT(discriminant)) / (2 * a);
        root2 := (-b - SQRT(discriminant)) / (2 * a);
```

```
        WRITELN('Root1 = ',root1); WRITELN;
        WRITELN('Root2 = ',root2); WRITELN;
    END
    ELSE BEGIN
        real_part := SQRT(-discriminant) / (2 * a);
        imag_part := -b / (2 * a);

        WRITELN('Root1 = (',real_part,') + i (',imag_part,')');
        WRITELN;
        WRITELN('Root2 = (',real_part,') - i (',imag_part,')');
        WRITELN;
    END; { IF }

END.
```

The C version is shown below:

Listing 6.4

```c
/* C program that solves the roots of a quadratic equation */
/* This version uses if-else clauses.                      */
#include <stdio.h>
#include "math.h"
main()
{
    float a, b, c, discriminant;
    float real_part, imag_part, root1, root2;
    printf("\t\tSOLVE FOR THE ROOTS OF A QUADRATIC EQUATION");
    printf("\n\n");
    printf("The equation is Y = A X^2 + B X + C\n");
    printf("\nEnter A : "); scanf("%f", &a);
    printf("\nEnter B : "); scanf("%f", &b);
    printf("\nEnter C : "); scanf("%f", &c);
    printf("\n\n");
    discriminant = b * b - 4.0 * a * c;
    if (discriminant >= 0.0)    {
        root1 = (-b + sqrt(discriminant)) / (2 * a);
        root2 = (-b - sqrt(discriminant)) / (2 * a);
        printf("Root1 = %f\n\n",root1);
        printf("Root2 = %f\n\n",root2);
    }
    else {
        real_part = sqrt(-discriminant) / (2 * a);
        imag_part = -b / (2 * a);
        printf("Root1 = (%f) + i (%f)\n\n",real_part,imag_part);
        printf("Root2 = (%f) - i (%f)\n\n",real_part,imag_part);
    } /* if */
}
```

Notice again the use of the braces to contain blocks of statements. In addition, notice how each statement ends with a semicolon, and that the close braces are NOT followed by semicolons.

You can nest **if-else** statements, just like in Pascal. The general syntax for nested if statements is

DECISION-MAKING 81

```
if (<test #1>)
    <single statement> | { <sequence of statements> }
else if (<test #2>)
    <single statement> | { <sequence of statements> }
else if (<test #3>)
    <single statement> | { <sequence of statements> }
else if (<test #4>)
    <single statement> | { <sequence of statements> }
...
else if (<test #n>)
    <single statement> | { <sequence of statements> }
else
    <single statement> | { <sequence of statements> }
```

The above general syntax suggests that the program flow cascades from one tested expression into another until one of two things occurs:

1. One of the tested expressions is found to be true (that is, nonzero).
2. The **else** clause is reached when all of the tested expressions are found to be false (that is, zero).

To illustrate the nested if statement, I will expand on my root-solving example one more time. The change is based on the fact that when the discriminant is positive, the roots are real and different; when it is 0, the roots are real and equal; and when it is negative, the roots are complex. To implement the above algorithm, I resort to a nested IF statement. The Pascal version is shown below:

Listing 6.5

```
PROGRAM Decision_Making_3;
{ Turbo Pascal program that solves the roots of a quadratic  }
{ equation this version uses IF-THEN-ELSE IF clauses.        }
VAR a, b, c,
    discriminant,
    real_part, imag_part,
    root1, root2           : REAL;
BEGIN
    WRITELN('SOLVE FOR THE ROOTS OF A QUADRATIC EQUATION':60);
    WRITELN; WRITELN;
    WRITELN('The equation is Y = A X^2 + B X + C');
    WRITELN; WRITELN;
    WRITE('Enter A : '); READLN(a); WRITELN;
    WRITE('Enter B : '); READLN(b); WRITELN;
    WRITE('Enter C : '); READLN(c); WRITELN;
    discriminant := b * b - 4.0 * a * c;
    IF (discriminant > 0.0) THEN BEGIN
        root1 := (-b + SQRT(discriminant)) / (2 * a);
        root2 := (-b - SQRT(discriminant)) / (2 * a);
        WRITELN('Root1 = ',root1); WRITELN;
        WRITELN('Root2 = ',root2); WRITELN;
    END
    ELSE IF discriminant = 0.0 THEN BEGIN { two identical roots }
        root1 := -b / (2 * a);
        WRITELN('Root1 = ',root1); WRITELN;
```

```pascal
            WRITELN('Root2 = ',root1); WRITELN;
        END
        ELSE BEGIN { discriminant < 0.0 }
            real_part := SQRT(-discriminant) / (2 * a);
            imag_part := -b / (2 * a);
            WRITELN('Root1 = (',real_part,') + i (',imag_part,')');
            WRITELN;
            WRITELN('Root2 = (',real_part,') - i (',imag_part,')');
            WRITELN;
        END; { IF }
END.
```

Run the above Pascal program and enter the values 2, -4, and 5 for **A**, **B**, and **C**, respectively. The screen image of the sample session is shown below:

```
            SOLVE FOR THE ROOTS OF A QUADRATIC EQUATION

The equation is Y = A X^2 + B X + C
Enter A : 2
Enter B : -4
Enter C : 5
Root1 = ( 1.22474487139152E+0000) + i ( 1.00000000000000E+0000)
Root2 = ( 1.22474487139152E+0000) - i ( 1.00000000000000E+0000)
```

Thus, the solution returns two complex roots.
The C version is listed below:

Listing 6.6

```c
/* C program that solves the roots of a quadratic equation */
/* This version uses nested if-else clauses.              */
#include <stdio.h>
#include "math.h"
main()
{
    float a, b, c, discriminant;
    float real_part, imag_part;
    float root1, root2;
    printf("\t\tSOLVE FOR THE ROOTS OF A QUADRATIC EQUATION");
    printf("\n\n");
    printf("The equation is Y = A X^2 + B X + C\n");
    printf("\nEnter A : "); scanf("%f", &a);
    printf("\nEnter B : "); scanf("%f", &b);
    printf("\nEnter C : "); scanf("%f", &c);
    printf("\n\n");
    discriminant = b * b - 4.0 * a * c;
    if (discriminant > 0.0)
    {
        root1 = (-b + sqrt(discriminant)) / (2 * a);
        root2 = (-b - sqrt(discriminant)) / (2 * a);
        printf("Root1 = %f\n\n", root1);
        printf("Root2 = %f\n\n", root2);
    }
    else if (discriminant == 0.0)
    { /* two identical roots */
```

```
            root1 = -b / (2 * a);
            printf("Root1 = %f\n\n",root1);
            printf("Root2 = %f\n\n",root1);
    }
    else
    { /* discriminant < 0.0 */
            real_part = sqrt(-discriminant) / (2 * a);
            imag_part = -b / (2 * a);
            printf("Root1 = (%f) + i (%f)",real_part,imag_part);
            printf("\n\n");
            printf("Root2 = (%f) - i (%f)",real_part,imag_part);
            printf("\n\n");
    }
}
```

Run the C program and enter the same coefficients used earlier (2, -4, and 5). The results are the same, but are displayed using fewer digits:

```
        SOLVE FOR THE ROOTS OF A QUADRATIC EQUATION
The equation is Y = A X^2 + B X + C
Enter A : 2
Enter B : -4
Enter C : 5
Root1 = (1.224745) + i (1.000000)
Root2 = (1.224745) - i (1.000000)
```

The next program also illustrates nested **if** statements while tackling a different problem. The program is a simple four-function calculator that is invoked to perform one operation (this program is enhanced in the next chapter to perform multiple operations). The program user is prompted to enter the first operand, the desired basic operation, and the second operand. Division by 0 is detected and an error message is displayed. In addition, if you type an invalid operator symbol you also get an error message.

Listing 6.7

```
PROGRAM Decision_Making_4;
Uses CRT;
{ simple Turbo Pascal program that implements a one-time }
{ simple four-function calculator                        }
VAR ok : BOOLEAN;
    op : CHAR;
    x, y, z : REAL;
BEGIN
    WRITE('Enter first number : '); READLN(x); WRITELN;
    WRITE('Enter operation [in +-/*] : '); op := ReadKey;
    WRITELN(op); WRITELN;
    WRITE('Enter second number : '); READLN(y); WRITELN;
    ok := TRUE; { assign optimistic default }
    IF op = '+' THEN
        z := x + y
    ELSE IF op = '-' THEN
        z := x - y
```

84 INTRODUCING C TO PASCAL PROGRAMMERS

```
      ELSE IF op = '*' THEN
         z := x * y
      ELSE IF op = '/' THEN
         IF y <> 0.0 THEN
            z := x / y
         ELSE BEGIN { division by zero }
            WRITELN('Error: Cannot divide by zero!');
            ok := FALSE
         END
      ELSE BEGIN { bad operator }
         WRITELN('You entered a bad operator');
         ok := FALSE
      END; { IF }

   WRITELN; WRITELN;
   IF ok THEN BEGIN {display results if available }
      WRITELN(x,' ',op,' ',y,' = ',z);
      WRITELN; WRITELN
   END;

END.
```

The C version is shown as

Listing 6.8

```c
/* simple C program that implements a one-time      */
/* simple four-function calculator                   */
#include <stdio.h>
#include "conio.h"
#define BOOLEAN char
#define TRUE 1
#define FALSE 0
main()
{
    BOOLEAN ok = TRUE;
    char op;
    float x, y, z;
    printf("Enter first number : "); scanf("%f", &x);
    printf("\nEnter operation [in +-/*] : "); op = getche();
    printf("\nEnter second number : "); scanf("%f", &y);
    printf("\n");
    if (op == '+')
       z = x + y;
    else if (op == '-')
       z = x - y;
    else if (op == '*')
       z = x * y;
    else if (op == '/')
     { if (y != 0.0)
          z = x / y;
        else
        { /* division by zero */
           printf("Error: Cannot divide by zero!\n");
           ok = FALSE;
```

```
        }
    }
    else
    { /* bad operator */
        printf("You entered a bad operator");
        ok = FALSE;
    }
    printf("\n\n");
    if (ok)    /* display results if available */
        printf("%f %c %f = %f\n\n\n",x,op,y,z);
}
```

Notice that the characters used in comparing the user-typed operator are enclosed in single quotes and not double quotes. Also observe the use of == as the relational operator for testing equality. The last **else** clause is used in both versions to detect invalid operator symbols.

THE switch STATEMENT

Looking at the last example, you may have thought that, as a veteran Pascal programmer, you would replace the nested loops with a CASE statement. Fortunately, C supports the **switch** statement which is similar to the CASE statement, with a few subtle differences. The general syntax for the switch statement is

```
switch (<variable> {
    case <constant1>
  [case <constant2>...]
        <one or more statements>;
        break;
    case <constant3>
  [case <constant4>...]
        <one or more statements>;
        break;
    ......
    default:
        <one or more statements>;
        break;
}
```

The difference between the C **switch** and Pascal CASE statements is greater than that between the C **if** and Pascal IF statements. The following aspects should be noted:

1. The **switch** value must be an integer-compatible value. You may use a constant, variable, expression, and function as the switch variable. You cannot use floating-point data types.
2. The value used in each **case** label must be a constant. Since C does not support a syntax for a range of values (in Pascal this is represented by "<first value>..<last value>"), you must use a separate case label FOR EACH VALUE.

Programming Hint

If the list of values is large and forms a continuous range, you may be better off using a nested if-else statement.

Program Translation

To translate a Pascal CASE statement into a switch statement in C, use the following general form:

```
Pascal:
    CASE <case-var> OF
        <case list #1> : <single statement> |
                        BEGIN <sequence of statements> END;
        <case list #2> : <single statement> |
                        BEGIN <sequence of statements> END;
        <other case lists >
        <case list #n> : <single statement> |
                        BEGIN <sequence of statements> END;
        ELSE <single statement> |
                        BEGIN <sequence of statements> END;
    END;
C:
    switch <case-var> {
        case <value #1.1>:
        case <value #1.2>:
        <other case values>
        case <value #1.n>:
            <single or multiple statements>
            break:
        case <value #2.1>:
        case <value #2.2>:
        <other case values>
        case <value #2.n>:
            <single or multiple statements>
            break:
        <other case lists >
        case <value #n.1>:
        case <value #n.2>:
        <other case values>
        case <value #n.n>:
            <single or multiple statements>
            break:
        default:
            <single or multiple statements>
            break:
    }
```

3. The **break** statement is used to exit the **switch** and resume after the end of the **switch** statement. If the **break** statement is omitted, program execution proceeds throughout the statements in the **case** labels that follow.
4. The **default** clause is used as a catch-all clause. Using **break** at the end of this clause is optional, but safer (and therefore recommended).

To illustrate the use of the **switch** statement, I present a new version of the simple calculator program. The Pascal version uses the CASE statement, while the C edition employs the **switch** statement. The Pascal listing is shown below:

Listing 6.9

```
PROGRAM Decision_Making_5;
Uses CRT;
{ simple Turbo Pascal program that implements a one-time  }
{ simple four-function calculator using the CASE statement. }
VAR ok : BOOLEAN;
    op : CHAR;
    x, y, z : REAL;
BEGIN
    WRITE('Enter first number : '); READLN(x); WRITELN;
    WRITE('Enter operation [in +-/*] : '); op := ReadKey;
    WRITELN(op); WRITELN;
    WRITE('Enter second number : '); READLN(y); WRITELN;
    ok := TRUE; { assign optimistic default }
    CASE op OF

      '+' : z := x + y;
      '-' : z := x - y;
      '*' : z := x * y;
      '/' : BEGIN
               IF y <> 0.0 THEN
                  z := x / y
               ELSE BEGIN { division by zero }
                  WRITELN('Error: Cannot divide by zero!');
                  ok := FALSE
               END
            END

    ELSE BEGIN { bad operator }
      WRITELN('You entered a bad operator');
      ok := FALSE
    END;
    END; { CASE }
    WRITELN; WRITELN;
    IF ok THEN BEGIN {display results if available }
       WRITELN(x,' ',op,' ',y,' = ',z);
       WRITELN; WRITELN
    END;
END.
```

The C version is listed on the next page:

Listing 6.10

```c
/* simple C program that implements a one-time simple  */
/* four-function calculator using the switch statement. */
#include <stdio.h>
#include "conio.h"
#define BOOLEAN char
#define TRUE 1
#define FALSE 0
main()
{
    BOOLEAN ok;
    char op;
    float x, y, z;
    printf("Enter first number : "); scanf("%f", &x);
    printf("\nEnter operation [in +-/*] : "); op = getche();
    printf("\nEnter second number : "); scanf("%f", &y);
    printf("\n");
    ok = TRUE; /* assign optimistic default */
    switch (op) {
      case '+' :
            z = x + y;
            break;
      case '-' :
            z = x - y;
            break;
      case '*' :
            z = x * y;
            break;
      case '/' :
            if (y != 0.0)
                z = x / y;
            else
            { /* division by zero */
                printf("\n Error: Cannot divide by zero!");
                ok = FALSE;
            }
            break;
      default :   /* bad operator */
            printf("\nYou entered a bad operator");
            ok = FALSE;
    } /* switch */
    printf("\n\n");
    if (ok)
        printf("\n %f %c %f = %f\n\n", x, op, y, z);
}
```

The two program versions illustrate the effect of translating programs that modestly use the CASE and **switch** statements. Keeping in mind the differences in syntax, the C version does not exhibit any feature that a Pascal programmer might find rather unusual.

The above program can be rewritten to use the assignment operators +=, -=, *=, and /=.

Listing 6.11

```c
/* simple C program that implements a one-time simple   */
/* four-function calculator using the switch statement. */
/* This modified program version illustrates how the    */
/* op =getche() assignment may be used inside a switch  */
/* expression. In addition, assignment operators are    */
/* used in calculating the results.                     */
#include <stdio.h>
#include "conio.h"
#define BOOLEAN char
#define TRUE 1
#define FALSE 0
main()
{
    BOOLEAN ok;
    char op;
    float x, y, z;
    printf("Enter first number : "); scanf("%f", &x);
    printf("\nEnter second number : "); scanf("%f", &y);
    printf("\n");
    ok = TRUE; /* assign optimistic default */
    z = x; /* initialize result with value of x */
    printf("Enter operation [in +-/*] : ");
    switch ( op = getche() ) {
      case '+' :
            z += y;
            break;
      case '-' :
            z -= y;
            break;
      case '*' :
            z *= y;
            break;
      case '/' :
            if (y != 0.0)
                z /= y;
            else
            { /* division by zero */
                printf("\n Error: Cannot divide by zero!");
                ok = FALSE;
            }
            break;
      default :   /* bad operator */
            printf("\nYou entered a bad operator");
            ok = FALSE;
    } /* switch */
    printf("\n\n");
    if (ok)
        printf("\n %f %c %f = %f\n\n", x, op, y, z);
}
```

The next program shows how the C **switch** statement handles translating Pascal CASE labels containing sets of discrete values and ranges of values. The program prompts you to type:

1. A month number, and reports its calendar quarter number.
2. A letter that is classified as being an upper-case letter, a lower-case letter, a digit, an arithmetic operator, or something weird (so to speak).

The Pascal listing is shown below:

Listing 6.12

```
PROGRAM Decision_Making_6;
Uses CRT;
{ Turbo Pascal program that demonstrates using the CASE statement
  containing CASE clauses made up of:
    1) Sets of discrete values.
    2) Ranges of values.
}
VAR month : INTEGER;
    ch : CHAR;
BEGIN
    { test numeric values for the CASE statement }
    WRITE('Enter month number : ');
    READLN(month); WRITELN;
    WRITE('Month number ',month,' is in ');
    CASE month OF
        { set of discrete values }
        1,2,3      : WRITE('the first');
        { range of values }
        4..6       : WRITE('the second');
        { range of values }
        7..9       : WRITE('the third');
        { one discrete value and a range of values }
        10, 11..12 : WRITE('the fourth');
        ELSE         WRITE('an unknown');
    END; { CASE }
    WRITELN(' quarter');
    WRITELN; WRITELN;
    { test character values for the CASE statement }
    WRITE('Enter a letter : ');
    ch := ReadKey;  WRITELN(ch); WRITELN;
    WRITE(ch,' is a ');
    CASE ch OF
        'A'..'Z' : WRITELN('uppercase letter');
        'a'..'z' : WRITELN('lowercase letter');
        '0'..'9' : WRITELN('digit');
        '+','-','*','/' : WRITELN('math operator');
        ELSE WRITELN('something weird!');
    END; { CASE }
END.
```

The translated C version converts each Pascal CASE label into a sequence of **case** labels. Notice that in translating the Pascal character ranges 'A'..'Z' and 'a'..'z', I omitted many of the **case** labels to keep the listing short.

The C listing is found below:

Listing 6.13

```c
/* C program that demonstrates using the switch statement
   containing case clauses made up of:
     1) Sets of discrete values.
     2) Ranges of values.
*/
#include <stdio.h>
#include "conio.h"
#define BOOLEAN char
#define TRUE 1
#define FALSE 0
main()
{
    int month;
    char ch;
    /* test numeric values for the CASE statement */
    printf("Enter month number : ");
    scanf("%d", &month); printf("\n");
    printf("Month number %d is in ",month);
    switch (month) {
        case 1:
        case 2:
        case 3:
            printf("the first");
            break;
        case 4 :
        case 5 :
        case 6 :
            printf("the second");
            break;
        case 7 :
        case 8 :
        case 9 :
            printf("the third");
            break;
        case 10 :
        case 11 :
        case 12 :
            printf("the fourth");
            break;
        default :
            printf("an unknown");
    } /* CASE */
    printf(" quarter\n\n\n");
    /* test character values for the CASE statement */
    printf("Enter a letter : ");
    ch = getche();
    printf("\n%c is a ", ch);
    switch (ch) {
        case 'A' :
        case 'B' :
        case 'C' :
```

```
            case 'D' :
            /* other case clauses for 'E' to 'Y' here */
            case 'Z' :
               printf("uppercase letter\n");
               break;
            case 'a' :
            case 'b' :
            case 'c' :
            case 'd' :
            /* other case clauses for 'e' to 'y' here */
            case 'z' :
               printf("lowercase letter\n");
               break;
            case '0' :
            /* other case clauses for '1' to '8' here */
            case '9' :
               printf("digit\n");
               break;
            case '+' :
            case '-' :
            case '*' :
            case '/' :
               printf("math operator\n");
               break;
            default :
               printf("something weird!\n");
         } /* CASE */
}
```

The above program demonstrates that you can often end up with a long list of **case** labels in C. If the values in the **case** labels form a continuous range, it becomes more worthwhile to resort to a nested **if-else** statement. The following C version does just that. The **switch** statement is converted into nested **if-else** statements. The following C version is a fully functioning translation of the original Pascal program:

Listing 6.14

```
/* C program that demonstrates using the if-else statement */
/* instead of the switch statement to eliminate the long   */
/* list of 'case' clauses.                                 */
#include <stdio.h>
#include "conio.h"
#define BOOLEAN char
#define TRUE 1
#define FALSE 0
/*define macro similar to Pascal's <var> IN [<low>..<high>] */
#define in_range(var,low,high) (var >= low && var <= high)
main()
{
    int month;
    char ch;
    /* test numeric values for the CASE statement */
```

```
    printf("Enter month number : ");
    scanf("%d", &month); printf("\n");
    printf("Month number %d is in ",month);
    /* use if-else without the in_range macro */
    if (month >= 1 && month < 4)
            printf("the first");
    else if (month >= 4 && month < 7)
            printf("the second");
    else if (month >= 7 && month < 10)
            printf("the third");
    else if (month >= 10 && month < 13)
            printf("the fourth");
    else
            printf("an unknown");
    printf(" quarter\n\n\n");
    /* test character values for the CASE statement */
    printf("Enter a letter : ");
    ch = getche();
    printf("\n%c is a ", ch);
    /* use the if-else with the in_range macro */
    if in_range(ch,'A','Z')
            printf("uppercase letter\n");
    else if in_range(ch,'a','z')
            printf("lowercase letter\n");
    else if in_range(ch,'0','9')
            printf("digit\n");
    else if (ch == '+' || ch == '-' || ch == '*' || ch =='/')
            printf("math operator\n");
    else
            printf("something weird!\n");
}
```

The nested **if-else** statements shorten the program and reduce the probability of typographical errors. The macro **in_range** is used to test whether or not a value falls within a certain range.

CHAPTER SUMMARY

C supports the **if** and **if-else** statements. The general syntax for the **if** statement is

```
if (<tested expression is not zero>)
    <single statement> | { <sequence of C statements> }
```
The general syntax for the **if-else** statement is
```
if (<tested expression is not zero>)
    <single statement> | { <sequence of C statements> }
else
    <single statement> | { <sequence of C statements> }
```

Nested **if-else** statements are allowed in C and have the following general syntax:
```
if (<tested expression #1 is not zero>)
    <single statement> | { <sequence of C statements> }
```

```
else if (<tested expression #2 is not zero>)
    <single statement> | { <sequence of C statements> }
else if (<tested expression #3 is not zero>)
    <single statement> | { <sequence of C statements> }
..........
else if (<tested expression #n is not zero>)
    <single statement> | { <sequence of C statements> }
else
    <single statement> | { <sequence of C statements> }
```

The tested expressions of a nested **if-else** statement are evaluated in sequence until either one of them returns a nonzero value, or until the **else** clause is reached.

Other rules for using the **if** statement are

1. The tested expression must be enclosed in parentheses.
2. The C language has no **then** keyword.
3. Block statements in C are enclosed in open and close braces. Each statement must end with a semicolon, including the last one in a block. The close brace must not be followed by a semicolon.

The C language supports the **switch** statement that closely resembles a nested **if-else** statement. The general syntax is

```
switch (<variable> {
   case <constant1>
   [case <constant2>...]
       <one or more statements>;
       break;
    case <constant3>
   [case <constant4>...]
       <one or more statements>;
       break;
   ......
   default:
       <one or more statements>;
       break;
}
```

The following must be observed when using a **switch** statement:

1. The **switch** value must be an integer-compatible value. You may use a variable, function, or expression to supply the **switch** value.
2. The **case** labels must only contain constants.
3. One **case** label is allowed for each constant value. C does not support ranges of values to be associated with a single **case** label.
4. The **break** statement must be used at the end of a **case** clause to force the program flow to resume after the end of the **switch** statement.
5. No braces are needed to contain statement blocks within each **case** clause.

CHAPTER

7

Loops

CHAPTER GOALS

This chapter examines the various types of loops supported by C. Topics include the following:
- The for loop.
- Exiting loops.
- The do-while loop.
- The while loop.
- Nested loops.

LOOPS: AN OVERVIEW

Loops are an essential programming construct that permits the repetitive execution of a sequence of statements and/or access to array members. Loops can be generally classified into three categories: fixed, conditional, and infinite. Fixed loops essentially iterate for a specific number of times that is known when the loop starts executing. Thus, exiting a fixed loop is guaranteed. Conditional loops execute the statements in the loop body, as long as or until a tested expression is true. Thus, the behavior of conditional loops falls between two extremes: one extreme being not executing at all; the other, looping infinitely! The programmer should be concerned more about the latter condition. Open loops, as the name suggests, are supposed to loop indefinitely (sounds like they're just asking for trouble!). At first glance, C appears to support only the fixed (that is, the **for** loop) and conditional loops. As you will discover later, even the **for** loop in C "has an interactive nature."

THE for LOOP

The **for** loop in C is a variant of the popular DO loop in FORTRAN, FOR-NEXT in BASIC, and FOR-DO in Pascal. The general syntax for a simple for loop is

```
for(<value init.>;<loop continuation test>;<increment statement>)
```

The <value init.> part employs a statement to initialize the loop control variable. The <loop continuation test> is a logical expression used to test for additional looping conditions. The <increment statement> is a C statement used to increment the loop control variable. There is no default increment value. However, you may increment by any value, including a value that is greater than unity. Compare this to Pascal's inflexible increment by one. Thus, you can see that the for loop is C is fairly different from the FOR loop in Pascal.

Program Translation

The general form for translating upward counting Pascal FOR loops into C is

Pascal:
```
    FOR <ForVar> := <First> TO <Last> DO
```
C:
```
    for (<ForVar> = <First>; <ForVar> <= <Last>; <ForVar>++)
```

For downward counting FOR loops use the following form:

Pascal:
```
    FOR <ForVar> := <Last> DOWNTO <First> DO
```
C:
```
    for (<ForVar> = <Last>; <ForVar> >= <First>; <ForVar>--)
```

The first example is a program that calculates the factorial of a number using a **for** loop. The program is written to return the factorials for numbers in the range of 1 to 50. Values outside that range return an error message. The Pascal version is shown below:

Listing 7.1

```
PROGRAM For_Loop_1;
{ Turbo Pascal program that calculates a
  factorial using a FOR loop              }
VAR factorial : REAL;
    i, n : BYTE;
BEGIN
    WRITE('Enter the factorial of [1..50] : ');
    READLN(n); WRITELN;
    IF (n > 0) AND (n <= 50) THEN BEGIN
        factorial := 1.0;
        FOR i := 1 TO n DO
            factorial := factorial * i;
        WRITELN(n,'! = ',factorial);
    END
    ELSE
```

                                                                LOOPS   97

```
        WRITELN('Sorry! Factorial is out of range);
END.
```

The C version is shown below:

Listing 7.2

```
/* C program that calculates a factorial using a for loop */
#include <stdio.h>
#define BYTE char
main()
{
    /* factorial is declared and also initialized */
    double factorial = 1.0;
    BYTE i, n;
    printf("Enter the factorial of [1..50] : ");
    scanf("%d", &n); printf("\n");
    if (n > 0 && n <= 50) {
        for (i = 1; i <= n; i++)
            /* ─     ─    ─
                    ^       ^        ^
                    |       |        |
                    |       |        increment i by 1
                    |       test loop terminating condition
                    initialize loop counter
            */
            factorial *= (double) i;
        printf("%d! = %lf\n",n,factorial);
    }
    else
        printf("Sorry! factorial is out of range\n");
}
```

Comparing the two versions, notice the following:

1. The C **for** loop initializes the loop variable **i** using the statement "i = 1;". The test **for** loop resumption is i **<= n** (DO NOT FORGET THE LESS THAN SIGN!). This means that as long as i is less than or equal to **n**, continue looping. The C loop control variable is incremented by 1 using "i++".
2. The **factorial** variable is initialized along with its declaration.
3. The value of **factorial** is updated in the **for** loop using an assignment operator and the type casting of the loop control variable.

C supports a **for** loop feature that departs from the typical FOR loops you have seen in Pascal, BASIC, and many other languages. This feature enables you to use multiple statements in the initialization and increment parts of the loop. This is best illustrated in the next example. The program calculates and displays the statistical mean and standard deviation for a range of integral numbers. The program prompts you to type integer values for the lower and upper range limits. For the sake of demonstration, I use a FOR loop counting downward in Pascal. The Pascal version is listed below:

Listing 7.3

```
PROGRAM For_Loop_2;
{ Turbo Pascal program that calculates the statistical average
  and standard deviation using a decremented FOR loop         }
VAR sum, sumx, sumxx,
    average, sdev    : REAL;
    i, low, high     : INTEGER;
BEGIN
    WRITE('Enter lower range : '); READLN(low);  WRITELN;
    WRITE('Enter upper range : '); READLN(high); WRITELN;
    { initialize statistical summations }
    sum := 0.0;
    sumx := 0.0;
    sumxx := 0.0;
    FOR i := high DOWNTO low DO BEGIN
        sum := sum + 1.0;
        sumx := sumx + i;
        sumxx := sumxx + SQR(i)
    END; { FOR }
    { calculate statistics }
    average := sumx / sum;
    sdev := SQRT((sumxx - SQR(sumx) / sum) / (sum - 1.0));
    WRITELN('Average       = ',average); WRITELN;
    WRITELN('Std. deviation = ',sdev); WRITELN;
END.
```

When you run the Pascal program, type 1 and 100 as the lower and upper range values, respectively. The screen image of the input and output is shown below:

```
Enter lower range : 1
Enter upper range : 100
Average         = 5.05000000000000E+0001
Std. deviation = 2.90114919758926E+0001
```

The C version is shown below:

Listing 7.4

```
/* C program that calculates the statistical average
   and standard deviation using a decremented for loop      */
#include <stdio.h>
#include "math.h"
/* define square pseudo-function */
#define SQR(x) ((x) * (x))
main()
{
    double sum, sumx, sumxx;
    double average, sdev;
    int i, low, high;
    printf("Enter lower range : "); scanf("%d", &low);
    printf("\nEnter upper range : "); scanf("%d", &high);
    printf("\n");
```

```
    for (i = high, sum = 0.0,
        /* initialize counter & summations    */
        sumx = 0.0, sumxx = 0.0;
        /* check loop termination condition */
        i >= low;
        /* decrement counter and increment data count */
        i--, sum++) {
        /* update summations using assignment operators
           & type casting */
        sumx += (double) i;
        sumxx += (double) SQR(i);
    } /* for */
    /* calculate statistics */
    average = sumx / sum;
    sdev = sqrt((sumxx - SQR(sumx) / sum) / (sum - 1.0));
    printf("Average        = %lf\n\n",average);
    printf("Std. deviation = %lf\n\n",sdev);
}
```

In comparing the two versions, notice the following features of C:

1. The variables for the statistical summations are initialized inside the C **for** loop, together with the data range index, **i**. The latter is set equal to the upper range limit. The comma operator is employed to delimit the various initialization statements.
2. The loop continuation test employs the logical expression "i >= low".
3. The loop increment part actually decrements the value of the index i and increments the value of **sum**. The comma operator is employed to delimit the various incrementing statements.
4. The main loop body increments the values of **sumx** and **sumxx**, using assignment operators and type casting.

When you run the C version, type 1 and 100 as the lower and upper range values, respectively. The screen image of the input and output is shown below:

```
Enter lower range : 1
Enter upper range : 100
Average        = 50.500000
Std. deviation = 29.011492
```

The above examples illustrated single **for** loops. The next program employs nested loops to draw a simple V-shaped histogram. The program also demonstrates the use of GOTOXY statements. Under the current setting, each vertical bar of asterisks appears when you press any key. The Pascal version appears below:

Listing 7.5

```
Program For_Loop3;
Uses CRT;
{ Turbo Pascal program that uses multiple loops to draw a simple
  histogram.
    The program also demonstrates the use of the GOTO statements
}
```

100 INTRODUCING C TO PASCAL PROGRAMMERS

```pascal
LABEL 999, 998;
CONST MAX_COL = 80;
      MID_COL = 40;
      MAX_ROW = 24;
{$DEFINE DEBUG} { debugging switch }
VAR i, x, xtransform, y : INTEGER;
    ch : CHAR;
BEGIN
    ClrScr;
    { draw X-axis }
    GotoXY(1,24);
    FOR x := 1 TO MAX_COL DO
        WRITE('_');
    { draw Y-axis }
    FOR y := 1 TO MAX_ROW DO BEGIN
        GotoXY(MID_COL,y);
        WRITE('|');
    END;
    FOR x := 1 TO MAX_COL-1 DO BEGIN
        {$IFDEF DEBUG}
            ch := ReadKey;
            IF ch IN ['Q','q'] THEN GOTO 999; { end program }
        {$ENDIF}
        { skip over median screen column }
        IF x = MID_COL THEN GOTO 998;
        xtransform := ABS(x - MID_COL) div 2;
        y := MAX_ROW - xtransform;
        IF y >= MAX_ROW THEN y := MAX_ROW - 1;
        { draw histogram bar }
        FOR i := y TO MAX_ROW-1 DO BEGIN
            GotoXY(x,i);
            WRITE('*');
        END; { FOR }
        998:
    END; { FOR }
    REPEAT
    UNTIL KeyPressed;
    999:
END.
```

When you run the program, the following (partial) screen image appears:

LOOPS **101**

```
**                                              |
****                                            |
******                                          |
********                                        |
**********                                      |
************                                    |
**************                                  |                              *
****************                                |                             **
******************                              |                            ***
********************                            |                          *****
**********************                          |                         ******
************************                        |                        ********
**************************                      |                      **********
****************************                    |                     ************
******************************                  |                    **************
********************************                |                  ****************
**********************************              |                 ******************
************************************            |                ********************
**************************************          |              **********************
****************************************        |             ***********************
******************************************      |            *************************
******************************************** | *************************
                                                |
```

The translated version is listed below:

Listing 7.6

```
/* C program that uses multiple loops to draw a simple
   histogram.
*/

#include <stdio.h>
#include "conio.h"
#include "math.h"
/* define empty debugging macro */
#define DEBUG
main()
{
    const int MAX_COL = 80;
    const int MID_COL = 40;
    const int MAX_ROW = 24;
    int i, x, xtransform, y;
    char ch = ' ';
    clrscr();
    /* draw X-axis */
    gotoxy(1,MAX_ROW);
    for (x = 1; x <= MAX_COL; x++)
        putchar('_');
    /* draw Y-axis */
    for (y = 1; y <= MAX_ROW; y++)   {
        gotoxy(MID_COL,y);
        putchar('|');
```

```
    }
    for (x = 1; x < MAX_COL; x++)   {
#ifdef DEBUG
        ch = getch();
        if (ch == 'Q' || ch == 'q')
            break; /* break out of outer loop */
#endif
        /* skip over median screen column */
        if (x == MID_COL)
            continue; /* resume at next the iteration of outer loop */
        xtransform = abs(x - MID_COL) / 2;
        y = MAX_ROW - xtransform;
        if (y >= MAX_ROW)
            y = MAX_ROW - 1;
        /* draw histogram bar */
        for (i = y; i < MAX_ROW; i++)   {
            gotoxy(x,i);
            printf("*");
        } /* for i */
    } /* for x */
    if (ch == 'q')
        ch = 'Q';
    do {
    /* nothing */
    } while (ch != 'Q' && !getch() );
}
```

Notice that in the Pascal program, a GOTO statement is used to jump to the end of the FOR loop:

```
{ skip over median screen column }
IF x = MID_COL THEN GOTO 998;
```

The C program employs the more elegant **continue** statement to resume at the next loop iteration. I could have used a **goto** in the C program (yes, they do exist in C), but I prefer to utilize the more civilized **continue** over the barbaric **goto**:

```
/* skip over median screen column */
if (x == MID_COL)
            continue; /* resume at next the iteration of outer loop */
```

Pascal does not support the formal infinite loop, although its descendants Modula-2 and Ada do. C may appear to be two-faced regarding infinite loops. At first glance, you may think that infinite loops are not supported by C, and you are right if you are looking for a distinct infinite loop construct. However, the way the **for** loop has been laid out by the C designers you can use it to implement an infinite loop. The trick is to employ no loop control variable, initialization, continuation test, and increment parts, as shown below:

```
for (;;) {
    <body of infinite loop>
}
```

You exit an infinite loop by using either the **exit** or **break** statements. The choice between these two statements depends on whether or not you want

LOOPS 103

to terminate the program using **exit**, or resume execution after the infinite loop with **break**.

The following Pascal program mimics an infinite loop by using a WHILE loop with the never-failing test (2 > 1). The program prompts you for a number, calculates and displays its square, and queries for more calculations. The process can be repeated indefinitely (or until your computer breaks down, whichever comes first!). The Pascal code is shown below:

Listing 7.7

```
Program Open_Loop;
{ Turbo Pascal program that demonstrates using the
  WHILE loop to emulate an infinite loop.                }
Uses CRT;
VAR ch : CHAR;
    x, y : REAL;
BEGIN
   { WHILE loop with empty parts }
   WHILE 2 > 1 DO BEGIN
      WRITELN; WRITELN;
      WRITE('Enter a number : ');
      READLN(x);
      y := x * x;
      WRITELN('(',x,')^2 = ',y); WRITELN; WRITELN;
      WRITE('More calculations? (Y/N) ');
      ch := ReadKey;
      WRITELN(ch);
      IF (ch <> 'y') AND (ch <> 'Y') THEN
         HALT(0);
   END;
END.
```

Run the above program and enter the numbers 5, 10, 33, and 12 at each prompt. The screen image is shown below:

```
Enter a number : 5
( 5.00000000000000E+0000)^2 =   2.50000000000000E+0001
More calculations? (Y/N) y
Enter a number : 10
( 1.00000000000000E+0001)^2 =   1.00000000000000E+0002
More calculations? (Y/N)  y
Enter a number : 33
( 3.30000000000000E+0001)^2 =   1.08900000000000E+0003
More calculations? (Y/N)  y
Enter a number : 12
( 1.20000000000000E+0001)^2 =   1.44000000000000E+0002
More calculations? (Y/N) n
```

The C version which contains the versatile **for** loop is shown below:

Listing 7.8

```
/* C program that demonstrates using the
   for loop to emulate an infinite loop.     */
#include <stdio.h>
```

```
#include "conio.h"
main()
{
   char ch;
   double x, y;
   /* for loop with empty parts */
   for (;;) {
      printf("\n\nEnter a number : ");
      scanf("%lf", &x);
      y = x * x;
      printf(" (%lg)^2 = %lg\n\n", x, y);
      printf("More calculations? (Y/N) ");
      ch = getche();
      if (ch != 'y' && ch != 'Y')
         exit(0);
   }
}
```

The following screen image is produced when entering the same numbers used with the Pascal program:

```
Enter a number : 5
 (5)^2 = 25
More calculations? (Y/N) y
Enter a number : 10
 (10)^2 = 100
More calculations? (Y/N) y
Enter a number : 33
 (33)^2 = 1089
More calculations? (Y/N) y
Enter a number : 12
 (12)^2 = 144
More calculations? (Y/N) n
```

EXITING LOOPS

C provides you with the two mechanisms to exit fixed and conditional loops. The first uses **break** to exit the loop and resume execution at the code that follows the loop. The second type of loop exit is **continue**. As the name suggests, the remainder of the loop is bypassed and the program proceeds to the beginning of the loop. The **break** can also be used to exit infinite loops.

The following program demonstrates exiting a fixed loop with a **continue** and exiting an infinite loop with a **break**. The fixed loop attempts to display the square root of numbers ranging from -2 to 10. Since square roots of negative numbers cannot be handled by the **sqrt** function, the **continue** statement is used to bypass the calculations in the loop when the argument of **sqrt** is negative. The second loop is an infinite loop that prompts the user for a number to calculate and displays its square root. If you enter a negative number, the **break** exits the infinite loop altogether. The C listing is shown below:

Listing 7.9

```
/* program that demonstrates the use of break and continue */
#include <stdio.h>
#include "math.h"
main()
{
   int i;
   double x, result;
   for (i = -2; i <= 10; i++) {
       x = (double) i;
       if (x < 0.0) continue;
       result = sqrt(x);
       printf("SQRT(%lg) = %lg\n", x, result);
   }
   for (;;) {
     printf("Enter a positive number ");
     printf("(exit using a negative number) : ");
     scanf("%lf", &x);
     if (x < 0.0) break;
     result = sqrt(x);
     printf("SQRT(%lg) = %lg\n", x, result);
   }
}
```

THE do-while LOOP

Another loop construct supported by C is the **do-while** loop. This is similar to the REPEAT-UNTIL loop, with one important difference: the logical expression used to reiterate the REPEAT loop must be logically negated to work with the **do-while** loop. In other words, the REPEAT-UNTIL NOT is equivalent to the **do-while**. The general syntax of the do-while loop is

```
do {
    <sequence of statements>
} while (<logical expression>);
```

Program Translation

To translate a REPEAT-UNTIL loop in Pascal into a do-while loop, use the following form:

Pascal:
```
REPEAT
    <sequence of statements>
UNTIL (<logical expression>);
```

C:
```
do {
    <sequence of statements>
} while ( !(<logical expression>) );
```

106 INTRODUCING C TO PASCAL PROGRAMMERS

The first example actually utilizes nested REPEAT (**do-while**) loops. The outer loop is used to prompt the user for a positive number. The inner loop implements Newton's algorithm to calculate the square root iteratively. The Pascal listing is shown below:

Listing 7.10

```
PROGRAM Repeat_it;
{ Turbo Pascal program that calculates the square root of a
  number by using Newton's root seeking algorithm and a
  REPEAT-UNTIL loop.
  The program contains two REPEAT loops:
     1) The outer loop is used to re-prompt the user for a
        positive number.
     2) The inner loop is used to iterate the refinement of the
        value for the sought square root.
}
CONST ACCURACY = 0.00001; { predefined accuracy }
VAR number, sqroot : REAL;
    done : BOOLEAN;
BEGIN
    REPEAT
        WRITE('Enter a positive number ');
        READLN(number); WRITELN;
        IF (number > 0.0) THEN BEGIN
            { calculate initial guess for the square root }
            sqroot := number / 2.0;
            { refine guess }
            REPEAT
                sqroot := (number / sqroot + sqroot) / 2.0;
            UNTIL ABS(number - sqroot * sqroot) < ACCURACY;
            WRITELN('SQR(',number:10:5,') = ',sqroot:10:5);
            done := TRUE
        END
        ELSE BEGIN
            WRITELN('Please enter a positive number!');
            done := FALSE;
        END;
        WRITELN;
    UNTIL done;
END.
```

The C version is listed below:

Listing 7.11

```
/* C program that calculates the square root of a number
   by using Newton's root seeking algorithm and a do-while loop.
   The program contains two do-while loops:
      1) The outer loop is used to reprompt the user for a
         positive number.
      2) The inner loop is used to iterate the refinement of the
         value for the sought square root.
```

```c
*/
#include <stdio.h>
/* import the fabs() function from math.h */
#include "math.h"
#define BOOLEAN char
 /* predefined accuracy */
#define ACCURACY   0.00001
#define TRUE 1
#define FALSE 0
main()
{
    float number, sqroot;
    BOOLEAN done;
    do {
        printf("Enter a positive number : ");
        scanf("%f", &number); printf("\n");
        if (number > 0.0)   {
            /* calculate initial guess for the square root */
            sqroot = number / 2.0;
            /* refine guess */
            do {
                sqroot = (number / sqroot + sqroot) / 2.0;
            } while
              ( !((fabs(number - sqroot * sqroot)) < ACCURACY) );
            printf("SQRT(%10.5f) = %10.5f",number,sqroot);
            done = TRUE;
        }
        else {
            printf("Please enter a positive number!\n");
            done = FALSE;
        }
        printf("\n");
    } while (!done);
}
```

In comparing both the Pascal and C versions, notice the following C features:

1. The **done** variable in C, used to control the outer **do-while** loop, is declared to be BOOLEAN. In this case, it is an alias for the **char** type, which in turn is integer-compatible. The outer loop tests the expression (**!done**) and examines the numeric value stored in **done**.
2. The **fabs()** function, used to return the absolute value for floating point types, is accessed by including the file "math.h".
3. In translating the logical expression in the Pascal UNTIL clause, the NOT operator in C is used to obtain the looping condition in the **do-while**.

When you run the C version, first enter -4. Since negative numbers are invalid entries, you will be prompted to enter a positive number. This time enter 5. The program displays the number you typed and its square root, as shown below:

```
Enter a positive number : -4
Please enter a positive number!
```

```
Enter a positive number : 5
SQRT(    5.00000) =     2.23607
```

The following program shows another example of translating REPEAT-UNTIL loops in Pascal into **do-while** loops in C. The program also contains nested REPEAT loops that implement an enhanced version of the four-function calculator program presented earlier. You might remember that the earlier versions performed one operation at a time. To perform multiple operations, you had to repeatedly invoke the compiled program from DOS. The REPEAT loop solves this frustrating aspect of the program. An outer REPEAT loop is used to prompt for the operands and operator, to calculate and display the results, and to prompt for additional calculations. The last part uses a separate REPEAT loop to ensure that your response is either a **Y** or an **N** (lower case is also valid). This Yes/No prompting is quite popular in all languages, and you most likely already employ it in your programs. The Pascal code is shown below:

Listing 7.12

```
PROGRAM Repeat_it2;
Uses CRT;
{ This program is a modified version of an earlier simple
  calculator program. The REPEAT loop is used as:
     1) An outer loop to enable the user to perform as many
        operations as desired.
     2) An inner loop to ensure that the user's input to
        Yes/No prompt is either an 'N' or a 'Y' (in both
        upper and lower case)
}
VAR ok : BOOLEAN;
    ans, op : CHAR;
    x, y, z : REAL;
BEGIN
    REPEAT
        WRITE('Enter first number : '); READLN(x); WRITELN;
        WRITE('Enter operation [in +-/*] : '); op := ReadKey;
        WRITELN(op); WRITELN;
        WRITE('Enter second number : '); READLN(y); WRITELN;
        ok := TRUE; { assign optimistic default }
        CASE op OF
           '+' : z := x + y;
           '-' : z := x - y;
           '*' : z := x * y;
           '/' : BEGIN
                    IF y <> 0.0 THEN
                       z := x / y
                    ELSE BEGIN { division by zero }
                       WRITELN('Error: Cannot divide by zero!');
                       ok := FALSE
                    END
                 END
           ELSE BEGIN { bad operator }
              WRITELN('You entered a bad operator');
              ok := FALSE
```

```
            END;
        END; { CASE }
        WRITELN; WRITELN;
        IF ok THEN BEGIN {display results if available }
            WRITELN(x,' ',op,' ',y,' = ',z);
            WRITELN; WRITELN
        END;
        REPEAT
            WRITE('Want to perform more operations ? (Y/N) ');
            ans := ReadKey;
            WRITELN(ans);
            WRITELN;
            ans := Upcase(ans);
        UNTIL ans IN ['Y','N'];
    UNTIL ans = 'N';
END.
```

The C version is shown below:

Listing 7.13

```
/* This program is a modified version of an earlier simple
   calculator program. The do loop is used as:
      1) An outer loop to enable the user to perform as many
         operations as desired.
      2) An inner loop to ensure that the user's input to
         Yes/No prompt is either an 'N' or a 'Y' (in both
         upper and lower case).
*/
#include <stdio.h>
#include "conio.h"
#define BOOLEAN char
#define TRUE 1
#define FALSE 0
#define Upcase(c) (c += 'A' - 'a')
#define is_yes_no(var) (var == 'Y' || var == 'N')
main()
{
    BOOLEAN ok;
    char ans, op;
    double x, y, z;
    do {
        printf("Enter first number : "); scanf("%lf", &x);
        printf("\nEnter operation [in +-/*] : ");
        op = getche();
        printf("\n\nEnter second number : "); scanf("%lf", &y);
        printf("\n");
        ok = TRUE; /* assign optimistic default */
        switch (op) {
          case '+' :
            z = x + y;
            break;
          case '-' :
            z = x - y;
            break;
```

```
            case '*' :
               z = x * y;
               break;
            case '/' :
               {
                  if (y != 0.0)
                     z = x / y;
                  else { /* division by zero */
                        printf("Error: Cannot divide by zero!");
                        ok = FALSE;
                       }
               }
               break;
            default : { /* bad operator */
               printf("You entered a bad operator");
               ok = FALSE;
              }
         } /* switch */
         printf("\n\n");
         if (ok)     /*display results if available */
            printf("%lf %c %lf = %lf\n\n", x, op, y, z);
         do {
               printf("Want to perform more operations ? (Y/N) ");
               ans = getche();
               printf("\n\n");
               if (ans > 'Z') /* character is a lower case ? */
                  ans = Upcase(ans);
            } while ( !(is_yes_no(ans)) );
      } while ( !(ans == 'N') );
}
```

In translating the above program from Pascal to C, note the following: The following Pascal statement:

```
ans := Upcase(ans);
```

is translated into:

```
if (ans > 'Z') /* character is a lower case ? */
   ans = Upcase(ans);
```

where **Upcase** is a macro-based pseudofunction that converts a lower-case character into upper case. The if statement is needed to avoid processing upper-case characters in **Upcase**, which results in wrong conversions.

The UNTIL clause, which uses a character set member test, in the Pascal version:

```
UNTIL ans IN ['Y','N'];
```

is translated into:

```
while ( !(is_yes_no(ans)) );
```

where **is_yes_no** is a macro-based pseudofunction defined as:

```
#define is_yes_no(var) (var == 'Y' || var == 'N')
```

Run the C version and enter the following operations:

```
 5 + 10
355 / 113
```

```
Enter first number : 5
Enter operation [in +-/*] : +
Enter second number : 10
5.000000 + 10.000000 = 15.000000
Want to perform more operations ? (Y/N) y
Enter first number : 355
Enter operation [in +-/*] : /
Enter second number : 113
355.000000 / 113.000000 = 3.141593
Want to perform more operations ? (Y/N) n
```

THE WHILE LOOP

C supports a **while** loop that is very similar to the WHILE loop in Pascal and BASIC. Therefore, translating between the Pascal WHILE and C while loops is very smooth. The general syntax for the **while** loop is:

```
while (<logical expression>)
    <single statement> | { <sequence of statements> }
```

Remember to enclose the logical expression of the **while** loop in parentheses.

As with the WHILE loop in Pascal, the C version first examines a logical expression before executing the loop body. Thus, if the tested expression fails the very first time, the statement(s) in the loop are bypassed and program execution resumes after the loop.

The first example modifies the last version of the calculator program. The new version prompts you to enter the operation first and then the value of the operands. This form of math is called **Polish Notation** and is seldom used. However, this version first prompts for the operation to enable you to enter the letter Q to exit, avoiding the mandatory input of the operands when you do not wish to perform any calculation. The Pascal version is shown below:

Listing 7.14

```
PROGRAM Do_While_1;
Uses CRT;
{ Turbo Pascal program that uses a WHILE loop to enable the
  user to perform several basic math operations.                }
VAR ok : BOOLEAN;
    op : CHAR;
    x, y, z : REAL;
BEGIN
    WRITE('Enter operation [+-/* or [Q] to quit] ');
    op := ReadKey;
    WRITELN(op); WRITELN;
    WHILE op <> 'Q' DO BEGIN
        WRITE('Enter two numbers delimited by a space : ');
        READLN(x,y); WRITELN;
        ok := TRUE;
        CASE op OF
            '+' : z := x + y;
```

```
            '-' : z := x - y;
            '*' : z := x * y;
            '/' : BEGIN
                    IF y <> 0.0 THEN
                        z := x / y
                    ELSE BEGIN
                        WRITELN('Cannot divide by zero');
                        WRITELN;
                        ok := NOT ok;
                    END
                  END
            ELSE BEGIN
                WRITELN('Bad operator');
                WRITELN;
                ok := NOT ok;
            END;
        END; { CASE }
        IF ok THEN WRITELN(x,' ',op,' ',y,' = ',z);
        WRITELN; WRITELN;
        WRITE('Enter operation [+-/* or [Q] to quit] ');
        op := ReadKey;
        WRITELN(op); WRITELN;
    END; { WHILE }
END.
```

Run the Pascal version and perform the following operations:

355 / 113
4.5 * 6.5

The screen image for the above operations is shown below:

```
Enter operation [+-/* or [Q] to quit] /
Enter two numbers delimited by a space : 355 113
  3.55000000000E+02 /  1.13000000000E+02 =  3.14159292035E+00
Enter operation [+-/* or [Q] to quit] *
Enter two numbers delimited by a space : 4.5 6.5
  4.50000000000E+00 *  6.50000000000E+00 =  2.92500000000E+01
Enter operation [+-/* or [Q] to quit] Q
```

The C version is listed below:

Listing 7.15

```
/* C program that uses a while loop to enable the
   user to perform several basic math operations.             */
#include <stdio.h>
#include "conio.h"
#define BOOLEAN char
#define TRUE 1
#define FALSE 0
main()
{
    BOOLEAN ok;
    char op;
    float x, y, z;
```

```
    printf("Enter operation [+-/* or [Q] to quit] ");
    op = getche();
    while (op != 'Q') {
        printf("\n");
        printf("Enter two numbers delimited by a space : ");
        scanf("%f %f", &x, &y); printf("\n");
        ok = TRUE;
        switch (op) {
            case '+' :
                z = x + y;
                break;
            case '-' :
                z = x - y;
                break;
            case '*' :
                z = x * y;
                break;
            case '/' :
                if (y != 0.0)
                    z = x / y;
                else {
                    printf("Cannot divide by zero\n\n");
                    ok = !ok;
                }
                break;
            default :
                printf("Bad operator\n\n");
                ok = ! ok;
        } /* switch */
        if (ok)
            printf("%f %c %f = %f\n", x, op, y, z);
        printf("\n\n");
        printf("Enter operation [+-/* or [Q] to quit] ");
        op = getche();
    } /* while */
}
```

Translating a **while** loop from Pascal to C is smoother than translating the for or **do-while** loops. The Pascal WHILE loop:

```
WHILE op <> 'Q' DO BEGIN
```

is converted into a very similar form:

```
while (op != 'Q') {
```

The above C program can be rewritten to take advantage of some of the unique C features. The expression tested by the **while** loop can be written as:

```
while ( (op = getche()) != 'Q') {
```

Two steps occur in the above logical expression. The first expression (**op = getche()**) is executed, allowing the program to read a character from the keyboard and assign it to variable **op**. The parentheses are used, because the relational operator, !=, has a higher precedence over the assignment operator. The second step is comparing the new content of **op** with the character **Q**.

114   INTRODUCING C TO PASCAL PROGRAMMERS

Thus, the **while** loop performs two tasks. This is an example of the terseness of C as compared with Pascal.

Programming Hint

C permits the use of an expression where a variable is allowed.

The modified C version is shown below:

Listing 7.16

```
/* C program that uses a while loop to enable the
   user to perform several basic math operations.          */
#include <stdio.h>
#include "conio.h"
#define BOOLEAN char
#define TRUE 1
#define FALSE 0
main()
{
    BOOLEAN ok;
    char op;
    float x, y, z;
    printf("`Enter operation [+-/* or [Q] to quit] ");
    while ( (op = getche()) != 'Q') {
        printf("\n");
        printf("Enter two numbers delimited by a space : ");
        scanf("%f %f", &x, &y); printf("\n");
        ok = TRUE;
        switch (op) {
            case '+' :
                z = x + y;
                break;
            case '-' :
                z = x - y;
                break;
            case '*' :
                z = x * y;
                break;
            case '/' :
                if (y != 0.0)
                    z = x / y;
                else {
                    printf("Cannot divide by zero\n\n");
                    ok = !ok;
                }
                break;
            default :
                printf("Bad operator\n\n");
                ok = ! ok;
```

```
        } /* switch */
        if (ok)
            printf("%f %c %f = %f\n", x, op, y, z);
        printf("\n\n");
        printf("Enter operation [+-/* or [Q] to quit] ");
    } /* while */
}
```

Run the C version and perform the following operations:

355 / 113
4.5 * 6.5

The screen image for the above operations is shown below:

```
Enter operation [+-/* or [Q] to quit] /
Enter two numbers delimited by a space : 355 113
355.000000 / 113.000000 = 3.141593
Enter operation [+-/* or [Q] to quit] *
Enter two numbers delimited by a space : 4.5 6.5
4.500000 * 6.500000 = 29.250000
Enter operation [+-/* or [Q] to quit] Q
```

The next program illustrates using **do-while** and **while** loops in C (REPEAT-UNTIL and WHILE loops in Pascal) to calculate factorials. The Pascal program uses a main REPEAT-UNTIL loop that contains two other loops:

1. A WHILE loop, to calculate the factorials.
2. A REPEAT-UNTIL, to verify the user's Yes/No input.

The Pascal version is listed below:

Listing 7.17

```
PROGRAM Do_While_2;
Uses CRT;
{ Turbo Pascal program that uses a WHILE loop to enable the
  user to calculate several factorials.                     }
VAR ans : CHAR;
    i, number : BYTE;
    factorial : REAL;
BEGIN
    REPEAT
        WRITE('Enter the factorial number : ');
        READLN(number); WRITELN;
        IF number IN [1..50] THEN BEGIN
            factorial := 1.0;
            i := number;
            WHILE i > 1 DO BEGIN
                factorial := factorial * i;
                DEC(i)
            END; { WHILE }
            WRITELN(number,'! = ',factorial);
        END
        ELSE
            WRITELN('Number is out of range');
        WRITELN;
```

116 INTRODUCING C TO PASCAL PROGRAMMERS

```
        REPEAT
            WRITE('Enter another factorial? (Y/N) ');
            ans := ReadKey; WRITELN(ans); WRITELN;
            ans := Upcase(ans);
        UNTIL ans IN ['Y','N'];
    UNTIL ans = 'N';
END.
```

Run the Pascal version and calculate the factorials for the numbers 5, 10, and 15. The screen image for the sample session is shown:

```
Enter the factorial number : 5
5! =   1.20000000000000E+0002
Enter another factorial? (Y/N) y
Enter the factorial number : 10
10! =  3.62880000000000E+0006
Enter another factorial? (Y/N) y
Enter the factorial number : 15
15! =  1.30767436800000E+0012
Enter another factorial? (Y/N) n
```

The C version is listed below:

Listing 7.18

```
/* C program that uses a while loop to enable the
   user to calculate several factorials.                    */
#include <stdio.h>
#include "conio.h"
#define BYTE unsigned char
#define touppercase(c) (c += 'A' - 'a')
main()
{
    char ans;
    BYTE i, number;
    double factorial;
    do {
        printf("Enter the factorial number : ");
        scanf("%d", &number); printf("\n");
        if (number >= 1 && number <= 50) {
            factorial = 1.0;
            i = number;
            while (i > 1)
                factorial *= (double) i--;
            printf("%d! = %lf\n", number, factorial);
        }
        else
            printf("Number is out of range\n");
        printf("\n\n");
        do {
            printf("Enter another factorial? (Y/N) ");
            ans = getche();
            printf("\n\n");
            if (ans > 'Z')
                touppercase(ans);
        } while ( !(ans == 'Y' || ans == 'N') );
```

LOOPS 117

```
    } while (ans != 'N');
}
```

In comparing the source code for both languages, notice the following:
The Pascal WHILE loop:
```
WHILE i > 1 DO BEGIN
    factorial := factorial * i;
    DEC(i);
END; { WHILE }
```
is directly converted into a terse form:
```
while (i > 1)
    factorial *= (double) i--;
```
which employs a postdecrement operator of i in the assignment operator statement. Using the postdecrement operator, the variable i is decreased after its value is multiplied by **factorial**.

Run the C version and calculate the factorials for the numbers 5, 10, and 15. The screen image for the sample session is shown:
```
Enter the factorial number : 5
5! = 120.000000
Enter another factorial? (Y/N) y
Enter the factorial number : 10
10! = 3628800.000000
Enter another factorial? (Y/N) y
Enter the factorial number : 15
15! = 1307674368000.000000
Enter another factorial? (Y/N) n
```

Most of the examples that have been presented so far manipulate numbers. Here is a program that examines the characters you type from the keyboard. Once you press a carriage return, the program displays the number of space-delimited words, characters, and total number of keys you pressed. The Pascal version is listed below:

Listing 7.19

```
PROGRAM Word_Count;
Uses CRT;
{ Turbo Pascal program that counts the number of words and
  characters typed from the keyboard, until a <CR> is pressed }
VAR ch : CHAR;
    num_word, num_char, num_keys : INTEGER;
BEGIN
    { initialize number of words, characters, and keystrokes }
    num_word := 1;
    num_char := 0;
    num_keys := 0;
    WRITELN(''Type a sentence'); WRITELN;
    ch := ReadKey;
    WHILE ch <> #13 DO BEGIN
        WRITE(ch);
        INC(num_keys);
```

118   INTRODUCING C TO PASCAL PROGRAMMERS

```
            if ch = ' ' THEN
                INC(num_word)
            ELSE
                INC(num_char);
            ch := ReadKey;
        END; { WHILE }
        IF num_keys = 0 THEN num_word := 0;
        WRITELN;
        WRITELN;
        WRITELN('You typed ',num_keys,' keys');
        WRITELN('              ',num_word,' words');
        WRITELN('              ',num_char,' non-space characters');
        WRITELN; WRITELN;
END.
```

Run the Pascal program version and type the sentence, "The rain in Spain stays mainly in Madrid". The screen image for the sample session is shown below:

```
Type a sentence
The rain in Spain stays mainly in Madrid
You typed 40 keys
         8 words
            33 non-space characters
```

The C version is shown below:

Listing 7.20

```
/* C program that counts the number of words and
   characters typed from the keyboard, until a <CR> is pressed */
#include <stdio.h>
#include "conio.h"
main()
{
    char ch;
    int num_word = 1, num_char = 0, num_keys = 0;
    printf("Type a sentence\n\n");
    while ( (ch = getche()) != '\r')  {
        num_keys++;
        if (ch == ' ')
            num_word++;
        else
            num_char++;
    } /* while */
    if (num_keys == 0)
        num_word = 0;
    printf("\n\n");
    printf("You typed %d keys\n",num_keys);
    printf("          %d words\n",num_word);
    printf("          %d non-space characters\n\n\n",num_char);
}
```

Run the C program version and type the same sentence used for the Pascal version. The screen image for the sample session is shown below:

```
Type a sentence
The rain in Spain stays mainly in Madrid
You typed 40 keys
          8 words
          33 non-space characters
```

CHAPTER SUMMARY

C supports a number of loop constructs.

The **for** loop is made of three parts: the initialization statements, loop continuation test, and increment/decrement statements. This is

```
for(<list of value initialization statements>;
    <loop continuation test>;
    <list of increment statements>)
```

The for loop in C is noted for the following:

- Each part of the **for** loop is optional. Eliminating all three parts results in having an infinite **for** loop that tends to execute indefinitely.

- The initialization and increment/decrement parts may contain multiple statements separated by commas. Thus, multiple loop control variables may be used in a **for** loop.

The **do-while** reiterates the loop body as long as a tested expression is true (that is, not 0). The general syntax of the **do-while** loop is

```
do {
    <sequence of statements>
} while (<logical expression>);
```

The **while** loop executes its statements as long as the tested condition is true (that is, nonzero). The general syntax for the **while** loop is

```
while (<logical expression>)
    <single statement> | { <sequence of statements> }
```

Loops are exited using the **break** statement. In the case of nested loops, the program resumes after the end of the loop where the **break** is placed. The **exit** statement is used to **exit** a loop and halt the program altogether.

CHAPTER

8

Simple Functions

CHAPTER GOALS

This chapter introduces you to simple functions in C and covers the following topics:

- Syntax of C functions.
- Parameters of functions.
- Returning function values.
- Local variables.
- Making a C function work like a procedure.
- Recursive functions.
- Exiting functions.

OVERVIEW

Functions play a major role in extending the small core of the C language. The designers of the C language made provisions for functions only. C does not support formal procedures. However, using the flexibility of C, you may place the function call alone in a statement and discard the returned function value. Thus, procedures in C are emulated by functions, and the new ANSI standard for C has come one step closer to formally recognizing that by supporting the **void** (that is, typeless) type.

C FUNCTIONS

Functions in C differ from those in Pascal in both syntax and functionality. There are two general forms for declaring a function. The first follows the K&R syntax:

```
<function type> <function name>(<list of parameters>)
<data type declaration for the parameters>
{
  <sequence of statements>;
  return <returned function value>;
}
```

The second follows the ANSI standard:

```
<function type> <function name>(<list of typed parameters>)
{
  <sequence of statements>;
  return <returned function value>;
}
```

Except for the following example, I will use the ANSI syntax for declaring parameters in a function.

The following points characterize functions in C:

1. The function type is declared before the function name. If the function type is omitted the default type of **int** is assumed.
2. C has no equivalent to the FUNCTION keyword in Pascal.
3. The arguments of a function are passed by value. To alter the value of one or more arguments, you must pass pointers to their addresses (this is discussed in Chapter 11).
4. The statements of a C function are enclosed in open and close braces.
5. While a function is permitted to have local variables, it cannot have nested functions.
6. The **return** keyword is used to return function values in C.

Programming Note

C allows only one level of routines and two levels of data (global and local). Functions are able to access global data objects (that is, data types, constants, and variables) and easily alter global variables. However, this is not considered sound programming practices among veteran C programmers.

Program Translation

To convert a simple Pascal function (with arguments that are passed by value) into a C function, use the general form:

Pascal:
```
FUNCTION this_func(<list of parameters>) : <returned type>;
<data objects declarations>
BEGIN
  <function body>
  this_func := <returned value>
END;
```

122 INTRODUCING C TO PASCAL PROGRAMMERS

> C:
> ```
> <returned type> this_func(<list of parameters>)
> <data objects declarations>
> {
>    <function body>;
>    return <returned value>;
> }
> ```
> NOTE: There is no semicolon after the close parenthesis that contains the parameter list.
>
> The parameter lists for simple functions are translated as follows:
> Pascal:
>   (<var_1> : <type1>, <var2>,..,<varn> : <type2>)
> C:
>   (<type1> <var_1>,<type2> <var2>,..,<type2> <varn>)

Parameters with the same data types cannot be grouped in C. Each parameter must be explicitly declared.

Using simple functions in C is very similar to using Pascal functions.

The following program illustrates how to write a simple C function. The program prompts you for an integer, calculates its squared value, and displays the data. A squaring function is used. The Pascal version is shown below:

Listing 8.1

```
PROGRAM Use_function_1;
{ Turbo Pascal program to implement a
  function to square integers          }
VAR i, j : INTEGER;
FUNCTION square(X : INTEGER) : INTEGER;
BEGIN
    square := X * X
END;
BEGIN
    WRITE('Enter number : '); READLN(i); WRITELN;
    j := square(i);
    WRITELN(i,'^2 = ',j);
    WRITELN; WRITELN;
END.
```

In translating the above Pascal code, I have implemented two versions of the squaring function: function **square1**, using the K&R syntax and **square2**, using the ANSI syntax.

Listing 8.2

```
/* C program to implement a function to square integers    */
/* Program shows the function in two syntax versions: K&R  */
/* and the new ANSI standard.                              */
#include <stdio.h>
main()
```

```
{
    int i, j;
    printf ("Enter number : "); scanf ("%d", &i);
    j = square1 (i);
    printf ("\n%d^ = %d using first version\n\n", i, j);
    j = square2 (i);
    printf ("\n%d^ = %d using second version\n\n", i, j);
}
/* this version follows K&R syntax */
int square1 (x)
int x;
{
    return x * x;
}
/* this version follows the new ANSI standard */
int square2 (int x)
{
    return x * x;
}
```

In comparing the Pascal and C versions, notice the following differences:

1. The function heading in Pascal is:
   `FUNCTION square (X : INTEGER) : INTEGER;`
   while in the ANSI C version it is:
   `int square2 (int x)`
   Notice that data type declaration for the function and argument are reversed, while simultaneously omitting colons in C. In addition, the function heading in C does not have a semicolon.

2. In C the **return** statement is employed (instead of an assignment to the function name) to yield the function's result. The expression returned need not be enclosed in parentheses.

3. Parameter passing in the above example was done by value. The value of the argument **i** was passed to the function for processing.

The above example illustrated an integer-type function. The next example shows one that returns a floating-point result. The program solves for the root of a user-defined nonlinear function. The iterative Newton's method is employed to obtain the sought results and is implemented in the function **root**. In addition, the user-defined function is placed in function **fofx**. The current program version has this function set to solve for the root of the following polynomial:

$f(X) = X^3 - 2 X^2 + 5 X + 5$

The **root** function takes three parameters: the initial guess, the sought accuracy of the solution, and the maximum number of iterations. The latter is supplied by a constant defined in the program. The function returns the value of the root, under normal circumstances, or the best guess for the root.

Listing 8.3

```pascal
PROGRAM Use_function_2;
{ Turbo Pascal program to solve for the root of a function }
CONST MAX_ITER = 30;
VAR accuracy, guess : REAL;
FUNCTION fofx(x : REAL) : REAL;
{ the nonlinear function whose root is sought }
BEGIN
    fofx := x * x * x - 2 * x * x + 5 * x + 5.0
END;
FUNCTION root(guess, accuracy : REAL; max_iter : INTEGER) : REAL;
{ function to solve for the sought root }
CONST SMALL = 1.0E-10;
      BIG = 0.01;
VAR iter : INTEGER;
    diff, h : REAL;
BEGIN
    IF accuracy > BIG THEN accuracy := BIG
    ELSE IF accuracy < SMALL THEN accuracy := SMALL;
    iter := 0; { initialize iteration counter }
    REPEAT
       { calculate differential increment }
       IF ABS(guess) > 1.0 THEN h := 0.01 * guess
                           ELSE h := 0.01;
       { calculate improvement in guess }
       diff := 2.0 * h * fofx(guess) /
                     (fofx(guess+h) - fofx(guess-h));
       { update guess }
       guess := guess - diff;
       { increment loop counter and test for divergence }
       INC(iter);
       IF iter > max_iter THEN diff := 0.0;
    UNTIL ABS(diff) < accuracy;
    root := guess;
END;
BEGIN
    WRITE('Enter guess and accuracy : ');
    READLN(guess,accuracy); WRITELN;
    WRITELN('Root = ',root(guess, accuracy, MAX_ITER));
    WRITELN; WRITELN;
END.
```

Run the Pascal version and enter 4 and 0.000001 as the initial guess and the sought accuracy, respectively. The root is approximately -0.7189. The screen image of the sample session is shown below.

```
Enter guess and accuracy : 4.0 0.000001
Root = -7.18934551346138E-0001
```

The C version is listed below:

Listing 8.4

```c
/* C program to solve for the root of a function */
#include <stdio.h>
#include "math.h"
/* need to declare local functions that are not of type int */
double root(double, double, int);
main()
{
   const int MAX_ITER = 30;
   double accuracy, guess;
   printf("Enter guess and accuracy : ");
   scanf("%lf %lf", &guess, &accuracy);
   printf("\nRoot = %lf\n\n",root(guess, accuracy, MAX_ITER));
}
double fofx(double x)
/* the nonlinear function whose root is sought */
{
    return (x * x * x - 2 * x * x + 5 * x + 5.0);
}
double root(double guess, double accuracy, int max_iter)
/* function to solve for the sought root */
{
    /* declare local constants */
    const double SMALL = 1.0E-10;
    const double BIG = 0.01L;
    /* declare local variables */
    int iter = 0;
    double diff, h;
    if (accuracy > BIG)
       accuracy = BIG;
    else if (accuracy < SMALL)
       accuracy = SMALL;
    do {
      /* calculate differential increment */
      if (fabs(guess) > 1.0)
         h = 0.01 * guess;
      else
         h = 0.01;
      /* calculate improvement in guess */
      diff = 2.0 * h * fofx(guess) /
                    (fofx(guess+h) - fofx(guess-h));
      /* update guess */
      guess -= diff;
      /* increment loop counter and test for divergence */
      if (++iter > max_iter)
         diff = 0.0;
    } while ( !((fabs(diff) < accuracy)) );
     /* OR use (fabs(diff) >= accuracy)   */
    return guess;
}
```

In comparing the listings of the two versions, notice the following C features:

1. The **main** function in the above C program has the following declaration:
   ```
   double root(double, double, int);
   ```
   This is called function prototyping and is mandatory for functions that return data types other than integers. Function prototyping informs the compiler of the exact data type of the function, as well as the number of parameters and their individual data types. Under the K&R (Kernighan & Ritchie) definition function protoyping existed, but no parameters were needed. With the advent of the ANSI C, the parameters of the function are also required in the prototype. This offers more compiler verification and prevents a program from passing the wrong number and/or types of parameters.

   As the above function prototyping declaration illustrates, the number and type of arguments are represented by their data types. If no arguments are used, then the keyword **void** must be inserted.

2. The declaration of function **root** in C, using the ANSI syntax, is
   ```
   double root(double guess, double accuracy, int max_iter)
   ```
   The above differs from declaring parameters in Pascal functions, and even global/local variables in C, in that each parameter must be accompanied by its data type. No mechanism is supported to shorten the parameter list by lumping parameters with the same data type. Thus, the following is not legal:

NOT LEGAL

```
double root(double guess, accuracy; int max_iter)
```

   You may spread the parameter list over multiple lines and even include comments, as in:
   ```
   double root(double guess,      /* supply initial guess    */
               double accuracy,   /* supply desired accuracy */
               int max_iter)      /* max number of iterations */
   ```
3. Both versions declare local constants and variables inside function **root**. The C declarations are
   ```
   /* declare local constants */
   const double SMALL = 1.0E-10;
   const double BIG = 0.01L;
   /* declare local variables */
   int iter = 0;
   double diff, h;
   ```

Programming Note

Since C allows single-level functions (that is, no nested functions) local data objects (constants, variables, etc.) are strictly accessible to the function within which they are declared. This also applies to function **main**. No routine inherits data objects from another.

SIMPLE FUNCTIONS

Run the above version and enter 4 and 0.000001 as the initial guess and the sought accuracy, respectively. The root is approximately -0.7189. You may want to try other initial guesses, all of which should yield the same solution. The screen image of the sample session is shown below.

```
Enter guess and accuracy : 4.0 0.000001
Root = -0.718935
```

In the earlier chapters I have employed macro-based pseudofunctions to work as simple C functions. The following program is a modified version of a previous one. It contains both the macro and actual function for comparison and performs the same tasks twice: once with the macros, the other utilizing the C functions. The C functions are named by inserting **fn_** before the corresponding macro name.

Listing 8.5

```
/* C program to compare macro-based pseudo-functions
   with actual functions.                                   */
#include <stdio.h>
#include "conio.h"
#include "scrncurs.h"
/* define data type macros */
#define BOOLEAN char
#define BYTE unsigned char
/* define boolean constants */
#define FALSE 0
#define TRUE 1
/* macros that define pseudo one-line functions */
#define boolean(x) ((x) ? "TRUE" : "FALSE")
#define abs(x) (((x) >= 0) ? (x) : -(x))
#define max(x,y) (((x) > (y)) ? (x) : (y))
#define min(x,y) (((x) > (y)) ? (y) : (x))
#define sqr(x) ((x) * (x))
#define cube(x) ((x) * (x) * (x))
#define reciprocal(x) (1 / (x))
#define XOR(test1,test2) (((test1 + test2) == TRUE) ? TRUE : FALSE)
/* macros used for character testing */
#define islower(c) (c >= 'a' && c <= 'z')
#define isupper(c) (c >= 'A' && c <= 'Z')
#define isdigit(c) (c >= '0' && c <= '9')
#define isletter(c) ((c >= 'A' && c <= 'Z') || (c >= 'a' && c <=
'z'))
/* macros used in character case conversions */
#define tolowercase(c) (c - 'A' + 'a')
#define touppercase(c) (c - 'a' + 'A' )
/* declare function prototypes */
/* int fn_abs(int), fn_max(int,int), fn_min(int,int); */
double fn_reciprocal(double);
BOOLEAN fn_XOR(BOOLEAN,BOOLEAN);
BOOLEAN fn_islower(char);
BOOLEAN fn_isupper(char);
BOOLEAN fn_isdigit(char);
BOOLEAN fn_isletter(char);
char fn_tolowercase(char);
```

```
char fn_touppercase(char);
main()
{
   BOOLEAN bool;
   BYTE i, j;
   int k, m;
   char ch, akey;
   double x = 0.10;
   printf("Enter an integer : "); scanf("%d", &k);
   printf("\n");
   printf("%d squared = %d ", k, sqr(k));
   printf("\n\n");
   printf("1 / %f = %f", x, reciprocal(x));
   printf(" \n\n");
   ch = 'A';
   printf("The lowercase of %c is %c", ch, tolowercase(ch));
   printf("\n\n");
   ch = 'g';
   printf("The uppercase of %c is %c", ch, touppercase(ch));
   printf("\n\npress any key to continue");
   akey = getch();
   clrscr;
   printf("\n\nType a letter or a digit : "); ch = getche();
   bool = isupper(ch);
   gotoxy(10,5);
   printf("character is uppercase : %s\n",boolean(bool));
   bool = islower(ch);
   gotoxy(10,6);
   printf("character is lowercase : %s\n",boolean(bool));
   bool = isletter(ch);
   gotoxy(10,7);
   printf("character is a letter  : %s\n",boolean(bool));
   bool = isdigit(ch);
   gotoxy(10,8);
   printf("character is a digit   : %s\n",boolean(bool));
   printf("\n");
   printf("Enter two integers (delimited by a space) : ");
   scanf("%d %d", &k, &m);
   printf("\n\n");
   printf("The largest  of the two numbers is %d\n\n",max(k,m));
   printf("The smallest of the two numbers is %d\n\n",min(k,m));
   printf("ABS(%d) = %d\n\n", k, abs(k));
   printf("\npress any key to continue");
   akey = getch();
   /* do same tasks using functions */
   clrscr;
   printf("Performing the same tasks using C functions\n\n\n");
   printf("Enter an integer : "); scanf("%d", &k);
   printf("\n");
   printf("%d squared = %d ", k, fn_sqr(k));
   printf("\n\n");
   printf("1 / %f = %f", x, fn_reciprocal(x));
   printf("\n\n");
   ch = 'A';
   printf("The lowercase of %c is %c", ch, fn_tolowercase(ch));
```

SIMPLE FUNCTIONS 129

```
      printf("\n\n");
      ch = 'g';
      printf("The uppercase of %c is %c", ch, fn_touppercase(ch));
      printf("\n\npress any key to continue");
      akey = getch();
      clrscr;
      printf("\n\nType a letter or a digit : "); ch = getche();
      bool = fn_isupper(ch);
      gotoxy(10,5);
      printf("character is uppercase : %s\n",boolean(bool));
      bool = fn_islower(ch);
      gotoxy(10,6);
      printf("character is lowercase : %s\n",boolean(bool));
      bool = fn_isletter(ch);
      gotoxy(10,7);
      printf("character is a letter  : %s\n",boolean(bool));
      bool = fn_isdigit(ch);
      gotoxy(10,8);
      printf("character is a digit   : %s\n",boolean(bool));
      printf("\n");
      printf("Enter two integers (delimited by a space) : ");
      scanf("%d %d", &k, &m);
      printf("\n\n");
      printf("The largest  of the two numbers is %d\n\n",fn_max(k,m));
      printf("The smallest of the two numbers is %d\n\n",fn_min(k,m));
      printf("ABS(%d) = %d\n\n", k, fn_abs(k));
}
/* declare functions that perform same tasks as macros */
int fn_abs(int x)
{
   if (x < 0)
      return (-x);
   else
      return x;
}
int fn_max(int x, int y)
{
   if (x > y)
      return x;
   else
      return y;
}
int fn_min(int x, int y)
{
   if (x > y)
      return y;
   else
      return x;
}
int fn_sqr(int x)
{
   return x * x;
}
int fn_cube(int x)
{
```

```c
    return x * x * x;
}
double fn_reciprocal(double x)
{
    return 1 / x;
}
BOOLEAN fn_XOR(BOOLEAN test1, BOOLEAN test2)
{
    if ((test1 + test2) != TRUE)
        return FALSE;
    else
        return !FALSE;
}
BOOLEAN fn_islower(char c)
{
    if (c >= 'a' && c <= 'z')
        return !FALSE;
    else
        return FALSE;
}
BOOLEAN fn_isupper(char c)
{
    if (c >= 'A' && c <= 'Z')
        return !FALSE;
    else
        return FALSE;
}
BOOLEAN fn_isdigit(char c)
{
    if (c >= '0' && c <= '9')
        return !FALSE;
    else
        return FALSE;
}
BOOLEAN fn_isletter(char c)
{
    if ((c >= 'A' && c <= 'Z') || (c >= 'a' && c <= 'z'))
        return !FALSE;
    else
        return FALSE;
}
char fn_tolowercase(char c)
{
    if (c >= 'A' && c <= 'Z')
        return (c - 'A' + 'a');
    else
        return c;
}
char fn_touppercase(char c)
{
    if (c >= 'a' && c <= 'z')
        return (c - 'a' + 'A');
    else
        return c;
}
```

SIMPLE FUNCTIONS   131

The functions that alter the case of a character work with any character. By contrast, the macro versions only work properly if a character with the intended case is supplied!

Run the above C program and enter the following twice, one for the code lines using the macros, the other for the code lines that invoke the functions:

1. The integer 5.
2. The letter g.
3. The integers 10 and 66.

```
Enter an integer : 5
5 squared = 25
1 / 0.100000 = 10.000000
The lowercase of A is a
The uppercase of g is G
press any key to continue <any key>
<the screen clears>
Type a letter or a digit : g
        character is uppercase : FALSE
        character is lowercase : TRUE
        character is a letter  : TRUE
        character is a digit   : FALSE
Enter two integers (delimited by a space) : 10 66
The largest  of the two numbers is 66
The smallest of the two numbers is 10
ABS(10) = 10
press any key to continue <any key>
<the screen clears>
Performing the same tasks using C functions
Enter an integer : 5
5 squared = 25
1 / 0.100000 = 10.000000
The lowercase of A is a
The uppercase of g is G
press any key to continue <any key>
Type a letter or a digit : g
        character is uppercase : FALSE
        character is lowercase : TRUE
        character is a letter  : TRUE
        character is a digit   : FALSE
Enter two integers (delimited by a space) : 10 66

The largest of the two numbers is 66
The smallest of the two numbers is 10
ABS(10) = 10
```

MAKING A C FUNCTION WORK AS A PROCEDURE

As a Pascal programmer, you may expect to see procedures implemented in C. This talk of *all functions and no procedures* should not dismay you. A popular saying states, "Where there is a will, there is a way." This is also true when it comes to making functions behave like procedures.

132 INTRODUCING C TO PASCAL PROGRAMMERS

The old technique, prior to the ANSI standard, was to employ an integer-typed function and place it in a statement all by itself. This causes the runtime system to ignore its returned value. To add clarity to such functions, macros were usually used to make **void** (the name often selected) synonymous with **int**. Thus, older C programs looked something like:

```
#defined void int
<other declarations>
void gotoxy(x, y)
int x, y;
{
<statements for function>
}
```

The committee for the ANSI standard decided to make **void** a predefined keyword used to declared functions that do not return any value. Therefore, the next time you hear or read about a void function in C, simply think of it as a procedure!

In the last example I illustrated how macros can work like normal simple functions in C. I deliberately retained a number of macros that manipulate the screen and cursor in file "scrncurs.h". Since these macros emulate procedures, not functions, I present them now in a modified version of the last program. I have removed the macro-based functions from the program, retained the set of functions, and added the screen/cursor control void functions **clrscr**, **gotoxy**, and **clreol**. These void functions, like their macro counterparts, work with the ANSI.SYS driver. The **wait-key** function is used to prompt you to press any key to resume with the program.

The void functions also require prototyping. The following declarations are inserted in the **main** function:

```
void clrscr(void);
void gotoxy(int,int);
void clreol(void);
void wait_key(void);
```

Void functions with a void argument list, like **clrscr**, **clreol**, and **wait_key**, still need parentheses (with no arguments) to be used. Also, notice that the void functions do not employ the return statement.

The C program is shown below:

Listing 8.6

```
/* C program to use void functions as procedures.          */
#include <stdio.h>
#include "conio.h"
/* define data type macros */
#define BOOLEAN char
#define BYTE unsigned char
/* define boolean constants */
#define FALSE 0
#define TRUE 1
#define boolean(x) ((x) ? "TRUE" : "FALSE")
/* declare function prototypes */
```

SIMPLE FUNCTIONS 133

```c
/* int fn_abs(int), fn_max(int,int), fn_min(int,int); */
double fn_reciprocal(double);
BOOLEAN fn_XOR(BOOLEAN,BOOLEAN);
BOOLEAN fn_islower(char);
BOOLEAN fn_isupper(char);
BOOLEAN fn_isdigit(char);
BOOLEAN fn_isletter(char);
char fn_tolowercase(char);
char fn_touppercase(char);
/* added set of screen management void-typed functions */
void clrscr(void);
void gotoxy(int,int);
void clreol(void);
/* void function used in waiting for a key to be presses */
void wait_key(void);
main()
{
   BOOLEAN bool;
   BYTE i, j;
   int k, m;
   char ch;
   double x = 0.10;
   printf("Enter an integer : "); scanf("%d", &k);
   printf("\n");
   printf("%d squared = %d ", k, fn_sqr(k));
   printf("\n\n");
   printf("1 / %f = %f", x, fn_reciprocal(x));
   printf("\n\n");
   ch = 'A';
   printf("The lowercase of %c is %c", ch, fn_tolowercase(ch));
   printf("\n\n");
   ch = 'g';
   printf("The uppercase of %c is %c", ch, fn_touppercase(ch));
   wait_key();
   clrscr();
   printf("\n\nType a letter or a digit : "); ch = getche();
   bool = fn_isupper(ch);
   gotoxy(10,5);
   printf("character is uppercase : %s\n",boolean(bool));
   bool = fn_islower(ch);
   gotoxy(10,6);
   printf("character is lowercase : %s\n",boolean(bool));
   bool = fn_isletter(ch);
   gotoxy(10,7);
   printf("character is a letter  : %s\n",boolean(bool));
   bool = fn_isdigit(ch);
   gotoxy(10,8);
   printf("character is a digit   : %s\n",boolean(bool));
   printf("\n");
   printf("Enter two integers (delimited by a space) : ");
   scanf("%d %d", &k, &m);
   printf("\n\n");
   printf("The largest  of the two numbers is %d\n\n",fn_max(k,m));
   printf("The smallest of the two numbers is %d\n\n",fn_min(k,m));
   printf("ABS(%d) = %d\n\n", k, fn_abs(k));
```

```c
}
/* declare functions that perform same tasks as macros */
int fn_abs(int x)
{
   if (x < 0)
      return (-x);
   else
      return x;
}
int fn_max(int x, int y)
{
   if (x > y)
      return x;
   else
      return y;
}
int fn_min(int x, int y)
{
   if (x > y)
      return y;
   else
      return x;
}
int fn_sqr(int x)
{
   return x * x;
}
int fn_cube(int x)
{
   return x * x * x;
}
double fn_reciprocal(double x)
{
   return 1 / x;
}
BOOLEAN fn_XOR(BOOLEAN test1, BOOLEAN test2)
{
   if ((test1 + test2) != TRUE)
      return FALSE;
   else
      return !FALSE;
}
BOOLEAN fn_islower(char c)
{
   if (c >= 'a' && c <= 'z')
      return !FALSE;
   else
      return FALSE;
}
BOOLEAN fn_isupper(char c)
{
   if (c >= 'A' && c <= 'Z')
      return !FALSE;
   else
      return FALSE;
```

```
}
BOOLEAN fn_isdigit(char c)
{
    if (c >= '0' && c <= '9')
        return !FALSE;
    else
        return FALSE;
}
BOOLEAN fn_isletter(char c)
{
    if ((c >= 'A' && c <= 'Z') || (c >= 'a' && c <= 'z'))
        return !FALSE;
    else
        return FALSE;
}
char fn_tolowercase(char c)
{
 return (c - 'A' + 'a');
}
char fn_touppercase(char c)
{
    return (c - 'a' + 'A');
}
/* set of void functions (i.e. procedures) to perform screen
   management and waiting for a key to be pressed           */
void clrscr(void)
{
    printf("\x1b[2J");
}
void gotoxy(int col,int row)
{
    printf("\x1b[%d;%dH", row, col);
}
void clreol(void)
{
    printf("\x1b[K");
}
void wait_key(void)
{
  char akey;
  printf("\n\npress any key to continue");
  akey = getch();
}
```

RECURSIVE FUNCTIONS

C supports recursive functions. Recursive function calls in C are practically the same as those in Pascal. Like Pascal, recursive functions need no special declaration.

The following simple program calculates factorials recursively. You are prompted to enter an integer, whose factorial is calculated and displayed. The recursive **factorial** function performs the task in question. The Pascal code is shown below:

Listing 8.7

```
PROGRAM Recursive_Factorials;
{ Turbo Pascal program that calculates factorials recursively }
VAR n : BYTE;
FUNCTION factorial(x : BYTE) : REAL;
{ recursive factorial function }
BEGIN
    IF x > 1 THEN factorial := x * factorial(x - 1)
             ELSE factorial := 1.0
END;
BEGIN
    WRITE('Enter factorial number : ');
    READLN(n); WRITELN;
    WRITELN(n,'! = ',factorial(n));
    WRITELN; WRITELN;
END.
```

Run the program twice and enter 5 and 10. The screen image is shown below:

```
Enter factorial number : 5
5! =  1.20000000000000E+0002
Enter factorial number : 10
10! =  3.62880000000000E+0006
```

The C code is listed below:

Listing 8.8

```
/* C program that calculates factorials recursively */
#include <stdio.h>
#define BYTE unsigned char
main()
{
    BYTE n;
    double factorial(BYTE);
    printf("Enter factorial number : ");
    scanf("%d", &n);
    printf("\n%d! = %lf\n\n\n", n, factorial(n));
}
double factorial(BYTE x)
/* recursive factorial function */
{
    if (x > 1)
       return (double) x * factorial(x - 1);
    else
       return 1.0L;
}
```

The C version is written to utilize type casting for the value returned by the function. The statements that invoke recursion are similar:

```
factorial := x * factorial(x - 1)        <- Pascal
return (double) x * factorial(x - 1);    <- C
```

Run the C version twice and enter 5 and 10. The screen image is shown below:

```
Enter factorial number : 5
5! = 120.000000
Enter factorial number : 10
10! = 3628800.000000
```

Functions in C are indeed very powerful. This chapter has merely introduced you to their basic aspects. In order to discuss the power and versatility of C functions, I will need to first discuss advanced data structures.

EXITING FUNCTIONS

In writing functions and procedures for certain applications, you may need to provide an early exit from a called routine. This may be due to one of two general cases:

1. The routine examines its arguments only to discover that they represent invalid data.
2. The function performs iterative searches for solutions. You may want to include code to detect arguments that provide data with trivial solutions. Under this condition, the function returns the sought answer without going through the extensive iterations or searches. In Pascal you employ the EXIT statement to leave a function or procedure and return to the caller. In C, you instead employ **return**. If you exit from a function, you might as well return a special value that is indicative of the special exit-condition. In the case of a void C function, simply use **return** with no expression associated with it.

CHAPTER SUMMARY

- C implements functions at a single level only. The general ANSI standard syntax for declaring functions is

    ```
    <function type> <function name>(<list of typed parameters>)
    {
      <local declarations>;
      <sequence of statements>;
      return <returned function expression>;
    }
    ```

- Functions in C do not require a special keyword to declare them. The parameter list consists of the data type and name of each parameter. The type is declared first, followed by the parameter itself. Spaces are used to delimit the data types and the parameters. Commas are used to separate the individual parameter declarations.

- A function that has no parameter can use the reserved word **void** in its parameter list. When such a function is invoked, empty parentheses must follow the function name.

- Arguments of C functions are essentially passed by value. Therefore, any variable passed as a parameter cannot have its value permanently altered by the function, unless the address of the variable is passed.
- Functions used in the **main** function must be prototyped (functions that return the **int** type are exempt). This is a special declaration that informs the compiler of the type of value returned by a function, along with the number of parameters and their exact data types.
- A C function may avoid returning a value and yet still perform a meaningful task. In this case, the function behaves like a procedure and can be placed all by itself in a statement. Under the ANSI standards, the **void** data type affirms the above special role of a function.
- C supports recursive functions.

CHAPTER

9

Pointers, Arrays, and Strings

CHAPTER GOALS

This chapter looks at advanced data types in C and covers the following topics:

- Storage classes.
- Scope of variables.
- Pointers to simple data types.
- Single and multidimensional arrays.
- Accessing arrays using pointers.
- Strings in C.

In this chapter we begin taking a deeper look into important data structures in C. While these include arrays and strings, one cannot stress enough the importance of pointers in C. Some programmers say that C is a language built on the four basic operations and pointers! If anything, their statement correctly indicates the importance of pointers in C. As a Pascal programmer, you have most likely used the Pascal pointer types. In C you will learn to rely on them more and use them with greater frequency and in a wider scope.

STORAGE CLASSES

C supports a number of storage classes (or modes, if you prefer) giving you more power to determine the lifetime of variables.

Automatic

This class contains the local dynamic variables with the following characteristics:
- They are created when the function is invoked.
- They disappear when the called function terminates.

In Pascal they are simply called local variables. This is also true in C.

Static

Once the variables in this class are created they retain their locations in memory and, consequently, their values, during the entire program execution. Thus, when a function with static local variables is first invoked, the static variables are allocated permanent memory addresses and initialized. When the function exits, the static variables still retain their values, which are accessible during subsequent function calls. To declare static variables, simply insert the reserved word **static** before the data type. There is no need to declare global variables as static, since they are present throughout the execution of the program anyway.

Pascal does not formally support static variables. In the next program I attempt to emulate static variables using variables that are passed by reference. The program prompts you to enter real numbers. After you do this, the program displays the current average. You may exit the program by entering 0.

The Pascal version is shown below:

Listing 9.1

```
PROGRAM Emulate_Static_Variables;
Uses CRT;
{ Turbo Pascal program that emulates static variables by passing
  them as arguments in a routine.                              }
VAR sum, sumx, sumxx : REAL;
    x : REAL;
FUNCTION average(    x       : REAL; { input   }
                 VAR sum,            { in/out  }
                     sumx,           { in/out  }
                     sumxx : REAL    { in/out }) : REAL;
{ function to return the statistical average }
BEGIN
    { update the statistical summations }
    sum := sum + 1.0;
    sumx := sumx + x;
    sumxx := sumxx + x * x;
    { calculate the average }
    average := sumx / sum;
END;
BEGIN
    clrscr;
    { initialize summations }
```

POINTERS, ARRAYS, AND STRINGS   141

```
    sum := 0.0;
    sumx := 0.0;
    sumxx := 0.0;
    WRITE('Enter number [0 to exit] : ');
    READLN(x); WRITELN;
    WHILE x <> 0.0 DO BEGIN
        WRITELN('current average = ',average(x,sum,sumx,sumxx));
        WRITELN;
        WRITE('Enter number [0 to exit] : ');
        READLN(x); WRITELN;
    END; { WHILE }
END.
```

Run the Pascal program version and enter the numbers 1, 2, 3, 4, 5, and 6. To exit, type 0. The screen image of the sample session is shown below:

```
Enter number [0 to exit] : 1
current average =  1.00000000000000E+0000
Enter number [0 to exit] : 2
current average =  1.50000000000000E+0000
Enter number [0 to exit] : 3
current average =  2.00000000000000E+0000
Enter number [0 to exit] : 4
current average =  2.50000000000000E+0000
Enter number [0 to exit] : 5
current average =  3.00000000000000E+0000
Enter number [0 to exit] : 6
current average =  3.50000000000000E+0000
Enter number [0 to exit] : 0
```

The C version, which uses static variables, is listed below:

Listing 9.2

```
/* C program that uses static variables in a routine. */
#include <stdio.h>
#include "scrncurs.h"
double average(double); /* declare function prototype */
main()
{
    double x;
    clrscr;
    printf("Enter number [0 to exit] : ");
    scanf("%lf", &x); printf("\n");
    while (x != 0.0)  {
        printf("current average = %lf\n\n",average(x));
        printf("Enter number [0 to exit] : ");
        scanf("%lf", &x); printf("\n");
    } /* while */
}
double average(double x)
/* function to return the statistical average       */
{
    /* declare and initialize local static variables */
```

142 INTRODUCING C TO PASCAL PROGRAMMERS

```
    static double sum = 0.0L, sumx = 0.0L, sumxx = 0.0L;
    /* update the statistical summations */
    sum++;
    sumx += x;
    sumxx += x * x;
    /* calculate the average */
    return sumx / sum;
}
```

Notice how the static variables are declared in the **average** function:
`static double sum = 0.0L, sumx = 0.0L, sumxx = 0.0L;`

The **static** storage class indicator is used to declare the **sum**, **sumx**, and **sumxx** variables as static. The declaration also initializes the values of these variables.

These static variables are kept hidden from the **main** function (unlike the Pascal version) while retaining their data between calls to function **average**. This represents an important tool in modern software engineering called data hiding. The details of the statistical summations are hidden from the function **main**.

Run the C version and enter the numbers 1, 2, 3, 4, 5, and 6. To exit, type 0. The screen image of the sample session is shown below:

```
Enter number [0 to exit] : 1
current average = 1.000000
Enter number [0 to exit] : 2
current average = 1.500000
Enter number [0 to exit] : 3
current average = 2.000000
Enter number [0 to exit] : 4
current average = 2.500000
Enter number [0 to exit] : 5
current average = 3.000000
Enter number [0 to exit] : 6
current average = 3.500000
Enter number [0 to exit] : 0
```

Another application for static variables is the following C function that calculates factorials. The function is designed to store the first 30 factorials in a static array (more about arrays later in this chapter). The first time the function is called, the first 30 factorials are systematically evaluated and stored in the static array. The call to the **super_fact** function examines the value of the argument: if it is less than 31, the sought result is obtained by simply recalling the appropriate static array element. If the argument is larger than 30, the factorial is calculated starting with 30! stored in the last static array element. This function is most suitable if the factorials requested are mostly those of lower numbers. The code for the function is

```
double super_fact(unsigned int n)
{
   static flag = 0;
   static double results[31];
```

```
    unsigned int i;
    double result = 1.0;
    if (flag == 0) {
       flag = 1;
       results[0] = 1.0;
       results[1] = 1.0;
       for (i = 2; i < 31; i++)
          results[i] := results[i-1];
    }
    if (n < 31)
       result = results[n];
    else {
       result = results[30];
       for (i = 31; i <= n; i++)
         result *= (double) i;
    }
       return result; /* return function value */
}
```

Extern

This type of storage class is mainly aimed at resolving accesses to data declared in external source code files. This usually occurs when you are working on a large software project that involves several source code files. The **extern** declaration tells the compiler to resolve the address allocation during the linking phase (when other files are included in the linking process).

The following partial code is stored in two files. The variables **mat_size** and **missing_code**, and the matrix **x** are all used in both programs. To prevent the compiler from allocating duplicate memory addresses for the above data objects, the **extern** class storage indicator is used in the second source file:

Source code in file # 1

```
#include <stdio.h>
int mat_size;
double missing_data;
double x[10][10];
main()
{
    printf("Enter matrix size : ");
    scanf("%d", &mat_size);
    printf("\n\nEnter code for missing data : ");
    scanf("%lf",&missing_data);

    /* sequence of other statements here */
}
```

Source code in file # 2

```
extern int mat_size;
extern double missing_data;
extern double x[10][10];
double determinant(void)
{
   /* calculate the determinant of square matrix */
   return <result>;
}
```

Register

Since the C language is used for systems design, program speed is of prime importance in these low-level applications. Manipulating data in the CPU registers is much faster than if the same data resides in memory. The **Register** storage class indicator instructs the compiler to use an available CPU register to store data from automatic variables. You can use the **Register** storage class with characters, integers, and pointers. A **Register** variable can be used as an array index or an initailization variable used to setup the values of an array. DO NOT USE THIS STORAGE CLASS UNTIL YOU BECOME A PRACTICING C PROGRAMMER.

SCOPE OF VARIABLES

As a Pascal programmer you learned that in every routine you must declare all of the data objects (that is, constants, types, and variables) before you begin listing the program code for that routine. Pascal does not allow you to declare new nondynamic variables once you go past the BEGIN keyword in the routine or main program. This means that every variable you employ in the routine must be declared regardless of the extent of its usage. For example, a local dummy variable used in one statement is declared in the same way as another local variable playing a major role in another statement. Both types of local variables have the same life span in the routine even though the dummy is idle most of that life span!

C allows you to rectify the above situation (especially if you have a large program with numerous variables that are used in a short range of lines) by allowing you to declare new data objects in separate blocks. The open and close braces are used to declare a new block. After the open brace, you may declare new variables that exist inside this block (and any nested blocks). When the corresponding close brace is encountered, the variables declared in that block are removed.

To illustrate the above C feature, I present the following program. It calculates the average and standard deviation of data you key in. The program prompts you for the number of data and then requests that you enter the data itself. The Pascal version illustrates how such a program is written in the way you have been familiar with (that is, declare all of the variables up front):

POINTERS, ARRAYS, AND STRINGS **145**

Listing 9.3

```
PROGRAM Basic_stat;
Uses CRT;
{ This Turbo Pascal program calculates the basic statistics for
  a given set of data. This program is translated into two C
  versions. The first is close to a mirror image of the Pascal
  code. The second version illustrates the feature in C that
  permits the declaration of variables in the middle of the
  code.
}
VAR x, sum, sumx, sumxx : REAL;
    mean, sdev : REAL;
    i, count : INTEGER;
BEGIN
    clrscr;
    REPEAT
        WRITE('Enter number of data (> 1) : ');
        READLN(count); WRITELN;
    UNTIL count > 1;
    { initialize statistical summations }
    sum := count;
    sumx := 0.0;
    sumxx := 0.0;
    FOR i := 1 TO count DO BEGIN
        WRITE('Enter a number : ');
        READLN(x); WRITELN;
        sumx := sumx + x;
        sumxx := sumxx + x * x
    END; { FOR }
    { calculate the mean and std. deviation }
    mean := sumx/ sum;
    sdev := SQRT((sumxx - sumx * sumx / sum) / (sum - 1.0));
    WRITELN('Mean            = ',mean); WRITELN;
    WRITELN('Std. deviation = ',sdev); WRITELN;
END.
```

The first C version is a straightforward translation of the program using the same declaration scheme as the Pascal version:

Listing 9.4

```
/* C program that is a translation of the Pascal program that
   calculates the basic statistics for a given set of data. This
   version shows the usual fashion for which all of the variables
   are declared at the beginning of the code in main(). All of
   the variables are visible (and accessible) throughout the
   code of main().                                            */
#include <stdio.h>
#include "math.h"
#include "scrncurs.h"
main()
{
    double x, sum, sumx, sumxx;
```

```
    double mean, sdev;
    int i, count;
    clrscr;
    do {
        printf("Enter number of data (> 1) : ");
        scanf("%d", &count); printf("\n");
    } while ( !(count > 1) );
    /* initialize statistical summations */
    sum = count;
    sumx = 0.0;
    sumxx = 0.0;
    for (i = 1; i <= count; i++)  {
        printf("Enter a number : ");
        scanf("%lf", &x); printf("\n");
        sumx += x;
        sumxx +=  x * x;
    } /* for */
    /* calculate mean and std. deviation */
    mean = sumx/ sum;
    sdev = sqrt((sumxx - sumx * sumx / sum) / (sum - 1.0));
    printf("Mean           = %lf\n\n",mean);
    printf("Std. deviation = %lf\n\n",sdev);
}
```

The modified C version is written in such a way that variables are created in blocks and are given a tailored life span. The above program is broken down into the following segments:

1. A **do-while** loop, to prompt you for the number of data.
2. A sequence of statements used to initialize the statistical summations.
3. A **for** loop that prompts you to enter the data.
4. A sequence of statements that are employed to calculate and display the results.

Using the above program segments, an outline is made and is included in the modified C program shown below:

Listing 9.5

```
/* This C program is a modified version of the last one.
   It uses multiple scope variables, a feature not supported
   by Pascal. This feature enables you to save memory by
   declaring large arrays and matrices that store temporary
   data inside new sub-levels of code. The memory space of
   these arrays is reclaimed once the end of the sub-level
   block is reached.                                      */
#include <stdio.h>
#include "math.h"
#include "scrncurs.h"
/*--------- outline for program level blocks ---------
main()
```

POINTERS, ARRAYS, AND STRINGS   147

```
{                            SCOPE OF VARIABLES
                            ─────────────────────────────
    <declarations>     count
                        |
    <do-while loop>     |
                        |
    { sub-level #1      |     sum,sumx,sumxx
      { sub-level #2    |           |           i,x
        <for loop>      |           |            |
                        |           |            |
      } end of #2       |           |            V
                        |           |
      {sub-level #2     |           |                   mean,sdev
       <calculations>   |           |                      |
       <output>         |           |                      |
      } end of #2       |           |                      V
    } end of #1         |           V
                        |
                        |
                        V
} end of main()
*/
main()
{
    /* only variable 'count' is visible throughout main */
    int count;
    clrscr;
    do {
       printf("Enter number of data (> 1) : ");
       scanf("%d", &count); printf("\n");
    } while ( !(count > 1) );
    { /* declare sub-level #1: the variable declared below
         are visible within this code block              */
      double sum = count, sumx = 0.0L, sumxx = 0.0L;
      { /* declare sub-level #2: all the variables from the
           previous levels plus 'i' and 'x' are visible
           within this code block                        */
        double x;
        int i;
        for (i = 1; i <= count; i++)  {
           printf("Enter a number : ");
           scanf("%lf", &x); printf("\n");
           sumx += x;
           sumxx +=  x * x;
        } /* for */
        /* end of sub-level #2, variable 'i' is no longer
           accessible */
      }
      { /* declare a second sub-level #2 */
        double mean, sdev;
        /* calculate mean and std. deviation */
        mean = sumx/ sum;
        sdev = sqrt((sumxx - sumx * sumx / sum) / (sum - 1.0));
        printf("Mean           = %lf\n\n"   ,mean);
```

```
        printf("Std. deviation = %lf\n\n ",sdev);
        /* end of second sub-level #2 */
        }
        /* end of sub-level #1 */
    }
}
```

The above program shows various scopes of variables in the program:
1. The variable **count** is available throughout the program.
2. The summation variables **sum**, **sumx**, and **sumxx** exist in the first sublevel block. They come into being after the end of the **do-while** loop.
3. The **for** loop control variable **i** and the input variable **x** exist only in the block containing the **for** loop. They are not needed anywhere else in the program.
4. The variables **mean** and **sdev** come into play only at the end. They appear in the latter part of the program. While declaring variables in the specific blocks reduces the overall memory requirements at runtime (the extent of reduction depends on the number of variables), there are a few drawbacks:

- The readability of the program suffers, since the declaraion of variables are scattered throughout the code. In addition, this variable-declaration scheme may encourage the program author to use the same identifier name for two entirely different purposes. This degrades the readability even further.
- The maintentance of this type of programs is also a bit more difficult. As a rule of thumb, poorly readable programs are hard to update and maintain.

POINTERS TO SIMPLE DATA TYPES

Pointers, by definition, are variables that hold addresses of other objects, such as variables, functions, and procedures. By using pointers to work with variables, you need to declare the pointer such that the type of data it handles is also defined. The latter data type can be either simple or complex. The above notion exists in C as well as Pascal. However, pointers in Pascal are less frequently employed to access simple data types. The bulk of such cases in Pascal involve reading specific memory locations to obtain information related to DOS or the hardware. In C, using pointers with simple data types is more common. One popular case is the need to pass pointers to simple variables as arguments to functions (this is discussed in Chapter 11) in order to have the contents of the variables swapped. In the language of Pascal programmers, C pointers are used to pass variables by reference to routines.

Pointers are declared in a manner similar to ordinary variables. The difference is that the asterisk is placed before the name of the pointer-typed identifier. The following is an example of pointer declarations:

POINTERS, ARRAYS, AND STRINGS   149

```
int *int_ptr; /* pointer to integer */
double *ptr; /* pointer to double */
char *string; /* pointer to a character */
```

The above syntax declares specific identifiers to be pointers to data types. This means that you can also include ordinary variables, as shown below:

```
int *int_ptr, my_int; /* pointer and integer */
double *ptr, my_double; /* pointer and double */
char *string, my_char; /* pointer and character */
```

C allows you to declare typed pointers by placing the asterisk after the name of the data type, as shown in the following example:

```
int* int_ptr; /* pointer to integer */
double* ptr; /* pointer to double */
char* string; /* pointer to a character */
```

Note that any other identifiers included with the above pointers are not pointers. Thus **int*** is interpreted by the compiler as a pointer-to-integer type. Similarly, the **double*** and **char*** are considered pointers to **double** and **char** types, respectively.

Like ordinary variables, pointers should also be initialized. The problem that uninitialized pointers create is common to all languages that support pointers. In most cases they lead to program crashes.

C pointers, like those in Pascal, must be initialized before they are utilized. The initialization of a pointer may be either through dynamic memory allocation or setting it to point to an existing object. Dynamic memory allocation and deallocation are carried out through functions imported from various C libraries, including "stdlib.h". The following basic pointer operations are important to remember:

1. To allocate dynamic space, use the **malloc** or the **calloc** routines. This **malloc** routine merely requires the number of bytes to allocate and returns a generic pointer to the allocated memory. Hence, the **sizeof** operator is required to determine the size of the memory space needed. Type casting is also required to assign the appropriate pointer type. If there is insufficient memory space, a NULL is returned to the pointer. The general format for using **malloc** is:

   ```
   <pointer> = (<ptr-type> *) malloc(sizeof(<ptr-type>));
   ```

   The **calloc** routine is similar and requests the number of data objects to create and the size of the individual object. In addition, **calloc** assigns zeros to the memory space allocated.

   ```
   <pointer> = (<ptr-type> *) calloc(<total>,sizeof(<ptr-type>));
   ```

   In Pascal the NEW statement is used to allocate dynamic memory. The size of the allcoated space is implicitly calculated by NEW, unlike C's **malloc** and **calloc**.

2. To deallocate the dynamic space associated with a pointer, use the routine **free**. It takes a pointer as its sole argument:

   ```
   free(<pointer>);
   ```

   The **free** function corresponds to the Pascal DISPOSE statement.

3. To assign the address of a variable to a pointer with compatible type, use the & character, as shown below:

    `<pointer> = &<variable>;`

4. To access the content of the memory location indicated by the pointer, use the * character in front of the pointer.

Program Translation

The declaration of pointers is translated using the following general form:
Pascal:
```
        <pointer> : ^<data type>;
```
C:
```
        <data type> *<pointer>;
```
To Translate the NEW statement in Pascal into **malloc** in C, use
Pascal:
```
        NEW(<pointer>);
```
C:
```
        <pointer> = (data type>*) malloc(sizeof(<data type>));
```
To translate the DISPOSE into **free**:
Pascal:
```
        DISPOSE(<pointer>);
```
C:
```
        free(<pointer>);
```
To store the address of an existing variable in a pointer:
Pascal:
```
        <pointer> := @<variable>;
```
C:
```
        <pointer> = &<variable>;
```
To use a preinitialized pointer:
Pascal:
```
        <pointer>^ := <expression>;
    or  <statement using <pointer>^ >
```
C:
```
        *<pointer> = <expression>;
    or  <statement using *<pointer> >
```

The following program illustrates the two main types of pointers: those that are used to allocate memory and point to it, and those that point to existing variables. The pointers **int_ptr1, long_ptr1**, and **char_ptr1** are used to allocate memory dynamically. The pointers **int_ptr2, long_ptr2**, and **char_ptr2** are employed to point to the variables **i, j**, and **c**, respectively. The ordinary variables are assigned values within the program. The program itself does not perform anything meaningful besides demonstrating the types of pointers. The Pascal listing is shown below:

Listing 9.6

```pascal
PROGRAM Simple_Pointers;
Uses CRT;
{ Turbo Pascal program that illustrates using pointers to access
  simple data types in Pascal.                              }
VAR int_ptr1, int_ptr2   : ^INTEGER; { pointers to integers }
    long_ptr1, long_ptr2 : ^LONGINT; { pointers to long integers }
    char_ptr1, char_ptr2 : ^CHAR;    { pointers to characters }
    i : INTEGER;
    j : LONGINT;
    c : CHAR;
BEGIN
    { create dynamic space associated with pointers }
    NEW(int_ptr1);
    NEW(long_ptr1);
    NEW(char_ptr1);
    { assign values to variables }
    i := 7;
    j := 76;
    c := 'I';
    { obtain pointers of variables }
    int_ptr2 := @i;
    long_ptr2 := @j;
    char_ptr2 := @c;
    REPEAT
        WRITE('Enter a positive number : ');
        READLN(int_ptr1^); WRITELN;
    UNTIL int_ptr1^ > 0;
    INC(int_ptr1^);
    long_ptr1^ := SQR(int_ptr1^ + int_ptr2^);
    WRITELN(int_ptr1^ + int_ptr2^,' squared = ',long_ptr1^);
    WRITELN;

    WRITELN(long_ptr2^,' squared = ',long_ptr2^ * long_ptr2^);
    WRITELN;
    DEC(int_ptr1^,3);
    char_ptr1^ := CHR(int_ptr1^);
    WRITELN(char_ptr1^,' has the ASCII code of ',int_ptr1^);
    WRITELN(char_ptr2^,' has the ASCII code of ',ORD(char_ptr2^));
    WRITELN; WRITELN;
    WRITELN; WRITELN;
    { dispose of the dynamic space associated with pointers }
    DISPOSE(int_ptr1);
    DISPOSE(long_ptr1);
    DISPOSE(char_ptr1);
END.
```

Run the Pascal version and type 66 in response to the prompt. The screen image for the sample session is shown below:

```
Enter a positive number : 66
74 squared = 5476
76 squared = 5776
```

@ has the ASCII code of 64
I has the ASCII code of 73

The C version is listed below:

Listing 9.7

```c
/* C program that illustrates using pointers to access
   simple data types in Pascal.                       */
#include <stdio.h>
#include <stdlib.h>
main()
{
    int *int_ptr1, *int_ptr2; /* pointers to integers */
    long *long_ptr1, *long_ptr2; /* pointers to long integers */
    char *char_ptr1, *char_ptr2; /* pointers to characters */
    int i = 7;
    long j = 76;
    char c = 'I';
    /* create dynamic space associated with pointers */
    int_ptr1 = (int*) malloc(sizeof(int));
    long_ptr1 = (long*) malloc(sizeof(long));
    char_ptr1 = (char*) malloc(sizeof(char));
    int_ptr2 = &i;
    long_ptr2 = &j;
    char_ptr2 = &c;
    do {
        printf("Enter a positive number : ");
        /* note that int_ptr1 needs no & in scanf */
        scanf("%d",int_ptr1); printf("\n");
    } while (*int_ptr1 <= 0);
    (*int_ptr1)++; - () are used to increment the number
                   - pointed to and not the address of the pointer
    *long_ptr1 = square(*int_ptr1 + *int_ptr2);
    printf("%d squared = %ld\n\n",*int_ptr1 + *int_ptr2,*long_ptr1);
    printf("%ld squared = %ld\n\n",*long_ptr2,
                                    ((*long_ptr2) * (*long_ptr2)));
    *int_ptr1 -= 3;
    *char_ptr1 = *int_ptr1;
    printf(" %c has the ASCII code of %d\n",*char_ptr1,*int_ptr1);
    printf(" %c has the ASCII code of %d\n",*char_ptr2,*char_ptr2);
    /* dispose of the dynamic space associated with pointers */
    free(int_ptr1);
    free(long_ptr1);
    free(char_ptr1);
}
/* define square function */
int square(int x)
{
   return x * x;
}
```

These two program versions illustrate the rules of translating pointers of simple data from Pascal to C. Let me emphasize the difference in dynamic allocation: C enables you to check whether or not a request to allocate memory returns a NULL pointer in the case of insufficient memory. For the novice C programmer, using **malloc** may seem to be a bit more elaborate than Pascal's NEW statement. The above example illustrates an area of Pascal pointers that is smoothly translated into C. Every operation in the Pascal version is duplicated in C, without resorting to programming tricks. One small aspect worth pointing out is that **int_ptr1** needs no & operator in **scanf** since it is already a pointer!

Run the C version and type 66 in response to the prompt. The screen image for the sample session is shown below:

```
Enter a positive number : 66
74 squared = 5476
76 squared = 5776
@ has the ASCII code of 64
I has the ASCII code of 73
```

ARRAYS IN C: AN OVERVIEW

Arrays are very important data structures. They enable us to easily manipulate a collection of data objects sharing the same data type. While C supports arrays of various dimensions, certain related rules and syntaxes must be observed:

1. The lower bound of any dimension in a C array is fixed as 0. C provides no formal mechanism or syntax to alter it.
2. When you declare an array, you define the number of members in each dimension AND NOT THE UPPER ARRAY BOUNDS.
3. Array indices are enclosed in brackets, just as in Pascal.
4. When using multidimensional arrays, each dimension is enclosed in a separate set of brackets.

   Examples of declaring and using arrays in C are shown below:

```
int i[10], j[44,5];
double x[10,100], y[8];
i[0] = 1;
i[9] = 10;
x[3][55] = 3.14;
y[4] = 7.9876;
```

ONE-DIMENSIONAL ARRAYS

This is the simplest class of arrays. The first array element has an index of 0. One-dimensional arrays are generally declared as:

```
<data type> <array_name>[<number of elements>];
```

Programming Note

The valid indices for a one-dimensional array defined above range between 0 and (<number of elements> - 1).

Program Translation

To translate a one-dimensional array from Pascal to C, use the following general rule:
Pascal:
```
    A : ARRAY[<Low>..<High>] OF <type>;
```
C:
```
    <type> A[<High>-<Low>+1];
```

The following program permits you to enter data from the keyboard and calculate the average for the entered numbers. The program is set up to handle up to 30 data points. You are prompted to enter the number of observations, and your input is validated. The program illustrates storing and accessing data from arrays in C. First, the Pascal version is shown below:

Listing 9.8

```
Program Simple_Arrays;
Uses CRT;
{ Turbo Pascal program that demonstrates the use of
  one-dimensional arrays. The average value of the array
  is calculated.                                        }
CONST MAX = 30;
VAR x : ARRAY [1..MAX] OF REAL;
    sum, sumX, mean : REAL;
    i, n : INTEGER;
BEGIN
    ClrScr;
    REPEAT { obtain number of data points }
        WRITE('Enter number of data points [2 to ',MAX,'] : ');
        READLN(n); WRITELN;
    UNTIL n IN [2..MAX];
    { prompt user for data }
    FOR i := 1 TO n DO BEGIN
        WRITE('X[',i,'] : ');
        READLN(x[i]); WRITELN;
    END;
    { initialize summations }
    sum := n;
    sumx := 0.0;
    { calculate sum of observations }
    FOR i := 1 TO n DO
        sumx := sumx + x[i];
    mean := sumx / sum; { calculate the mean value }
    WRITELN; WRITELN;
    WRITELN('Mean = ',mean); WRITELN; WRITELN;
END.
```

The C version is shown below:

Listing 9.9

```c
/* C program that demonstrates the use of one-dimension
   arrays. The average value of the array is calculated. */
#include <stdio.h>
#include "scrncurs.h"
#define MAX 30
main()
{
    double x[MAX];
    double sum, sumx = 0.0, mean;
    int i, n;
    clrscr;
    do { /* obtain number of data points */
        printf("Enter number of data points [2 to %d] : ",MAX);
        scanf("%d", &n); printf("\n");
    } while (n < 2 || n > MAX);
    /* prompt user for data */
    for (i = 0; i < n; i++) {
        printf("X[%d] : ",i);
        scanf("%lf", &x[i]); printf("\n");
    }
    /* initialize summations */
    sum = n;
    /* calculate sum of observations */
    for (i = 0; i < n; i++)
        sumx += x[i];
    mean = sumx / sum; /* calculate the mean value */
    printf("\n\n");
    printf("Mean = %lf\n\n",mean);
}
```

Since C fixes the lower array limit at 0, the translation of the Pascal code has to undergo a number of adjustments. The same changes are performed on both for loops. The Pascal FOR-DO loops are

```
FOR i := 1 TO n DO BEGIN
```

with the loop control variable varying between 1 and the number of data points, **n**. Since C starts indexing at 0, the for loop is written as:

```
for (i = 0; i < n; i++) {
```

Notice that the loop continuation test is (i < n), instead of the usual (i <= n). The (i < n) expression may be replaced with (i <= (n-1)), but that takes slightly longer to execute.

Another change performed on the C code is the prompting statement:

```
printf("X[%d] : ",i);
```

Notice that I used **i**, to display C array indices that are shifted downward by one, compared to the Pascal version.

The array elements receive their values from the keyboard using the **scanf** function. Each array member, **x[i]**, uses an ampersand character to provide its address to **scanf**.

Arrays can be initialized, just like simple variables. The list of initial values is enclosed in open and close braces that may be spread over multiple lines. If there are fewer values in the initialization list than the size of the arrays, the balance of array elements are assigned zeros. Putting more data in the initialization list than there are elements in the array causes the compiler to flag an error. To illustrate array initialization, I present a modified version of the above C program. The array is internally supplied with data and the whole process of prompting the user for data is eliminated. The program simply displays the mean value (not too useful, but it shows how to initialize arrays). The listing is shown below:

Listing 9.10

```
/* C program that demonstrates the use of one-dimension
   arrays. The average value of the array is calculated.
   The array has its values preassigned internally.
*/
#include <stdio.h>
#include "scrncurs.h"
#define MAX 10
main()
{
    double x[MAX] = { 12.2, 45.4, 67.2, 12.2, 34.6, 87.4,
                      83.6, 12.3, 14.8, 55.5 };
    double sum = MAX, sumx = 0.0, mean;
    int i, n = MAX;
    clrscr;
    /* calculate sum of observations */
    for (i = 0; i < n; i++)
        sumx += x[i];
    mean = sumx / sum; /* calculate the mean value */
    printf("\n\n");
    printf("Mean = %lf\n\n",mean);
}
```

If you are one of those programmers who gets tired counting items in an initialization list, C has some real good news for you: arrays may be sized and also initialized by the list of values! This means that the array size requirement can be removed, and the compiler does the work for you.

I present yet another version of the above program. This one removes explicit dimensioning from the arrays **x** and relies on the size of the initialization list to automatically supply the tailored array size.

Programming Hint

When using arrays that are implicitly sized, you may want to add a few extra dummy values. This reserves space for additional valid data to be inserted at run-time.

The C listing is shown below:

Listing 9.11

```
/* C program that demonstrates the use of one-dimension
   arrays. The average value of the array is calculated.
   The array has its values preassigned internally.
*/
#include <stdio.h>
main()
{
    double x[] = { 12.2, 45.4, 67.2, 12.2, 34.6, 87.4,
                   83.6, 12.3, 14.8, 55.5 };
    double sum,  sumx = 0.0, mean;
    int i, n;
    n = sizeof(x) / sizeof(double);
    sum = n;
    /* calculate sum of observations */
    for (i = 0; i < n; i++)
        sumx += x[i];
    mean = sumx / sum; /* calculate the mean value */
    printf("\n\n");
    printf("Number of data points = %d\n",n);
    printf("Mean = %lf\n\n",mean);
}
```

Since the constant **MAX** is no longer used in the above program to specify the size of the array **x**, another method is used to obtain the size. The **sizeof(x)** returns the total number of bytes occupied by the array **x**, while **sizeof(double)** returns the size of each array member. Their ratio yields the actual number of elements. A sample session produces the results shown below:

```
Number of data points = 10
Mean = 42.5200000
```

MULTIDIMENSIONAL ARRAYS

Multidimensional arrays offer an extension to one-dimensional arrays. Each dimension offers an additional access attribute. Two-dimensional arrays (or matrices) are very popular, and three-dimensional arrays are also used, but less frequently than matrices. Declaring two- and three-dimensional arrays employs the following general syntax:

```
<type> <array-name>[<size1>][<size2>];
<type> <array-name>[<size1>][<size2>][<size3>];
```

Each dimension starts with index 0, and the declaration states the number of elements in each dimension.

158 INTRODUCING C TO PASCAL PROGRAMMERS

Program Translation

To translate a two-dimensional array from Pascal to C, use the following general rule:

Pascal:
```
        A : ARRAY[<Low1>..<High1>,<Low2>..<High2>] OF <type>;
```
C:
```
        <type> A[<High1>-<Low1>+1][<High2>-<Low2>+1];
```

For reasons that will become more apparent later, it is important to understand how multidimensional arrays are stored. Most, if not all, compilers store such arrays in a contiguous form (that is, one long array), but are smart enough to access elements of the different dimensions. While this is not a major issue in Pascal, it is in C. To explain the storage scheme, I begin by adopting a convention for referring to the dimensions in general. The following schema defines the dimension numbering and the notion of high- and low-order dimension. Here, I deliberately present a six-dimensional array as a useful, if extreme, case:

```
    1     2     3     4     5     6   <- dimension number
A  [10]  [8]   [6]   [4]   [2]   [2]
 higher dimension order --->
```

The very first element of a multi-dimensional array has 0 for all of its indices. Its value is stored as the first memory location in the contiguous array. The second value comes from the elements with 1 as the index in the highest dimension number (that is, higher dimension order). Similarly, the subsequent values come from that dimension until the upper limit is reached. This bumps the index counter of the next highest dimension by one and the index of the highest dimension is once more set to 0. This process is repeated until every element of all the dimensions is accessed. Pictorially, the entire process resembles filling your car with gas: the rightmost digits are the ones that turn the fastest, followed by the one immediately to their left, and so on.

To illustrate the above storage scheme, consider the following three-dimensional array with 12 elements:

```
int x[2][3][2];
```

It is stored as:

```
                <-- starting memory address
x[0][0][0]
x[0][0][1]      <- 3rd dimension is filled
x[0][1][0]
x[0][1][1]      <- 3rd dimension is filled
x[0][2][0]
x[0][2][1]      <- 3rd & 2nd dimension are filled
x[1][0][0]
x[1][0][1]      <- 3rd dimension is filled
x[1][1][0]
x[1][1][1]      <- 3rd dimension is filled
x[1][2][0]
x[1][2][1]      <- all dimensions are filled
```

The following program illustrates basic matrix manipulation. The program handles a matrix of up to 10 columns and 30 rows. You are prompted to enter the number of rows and columns, within this range. Once you have specified the size of your data table, you are prompted to key-in the data. The program calculates and displays the mean value for each column in your data table. The Pascal version is shown below:

Listing 9.12

```
Program Two_Dim_Arrays;
Uses CRT;
{ Turbo Pascal program that demonstrates the use of
  two-dimension arrays. The average value of each matrix
  column is calculated.                                  }
CONST MAX_COL = 10;
      MAX_ROW = 30;
VAR x : ARRAY [1..MAX_ROW,1..MAX_COL] OF REAL;
    sum, sumX, mean : REAL;
    i, j, rows, columns : INTEGER;
BEGIN
    ClrScr;
    REPEAT
        WRITE('Enter number of rows [2 to ',MAX_ROW,'] : ');
        READLN(rows); WRITELN;
    UNTIL rows IN [2..MAX_ROW];
    REPEAT
        WRITE('Enter number of columns [1 to ',MAX_COL,'] : ');
        READLN(columns); WRITELN;
    UNTIL columns IN [1..MAX_COL];
    FOR i := 1 TO rows DO BEGIN
        FOR j := 1 TO columns DO BEGIN
            WRITE('X[',i,',',j,'] : ');
            READLN(x[i,j]); WRITELN;
        END;
        WRITELN;
    END;
    FOR j := 1 TO columns DO BEGIN
        sum := rows;
        sumx := 0.0;
        FOR i := 1 TO rows DO
            sumx := sumx + x[i,j];
        mean := sumx / sum;
        WRITELN; WRITELN;
        WRITELN('Mean for column ',j,' = ',mean);
    END; { FOR j }
    WRITELN; WRITELN;
END.
```

The translated C version is:

Listing 9.13

```
/* C program that demonstrates the use of two-dimension arrays.
   The average value of each matrix column is calculated. */
#include <stdio.h>
```

```c
#include "conio.h"
#define MAX_COL 10
#define MAX_ROW 30
main()
{
    double x[MAX_ROW][MAX_COL];
    double sum, sumx, mean;
    int i, j, rows, columns;
    clrscr();
    do {
        printf("Enter number of rows [2 to %d] : ",MAX_ROW);
        scanf("%d", &rows); printf("\n");
    } while (rows < 2 || rows > MAX_ROW);
    do {
        printf("Enter number of columns [1 to %d] : ",MAX_COL);
        scanf("%d", &columns); printf("\n");
    } while (columns < 1 || columns > MAX_COL);
    for (i = 0; i < rows; i++)  {
        for (j = 0; j < columns; j++)  {
            printf("X[%d][%d] : ",i,j);
            scanf("%lf", &x[i][j]); printf("\n");
        }
        printf("\n");
    }
    for (j = 0; j < columns; j++)  {
        sum = rows;
        sumx = 0.0;
        for (i = 0; i < rows; i++)
            sumx += x[i][j];
        mean = sumx / sum;
        printf("\n\n");
        printf("Mean for column %d = %lf\n",j,mean);
    } /* for j */
    printf("\n\n");
}
```

The special changes made to the C version during translations deal with decrementing the array indices by one. The Pascal FOR-DO loops:

```
FOR i := 1 TO rows DO BEGIN
    FOR j := 1 TO columns DO BEGIN
```

are translated into:

```
for (i = 0; i < rows; i++)  {
    for (j = 0; j < columns; j++)  {
```

where the initial values of the loop control variables (also used to access the matrix) are set to 0. The first loop continuation expression is written as (i < rows), instead of (i <= rows). Similarly, the second loop continuation expression is written as (j < columns).

The **scanf** function employs &x[i][j] to read values from the keyboard and stores them in the array:

```
scanf("%lf", &x[i][j]); printf("\n");
```

In the next section I will show you how to use better alternate forms.

POINTERS, ARRAYS, AND STRINGS   161

As with one-dimensional arrays, multidimensional arrays can be initialized with a list of values. The list of initial values is stored using the same scheme for contiguous array storage, discussed earlier. The above C program is rewritten to have the matrix obtain data from within the program itself. No user input is required in the following version:

Listing 9.14

```
/* C program that demonstrates the initialization of a
   two-dimension array.
   The average value of each matrix column is calculated. */
#include <stdio.h>
#include "conio.h"
#define MAX_COL 3
#define MAX_ROW 5
main()
{
    double x[MAX_ROW][MAX_COL] = { /* — data for row 1 — */
                                   { 1.1, 2.1, 3.1, 4.2, 5.5 },
                                   /* — data for row 2 — */
                                   { 6.6, 7.7, 8.8, 6.4, 1.2 },
                                   /* — data for row 3 — */
                                   { 9.8, 2.3, 4.5, 7.8, 4.3 }
                                 };
    double sum, sumx, mean;
    int i, j, rows = MAX_ROW, columns = MAX_COL;
    clrscr();
    for (i = 0; i < rows; i++)  {
        for (j = 0; j < columns; j++)  {
            printf("X[%d][%d] : ",i,j);
            scanf("%lf", &x[i][j]); printf("\n");
        }
        printf("\n");
    }
    for (j = 0; j < columns; j++)  {
        sum = rows;
        sumx = 0.0;
        for (i = 0; i < rows; i++)
            sumx += x[i][j];
        mean = sumx / sum;
        printf("\n\n");
        printf("Mean for column %d = %lf\n",j,mean);
    } /* for j */
    printf("\n\n");
}
```

ACCESSING ARRAYS WITH POINTERS

In the grand scheme of things, all program variables are translated into memory addresses when the compiler processes the source code. Even the simple variables you employ are replaced by addresses and pointers. The side of C that makes it a high-level assembler enables you to employ memory addressing techniques in your source code. The real power of obtaining the address of a data object is that you've got its number, so to speak! Knowing where a data object is stored in memory permits you to alter its value directly and not waste the program's time with resolving array indices.

Our safari through the jungle of pointers in C really begins with using them to access arrays. When you access an array element, say x[i], the C compiler performs two referencing operations. First, the array name, **x**, is translated into a memory address where the first element of the array resides. The second step is to use the index value, **i**, to calculate the offset from the beginning of the array location. Thus, the sought memory address of x[i] is:

i'th element address = address of **x** + **i** * basic type size

The above discussion is not a mere explanation of what the compiler does. It opens new doors when you learn that C permits you to obtain the base-address of an array. Consider the following declaration that defines an array of integers and an integer-based pointer:

```
int x[100];
int *ptr;
```

C allows you to write the following statement and store the base address of array **x** in the compatible pointer **ptr**:

```
ptr = &x[0];
```
or
```
ptr = x;
```

This means that the name of an array (with any number of dimensions) is equivalent to the address of its first element.

Programming Note

<array_name> is equivalent to &<array_name>[0]..[0]

Going back to the address-calculating equation, I rewrite it by substituting (address of **x**) by **ptr**:

i'th element address = **ptr** + **i** * basic type size

C makes the above equation even easier to use, thanks to pointer arithmetic. You may have wondered all along about the benefits of associating a data type with a pointer. In C, when you increment or decrement a C pointer by, say **n**, you are automatically altering its address by **n** times the size of its associated data type. Thus, the above address-calculating equation is finally written as:

i'th element address = **ptr** + **i**

The above equation says that given a pointer to the base memory of a one-dimensional array, you may access any i'th element by using its address, expressed by **(ptr + i)**.

To demonstrate the use of pointers in accessing one-dimensional arrays, I present a modified version of the program that calculates the average value of an array. This program modifies the previous version in the following ways:

POINTERS, ARRAYS, AND STRINGS

1. The array name is used as a pointer to store data in the array.
2. A double-type pointer **real_ptr** is also used to demonstrate array access using a separate pointer.
   The program is shown below:

Listing 9.15

```
/* C program that demonstrates the use of pointer with
   one-dimension arrays. Program calculates the average
   value of the data found in the array.
*/
#include <stdio.h>
#include "conio.h"
#define MAX 30
main()
{
    double x[MAX];
    /* declare pointer and initialize with base
       address of array x */
    double *real_ptr = x;  /* same as = &x[0] */
    double sum, sumx = 0.0, mean;
    int i, n;
    clrscr();
    do {
        printf("Enter number of data points [2 to %d] : ",MAX);
        scanf("%d", &n); printf("\n");
    } while (n < 2 || n > MAX);
    for (i = 0; i < n; i++) {
        printf("X[%d] : ",i);
        /* use the pointer form (x+i) to store data in x[i] */
        scanf("%lf", x+i); printf("\n");
    }
    sum = n;
    for (i = 0; i < n; i++)
    /* use the pointer form *(real_ptr + i) to access x[i] */
        sumx += *(real_ptr + i);
    mean = sumx / sum;
    printf("\n\n");
    printf("Mean = %lf\n\n",mean);
}
```

Notice the following:
1. The **scanf** statement is written as:
   scanf("%lf", x+i);
   instead of the equivalent form:
   scanf("%lf", &x[i]);
   since x+i is equivalent to &x[i].
2. The pointer **real_pointer** is simultaneously declared and initialized using:
   double *real_ptr = x;

The pointer stores the base-address of array **x**. The expression "*(real_ptr + i)" is used instead of **x[i]**. The relationship can be developed using the following steps:

1. Given x[i] is equivalent to *(x + i).
2. Also given, the assignment real_ptr = x.
3. Therefore, x[i] is equivalent to *(real_ptr + i).

In the above program the address stored in pointer **real_ptr** remains that of the base-address of array **x**. By using pointer arithmetic with the loop index **i**, the program systematically varies the offset to access the array elements. C offers another important alternative that enables you to scroll-access the elements of an array without using the help of an offset value. The technique simply involves using the increment or decrement operators with pointers. You still need to initialize the pointer to the base-address of an array and then use the ++ operator to access array elements. Each time a "<pointer>++" expression is used, the pointer is advanced to the next element. This new feature is demonstrated in the following version that modifies the last one:

Listing 9.16

```
/* C program that demonstrates the use of pointers with
   one-dimension arrays. The average value of the array
   is calculated. This program modifies the previous version
   in the following way:  the real_ptr is used to access the
   array without any help from any loop control variable.
   This is accomplished by 'incrementing' the pointer, and
   consequently incrementing its address. This program
   illustrates pointer arithmetic that alters the pointer's
   address.
 */
#include <stdio.h>
#include "conio.h"
#define MAX 30
main()
{
    double x[MAX];
    double *real_ptr = x;
    double sum, sumx = 0.0, mean;
    int i, n;
    clrscr();
    do {
        printf("Enter number of data points [2 to %d] : ",MAX);
        scanf("%d", &n); printf("\n");
    } while (n < 2 || n > MAX);
    /* loop variable i is not directly involved in accessing
       the elements of array x                               */
    for (i = 0; i < n; i++) {
        printf("X[%d] : ",i);
    /* increment pointer real_ptr after taking a reference */
        scanf("%lf", real_ptr++); printf("\n");
    }
```

POINTERS, ARRAYS, AND STRINGS 165

```
    /* restore original address by using pointer arithmetic */
    real_ptr -= n;
    sum = n;
    /* loop variable i serves as a simple counter */
    for (i = 0; i < n; i++)
    /* increment pointer real_ptr after taking a reference */
        sumx += *(real_ptr++);
    mean = sumx / sum;
    printf("\n\n");
    printf("Mean = %1f\n\n",mean);
}
```

The above program in C first initializes the **real_ptr** pointer to the base-address of array **x**. The **real_ptr** is employed in the **scanf** function to store keyed data in the array **x** using:

`scanf("%lf", real_ptr++);`

At the end of the input for loop, the pointer **real_ptr** points to the tail of the array **x**. To reset it to the base-address, the following assignment operator is employed:

`real_ptr -= n;`

This makes **real_ptr** point to the address of **x[0]**. The same incrementing technique is used to calculate the total sum of data in the second **for** loop:

`sumx += *(real_ptr++);`

The above version most likely seems very peculiar to the eyes of the Pascal programmer, since neither the array name **x** nor a loop index is used to access the array!

The following program is a second example that illustrates the use of pointers to access arrays. The program is the Sieve benchmark, perhaps the most popular benchmark for microcomputers. The first listing is in Pascal, the second is in C and uses ordinary arrays, and the third is a C version using pointers:

Listing 9.17

```
PROGRAM Sieve_Benchmark;
{ Turbo Pascal program that performs the sieve benchmark }
CONST SIZE = 7000;
VAR I, PRIME, K, COUNT, ITER : INTEGER;
    FLAGS : ARRAY [0..SIZE] OF BOOLEAN;
BEGIN
    WRITELN('START 50 ITERATIONS');
    FOR ITER := 1 TO 50 DO BEGIN
        COUNT := 0;
        FOR I := 0 TO SIZE DO FLAGS[I] := TRUE;
        FOR I := 0 TO SIZE DO
            IF FLAGS[I] THEN BEGIN
                PRIME := I + I + 3;
                K := I + PRIME;
                WHILE K <= SIZE DO BEGIN
                    FLAGS[K] := FALSE;
```

166 INTRODUCING C TO PASCAL PROGRAMMERS

```
                    K := K + PRIME
                END;
                COUNT := COUNT + 1
            END;
        END;
    END;
    WRITELN(COUNT,' PRIMES');
END.
```

The C version employing arrays without pointers is shown below:

Listing 9.18

```c
/* C program that performs the sieve benchmark */
#include <stdio.h>
#define BOOLEAN unsigned char
#define TRUE 1
#define FALSE 0
#define SIZE 7001
main()
{
    int i, prime, k, count, iter;
    BOOLEAN flags[SIZE];
    printf("START 50 ITERATIONS\n");
    for (iter = 1; iter <= 50; iter++)   {
        count = 0;
        for (i = 0; i < SIZE; i++)   flags[i] = TRUE;
        for (i = 0; i < SIZE; i++) {
            if (flags[i])   {
                prime = i + i + 3;
                k = i + prime;
                while (k < SIZE)   {
                    flags[k] = FALSE;
                    k += prime;
                }
                count++;
            }
        }
    }
    printf("%d primes\n",count);
}
```

The C version that uses pointers is shown below:

Listing 9.19

```c
/* C program that performs the sieve benchmark, version 2 */
#include <stdio.h>
#define BOOLEAN unsigned char
#define TRUE 1
#define FALSE 0
#define SIZE 7001
main()
{
```

```
    int i, prime, k, count, iter;
    BOOLEAN flags[SIZE];
    BOOLEAN *ptr;
    printf("START 50 ITERATIONS\n");
    for (iter = 1; iter <= 50; iter++)   {
        count = 0;
        for (i = 0, ptr = flags; i < SIZE; i++, ptr++)
            *ptr = TRUE;
        for (i = 0, ptr = flags; i < SIZE; i++) {
            if (*(ptr + i))   {
                prime = i + i + 3;
                k = i + prime;
                while (k < SIZE)   {
                    *(ptr + k) = FALSE;
                    k += prime;
                }
                count++;
            }
        }
    }
    printf("%d primes\n",count);
}
```

In comparing the two C versions, notice the following differences:

1. The loop that initializes the **flags** array has been changed from:

    for (i = 0; i < SIZE; i++)   flags[i] = TRUE;

    to:

    for (i = 0, ptr = flags; i < SIZE; i++, ptr++)
      *ptr = TRUE;

    using the incremented pointer method to store values in the array **flags**.

2. The other references to **flags** are replaced by "***(ptr + <index>)**". This method is employed because a pointer is utilized in accessing random array members.

Accessing multidimensional arrays using pointers is slightly more elaborate than the case of one-dimensional arrays. Remember that for simple arrays you need the base-address of the array and one offset (that is, the index) to the sought array element. In the case of multidimensional arrays you need an offset for each dimension. Perhaps a better way of looking at it is, taking the case of matrices, to consider multidimensional arrays as arrays of arrays. To access a matrix, you need a pointer to the array that represents the proper row that contains an array of data. You need a second pointer to pick the exact element out of the selected row. In effect, you are using a pointer to a pointer, something fairly common in C.

To illustrate and further discuss the access of matrix elements, I now present a modified version of an earlier listing. The program illustrates the pointer-access method for both input and data access:

Listing 9.20

```
/*
  C program that demonstrates the use of pointers to access
  two-dimension arrays. The average value of each matrix column
  is calculated.
*/
#include <stdio.h>
#include "conio.h"
#define MAX_COL 10
#define MAX_ROW 30
main()
{
    double x[MAX_ROW][MAX_COL];
    double sum, sumx, mean;
    int i, j, rows, columns;
    clrscr();
    do {
        printf("Enter number of rows [2 to %d] : ",MAX_ROW);
        scanf("%d", &rows); printf("\n");
    } while (rows < 2 || rows > MAX_ROW);
    do {
        printf("Enter number of columns [1 to %d] : ",MAX_COL);
        scanf("%d", &columns); printf("\n");
    } while (columns < 1 || columns > MAX_COL);
    for (i = 0; i < rows; i++)  {
        for (j = 0; j < columns; j++)  {
            printf("X[%d][%d] : ",i,j);
            scanf("%lf", *(x+i)+j); printf("\n");
        }
        printf("\n");
    }
    for (j = 0; j < columns; j++)  {
        sum = rows;
        sumx = 0.0;
        for (i = 0; i < rows; i++)
            sumx += *(*(x+i)+j);
        mean = sumx / sum;
        printf("\n\n");
        printf("Mean for column %d = %lf\n\n",j+1,mean);
    } /* for j */
    printf("\n\n");
}
```

The ordinary access of the i'th row and j'th column of a matrix **x** is the reference **x[i][j]**. This is seen, as I stated earlier, as the j'th element of the one-dimensional array **x[i]**. From previous discussion, you know that **x[i]** and ***(x + i)** are equivalent, and that is the starting point. Thus, **x[i][j]** is equivalent to ***(x + i)[j]**. To take a pointer reference for index j we temporarily view ***(x + i)** as if it were the base-address of an array **y**, giving us **y[j]**. The pointer reference of the latter form is, by induction, ***(y + j)**. Replacing y with ***(x + i)** gives the final form ***(*(x + i) + j)**.

Programming Hint

When a pointer reference of a matrix x[i][j] is used to access its elements, you employ *(*(x +i) + j).

The address of the location of x[i][j] using pointers is *(x+i)+j.

The general pointer-access form for a multi-dimensional array,

x[i][j]..[n][m]
is,
*(*(..*(*(x+i) + j)..) + n) + m)

The lower-order dimensions are nested deeper than the higher-order dimensions.

STRINGS IN C

Up until now, the examples presented were predominantly numeric, with a few aimed at character manipulation. You may have grown suspicious about the absence of strings in all of these examples. The reason is that strings in C have two main ingredients: arrays and pointers. C regards strings as arrays of characters that end with the null character (i.e., '\0'). This null character MUST BE PRESENT IN ALL STRINGS AND MUST BE TAKEN INTO ACCOUNT WHEN DIMENSIONING A STRING.

Programming Notes

As a veteran Turbo Pascal programmer and novice in C, it is important to remember the following two features that you have taken for granted in Pascal BUT ARE NOT SUPPORTED IN C:

1. C does not allow statements that assign strings to other strings.
2. C does not support string concatenation using the + operator.

Programming Notes

Strings in C are not limited to 255 characters. The size of a string is limited by either the memory model used or the available memory space.

The first program performs simple character translation on a string. It prompts you for a string, the character to be replaced, and its replacement. The Pascal version, which should look trivial, is first presented on the following page:

170 INTRODUCING C TO PASCAL PROGRAMMERS

Listing 9.21

```
Program Translate_String_Characters;
Uses CRT;
{ Turbo Pascal program that demonstrates how a string is
  sometimes treated as an array of characters. Program
  examines the characters of a string and translates those
  that match.                                              }
VAR strng : STRING[80];
    old_char, new_char : CHAR;
    i : BYTE;
BEGIN
    ClrScr;
    WRITELN('Enter a string');
    READLN(strng); WRITELN; WRITELN;
    WRITE('Enter character to replace : ');
    READLN(old_char); WRITELN;
    WRITE('Enter new character : ');
    READLN(new_char); WRITELN;
    FOR i := 1 TO Length(strng) DO
        IF strng[i] = old_char THEN
            strng[i] := new_char;
    WRITELN;
    WRITELN('The translated string is');
    WRITELN(strng); WRITELN; WRITELN;
END.
```

The C version uses the **gets** and **puts** functions to enter and display strings. These functions are specialized in basic string I/O and are used most, if not all, of the time instead of **scanf**. The C listing is shown below:

Listing 9.22

```
/* C program that demonstrates how a string is
   sometimes treated as an array of characters. Program
   examines the characters of a string and translates those
   that match.                                              */
#include <stdio.h>
#include "conio.h"
#define BYTE unsigned char
main()
{
    char strng[81];
    char old_char, new_char;
    BYTE i;
    clrscr();
    printf("Enter a string\n");
    gets(strng); printf("\n\n");
    printf("Enter character to replace : ");
    old_char = getche(); printf("\n");
    printf("Enter new character : ");
    new_char = getche(); printf("\n");
    /* string index starts at zero */
    for (i = 0; strng[i] != '\0'; i++)
```

```
        if (strng[i] == old_char)
            strng[i] = new_char;
    printf("\nThe translated string is\n");
    puts(strng); printf("\n\n");
}
```

In comparing the listings of the two languages, notice the following:

1. The string is sized to contain 81 characters instead of 80. This is to account for the null character '\0'.
2. Processing the characters in the Pascal strings employs a FOR-DO loop and the predefined **Length** function:

   ```
   FOR i := 1 TO Length(strng) DO
   ```

   While C programs can import the equivalent of the Pascal **Length** function, a more popular approach (because it is faster) is to detect the null character in the C string, as shown:

   ```
   for (i = 0; strng[i] != '\0'; i++)
   ```

   The loop continuation test makes use of the fact that EVERY UNCORRUPTED C STRING ENDS WITH THE NULL CHARACTER.
3. Accessing individual characters in Pascal and C strings is similar.
4. The arguments for the **gets** and **puts** functions are the pointers to strings, represented in this case by the bare array names.

Newcomers to C learn sooner or later that string manipulation using pointers is a very popular way of handling strings. The use of string pointers with **gets** and **puts** is just the tip of the iceberg, so to speak. The above program is rewritten to use pointers and is listed below:

Listing 9.23

```
/* C program that demonstrates how a string is
   accessed using a character-pointer. The program
   examines the characters of a string and translates those
   that match.                                          */
#include <stdio.h>
#include "conio.h"
#define BYTE unsigned char
main()
{
    char strng[81];
    char *ptr = strng;
    char old_char, new_char;
    BYTE i;
    clrscr();
    printf("Enter a string\n");
    gets(strng); printf("\n\n");
    printf("Enter character to replace : ");
    old_char = getche(); printf("\n");
    printf("Enter new character : ");
    new_char = getche(); printf("\n");
    for (/* no initialization is needed */;*ptr != '\0'; ptr++) {
```

172   INTRODUCING C TO PASCAL PROGRAMMERS

```
        if (*ptr == old_char)
            *ptr = new_char;
    }
/* ———————— OR USE THE FOLLOWING FORM ————————
    while (*ptr != '\0') {
        if (*ptr == old_char)
            *ptr = new_char;
        ptr++;
    }
*/
/* ———————— OR USE THE FOLLOWING FORM ————————
    for (i = 0; *(ptr+i) != '\0'; i++)
        if (*(ptr+i) == old_char)
            *(ptr+i) = new_char;
*/
    printf("\nThe translated string is\n");
    puts(strng); printf("\n\n");
}
```

The above C program uses the pointer-increment technique to access the string characters. The **for** loop requires no initialization, since it is already carried with the pointer declaration.

The program has, in commented form, two alternate loops. The first is a **while** loop that tests the expression (*ptr != '\0'). The second is a for loop that employs a loop control variable. It is also used to provide an offset address in *(ptr+i) to access the i'th string character.

Run the C program and enter the string, "The number is 1.5432D+02". Replace the character **D** with **e**. The screen image of the sample session is

```
Enter a string
The number is 1.5432D+02
Enter character to replace : D
Enter new character : e
The translated string is
The number is 1.5432e+02
```

The above example is useful to introduce you to the basic string-handling techniques. Turbo Pascal has a number of predefined string-handling functions, such as the frequently used POS, DELETE, and INSERT. The following program displays the message "I am a Turbo Pascal Programmer." and performs the following changes on it:

1. Replaces the word "Pascal" with "C".
2. Inserts the words "very good" before the word "Turbo".
3. Replaces "I" with "You".

The Pascal listing is shown below:

Listing 9.24

```
Program String_Test1;
Uses CRT;
{ Turbo Pascal program that uses predefined string functions and
  procedures to manipulate strings. Program also uses string
```

POINTERS, ARRAYS, AND STRINGS 173

```
  constants, typed string constants and string variables. }
CONST TITLE = 'STRING TEST PROGRAM';
      PHRASE : STRING[40] = 'I am a Turbo Pascal Programmer.';
VAR strlen, char_pos, char_count : BYTE;
    strng : STRING[80];
BEGIN
    ClrScr;
    strlen := Length(TITLE);
    GotoXY(40 - strlen div 2, 1);
    WRITELN(TITLE);
    WRITELN; WRITELN;
    WRITELN(PHRASE); WRITELN;
    strng := PHRASE;
    char_pos := Pos('Pascal',PHRASE);
    char_count := Length('Pascal');
    Delete(strng, char_pos, char_count);
    Insert('C',strng,char_pos);
    WRITELN(strng); WRITELN;
    char_pos := Pos('Turbo',strng);
    Insert('very good ',strng,char_pos);
    WRITELN(strng); WRITELN;
    { manipulate the typed constant string as a variable }
    PHRASE := strng;
    Delete(PHRASE, 1, 4);
    PHRASE := 'You are' + PHRASE;
    WRITELN(PHRASE); WRITELN;
END.
```

Run the Pascal version, and the following is displayed (no input from the user is needed):

```
                    STRING TEST PROGRAM
I am a Turbo Pascal Programmer.
I am a Turbo C Programmer.
I am a very good Turbo C Programmer.
You are a very good Turbo C Programmer.
```

When I translated the above program, I wrote C routines that mimic the Pascal POS, INSERT and DELETE routines. These C functions are declared in function **main**.

Listing 9.25

```c
/* C program that uses predefined string functions and
   procedures to manipulate strings. Program also uses string
   constants, typed string constants and string variables. */
#include <stdio.h>
#include <string.h>
#include "conio.h"
#define BYTE unsigned char
main()
{
    const char *TITLE = "STRING TEST PROGRAM";
    const char PHRASE[40] = "I am a Turbo Pascal Programmer.";
    BYTE strlen_, char_pos, char_count;
    char* strng;
```

```c
    /* declare prototype for delete() and insert() functions */
    void delete(char*, unsigned int, unsigned int);
    void insert(char*, char*, unsigned int);
    clrscr();
    strlen_ = strlen(TITLE);
    gotoxy(40 - strlen_ / 2, 1);
    puts(TITLE);
    printf("\n\n");
    printf("%s\n\n", PHRASE);
    strng = PHRASE;
    char_pos = strpos(strng,"Pascal");
    char_count = strlen("Pascal ");
    delete(strng, char_pos, char_count);
    insert("C ", strng, char_pos);
    puts(strng); printf("\n");
    char_pos = strpos(strng,"Turbo");
    insert("very good ", strng, char_pos);
    puts(strng); printf("\n");
    delete(strng, 0, 4);
    insert("You are", strng, 0);
    puts(strng); printf("\n");
}
/*─────────── string operation routines ───────────
These routines mimic frequently-used Turbo Pascal string routines.
──────────────────────────────*/
int strpos(char* str, char* substr)
{
  int i = 0, j, k;
  while (*str != '\0') {
      for (j = i, k = 0; *str == *substr; j++, k++) {
          substr++;
          str++;
          if (*substr == '\0') return i;
      }
      str++;
      i++;
  }
  /* no match found */
  return (-1);
}
void delete(char* str, unsigned int first, unsigned int count)
{
  int length, last;
  int i, j, k;
  length = strlen(str);
  /* validity of parameters */
  if (first < length && first >= 0 &&
      count < length && count >= 0)   {
      last = first + count - 1;
      for (i = 0, k = 0; *(str + i) != '\0'; i++)
          if (i < first || i > last)
              *(str + k++) = *(str + i);
      /* k is already pointing to the next character */
      *(str + k) = '\0';
  }
}
```

```
void insert(char* substr, char* str, unsigned int index)
{
  int i, j, strlim;
  char tmpstr[101];
  strlim = strlen(str) - 1;
  if (index < 0) index = 0;
  if (index >= strlim) {
     i = 0;
     j = strlim + 1;
     while ( *(str + j++) = *(substr + i++) );
  }
  else {
     i = 0;
     if (index > 0) {
        for (; i < index; i++)
           *(tmpstr + i) = *(str + i);
     }
     for (j = 0; *(substr + j) != '\0'; i++, j++)
        *(tmpstr + i) = *(substr + j);
     for (j = index; *(str + j) != '\0'; i++, j++)
        *(tmpstr + i) = *(str + j);
     /* index i is already pointer to the end-of-string */
     *(tmpstr + i) = '\0';
     strcpy(str, tmpstr);
  }
}
```

Notice the following aspects of the C version:

1. The **TITLE** identifier is declared as a constant character-typed pointer. It always points to the starting memory location containing the constant string "STRING TEST PROGRAM". This type of pointer is indeed fixed.
   `const char *TITLE = "STRING TEST PROGRAM";`

2. The array **PHRASE** is a constant that holds 40 characters, at most (including the null string terminator).
   `const char PHRASE[40] = "I am a Turbo Pascal Programmer.";`

3. The prototypes of the string-handling functions I defined are declared as follows:
   `void delete(char*, unsigned int, unsigned int);`
   `void insert(char*, char*, unsigned int);`
   Notice that pointer-typed parameters are declared using the general syntax "<data type>*".

4. The function **strlen** is used to return the length of various strings throughout the program.

Run the C version and the following is displayed (no input from the user is needed):

```
                    STRING TEST PROGRAM
I am a Turbo Pascal Programmer.
I am a Turbo C Programmer.
I am a very good Turbo C Programmer.
You are a very good Turbo C Programmer.
```

I have deliberately resorted to writing my own string-handling functions to mimic some of those used in Pascal. There is nothing wrong with that, since it follows the spirit of C which encourages you to expand on the language by developing your own routines. The library "string.h" contains a number of functions that enable you to perform C-style string-manipulation. Turbo C offers a library of strings with the following functions (if you are using another C compiler, the string functions may differ). I will present a special format to permit easier reference:

```
FUNCTION NAME: strcat
PROTOTYPE: char* strcat(char* /*target*/, char* /*source*/);
CATEGORY: Concatenation
PURPOSE: Appends the contents of the source string to the target
string.
EXAMPLE:
     char* strng = "Turbo";
     strcat(strng," Pascal");
The strng pointer now points to "Turbo Pascal".
```

```
FUNCTION NAME: strchr
PROTOTYPE: char* strchr(char* /*target*/, char /*pattern*/);
CATEGORY: Searching
PURPOSE: Examines the target string for the first occurrence of the
pattern character.
EXAMPLE:
    char* strng;
    strng = strchr("C:TURBOC:INCLUDE:STRING.H", ':');
makes strng points to "TURBOC:INCLUDE:STRING.H".
```

```
FUNCTION NAME: strcmp
PROTOTYPE: int strcmp(char* /*strng1*/, char* /*strng2*/);
CATEGORY: String Comparison
PURPOSE: Compares two strings. The integer result indicates the
outcome of the comparison:
         < 0   when strng1 is less than strng2
         = 0   when strng1 is equal to strng2
         > 0   when strng1 is greater than strng2
EXAMPLE:
    char* strng1 = "Turbo C";
    char* strng2 = "Turbo Pascal";
    int i;

    i = strcmp(strng1, strng2);

returns a positive value since "Turbo C" is greater than "Turbo
Pascal".
```

```
FUNCTION NAME: strcpy
PROTOTYPE: char* strcpy(char* /*target*/, char* /*source*/);
CATEGORY: Copying
PURPOSE: Copies one string into another.
EXAMPLE:
     char* strng;
     strcat(strng,"Turbo Pascal");
The strng pointer now points to "Turbo Pascal".
```

POINTERS, ARRAYS, AND STRINGS   177

FUNCTION NAME: strcspn
PROTOTYPE: int strcspn(char* /*strng1*/, char* /*strng2*/);
CATEGORY: Searching
PURPOSE: Scans string1 and returns the length of the leftmost substring that totally void of the characters of the substring strng2.
EXAMPLE:
    char* strng = "The rain in Spain";
    int i;
    i = strcspn(strng," in");
assigns 8 (the length of "The rain") to the variable **i**.

FUNCTION NAME: strdup
PROTOTYPE: char* strdup(char* /*strng*/);
CATEGORY: Copying
PURPOSE: Duplicates the string-typed argument. The **malloc** routine is called to allocate the required space.
EXAMPLE:
    char* strng1 = "The reign in Spain";
    char* strng2;

    strng2 = strdup(strng1);
copies the contents of **strng1** into **strng2** after calling **malloc** to allocate the memory space for **strng2**.

FUNCTION NAME: stricmp
PROTOTYPE: int stricmp(char* /*strng1*/, char* /*strng2*/);
CATEGORY: String Comparison
PURPOSE: Compares two strings without making a distinction between upper- and lower-case characters. The integer result indicates the outcome of the comparison:
    < 0   when strng1 is less than strng2
    = 0   when strng1 is equal to strng2
    > 0   when strng1 is greater than strng2
EXAMPLE:
    char* strng1 = "Turbo pascal";
    char* strng2 = "Turbo Pascal";
    int i;

    i = stricmp(strng1, strng2);

assigns 0 to **i** since both strings are the same, ignoring case sensitivity.

FUNCTION NAME: strlen
PROTOTYPE: unsigned strlne(char* /*source*/);
CATEGORY: Searching
PURPOSE: Returns the length of a string.
EXAMPLE:

    char* str = "1234567890";
    unsigned i;

    i = strlen(str);
assigns 10 to the variable **i**.

FUNCTION NAME: strlwr
PROTOTYPE: char* strlwr(char* /*source*/);
CATEGORY: Changing
PURPOSE: Converts the upper-case characters of a string to lower-case.
EXAMPLE:
    char* str = "HELLO THERE";
    strlwr(str);
Pointer **str** now points to the string "hello there".

FUNCTION NAME: strncat
PROTOTYPE: char* strncat(char* /*target*/, char* /*source*/,
                         int /*numchars*/);
CATEGORY: Concatenation
PURPOSE: Appends, at most, numchars characters from the source string to the target string.
EXAMPLE:
    char* str1 = "Hello I am ";
    char* str2 = "Thomas Jones";
    strncat(str1, str2, 6);
The pointer **str1** now points to "Hello I am Thomas".

FUNCTION NAME: strncmp
PROTOTYPE: int strncmp(char* /*strng1*/, char* /*strng2*/,
                       int /*numchars*/);
CATEGORY: String Comparison
PURPOSE: Compares a specified number of leading characters in two strings. The integer result indicates the outcome of the comparison:
        < 0   when strng1 is less than strng2
        = 0   when strng1 is equal to strng2
        > 0   when strng1 is greater than strng2
EXAMPLE:
    char* strng1 = "Turbo C";
    char* strng2 = "Turbo Pascal";
    int i;

    i = strncmp(strng1, strng2, 7);

Assigns a positive value to **i** since "Turbo C" is greater than "Turbo P".

FUNCTION NAME: strncpy
PROTOTYPE: char* strncpy(char* /*target*/, char* /*source*/,
                         int /*numchars*/);
CATEGORY: Copying
PURPOSE: Copies a number of characters from the source string to the target string. Character truncation or padding may be performed, if necessary.
EXAMPLE:
    char* str1 = "Pascal";
    char* str2 = "Hello there";
    strncpy(str1, str2, 6);
The pointer **str1** now points to the string "Hello ".

POINTERS, ARRAYS, AND STRINGS   **179**

FUNCTION NAME: strnicmp
PROTOTYPE: int strnicmp(char* /*strng1*/, char* /*strng2*/,
                        unsigned /*numchars*/);
CATEGORY: String Comparison
PURPOSE: Compares a specified number of leading characters in two strings, ignoring the differences in the character case. The integer result indicates the outcome of the comparison:
    < 0 when strng1 is less than strng2
    = 0 when strng1 is equal to strng2
    > 0 when strng1 is greater than strng2
EXAMPLE:
    char* strng1 = "turbo c";
    char* strng2 = "Turbo Pascal";
    int i;

    i = strnicmp(strng1, strng2, 7);

Assigns a positive value to **i** since "turbo c" is greater than "Turbo P" when case sensitivity is ignored.

FUNCTION NAME: strnset
PROTOTYPE: char* strnset(char* /*target*/, char /*pattern*/,
                         int /*numchars*/);

CATEGORY: Changing
PURPOSE: Overwrites a number of characters in a string with duplicate copies of a single character.
EXAMPLE:
    char* message = "The Pirates of Pinzanee";
    char ch = '+';
    int i = 4;
    strnset(message, ch, i);
The character pointer **message** now points to the text "++++Pirates of Pinzanee".

FUNCTION NAME: strpbrk
PROTOTYPE: char* strpbrk(char* /*target*/, char* /*pattern*/);
CATEGORY: Searching
PURPOSE: Searches the target string for the first occurrence of ANY CHARACTER in the pattern of characters.
EXAMPLE:
    char* str = "Hello there how are you";
    char* substr = "hr";
    char* ptr;
    ptr = strpbrk(str, substr);
    puts(ptr);
This displays "here how are you", since the letter 'h' is encountered in the string before the letter 'r'.

FUNCTION NAME: strrchr
PROTOTYPE: char* strrchr(char* /*target*/, char /*pattern*/);
CATEGORY: Searching
PURPOSE: Searches a string for the LAST occurrence of the pattern character.

EXAMPLE:
```
   char* str = "Hello there how are you";
   /* 'r' occurs here     ^    and   ^ */
   char substr = 'r';
   char* ptr;
   ptr = strrchr(str, substr);
   puts(ptr);
```
Displays "re you".

FUNCTION NAME: strrev
PROTOTYPE: char* strrev(char* /*string*/);
CATEGORY: Changing
PURPOSE: Reverses the order of the string characters.
EXAMPLE:
```
   char* string = "Hello";
   strrev(string);
   puts(string);
```
Displays "olleH".

FUNCTION NAME: strset
PROTOTYPE: char* strset(char* /*target*/, char /*pattern*/);
CATEGORY: Changing.
PURPOSE: Replaces the contents of a string with the pattern character.
EXAMPLE:
```
   char* str = "Hello there how are you";
   char substr = '+';
   strset(str, substr);
   puts(str);
```
Displays "+++++++++++++++++++++++" since the strset function replaces every character of string **str** with '+'.

FUNCTION NAME: strspn
PROTOTYPE: int strspn(char* /*target*/, char* /*pattern*/);
CATEGORY: Searching
PURPOSE: Returns the number of characters in the leading part of the string that matches any character in the string pattern.
EXAMPLE:
```
   char* str = "Turbo C 1.5";
   char* substr = "T bour";
   int index;
   index = strspn(str, substr);
```
The variable **index** is assigned the value of 6, since the characters in **substr** found a match in every one of the first six characters of **str**.

FUNCTION NAME: strstr
PROTOTYPE: char* strstr(char* /*string*/, char* /* substr*/);
CATEGORY: Searching
PURPOSE: Scans a string for the first occurrence of a substring.
EXAMPLE:
```
   char* str = "Hello there! how are you";
   char* substr = "how";
   char* ptr;
```

POINTERS, ARRAYS, AND STRINGS   181

```
    ptr = strstr(str, substr);
    puts(ptr);
```
Displays "how are you" since the string search matched "how". The
pointer **ptr** points to the rest of the original string starting with
"how".

FUNCTION NAME: strtod
PROTOTYPE: double strtol(char*, char**);
CATEGORY: Conversion
PURPOSE: Converts a string into a double. String conversion is
stopped when an unrecognizable character is scanned.
EXAMPLE:
```
#include <stdio.h>
#include "string.h"
main()
{
    char strng[31];
    char** c;
    double x;
    printf("Enter an integer : ");
    gets(strng);
    x = strtod(strng,c);
    printf("%lf\n",x);
}
```

FUNCTION NAME: strtok
PROTOTYPE: char* strtok(char* /*target*/, char* /*delimiters*/);
CATEGORY: Searching
PURPOSE: Searches the target string for tokens. A string supplies the
set of delimiter characters. The following example shows how this
function works in returning the tokens in a string.
EXAMPLE:
```
#include <stdio.h>
#include "string.h"
#include <conio.h>
main()
{
    char* str = "(Base_Cost+Profit) * Margin";
    char* tkn = "+* ()";
    char* ptr = str;
    clrscr();
    puts(str);
    /* the first call looks normal */
    ptr = strtok(str, tkn);
    printf("\n\nis broken into: %s",ptr);
    do {
        /* must make first argument a NULL character */
        ptr = strtok('\0'', tkn);
        if (ptr) printf(" ,%s",ptr);
    } while (ptr);
    printf("\n\n");
}
```
Displays the following when the program is run:
(Base_Cost+Profit) * Margin
is broken into: Base_Cost, Profit, Margin

182 INTRODUCING C TO PASCAL PROGRAMMERS

FUNCTION NAME: strtol
PROTOTYPE: long strtol(char*, char**, int /*base*/);
CATEGORY: Conversion
PURPOSE: Converts a string into a long integer. String conversion is stopped when an unrecognizable character is scanned. String image may be that of decimal, octal, and hexadecimal numbers.
EXAMPLE:
```
#include <stdio.h>
#include "string.h"
main()
{
    char strng[31];
    char** c;
    long i;
    printf("Enter an integer : ");
    gets(strng);
    i = strtol(strng,c,10);
    printf("%ld\n",i);
}
```

FUNCTION NAME: strupr
PROTOTYPE: char* strupr(char*);
CATEGORY: Changing
PURPOSE: Converts the lower-case characters of a string into upper-case.
EXAMPLE:
```
    char* strng = "big letters";
    strupr(strng);
```
The pointer **strng** now points to the string "BIG LETTERS".

CHAPTER SUMMARY

- Storage classes. There are four storage classes in C:
  1. Automatic. The local variables of a function are automatically allocated and deallocated (at run-time) when the function is invoked and terminated, respectively.
  2. Static. The local variables of a function retain their values after their function terminates its action.
  3. Extern. This storage class is used in multifile projects to avoid duplicating memory space for the same variables. The linker is involved in resolving the references to **extern** variables.
  4. Register. Uses the CPU registers, instead of memory location, to manipulate variables that are characters, integers, or pointers.
- Scope of variables. C enables you to declare variables between program statements and enclose them in a statement block. The scope of these variables extends throughout the same block. At the end of the block they cannot be accessed, since their memory space is reclaimed.

POINTERS, ARRAYS, AND STRINGS 183

- Pointers to simple data types. Pointers are declared in C using one of two forms:
  ```
  <type>* <pointer>;
  <type> *<pointer>;
  ```
  The first form declares a pointer-type and is able to define one or more pointers. In the second form, the identifier <pointer> is declared as pointer to the stated <type>, and can be preceeded or followed by the declaration of ordinary variables.

  Pointers can take the address of a variable and consequently access its contents using the ampersand operator:
  ```
  <pointer> = &<variable>;
  ```
  You can also allocate dynamic memory and use a pointer to access that memory location, utilizing the **malloc** functions (one of few functions):
  ```
  <pointer> = (<pointer type> *) malloc(sizeof(<pointer type>));
  ```
  You can deallocate dynamic memory by using the **free** function:
  ```
  free(<pointer>);
  ```

- Single and multidimensional arrays. C supports arrays of a varying number of dimensions. The following rules are observed in declaring and using arrays:
  1. The lower bound of each dimension is fixed at 0.
  2. When declaring an array, you specify the number of elements in each dimension and not the upper-bound limit.
  3. The square brackets are used to hold the indices of arrays.
  4. Declaring and using multidimensional arrays involves the use of separate sets of brackets for each dimension. An example is declaring the following matrix:
  ```
  double table[10][45];
  ```
  and for accessing matrix elements:
  ```
  table [5][11] = 12.3;
  ```
  Multidimensional arrays are stored in a contiguous form such that the elements of the higher dimensions are closer to each other. By contrast, the elements of the lower dimensions are stored farther away from each other.

- Accessing arrays using pointers. Accessing one-dimensional arrays involves the following rules:

  The bare name of the array is a pointer to its first element, as shown in the following example:
  ```
  int a[10], *ptr;
  ptr = a;       /* or */
  ptr = &a[0];
  ```

To access the i'th element of an array you can substitute the traditional form <array_name>[i] with *(<array_name> + i), as shown in the example below:

```
for (i = 0; i < 10; i++)
    a[i] = i;
```

which has the same net effect as:

```
for (i = 0; i < 10; i++)
    *(a+i) = i;
```

The array name can be replaced with a pointer to the base-address of the array, as shown below:

```
ptr = a;
for (i = 0; i < 10; i++)
    *(ptr+i) = i;
```

Ultimately, you can access the element of an array in sequence by incrementing a pointer:

```
for (i = 0, ptr = a; i < 10; i++, ptr++)
    *ptr = i;
```

The handling of multidimensional arrays with pointers involves the use of pointers to other pointers. For example, the traditional reference to an i'th row and j'th column of matrix elements is **x[i][j]**. This is replaced by ***(*(x+i) +j)** (or ***(*(ptr+i) +j)**) if the pointer **ptr** has the base-address of matrix **x**).

- Strings in C. C regards strings as arrays of characters that are terminated with the NULL (ASCII zero) character. C strings are not limited to 255 characters; instead, they are limited by the memory model used or the availability of memory. When declaring an array you must account for the extra space used by the null character.

Character-typed pointers are very frequently used to manipulate strings and are extensively used in string functions. C relies on libraries to provide you with a rich set of string handling functions. Normal string assignments cannot be performed using the = operator and you cannot concatenate strings using the + operator. Every task related to string handling is performed using the library of string functions "string.h". Strings (that is, arrays of characters) and their pointers can be initialized during declaration using the = operator.

CHAPTER

10

Enumerated and Structured Data Types

CHAPTER GOALS

This chapter complements the previous one. The focus is on enumerated and structured data types that permit the programmer to define his or her own types. The chapter covers the following aspects:

- Type redefinition in C.
- Enumerated data types.
- Structured data types.
- Bitfields.
- Pointers to structures.
- Unions.
- Pointers to unions.
- Far pointers.

One of the advantages of languages such as Pascal, Ada, Modula-2, and C is the ability to create user-defined data structures. They enable you to define simple or elaborate data types that are better able to model real world applications and enhance program readability. This chapter looks at enumerated types, C record structures (simply called structures in C), and unions (similar to variant records in Pascal).

TYPE REDEFINITION IN C

As a Pascal programmer, you define new data types in the TYPE program section and assign to them identifier names. C has the **typedef** declaration that offers a similar mechanism. The general syntax for using **typedef** is:

```
typedef <older or longer type name> <newer or shorter name>;
```

In all of the examples that were presented I employed macro substitution to mimic **typedef**. The **typedef** creates aliases of data types known to the compiler. By contrast, the preprocessor merely substitutes the macro names with their equivalent type identifiers before code compilation begins.

Consider the case of the BOOLEAN macro-based pseudotype that I frequently used in the last chapters:

```
#define BOOLEAN unsigned char
```

This can be written utilizing **typedef** as:

```
typedef unsigned char BOOLEAN;
```

or, better yet, using a lower-case identifier name:

```
typedef unsigned char boolean;
```

The **typedef** works well with the names of structures and unions that I present in the next sections. Moreover, **typedef** can be used to redefine the identifier for a data type before or during the type declaration.

You can also employ **typedef** to define the identifier types that represent arrays. In this case, the general syntax for using **typedef** differs slightly and is shown below:

```
typedef <data type> <array-typename>[<size>];
```

The above **typedef** form defines the <array-typename> that can be used just like any other type. Examples are

```
#define MAX_ARRAY 10
typedef double real_array[MAX_ARRAY];
typedef char STRING80[81];
main()
{
   real_array x;  /* same as double x[MAX_ARRAY] */
   STRING80 name; /* same as char name[81] */
   /* other declarations and statements */
}
```

The above **typedef** statements define both a double-typed array **real_array** and STRING80 as an array of characters. These types are used to declare the variables **x** and **name**. Notice that during the declaration of the variables, you do not restate the size of the array; the compiler obtains that information from the **typedef** declarations.

Multidimensional array type names are similarly defined using **typedef**. You simply add the second dimension, as shown below:

```
#define MAX_ROW 10
#define MAX_COL 20
typedef double matrix[MAX_ROW][MAX_COL];
main()
{
   matrix x;
   /* other declarations and statements */
}
```

ENUMERATED AND STRUCTURED DATA TYPES

In addition to creating type identifiers that are associated with fixed arrays, the versatile **typedef** can be used to create open array types that are used as function parameters (more about this later). The syntax is basically the same, with one difference: the size of one dimension is removed, as shown below:

```
#define MAX_COL 20
typedef int open_array[];
typedef float open_matrix[][MAX_COL];
```

The above **typedef** statements define the one- and two-dimensional open arrays **open_array** and **open_matrix**, respectively. The **open_matrix** retains the size of the second dimension, for reasons that will be explained in the next chapter.

ENUMERATED DATA TYPES

Enumerated data types are supported by both Pascal and C. As a Pascal programmer, you have most likely utilized them to create ordinal data types with lists of values constructed using English (or English-like) words.

> **Programming Note**
>
> C does not support sets like Pascal does.

C enumerated types are declared in a manner very similar to that in Pascal. The general syntax is

```
enum <type> { <list of enumerated values> };
```
An example of a declaration is

```
enum colors { black, red, blue, green, yellow, white };
```

Like Pascal, C assigns integers to the values of an enumerated list. Thus, **black** is assigned 0, **red** is assigned 1, and so on. With this numbering scheme you should feel right at home with enumerated C types.

> **Programming Note**
>
> Like Pascal, members of enumerated types in C MUST be unique. You cannot define the same enumerated list member in two lists. The difference between Pascal and C is that identifiers in C are case-sensitive, while in Pascal they are not. Thus, you can duplicate members of enumerated types by altering their character case. Be aware that this can also easily breed mix-ups.

Compared to Pascal, C offers an additional capability regarding the assignment of values to the members of an enumerated list. You can explicitly assign values, in ascending order, to all or some of the members of the list. For example, I can write the color enumerated type declaration as:

```
enum colors { black  = 1,
              red    = 2,
              blue   = 3,
              green  = 5,
              yellow = 7,
              white  = 11 };
```

In the above declaration I chose to assign prime numbers as values for the individual color names. This assigns 1 to **black**, 2 to **red**, and so on. The above is an example where all of the members are assigned explicit values. You can assign values to selected members of the list, as shown below:

```
enum colors { black  = 1,
              red,
              blue,
              green  = 5,
              yellow = 7,
              white };
```

While **black** is explicitly assigned 1, **red** is assigned the value of **black** plus 1 (that is, 2). Similarly **blue** is assigned 3 (the value of **red** plus 1), and **white** is assigned 8 (the value of **yellow** plus 1).

Declaring variables that are of enumerated types follows one of three methods:

1. The declaration of variables may accompany the enumerated type definition:

   ```
   enum <type> {<list of enumerated values>} <list of variables>;
   ```

   An example is

   ```
   enum colors {black, red, blue, green, yellow, white}
                border_color, foreground, background;
   ```

2. The separate declaration of enumerated variables:

   ```
   enum <type> {<list of enumerated values>};
   enum <type> <list of variables>;
   ```

   An example is

   ```
   enum colors { black, red, blue, green, yellow, white };
   enum colors border_color, foreground, background;
   ```

3. Using the **typedef** to give the enumerated type a short type name:

   ```
   typedef enum <type> {<list of enumerated values>} <new type>;
   <new type> <list of variables>;
   ```

   An example is

   ```
   typedef enum enum_colors { black, red, blue, green,
                              yellow, white } color;
   color border_color, foreground, background;
   ```

ENUMERATED AND STRUCTURED DATA TYPES 189

> **Programming Hint**
>
> It is a good practice to make the first member of an enumerated list represent a null value. This enables you to employ it in trapping invalid values. An example is shown below:
>
> ```
> enum weekdays { Nullday, Sunday, Monday, Tuesday,
>                 Wednesday, Thusday, Friday, Saturday };
> ```
>
> where **Nullday** is the member of the enumerated list that represents an invalid weekday name.

> **Programming Hint**
>
> By utilizing enumerated types and the **typedef**, you can easily declare a boolean type in C using the following:
> ```
> enum BOOLEAN { FALSE, TRUE };
> typedef enum BOOLEAN boolean;
> ```

You can declare enumerated-type variables and initialize them using one of the values in the enumerated list. For example, you may declare the variable **border_color** as **enum colors** and initialize it with the enumerated value **red**:

```
enum colors border_color = red;
```

Turbo C permits you to utilize all of the relational operators with enumerated types.

The following program illustrates the use of enumerated data types to represent and classify the days of the week. The program prompts you to enter a day number (Sunday is 1, Monday is 2, and so on) and display one of the following messages, depending on the number you typed:

1. "Oh! The weekend!" if you typed 1 or 7.
2. "T.G.I.F.!!" if you entered 6.
3. "Work, work, work!" if you typed a number in the range of 2 to 5.

The Pascal listing is shown below:

Listing 10.1

```
Program Test_Enum;
{$V-}
Uses CRT;
{ Turbo Pascal program that demonstrates
  the use of enumerated types              }
TYPE WeekDays = (NullDay, Sunday, Monday, Tuesday,
                 Wednesday, Thursday, Friday, Saturday);
     LSTRING = STRING[80];
VAR day  : WeekDays;
    akey : CHAR;
    more : BOOLEAN;
```

190 INTRODUCING C TO PASCAL PROGRAMMERS

```
    j : WORD;
FUNCTION Enum_Val(i : BYTE) : WeekDays;
{ function to return the i'th enumerated list member }
VAR jour : WeekDays;
BEGIN
    jour := NullDay;
    INC(jour, i);
    Enum_Val := jour
END;
BEGIN
    ClrScr;
    REPEAT
        REPEAT
            WRITE('Enter a day number (Sun=1, Mon=2, etc) : ');
            READLN(j); WRITELN;
        UNTIL j IN [1..7];
        day := Enum_Val(j); { use enumerated function }
        CASE day OF
            Sunday, Saturday : WRITELN('Oh! The weekend!');
            Friday : WRITELN('T.G.I.F.!!');
            Monday..Thursday : WRITELN('Work, work, work!');
        END;
        WRITELN; WRITELN;
        WRITE('more? (Y/N) '); akey := ReadKey;
        IF akey IN ['Y','y'] THEN more := TRUE
                             ELSE more := FALSE;
        WRITELN; WRITELN;
    UNTIL NOT more;
END.
```

The Pascal program uses function **Enum_Val** to obtain the i'th member of an enumerated list. The function employs a small program trick to obtain the sought enumerated member.

The C version is shown below:

Listing 10.2

```
/* C program that demonstrates the use of enumerated types */
#include <stdio.h>
#include "conio.h"
/* make global enumerated definitions */
enum WeekDays { NullDay, Sunday, Monday, Tuesday,
                Wednesday, Thursday, Friday, Saturday };
enum BOOLEAN { FALSE, TRUE };
main()
{
    enum WeekDay day;
    char akey;
    enum BOOLEAN more;
    unsigned char j;
    /* define prototype of enumerated function */
    enum WeekDay enum_val(unsigned char);
    clrscr();
    do {
        do {
```

```c
            printf("Enter a day number (Sun=1, Mon=2, etc) : ");
            scanf("%d", &j); printf("\n");
         } while (j < 1 || j > 7);
         day = enum_val(j); /* use enumerated function */
         switch (day) {
            case Sunday:
            case Saturday:
               puts("Oh! The weekend!"); break;
            case Friday:
               puts("T.G.I.F.!!"); break;
            case Monday:
            case Tuesday:
            case Wednesday:
            case Thursday:
               puts("Work, work, work!"); break;
         }
         printf("\n\n");
         printf("more? (Y/N) "); akey = getche();
         more = (akey == 'Y' || akey == 'y') ? TRUE : FALSE;
         printf("\n\n");
      } while (more == TRUE);
}
enum WeekDay enum_val(unsigned char i)
/* enumerated function to get the i'th enumerated element */
{
   enum WeekDay jour;
   jour = NullDay;
   jour += i;
   return jour;
}
```

The above C program defines two enumerated types: **WeekDay** and **BOOLEAN**. The function **enum_val** is prototyped in **main** as:
enum WeekDay enum_val(unsigned char);

The C version is noted for its longer **switch** statement, which is compared to the CASE statement in Pascal. Since Pascal and C are able to assign the same numbers to the members of an enumerated list, converting enumerated types is a smooth operation. However, porting such programs from C to Pascal can be made more complex if explicit and noncontinuous values are assigned to C enumerated members.

Run the C program and enter day numbers 2, 6, and 1. The screen image for the sample session is shown below:
```
Enter a day number (Sun=1, Mon=2, etc) : 2
Work, work, work!
more? (Y/N) y
Enter a day number (Sun=1, Mon=2, etc) : 6
T.G.I.F.!!
more? (Y/N) y
Enter a day number (Sun=1, Mon=2, etc) : 1
Oh! The weekend!
more? (Y/N) n
```

The above C version can be altered to use **typedef** and remove the **enum_val** function. Removing the latter function is possible since C handles

192 INTRODUCING C TO PASCAL PROGRAMMERS

conversions between enumerated values and integers more easily than Pascal. A second program modification replaces the **switch** statement with an **if** statement. The modified program is

Listing 10.3

```
/* C program that demonstrates the use of enumerated types.
   This program is a modified version of the previous one.
   The differences are:
   1) The 'typedef' is used to define new data type identifiers.
   2) The function enum_val() is removed, since C tackles
      enumerated values more flexibly than Pascal.
   3) The switch statement is replaced by a battery of if
      statements.
*/
#include <stdio.h>
#include "conio.h"
main()
{
    enum WeekDays { NullDay, Sunday, Monday, Tuesday,
                    Wednesday, Thursday, Friday, Saturday };
    enum BOOLEAN { FALSE, TRUE };
    /* use typedef with enumerated types */
    typedef enum WeekDays week;
    typedef enum BOOLEAN boolean;
    /* use typedef to alias the predefined type
       unsigned char as byte                      */
    typedef unsigned char byte;
    week day;
    char akey;
    boolean more;
    byte j;
    clrscr();
    do {
        do {
           printf("Enter a day number (Sun=1, Mon=2, etc) : ");
           scanf("%d", &j); printf("\n");
        } while (j < 1 || j > 7);
        day = j; /* convert integer to enumerated type */
        if (day == Sunday || day == Saturday)
               puts("Oh! The weekend!");
        else if (day == Friday)
               puts("T.G.I.F.!!");
        else if (day >= Monday && day <= Thursday)
               puts("Work, work, work!");

        printf("\n\n");
        printf("more? (Y/N) "); akey = getche();
        more = (akey == 'Y' || akey == 'y') ? TRUE : FALSE;
        printf("\n\n");
    } while (more == TRUE);
}
```

In the above program, the declarations for the enumerated data types are placed inside **main**. The **typedef** is used to rename the following data types:

```
typedef enum WeekDays week;
typedef enum BOOLEAN boolean;
typedef unsigned char
```

Also notice that the statement:

```
day = j; /* convert integer to enumerated type *
```

has replaced

```
day = enum_val(j);
```

in the previous C program version.

STRUCTURED DATA TYPES

Record structures in Pascal are very powerful since they enable you to connect between logically related variables that are of different or identical data types. C supports structures that closely resemble Pascal records. The general syntax for declaring a structure is

```
struct <structure name or tag>
    {
     <list of structure components or fields>
    };
```

An example for a simple data structure is one that represents the components of a complex number:

```
struct complex_math
   {
    double real;
    double imaginary;
   };
```

Another example is a structure that represents personal data:

```
struct personal_data
  {
    char first_name[11];
    char middle_initial;
    char last_name[11];
    char address [41];
    char city[21];
    char state[3];
    char zip[10];
    int weight;
    double height;
  };
```

The above structure blends fields of various types, which is what structures are meant to do.

> **Program Translation**
>
> Translating Pascal records into C structures involves the following general form:
>
> Pascal:
> ```
>     <record_type> = RECORD
>                 <field1> : <type1>;
>                 <field2> : <type2>;
>                 <other fields>;
>                 <fieldn> : <typen>;
>     END;
> ```
> C:
> ```
>     struct <record_type>
>             {
>                 <type1> <field1>;
>                 <type2> <field2>;
>                 <other fields>;
>                 <typen> <fieldn>;
>             };
> ```

Declaring structured variables employs the following general syntax:

```
struct <structure name> <list of structured variables>;
```

Examples for declaring structured variables are

```
struct complex_math c1, c2, c3;
struct personal_data me, you, dog_named_boo;
```

You can also declare structured variables with the structure definition statement. For example, the following statement both defines the **complex_math** structure and declares three corresponding variables **c1**, **c2**, and **c3**:

```
struct complex_math
   {
   double real;
   double imaginary;
   } c1, c2, c3;
```

The data structure definition statement may also include a **typedef** clause that is usually intended to give a shorter name for the structure type. For example, the following defines the data structure **complex_math** and gives it the shorthand name **complex**. Now you may declare complex variables using just **complex**, instead of the longer form "struct complex_math":

```
typedef struct complex_math
   {
   double real;
   double imaginary;
   } complex;
complex c1, c2, c3;
```

ENUMERATED AND STRUCTURED DATA TYPES 195

Program Translation

Translating the declaration of record-typed variables into C structured variables employs the following general form:
   Pascal:
      VAR
         <record_var> : <record_name>;
   C:
      struct <record_name> <record_var>;
   or
      <typedefed record_name> <record_var>

Accessing the fields of a structured variable in C uses the dot notation, just like in Pascal. Using the **complex_math** structure, the following code illustrates storing and recalling data from fields of structured variables:

```
struct complex_math c1, c2, c3;
c1.real = 12.3;
c1.imaginary = 34.5;
c2.real = 92.3;
c2.imaginary = 94.5;
c3.real = c1.real + c2.real;
c3.imaginary = c1.imaginary + c2.imaginary;
printf("c3 = (%ld) +/- i (%ld)\n\n",c3.real,c3.imaginary)
```

Structured variables can be initialized, just like typed constants in Turbo Pascal. To initialize a **complex_math** structured variable, you may rewrite the above code as:

```
struct complex_math
   {
     double real;
     double imaginary;
   };
struct complex_math c1 = { 12.3, 34.5 };
struct complex_math c2 = { 92.3, 94.5 };
c3.real = c1.real + c2.real;
c3.imaginary = c1.imaginary + c2.imaginary;
printf("c3 = (%ld) +/- i (%ld)\n\n",c3.real,c3.imaginary);
```

Similarly you may initialize a **personal_data** variable using:

```
struct personal_data
   {
     char first_name[11];
     char middle_initial;
     char last_name[11];
     char address [41];
     char city[21];
     char state[3];
     char zip[10];
     int weight;
     double height;
   };
```

```
struct personal_data me = {"Namir", 'C', "Shammas",
                           "4823 LondonTown Street",
                           "OldYork", "ZZ", "00000",
                           170, 5.75 };
```

C does not provide the equivalent of the Pascal WITH. Consequently, the reference to fields of structures must include the structure names.

Declaring arrays that are structures is very similar to declaring arrays of simple types. The following example declares an array to store complex data and also initializes it:

```
struct complex_math
   {
     double real;
     double imaginary;
   };
struct complex_math c[3] = { { 1.1, 2.2 },
                             { 3.3, 4.4 },
                             { 5.5, 6.6 } };
```

ACCESSING ARRAYS OF STRUCTURES

You can declare and access an array of structures just like Pascal record arrays, using the following general syntax.

For accessing scalar fields in an array of structures:

```
struct_array_var[index].struct_field
```

Or, for accessing single elements of array-typed fields in an array of structures:

```
struct_array_var[index].struct_field[field_index]
```

The next program is an example that uses the following structure:

```
struct personal_data_struct
   {
      char name[31];
      byte age;
      float weight;
   };
```

An array of ten records is created. The program prompts you to enter the data for the fields of each record structure. Using the bubble sort method, the array is sorted according to the **name** field. The Pascal program is shown below:

Listing 10.4

```
Program Test_Records1;
Uses CRT;
{ Turbo Pascal program declares a record type and sorts
  an array of records                                    }
CONST NDATA = 10; { number of data points }
TYPE personal_data = RECORD
        name : STRING[30];
```

```
            age : BYTE;
            weight : REAL;
        END;
VAR i, j : BYTE;
    tempo : personal_data;
    person : ARRAY [1..NDATA] OF personal_data;
BEGIN
    FOR i := 1 TO NDATA DO BEGIN
        ClrScr;
        { put form on the screen }
        GotoXY(5, 1); WRITE('Entering record number ',i);
        GotoXY(5, 3); ClrEol; WRITE('Name    : ');
        GotoXY(5, 5); ClrEol; WRITE('Age     : ');
        GotoXY(5, 7); ClrEol; WRITE('Weight  : ');
        { input data from the form }
        GotoXY(14, 3); READLN(person[i].name);
        GotoXY(14, 5); READLN(person[i].age);
        GotoXY(14, 7); READLN(person[i].weight);
    END;
    ClrScr;
    WRITELN('THE SORTED LIST OF RECORDS IS');
    WRITELN;
    { sort and display the records }
    FOR i := 1 TO NDATA-1 DO BEGIN
        FOR j := i+1 TO NDATA DO
            IF person[i].name > person[j].name
            THEN BEGIN
                tempo := person[i];
                person[i] := person[j];
                person[j] := tempo;
            END; { IF }
        { display each ordered record }
        WITH person[i] DO
            WRITELN(name:30,' ',age:5,' ',weight:10);
    END; { FOR i }
    { display last record }
    WITH person[NDATA] DO
        WRITELN(name:30,' ',age:5,' ',weight:10);
END.
```

The C version is listed below:

Listing 10.5

```
/* C program declares a structure type and sorts an array of
   records.
*/
#include <stdio.h>
#include <string.h>
#include "conio.h"
#define NDATA 10   /* number of data points */
main()
{
    typedef unsigned int byte;
```

INTRODUCING C TO PASCAL PROGRAMMERS

```
    /* declare structure and define its name */
        /* declare structure & its name
                    _____
                V                       V    */
    typedef struct personal_data_struct
                {
                    char name[31];
                    byte age;
                    float weight;
                } personal_data; /* <- give it an alias typedef */
    byte i, j;
    /* use typedef name in declaring structures */
    personal_data tempo, person[NDATA];
    clrscr();
    for (i = 0; i < NDATA; i++)   {
        clrscr();
        /* put form on the screen */
        gotoxy(5, 1);
        printf("Entering record number %d",i+1);
        gotoxy(5, 3); clreol(); puts("Name    : ");
        gotoxy(5, 5); clreol(); puts("Age     : ");
        gotoxy(5, 7); clreol(); puts("Weight  : ");
        /* input data from the form */
        gotoxy(14, 3); scanf("%s", &person[i].name);
        gotoxy(14, 5); scanf("%d", &person[i].age);
        gotoxy(14, 7); scanf("%f", &person[i].weight);
    }
    clrscr();
    printf("THE SORTED LIST OF RECORDS IS\n\n");
    /* sort and display the records */
    for (i = 0; i < (NDATA-1); i++)   {
        for (j = i+1; j < NDATA; j++)
            if (strcmp(person[i].name,person[j].name) > 0) {
                tempo = person[i];
                person[i] = person[j];
                person[j] = tempo;
            } /* if */
        /* display each ordered record */
        printf("%30s   %5d   %10f\n", person[i].name,
                    person[i].age, person[i].weight);
    } /* for i */
    /* display last record */
    printf("%30s   %5d   %10f\n", person[NDATA-1].name,
                    person[NDATA-1].age,
                    person[NDATA-1].weight);
}
```

Notice the following in the C program:

1. The **typedef** is incorporated in the structure declaration to define the shorter structure name **personal_data**:

    ```
    typedef struct personal_data_struct
            {
                char name[31];
    ```

ENUMERATED AND STRUCTURED DATA TYPES   199

```
        byte age;
        float weight;
    } personal_data;
```

The **personal_data** identifier is used to declare the structured variables in:

```
personal_data tempo, person[NDATA];
```

instead of the longer and more formal form:

```
struct personal_data_struct tempo, person[NDATA];
```

2. To use **scanf**, you need the address of the variable or field receiving the keyed-in data. To input data to the **name** field of the i'th structure array, use **&person[i].name**. Similarly, the **&person[i].age** and **&person[i].weight** are used to store data in the other fields of each structure array member:

```
gotoxy(14, 3); scanf("%s", &person[i].name);
gotoxy(14, 5); scanf("%d", &person[i].age);
gotoxy(14, 7); scanf("%f", &person[i].weight);
```

3. Since the array sorting is based on the **name** field, the **strcmp** function is used to compare the string-typed fields of different array members:

```
if (strcmp(person[i].name,person[j].name) > 0) {
```

4. Swapping structures in C and in Pascal is very similar, since both languages permit the assignment of variables of the same structures:

```
tempo = person[i];
person[i] = person[j];
person[j] = tempo;
```

Run the above program using the following data:

Name	Age	Weight
Love	65	179
Short	31	188
Zelnick	33	178
Johnson	22	190
DeArras	35	188
Faraday	45	210
Bond	55	190
Rollins	24	166
Shammas	33	170
Martin	36	126

The screen image for entering the first record is

```
Entering record number 1
Name   : Love
Age    : 65
Weight : 179
```

The other screen images are similar. The image of the sorted output list is shown below:

THE SORTED LIST OF RECORDS IS

Bond	55	190.000000
DeArras	35	188.000000
Faraday	45	210.000000
Johnson	22	190.000000
Love	65	179.000000
Martin	36	126.000000
Rollins	24	166.000000
Shammas	33	170.000000
Short	31	188.000000
Zelnick	33	178.000000

C structures can be nested, just as in Pascal. This gives you additional power in expressing elaborate real-world problems (in terms of nested structures). Consider the following data structure that describes a few aspects of the basic personal data:

```
struct single
   {
     char first_name[31];
     char last_name[31];
     int  age;
     int  weight;
   };
```

The above structure can be used in declaring this structure:

```
struct family
   {
     struct single wife;
     struct single husband;
     int num_cars;
     int num_children;
     double total_income;
   };
```

The **family** structure has two fields that are *single* structures and three simple-typed fields. Variables that have nested structures may be initialized, and the braces are used to observe the order and hierarchy of fields and nested structures. For example, a variable of type **family** may be initialized in the following manner:

```
struct family our_house = { { "Bobbi", "Shammas", 31, 135 },
                            { "Namir", "Shammas", 33, 170 },
                            2, 1, 40.0 };
```

Accessing variables that contain nested structures is identical to the notation used in Pascal. The following is a list of fields in the **our_house** identifier:

ENUMERATED AND STRUCTURED DATA TYPES 201

Component	Field in single	in family
our_house.husband.name[0]	last_name	husband
our_house.wife.age	age	wife
our_house.wife.weight	weight	wife
our_house.num_cars	...	num_cars

The following program handles nested record structures. The program prompts you to enter personal data and information related to a car owned by that person. The **car_info** structure handles the data related to a car. The same record is nested in a **personal_data** structure that also defines the fields for personal information. The Pascal version is shown below:

Listing 10.6

```
Program Test_Records2;
Uses CRT;
{ Turbo Pascal program declares a nested record type and
  sorts an array of records                                      }
CONST NDATA = 3; { number of data points }
TYPE car_info = RECORD
        make : STRING[20];
        year : WORD;
        doors : BYTE;
    END;
    personal_data = RECORD
        name : STRING[30];
        age : BYTE;
        weight : REAL;
        car : car_info
    END;
VAR i, j : BYTE;
    tempo : personal_data;
    person : ARRAY [1..NDATA] OF personal_data;
BEGIN
    FOR i := 1 TO NDATA DO BEGIN
        ClrScr;
      { put form on the screen }
        GotoXY(5, 1); WRITE('Entering record number ',i);
        GotoXY(5, 3); WRITE('Name             : ');
        GotoXY(5, 5); WRITE('Age              : ');
        GotoXY(5, 7); WRITE('Weight           : ');
        GotoXY(5, 9); WRITE('Car make         : ');
        GotoXY(5,11); WRITE('Model year       : ');
        GotoXY(5,13); WRITE('Number of doors  : ');
      { input data from the form }
        GotoXY(25, 3); READLN(person[i].name);
        GotoXY(25, 5); READLN(person[i].age);
        GotoXY(25, 7); READLN(person[i].weight);
        GotoXY(25, 9); READLN(person[i].car.make);
        GotoXY(25,11); READLN(person[i].car.year);
        GotoXY(25,13); READLN(person[i].car.doors);
    END;
```

```pascal
    ClrScr;
    WRITELN('THE SORTED LIST OF RECORDS IS');
    WRITELN;
    { sort and display the records }
    FOR i := 1 TO NDATA-1 DO BEGIN
        FOR j := i+1 TO NDATA DO
            IF person[i].name > person[j].name
            THEN BEGIN
                tempo := person[i];
                person[i] := person[j];
                person[j] := tempo;
            END; { IF }
        { display each ordered record }
        WITH person[i] DO
            WRITELN(name:20,' ',age:5,' ',weight:10,' ',
                    car.make:20,' ',car.year:4,' ',car.doors:2);
    END; { FOR i }
    { display last record }
    WITH person[NDATA] DO
        WRITELN(name:20,' ',age:5,' ',weight:10,' ',
                car.make:20,' ',car.year:4,' ',car.doors:2);
END.
```

The translated C version is listed below:

Listing 10.7

```c
/* C program declares a nested record type and
   sorts an array of records                                    */
#include <stdio.h>
#include <string.h>
#include "conio.h"
#define NDATA  10 /* number of data points */
main()
{
    typedef unsigned char byte;
    typedef unsigned int word;
    struct car_info {
        char make[21];
        word year;
        byte doors;
    };
    struct personal_data {
        char name[31];
        byte age;
        float weight;
        struct car_info car;
    };
    byte i, j;
    struct personal_data tempo;
    struct personal_data person[NDATA];
    for (i = 0; i < NDATA; i++)   {
        clrscr();
        /* put form on the screen */
        gotoxy(5, 1); printf("Entering record number %d",i+1);
```

ENUMERATED AND STRUCTURED DATA TYPES

```
        gotoxy(5, 3); printf("Name             : ");
        gotoxy(5, 5); printf("Age              : ");
        gotoxy(5, 7); printf("Weight           : ");
        gotoxy(5, 9); printf("Car make         : ");
        gotoxy(5,11); printf("Model year       : ");
        gotoxy(5,13); printf("Number of doors  : ");
        /* input data from the form */
        gotoxy(25, 3); scanf("%s", &person[i].name);
        gotoxy(25, 5); scanf("%d", &person[i].age);
        gotoxy(25, 7); scanf("%f", &person[i].weight);
        gotoxy(25, 9); scanf("%s", &person[i].car.make);
        gotoxy(25,11); scanf("%d", &person[i].car.year);
        gotoxy(25,13); scanf("%d", &person[i].car.doors);
    }
    clrscr();
    printf("THE SORTED LIST OF RECORDS IS\n\n");
    /* sort and display the records */
    for (i = 0; i < NDATA-1; i++)   {
        for (j = i+1; j < NDATA; j++)
            if (strcmp(person[i].name,person[j].name) > 0) {
                tempo = person[i];
                person[i] = person[j];
                person[j] = tempo;
            } /* if */
        /* display each ordered record */
        printf("%20s %5d %10f %20s %4d %2d\n",
                    person[i].name,
                    person[i].age,
                    person[i].weight,
                    person[i].car.make,
                    person[i].car.year,
                    person[i].car.doors);
    } /* for i */
    /* display last record */
        printf("%20s %5d %10f %20s %4d %2d\n",
                    person[NDATA-1].name,
                    person[NDATA-1].age,
                    person[NDATA-1].weight,
                    person[NDATA-1].car.make,
                    person[NDATA-1].car.year,
                    person[NDATA-1].car.doors);
}
```

The C version is a close translation of the original Pascal program. Accessing fields in nested C structures is identical to that in Pascal. For example, to access the **make** field nested in the **car** field, the data path **person[i].car.make** is employed.

BITFIELDS IN C

C enables you to use bitfields with its structures. This permits you to perform bit-level access and manipulation to query or set information about the hardware and the operating system. The general syntax for defining bitfields is

```
struct <structure name>
    {
        <type 1> <field 1> : <field length 1>;
        <type 2> <field 2> : <field length 2>;
        <type 3> <field 3> : <field length 3>;
        <other fields declared here>;
        <type n> <field n> : <field length n>;
    };
```

The bitfields access a memory address in the following fashion: the first bitfield points to the least significant bit, the last bitfield points to the most significant bit. In other words, the sequence of bitfields accesses memory addresses from least to most significant bits.

For example, you can define a structure to query the keyboard status by examining the single bits:

```
typedef struct kbd_status_type {
            unsigned int leftshift   : 1;
            unsigned int rightshift  : 1;
            unsigned int ctrl        : 1;
            unsigned int alt         : 1;
            unsigned int scrollock   : 1;
            unsigned int numlock     : 1;
            unsigned int capslock    : 1;
            unsigned int insert      : 1;
        };
```

The bitfields can be used by declaring a variable and making field references using the dot operator, as with ordinary structures.

The following example uses a bitfield structure and assigns values to it (0 or 1 to each bitfield). The program then writes the bitfield structure into memory location 0000:0417 to alter the status of the keyboard. If your keyboard has an LED for the [Caps Lock], [Num Lock], and [Scroll Lock], watch them come on when the program runs. The program uses a far pointer to access the sought memory location. In addition, it uses a function of type **int** to carry out writing the bitfields to the memory location. This is a required trick to make the runtime system convert the bitfield structure into a character-typed argument that is used by the pointer. Any attempts to perform the same operation in the **main** function is resisted by the compiler. The C listing is shown below:

Listing 10.8

```
/* C program that alters the status of the keyboard by
   writing bitfields to memory location hex 0000:0417  */
#include <stdio.h>
#define ON  1
#define OFF 0
typedef struct kbd_status_type {
            unsigned int leftshift   : 1;
            unsigned int rightshift  : 1;
            unsigned int ctrl        : 1;
            unsigned int alt         : 1;
            unsigned int scrollock   : 1;
```

```
            unsigned int numlock   : 1;
            unsigned int capslock  : 1;
            unsigned int insert    : 1;
   } kbd_status;
main()
{
   kbd_status kbd;
   kbd.leftshift = OFF;
   kbd.rightshift = OFF;
   kbd.ctrl = OFF;
   kbd.alt = OFF;
   kbd.scrollock = ON;
   kbd.numlock = ON;
   kbd.capslock = ON;
   kbd.insert = OFF;
   adjust_kbd(kbd);
   if (kbd.leftshift == 1)
      printf("Left Shift is on\n");
   if (kbd.rightshift == 1)
      printf("Right Shift is on\n");
   if (kbd.ctrl == 0)
      printf("Ctrl key is off\n");
   else
     printf("Ctrl key is on\n");
   if (kbd.alt == 0)
      printf("Alt key is off\n");
   else
     printf("Alt key is on\n");
   if (kbd.scrollock == 1)
      printf("Scroll Lock is on\n");
   if (kbd.numlock == 1)
      printf("Num Lock key is on\n");
   if (kbd.capslock == 1)
      printf("Caps key is on \n");
   if (kbd.insert == 1)
      printf("Insert key is on\n");
}
int adjust_kbd(char status)
{
   int far *farptr;
   farptr = (int far *) 0x417;
   /* read bitfields into memory location */
   *(farptr) = status;
}
```

USING POINTERS TO STRUCTURES

The use of pointers to user-defined record structures is popular in Pascal and C. Using this genre of pointer plays an even bigger role in C. One such reason is that pointers to structures enable you to pass structures to functions and have them alter their contents.

Declaring pointers to structures follows the general rules of pointer declaration in C. So, there are no new rules to learn or observe; likewise, there is no special syntax. On the other hand, using structure pointers follows some new syntactical rules. Of course, you must initialize the pointer before using it. Accessing any field in the structure is performed using the following general syntax:

`<structure-pointer> -> <selected field>`

> ### Program Translation
>
> Translating pointers to record structures from Pascal to C uses the following rule:
> Pascal:
> ```
>     Declaration:        VAR <pointer> : ^<record>;
>     Initialization:     NEW(<pointer>);
>     Pointer reference:  <pointer>^.<selected field>
> ```
> C:
> ```
>     Declaration:        <record> *<pointer>;
>     Initialization:     <pointer> = (<record> *)
>                                      malloc(sizeof(<record>));
>                         OR
>                         <pointer> = &<record_var>;
>     Pointer reference:  <pointer>-><selected field>
> ```

The following C program is a modified version of the last one. The ten-member array **person** is still declared, but its elements are manipulated using a new structure pointer **ptr**. The listing is shown below:

Listing 10.9

```
/* C program declares a structure type and sorts an array
   of records. This version employs pointers to structures.
*/
#include <stdio.h>
#include <string.h>
#include "conio.h"
#define NDATA 10   /* number of data points */
main()
{
   typedef unsigned int byte;
   /* declare structure and define its name */
        /* declare structure & its name
           ----------------------------
            v                       v    */
   typedef struct personal_data_struct
           {
             char name[31];
             byte age;
             float weight;
           } personal_data; /* <- give it an alias typedef */
   byte i, j;
   /* use typedef name in declaring structures */
   personal_data tempo, person[NDATA];
   /* assign pointer and initialize to base-address of
      structure array 'person' */
```

```
    personal_data *ptr = &person;
    for (i = 0; i < NDATA; i++)   {
        clrscr();
        /* put form on the screen */
        gotoxy(5, 1);
        printf("Entering record number %d",i+1);
        gotoxy(5, 3); puts("Name    : ");
        gotoxy(5, 5); puts("Age     : ");
        gotoxy(5, 7); puts("Weight  : ");
        /* input data from the form */
        gotoxy(14, 3); scanf("%s", &(ptr->name));
        gotoxy(14, 5); scanf("%d", &(ptr->age));
        gotoxy(14, 7); scanf("%f", &(ptr->weight));
        ptr++; /* increment address of pointer */
    }
    clrscr();
    printf("THE SORTED LIST OF RECORDS IS\n\n");
    ptr = &person; /* restore the base pointer address */
    /* sort and display the records */
    for (i = 0; i < NDATA-1; i++)   {
        for (j = i+1; j < NDATA; j++)
            if (strcmp((ptr+i)->name, (ptr+j)->name) > 0)  {
                tempo = *(ptr+i);
                *(ptr+i) = *(ptr+j);
                *(ptr+j) = tempo;
            }
            /* if */
        /* display each ordered record */
        printf("%30s   %5d   %10f\n", (ptr+i)->name,
                                      (ptr+i)->age,
                                      (ptr+i)->weight);
    } /* for i */
    /* display last record */
    printf("%30s   %5d   %10f\n", (ptr + NDATA-1)->name,
                                  (ptr + NDATA-1)->age,
                                  (ptr + NDATA-1)->weight);
}
```

Examine the above listing and notice the following:

1. The structure pointer is initialized using:

    `personal_data *ptr = &person;`

    which stores the base-address of array **person** into **ptr**.

2. The input of the data is performed using the pointer-increment method. The ampersand provides **scanf** with the location of the field receiving the data. For example, since **(ptr->name)** is the reference to the name field of the current record, &(ptr->name) is its address.
    ```
    gotoxy(14, 3); scanf("%s", &(ptr->name));
    gotoxy(14, 5); scanf("%d", &(ptr->age));
    gotoxy(14, 7); scanf("%f", &(ptr->weight));
    ptr++; /* increment address of pointer */
    ```

3. After the input process is terminated, the structure pointer **ptr** is reset to the base-address of array **person**. The nested for loops that perform the

208 INTRODUCING C TO PASCAL PROGRAMMERS

bubble sort use **ptr** with an offset index to access data at random from array **person**:

```
if (strcmp((ptr+i)->name, (ptr+j)->name) > 0) {
    tempo = *(ptr+i);
    *(ptr+i) = *(ptr+j);
    *(ptr+j) = tempo;
}
```

4. The output of the sorted data is carried out using:

```
printf("%30s  %5d  %10f\n", (ptr+i)->name,
                            (ptr+i)->age,
                            (ptr+i)->weight);
```

Notice that the **(ptr+i)** component is the pointer to the i'th array element. It is a compound pointer that is employed in selecting the required fields using the -> selector.

The above program version can be modified to remove the array **person** and instead use an array of pointers. In a way, this simplifies the field referencing. Of course, calls to the **malloc** routine are made to allocate space for each structure. The modified listing is shown below:

Listing 10.10

```
/* C program declares a structure type and sorts an array
   of records. This version employs pointers to structures.
*/
#include <stdio.h>
#include <string.h>
#include "conio.h"
#define NDATA 10  /* number of data points */
main()
{
    typedef unsigned int byte;
    /* declare structure and define its name */
            /* declare structure & its name
               ------------------------------
               v                            v   */
    typedef struct personal_data_struct
            {
              char name[31];
              byte age;
              float weight;
            } personal_data; /* <- give it an alias typedef */
    byte i, j;
    /* use typedef name in declaring structures */
    personal_data tempo, *ptr[NDATA];
    /* dynamically allocate space for the data */
    for (i = 0; i < NDATA; i++)
        ptr[i] = (personal_data *) malloc(sizeof(personal_data));
    for (i = 0; i < NDATA; i++)  {
        clrscr();
        /* put form on the screen */
        gotoxy(5, 1);
```

```
            printf("Entering record number %d",i+1);
            gotoxy(5, 3); puts("Name    : ");
            gotoxy(5, 5); puts("Age     : ");
            gotoxy(5, 7); puts("Weight  : ");
            /* input data from the form */
            gotoxy(14, 3); scanf("%s", &(ptr[i]->name));
            gotoxy(14, 5); scanf("%d", &(ptr[i]->age));
            gotoxy(14, 7); scanf("%f", &(ptr[i]->weight));
        }
        clrscr();
        printf("THE SORTED LIST OF RECORDS IS\n\n");
        /* sort and display the records */
        for (i = 0; i < NDATA-1; i++)  {
            for (j = i+1; j < NDATA; j++)
                if (strcmp(ptr[i]->name,ptr[j]->name) > 0) {
                    tempo = *ptr[i];
                    *ptr[i] = *ptr[j];
                    *ptr[j] = tempo;
                }
                /* if */
            /* display each ordered record */
            printf("%30s  %5d  %10f\n", ptr[i]->name,
                                         ptr[i]->age,
                                         ptr[i]->weight);
        } /* for i */
        /* display last record */
        printf("%30s  %5d  %10f\n", ptr[NDATA-1]->name,
                                     ptr[NDATA-1]->age,
                                     ptr[NDATA-1]->weight);
}
```

Compare the form of pointer access to the fields between this version and its predecessor. The code above offers more uniform referencing to pointers.

Nested structures can also be accessed by pointers. The -> field selector is used only once, after the pointer. Accessing deeply nested fields involves the dot notation. The following program is a modification of the last nested-record example. This version uses pointers to access the record structures.

Listing 10.11

```
/* C program declares a nested record type and sorts an array
   of records. This version uses pointers to structures for
   manipulating the various records.
*/
#include <stdio.h>
#include <string.h>
#include "conio.h"
#define NDATA 10 /* number of data points */
main()
{
    typedef unsigned char byte;
    typedef unsigned int word;
    struct car_info {
```

```c
      char make[21];
      word year;
      byte doors;
   };
   struct personal_data {
      char name[31];
      byte age;
      float weight;
      struct car_info car;
   };
byte i, j;
struct personal_data tempo;
struct personal_data person[NDATA], *ptr = &person;
for (i = 0; i < NDATA; i++)   {
   clrscr();
   /* put form on the screen */
   gotoxy(5, 1); printf("Entering record number %d",i+1);
   gotoxy(5, 3); printf("Name              : ");
   gotoxy(5, 5); printf("Age               : ");
   gotoxy(5, 7); printf("Weight            : ");
   gotoxy(5, 9); printf("Car make          : ");
   gotoxy(5,11); printf("Model year        : ");
   gotoxy(5,13); printf("Number of doors   : ");
   /* input data from the form */
   gotoxy(25, 3); scanf("%s", ptr->name);
   gotoxy(25, 5); scanf("%d", &(ptr->age));
   gotoxy(25, 7); scanf("%f", &(ptr->weight));
   gotoxy(25, 9); scanf("%s", &(ptr->car.make));
   gotoxy(25,11); scanf("%d", &(ptr->car.year));
   gotoxy(25,13); scanf("%d", &(ptr->car.doors));
   ptr++; /* increment pointer address */
}
ptr = person; /* reset base pointer address */
clrscr();
printf("THE SORTED LIST OF RECORDS IS\n\n");
/* sort and display the records */
for (i = 0; i < NDATA-1; i++)   {
   for (j = i+1; j < NDATA; j++)
      if (strcmp((ptr+i)->name, (ptr+j)->name) > 0) {
         tempo = *(ptr+i);
         *(ptr+i) = *(ptr+j);
         *(ptr+j) = tempo;
      } /* if */
   /* display each ordered record */
   printf("%20s %5d %10f %20s %4d %2d\n",
            (ptr + i)->name,
            (ptr + i)->age,
            (ptr + i)->weight,
            (ptr + i)->car.make,
            (ptr + i)->car.year,
            (ptr + i)->car.doors);
} /* for i */
/* display last record */
   printf("%20s %5d %10f %20s %4d %2d\n",
```

```
            (ptr + NDATA-1)->name,
            (ptr + NDATA-1)->age,
            (ptr + NDATA-1)->weight,
            (ptr + NDATA-1)->car.make,
            (ptr + NDATA-1)->car.year,
            (ptr + NDATA-1)->car.doors);
}
```

UNIONS AND POINTERS TO UNIONS

In a nutshell, a union in C is equivalent to variant Pascal records without the fixed record part. The general syntax for declaring a union structure is

```
union <union_structure_name>
     {
      <type 1> <field 1>;
      <type 2> <field 2>;
      <other fields>
      <type n> <field n>;
     };
```

As with variant records in Pascal, C allocates space for unions to accommodate the largest field. The various fields of a union share the same memory space. Making the fields equal (or approximately equal) enables you to make good use of the union's memory space at all times.

The following is an example for declaring a union data type:

```
typedef unsigned char byte;
union eight_byte_storage
   {
       double  dblvar;
       long    solong[2]
       int     intvar[4];
       long    solong[2]
       byte    onebyte[8];
   };
```

The size of the **eight_byte_storage**, as the name implies, is eight bytes. This is enough to accommodate a single double-typed variable; an array of two long integers; an array of four integers; and an array of eight bytes. In this example, all the fields of the union structure occupy the same memory space.

Program Translation

To translate a variant Pascal record into an equivalent C structure, you need to make use of nested structures, as shown below:
   Pascal:
```
      <record-type> = RECORD
         <fields for fixed part>;
         CASE <identifier> OF
            <fields for variant part>;
      END;
```

> **C:**
> ```
>     union <variant_part_union>
>         {
>             <fields for variant part>;
>         };
>     struct <fixed_part_struct>
>         {
>             <fields for fixed part>;
>         };
>     struct <record-type>
>         {
>             struct <fixed_part_struct> <fixed_part>;
>             union  <variant_part_union> <variant_part>;
>         };
> ```

Accessing the fields of a union involves the same notations as those for structures. The following example illustrates accessing fields using a variable and a pointer:

```
typedef unsigned char byte;
union eight_byte_storage
   {
      double  dblvar;
      long    solong[2];
      int     intvar[4];
      long    solong[2];
      byte    onebyte[8];
   } union_var, *unionptr = &union_var;
union_var.dblvar = 1.2345e+02;
union_var.dblvar *= 2.0;
union_ptr->solong[0] = 1234L;
union_ptr->solong[1] = union_ptr->solong[0] % 124L;
```

Unlike arrays and structures, unions cannot easily be initialized. For example, the following C program attempts to initialize a four-element union array. When you run the program the only correct value displayed corresponds to variable **x**, which happens to be the first field in the union. If you make the long integer field the first one, the program correctly displays the long integer and integer fields, but fails to show the correct contents of **s[1].x**.

```
/* C program that demonstrate the problems with attempting to
   initialize an array of unions.
*/
#include <stdio.h>
main()
{
    union rec_type {
              double x;
              long   n;
              int    i;
            };
    typedef union rec_type rec;
    rec s[4] = { 3, 3.14, 4, 70000 };
    printf("%d\n", (int) s[0].i);
```

```
    printf("%lg\n", (double) s[1].x);
    printf("%d\n", (int) s[2].i);
    printf("%ld\n", (long) s[3].n);
}
```

Unions are useful when writing programs that handle data which can be represented in alternate ways. A popular example is complex numbers. They can be represented using rectangular (that is, Cartesian) or polar coordinates. To relate a Cartesian point (X,Y) and its equivalent vector having an angle A and modulus R, use these equations:

A = ArcTan(Y / X)   and   R = (X^2 + Y^2) ^(0.5)
X = R * cos(A)   and   Y = R * sin(A)

The following program enables you to add complex numbers using data in either cartesian or polar form. The Pascal source code is

Listing 10.12

```
Program Test_Variant_Records;
{$V-}
Uses CRT;
{ Turbo Pascal program that demonstrates variant record types }
TYPE Complex = RECORD
        CASE BOOLEAN OF
            TRUE  : (xcoord, ycoord : REAL);
            FALSE : (angle, modulus : REAL);
        END;
VAR a, b, c : Complex;
    rectangular : BOOLEAN;
    ch : CHAR;
PROCEDURE Add_Complex;
VAR x, y : REAL;
BEGIN
    IF rectangular THEN BEGIN
        c.xcoord := a.xcoord + b.xcoord;
        c.ycoord := a.ycoord + b.ycoord
    END
    ELSE BEGIN
        x := a.modulus * cos(a.angle) + b.modulus * cos(b.angle);
        y := a.modulus * sin(a.angle) + b.modulus * sin(b.angle);
        c.angle := arctan(y/x);
        c.modulus := SQRT(x*x + y*y);
    END;
END;
PROCEDURE Get_Input;
BEGIN
    WRITE('Use Rectangular or Polar coordinates? (R/P) ');
    ch := Upcase(ReadKey); WRITELN(ch); WRITELN;
    IF ch <> 'P' THEN rectangular := TRUE
                 ELSE rectangular := FALSE;
    IF rectangular THEN BEGIN
        WRITE('Enter first complex number (x y coord) : ');
        READLN(a.xcoord, a.ycoord); WRITELN;
        WRITE('Enter second complex number (x y coord) : ');
```

214   INTRODUCING C TO PASCAL PROGRAMMERS

```
            READLN(b.xcoord, b.ycoord); WRITELN;
        END
        ELSE BEGIN
            WRITE('Enter first complex number (modulus angle) : ');
            READLN(a.modulus, a.angle); WRITELN;
            WRITE('Enter second complex number (modulus angle) : ');
            READLN(b.modulus, b.angle); WRITELN;
        END;
END;
PROCEDURE Show_Results;
BEGIN
    IF rectangular THEN
        WRITELN('Result = (',c.xcoord,') + (',c.ycoord,')')
    ELSE
        WRITELN('Result = ',c.modulus,' @ ',c.angle,' radians');
END;
BEGIN
    ClrScr;
    WRITELN('PROGRAM TO ADD COMPLEX NUMBERS':50);
    WRITELN; WRITELN;
    REPEAT
        Get_Input;
        Add_Complex;
        Show_Results;
        WRITELN; WRITELN;
        WRITE('Add more numbers? Y/N ');
        ch := UpCase(ReadKey);
        WRITELN; WRITELN;
    UNTIL ch <> 'Y';
END.
```

The translated C version is

Listing 10.13

```
/* C program that demonstrates variant record types using
   the union structure                                        */
#include <stdio.h>
#include "conio.h"
#include <math.h>
struct rect_type {
                double xcoord;
                double ycoord;
            };
struct polar_type {
                double angle;
                double modulus;
            };
union Complex {
                struct rect_type rect;
                struct polar_type polar;
            };
enum boolean_type { TRUE, FALSE };
typedef enum boolean_type boolean;
```

ENUMERATED AND STRUCTURED DATA TYPES 215

```c
/* declare global variables */
union Complex a, b, c;
boolean rectangular;
char ch;
/* declare prototype of user-defined functions */
void get_input(void), add_complex(void), show_results(void);
main()
{
    clrscr();
    printf("\t\tPROGRAM TO ADD COMPLEX NUMBERS\n\n\n");
    do {
        get_input();
        add_complex();
        show_results();
        printf("\n\n");
        printf("Add more numbers? Y/N ");
        ch = getche();
        if (ch >= 'a' && ch <= 'z') ch += 'A' - 'a';
        printf("\n\n");
    } while (ch == 'Y');
}
void add_complex(void)
{
  double x, y;
  if (rectangular == TRUE) {
      c.rect.xcoord = a.rect.xcoord + b.rect.xcoord;
      c.rect.ycoord = a.rect.ycoord + b.rect.ycoord;
  }
  else {
      x = a.polar.modulus * cos(a.polar.angle) +
          b.polar.modulus * cos(b.polar.angle);
      y = a.polar.modulus * sin(a.polar.angle) +
          b.polar.modulus * sin(b.polar.angle);
      c.polar.angle = atan(y/x);
      c.polar.modulus = sqrt(x*x + y*y);
  }
}
void get_input(void)
{
    printf("Use Rectangular or Polar coordinates? (R/P) ");
    ch = getche();
    if (ch >= 'a' && ch <= 'z') ch += 'A' - 'a';
    printf("\n\n");
    if (ch != 'P')
        rectangular = TRUE;
    else
        rectangular = FALSE;
    if (rectangular == TRUE)   {
        printf("Enter first complex number (x y coord) : ");
        scanf("%lf %lf", &(a.rect.xcoord), &(a.rect.ycoord));
        printf("\n");
        printf("Enter second complex number (x y coord) : ");
        scanf("%lf %lf", &(b.rect.xcoord), &(b.rect.ycoord));
        printf("\n");
    }
```

216 INTRODUCING C TO PASCAL PROGRAMMERS

```
        else {
            printf("Enter first complex number (modulus angle) : ");
            scanf("%lf %lf", &(a.polar.modulus), &(a.polar.angle));
            printf("\n");
            printf("Enter second complex number (modulus angle) : ");
            scanf("%lf %lf", &(b.polar.modulus), &(b.polar.angle));
            printf("\n");
        }
}
void show_results(void)
{
    if (rectangular == TRUE)
        printf("Result = (%lf) + (%lf)\n",
               c.rect.xcoord,c.polar.ycoord);
    else
        printf("Result = %lf @ %lf radians\n",
               c.polar.modulus,c.polar.angle);
}
```

Notice the important difference between using Pascal variant records and C unions. Since the C union contains nested structures you need to fully specify the variable name, unlike Pascal.

The above C version may be rewritten to use pointers to unions, instead of variables. Accessing the fields of a union uses the -> selector, just like with structures. The modified C version is

Listing 10.14

```
/* C program that demonstrates variant record types using
   the union structure                                    */
#include <stdio.h>
#include "conio.h"
#include <math.h>
#include <alloc.h>
struct rect_type {
                double xcoord;
                double ycoord;
            };
struct polar_type {
                double angle;
                double modulus;
            };
union Complex {
                struct rect_type rect;
                struct polar_type polar;
            };
enum boolean_type { TRUE, FALSE };
typedef enum boolean_type boolean;
union Complex *a, *b, *c;
boolean rectangular;
char ch;
/* declare prototype of user-defined functions */
void get_input(void), add_complex(void), show_results(void);
```

ENUMERATED AND STRUCTURED DATA TYPES 217

```c
main()
{
    /* allocate dynamic memory for pointers */
    a = (union Complex *) malloc(sizeof(union Complex));
    b = (union Complex *) malloc(sizeof(union Complex));
    c = (union Complex *) malloc(sizeof(union Complex));
    clrscr();
    printf("\t\tPROGRAM TO ADD COMPLEX NUMBERS\n\n\n");
    do {
        get_input();
        add_complex();
        show_results();
        printf("\n\n");
        printf("Add more numbers? Y/N ");
        ch = getche();
        if (ch >= 'a' && ch <= 'z') ch += 'A' - 'a';
        printf("\n\n");
    } while (ch == 'Y');
}
void add_complex(void)
{
    double x, y;
    if (rectangular == TRUE) {
        c->xcoord = a->rect.xcoord + b->rect.xcoord;
        c->ycoord = a->rect.ycoord + b->rect.ycoord;
    }
    else {
        x = a->polar.modulus * cos(a->polar.angle) +
            b->polar.modulus * cos(b->polar.angle);
        y = a->polar.modulus * sin(a->polar.angle) +
            b->polar.modulus * sin(b->polar.angle);
        c->polar.angle = atan(y/x);
        c->polar.modulus = sqrt(x*x + y*y);
    }
}
void get_input(void)
{
    printf("Use Rectangular or Polar coordinates? (R/P) ");
    ch = getche();
    if (ch >= 'a' && ch <= 'z') ch += 'A' - 'a';
    printf("\n\n");
    if (ch != 'P')
        rectangular = TRUE;
    else
        rectangular = FALSE;
    if (rectangular == TRUE)  {
        printf("Enter first complex number (x y coord) : ");
        scanf("%lf %lf", &(a->rect.xcoord), &(a->polar.ycoord));
        printf("\n");
        printf("Enter second complex number (x y coord) : ");
        scanf("%lf %lf", &(b->rect.xcoord), &(b->rect.ycoord));
        printf("\n");
    }
    else {
        printf("Enter first complex number (modulus angle) : ");
```

218 INTRODUCING C TO PASCAL PROGRAMMERS

```
            scanf("%lf %lf", &(a->polar.modulus), &(a->polar.angle));
            printf("\n");
            printf("Enter second complex number (modulus angle) : ");
            scanf("%lf %lf", &(b->polar.modulus), &(b->polar.angle));
            printf("\n");
        }
    }
    void show_results(void)
    {
        if (rectangular == TRUE)
            printf("Result = (%lf) + (%lf)\n",
                    c->rect.xcoord, c->rect.ycoord);
        else
            printf("Result = %lf @ %lf radians\n",
                    c->polar.modulus, c->polar.angle);
    }
```

Run either version of the C programs and add the following numbers:
1. (1,1) and (2,2).
2. (10 @ angle 1 radian) and (20 @ angle 1 radian).
   The screen image for the sample session is shown below:

```
        PROGRAM TO ADD COMPLEX NUMBERS
Use Rectangular or Polar coordinates? (R/P)  r
Enter first complex number (x y coord) : 1 1
Enter second complex number (x y coord) : 2 2
Result = (3.000000) + (3.000000)
Add more numbers? Y/N y
Use Rectangular or Polar coordinates? (R/P)  p
Enter first complex number (modulus angle) : 10 1
Enter second complex number (modulus angle) : 20 1
Result = 30.000000 @ 1.000000 radians
Add more numbers? Y/N n
```

FAR POINTERS

Pointers contain the addresses of the variables to which they point. In turn, addresses in the 8088 and 80x86 CPU family are divided into 64K segments. An absolute address is made up of a segment address and an offset address. Near pointers occupy two bytes and contain the offset address of the current data segment. They can access the addresses of variables *within reach*, so to speak. Thus, two-byte pointers work fine with the compact and small memory models. Other memory models require the use of the four-byte far pointers. The additional two-bytes are utilized to store the data segment address. Consequently, far pointers can access data located anywhere.

   As a novice C programmer, you will most likely start writing small C applications and use the small or compact compiler models (see Appendix E).

ENUMERATED AND STRUCTURED DATA TYPES 219

You need not be concerned too much about far pointers now. However, you still need to use them if your programs, regardless of the compiler model they use, tap into the hardware or operating system addresses. This is because such memory locations are not in the current data segment of your application. The example for using the bitfield structure also employed a far pointer to write the data to the hex location 0000:0417. Other applications may similarly set or query the hardware or the operating system. Here, I present a simple application that writes characters directly to the screen. The version for a color monitor is

Listing 10.15

```
/* C program that uses a far pointer to write directly to
   a color video screen.
*/
#include <stdio.h>
#include "conio.h"
#define COLOR_VIDEO 0xB8000000 /* address of a color monitor */
#define DISPLAY_ATTR 0x0100
main()
{
  int far *screen_ptr;
  int i;
  long attr = DISPLAY_ATTR;
  const int BYTES = 2000;
  char ch;
  while ((ch = getche()) != 'Q') {
     clrscr();
     screen_ptr = (int far *) COLOR_VIDEO;
     for (i = 0; i < BYTES; i++)
        *(screen_ptr + i) = ch | attr;
     attr += 0x0100;
  }
}
```

And the version for a monochrome monitor is

Listing 10.16

```
/* C program that uses a far pointer to write directly to
   a monochrome video screen.
*/
#include <stdio.h>
#include "conio.h"
#define COLOR_VIDEO 0xB0000000 /* address of a monochrome monitor */
#define DISPLAY_ATTR 0x0700
main()
{
  int far *screen_ptr;
  int i;
  const int BYTES = 2000;
  char ch;
```

```
while ((ch = getche()) != 'Q') {
   clrscr();
   screen_ptr = (int far *) COLOR_VIDEO;
   for (i = 0; i < BYTES; i++)
      *(screen_ptr + i) = ch | DISPLAY_ATTR;
   }
}
```

The far pointer **screen_ptr** is assigned the address of the physical screen, enabling it to display characters very quickly. The color monitor version also changes display attributes with every character you type (except the shifted [Q] key, used to exit).

CHAPTER SUMMARY

- You can rename data type identifiers using **typedef**. The general syntax is

    ```
    typedef <old type> <new type>;
    ```

    Examples are as follows:

    ```
    typedef   unsigned char     byte;
              old name          new name
    typedef struct personal_data_struct    personal_data;
                     old name                  new name
    typedef struct complex_math
              {
                 double  real;
                 double  imaginary;
              } Complex /* <- new type name */;
       typedef union two_bytes
                 {
                    char  ch[2];
                    int   one;
                 } deux_bytes /* <- new type name */;
    ```

- Enumerated data types. C enables you to define enumerated types, following the general syntax:

    ```
    enum <type> {<enumerated values list>} <enum variable list>;
    ```

    An example of a declaration is

    ```
    enum colors { black, red, blue, green, yellow, white }
              grass_color, tv_color;
    ```

    The identifiers used in enumerated lists are unique and cannot be used in another enumerated list. By default, the compiler assigns 0 to the first element in the enumerated list, 1 to the second member, and so on. You can override these assigned values by inserting "= <value>" after some or all of the enumerated list members. Explicitly assigned values must be in ascending order. An example is

    ```
    enum colors { black = 2,
    ```

```
                    red    = 5,
                    blue,  /* <- assigned 6 by compiler */
                    green, /* <- assigned 7 by compiler */
                    yellow = 25,
                    white  /* <- assigned 26 by compiler */ };
```

- Structured data types. C supports structured data types that are declared using the following general format:

```
struct <structure name>
    {
        <type 1> <field 1>;
        <type 2> <field 2>;
        <other fields>;
        <type n> <field n>;
    };
```

The fields in a C structure can be of any simple or user-defined type, including other structures. An example is

```
enum colors { black, red, blue, green, yellow, white };
struct level1
    {
        int a;
        double b;
    };
struct level2
    {
        enum colors        screen_color;
        struct level1      level1_field;
        char               name[30];
        int                index;
    };
```

Accessing fields of structures employs the dot notation that defines a data path. An example of this would be

```
struct level2 object;
object.index accesses the index field.
object.level1_field.a accesses the nested field.
object.screen_color accesses the enumerated colors field.
```

- Pointers to structures. Pointers can be used to access and manipulate the fields structures. The general format is

```
<pointer> -> <selected field>
```

If the <selected field> is made up of nested records, you access the nested fields using the dot notation, as in:

```
<pointer> -> <selected field>.<subfield1>
```

As with any other type of pointer, this class of pointer is either used to point to existing structured variables or is engaged in dynamic allocation.

- Unions. This class of structure stores its fields in the same memory location (that is, the fields overlap). The general syntax for declaring unions is

```
union <union_name>
    {
```

```
    <type 1> <field 1>;
    <type 2> <field 2>;
    <other fields>;
    <type n> <field n>;
};
```

The size of the union is equal to the size of the largest field.

The fields in a C union can be of any simple or user-defined type, including other structures or unions. An example is

```
enum colors { black, red, blue, green, yellow, white };
struct record
  {
     int a;
     double b;
  };
union variant
  {
     enum colors     screen_color;
     struct record   record_field;
     char            name[30];
     int             index;
  };
```

Accessing fields of unions employs the dot notation that defines a data path. For example:

```
union record object;
object.index accesses the index field.
object.level1_field.a accesses the nested field.
object.screen_color accesses the enumerated colors field.
```

- Pointers to unions. Pointers can be used to access and manipulate the fields in a structure. The general format is

  ```
  <pointer> -> <selected field>
  ```

  If the <selected field> is made up of nested records, you access the nested fields using the dot notation, as in:

  ```
  <pointer> -> <selected field>.<subfield1>
  ```

  As with any other type of pointer, this class of pointer is either used to point to existing union variables or is engaged in dynamic allocation.

CHAPTER

11

Advanced Functions

CHAPTER GOALS

This chapter looks at advanced features of C functions, including the following:
- Using arrays as function arguments.
- Using strings as function arguments.
- Using structures as function arguments.
- Passing addresses of arguments.
- Accessing the arguments of function **main**.
- Pointers to functions.
- Functions with a variable number of arguments.

C is a language with a small core that is extended by using function libraries. In Chapter 8 I presented functions that tackled arguments with simple types and returned simple results. Realistic and useful applications are expected to use more advanced data structures, such as arrays, strings, structures, and unions. This chapter demonstrates the power of functions in handling more advanced problems.

USING ARRAYS AS ARGUMENTS

When arrays are arguments passed to functions, you need to observe the following declarations:

224   INTRODUCING C TO PASCAL PROGRAMMERS

1. In function prototyping, an array-argument should be declared as a pointer to that array's type:

   ```
   <type> <array>[<size>];
   <function_type> <function>(<type>*, <other arguments>);
   ```

2. When the function is declared, you state the array type and its name, and use empty brackets, as shown below:

   ```
   <function_type> <function>(<type> <array>[], <other arguments>);
   ```

   A second and equally valid form employs a pointer-type declaration, as indicated below:

   ```
   <function_type> <function>(<type>* <array>, <other arguments>);
   ```

> ### Program Translation
>
> Pascal requires you to define an identifier type for the arrays that are passed as arguments to procedures and functions. C does not require such declarations.
>
> In Pascal you pass an array by reference using the VAR declaration; otherwise, you pass it by value. In C, you normally pass an array by employing a pointer to its base-address. C DOES NOT SUPPORT THE SPACE-WASTING PROCESS OF PASSING ARRAYS BY VALUE.
>
> Because of these two features in C, you can write functions that serve as general-purpose routines for array manipulation.

The following program fills an array of 100 elements with random numbers in the range of 0 to 1000. The **median** function scans its array-type parameter for the smallest and biggest values. Based on these statistics, it calculates the median value. The Pascal source code is shown below:

Listing 11.1

```
Program Pass_Array;
{ Turbo Pascal program that passes an array to a function to
  calculate the median value of the array elements. The array
  itself is generated as random numbers.                     }
CONST MAX = 100;
TYPE int_array = ARRAY [1..MAX] OF WORD;
VAR data : int_array;
    i : WORD;
FUNCTION median(x     : int_array; { input }
                count : WORD       { input }) : WORD;
VAR big, small : WORD;
    j : WORD;
BEGIN
    big := x[1];
    small := x[1];
    FOR j := 2 TO MAX DO BEGIN
        IF big < x[j] THEN big := x[j];
        IF small > x[j] THEN small := x[j]
    END;
```

```
        median := small + (big - small) div 2;
END;
BEGIN
    randomize;
    { fill array with random values }
    FOR i := 1 TO MAX DO
        data[i] := Trunc(1000 * random);
    WRITELN;
    WRITE('The median of ',MAX,' random numbers = ');
    WRITELN(median(data, MAX));
    WRITELN; WRITELN;
END.
```

I ran the program several times and obtained the following results (the results you obtain will most likely be different, since the sequence of random numbers that your runtime system generates will be different):

```
The median of 100 random numbers = 499
The median of 100 random numbers = 497
The median of 100 random numbers = 489
The median of 100 random numbers = 502
The median of 100 random numbers = 495
The median of 100 random numbers = 497
The median of 100 random numbers = 498
The median of 100 random numbers = 504
The median of 100 random numbers = 503
The median of 100 random numbers = 503
```

The C version is listed below:

Listing 11.2

```
/* C program that passes an array to a function to
   calculate the median value of the array elements. The array
   itself is generated as random numbers.                    */
#include <stdio.h>
#include "stdlib.h"
#define MAX 100
typedef unsigned int word;
typedef word int_array[MAX];
main()
{
    int_array data;
    word i;
    word median(word*, word);
    randomize();
    /* fill array with random values */
    for (i = 0; i < MAX; i++)
        data[i] = random(1000);
    printf("\n");
    printf("The median of %d random numbers = ",MAX);
    printf("%d\n\n\n", median(data, MAX));
}
word median(word x[], word count)
{
    word big = x[0], small = x[0];
```

```
    word j;
    for (j = 1; j < count; j++)   {
        if (big < x[j])   big = x[j];
        /* use pointer form */
        if (small > *(x+j))   small = *(x+j);
    }
    return (small + (big - small) / 2);
}
```
In the above C program the prototype of the function **median** is declared as:

`word median(word*, word);`

and the function heading is declared as:

`word median(word x[], word count)`

As stated earlier, no specific array size is required in declaring a parameter which is an array; hence, the **x[]** is used. The local variables **small** and **big** are both initialized to **x[0]** in the same statement where they are declared. The **median** function is called in function **main** using:

`printf("%d\n\n\n", median(data, MAX));`

Keep in mind that the identifier name **data** is a pointer to the base-address of the same array.

Another way in which the **median** function can be declared explicitly employs a pointer, as shown below:

`word median(word *x, word count)`

The statements of the **median** are rewritten to use more efficient pointers instead of array indexing. The local variables **small** and **big** are now initialized using ***x** instead of **x[0]**. Using the pointer-incrementing method, the contents of the array **x** are examined in sequence. The new C program version is shown below:

Listing 11.3

```
/* C program that passes an array to a function to
   calculate the median value of the array elements. The array
   itself is generated as random numbers. This version makes
   better use of pointers in function median.            */
#include <stdio.h>
#include "stdlib.h"
#define MAX 100
typedef unsigned int word;
main()
{
    word data[MAX];
    word i;
    word median(word*, word);
    randomize();
    /* fill array with random values */
    for (i = 0; i < MAX; i++)
        data[i] = random(1000);
    printf("\n");
    printf("The median of %d random numbers = ",MAX);
    printf("%d\n\n\n", median(data, MAX));
```

```c
}
word median(word *x, word count)
{
    word big = *x, small = *x;
    word j;
    for (j = 1; j < count; j++)   {
        x++; /* increment pointer address */
        if (big < *x)  big = *x;
        if (small > *x)  small = *x;
    }
    return (small + (big - small) / 2);
}
```

I ran the above C program version several times and obtained the following results (the results you obtain will most likely be different, due to a different sequence of random numbers that your system will generate):

```
The median of 100 random numbers = 495
The median of 100 random numbers = 495
The median of 100 random numbers = 495
The median of 100 random numbers = 501
The median of 100 random numbers = 501
The median of 100 random numbers = 501
The median of 100 random numbers = 501
The median of 100 random numbers = 501
The median of 100 random numbers = 501
The median of 100 random numbers = 501
The median of 100 random numbers = 501
```

In Pascal you have learned that most implementations do not allow functions to return advanced data types, such as arrays and records. Instead, the functions can use pointers to arrays and record structures. The majority of Pascal programmers solve this limitation by using procedures and employing array or record parameters passed by reference. The good news is that in C this limitation does not exist!

USING STRINGS AS ARGUMENTS

Since strings are arrays of characters, the rules for arrays presented in the last section also apply to them. The following program contains a function that converts lower-case characters into upper-case. The Pascal listing is shown below:

Listing 11.4

```
Program Pass_String;
{$V-}
{ Turbo Pascal program that passes a string to a function to
  return the uppercase version of the string.              }
TYPE STRING80 = STRING[80];
     STRING255 = STRING[255];
VAR strng : STRING255;
```

```
    freq : WORD;
FUNCTION uppercase(strng : STRING80) : STRING80;
VAR i : BYTE;
BEGIN
    { loop to convert each character to uppercase }
    FOR i := 1 TO Length(strng) DO
        strng[i] := UpCase(strng[i]);
    uppercase := strng;
END;
BEGIN
    REPEAT
        WRITE('Enter string : ');
        READLN(strng);
        IF strng <> '' THEN BEGIN
            WRITELN(uppercase(strng));
            WRITELN;
        END;
    UNTIL strng = '';
    WRITELN; WRITELN;
END.
```

The translated C version is shown below:

Listing 11.5

```
/* C program that passes a string to a function to
   return the uppercase version of the string.          */
#include <stdio.h>
typedef unsigned int word;
char* uppercase(char*);
main()
{
    char strng[256];
    word freq;
    do {
        printf("Enter string : ");
        gets(strng);
        if (*strng != '\0')  {
            puts(uppercase(strng));
            printf("\n");
        }
    } while (*strng != '\0');
    printf("\n\n");
}
char* uppercase(char strng[])
{
    int count = 0;
    int ascii_shift = 'A' - 'a';
    char copystr[256];
    char* strptr = copystr;
    do {
        copystr[count++] = strng[count];
    } while (strng[count] != '\0');
    copystr[count] = '\0';
    count = 0; /* reset counter variable */
```

```
    /* loop to convert each character to uppercase */
    while ( *strptr != '\0' ) {
        if ((*strptr >= 'A' && *strptr <= 'Z') ||
            (*strptr >= 'a' && *strptr <= 'z'))
           *strptr += ascii_shift;
        count++;
        strptr++;
    }
    strptr -= count;
    return strptr;
}
```

Notice the following about the above C program:

1. The function **uppercase** does not require a data type identifier that resembles STRING80 in the Pascal version.

2. The function **uppercase** is prototyped as follows:

   `char* uppercase(char*);`

   Since it takes an array of characters as its sole argument, the **char*** is used. The function result is set as **char*** because it also returns a pointer to the array of characters.

3. Despite the significant differences between implementing **uppercase** in Pascal and C, both are invoked in a similar way; in Pascal:

   `WRITELN(uppercase(strng));`

   and in C:

   `puts(uppercase(strng));`

4. The statements that make up function **uppercase** in C employ the identifier **strng** as a pointer used to scroll through the string characters. When the pointer reaches the null character it has no way of returning to (or supplying the **return** statement with) its original address. There are at least two solutions to this problem:

   - A local pointer stores the base-address of the string; then, that pointer is used in the **return** statement.

   - Employ a local variable to count the number of times the pointer has been incremented. After the while loop, decrement the string pointer address by the counter's value. This puts the string pointer back to the base-address of the string argument. The reset pointer is then returned. This is the solution used in the program to avoid altering the address of the **strng** pointer after the **uppercase** function terminates.

USING STRUCTURES AS ARGUMENTS

Structures can be passed by value or by reference to a function. In this section I discuss passing structure types by value. This process is very similar to passing simple data types to functions. The following steps should be observed:

1. Declare the structured type as global. This makes it accessible to all routines that need it. Declaring the type within **main** makes the structure visible only to **main**! You may want to use **typedef** to shorten the structure declaration, but that is left to your discretion.
2. Prototype the function using the structures in a way similar to using simple data types.
3. Declare the function with structures just like any function with simple type. The data type of the returned result may be either a simple or structured type.

The following program calculates the spatial distance between two points in space. The **coordinates** record structure is used to logically relate the three-dimensional coordinates of a point in space. The distance is calculated by the **distance** function, that accepts arguments that are record structures, and returns a floating-point result. The Pascal version is shown below:

Listing 11.6

```
Program Pass_Structure;
Uses CRT;
{$V-}
{ Turbo Pascal program that passes a record to a function to
  calculate the distance between two space coordinates.     }
TYPE coordinates = RECORD
                        X, Y, Z : REAL;
                   END;
VAR coord1, coord2 : coordinates;
FUNCTION distance(coord1, coord2 : coordinates) : REAL;
VAR delta_x, delta_y, delta_z : REAL;
BEGIN
    delta_x := coord1.X - coord2.X;
    delta_y := coord1.Y - coord2.Y;
    delta_z := coord1.Z - coord2.Z;
    distance := SQRT(delta_x * delta_x +
                     delta_y * delta_y +
                     delta_z * delta_z);
END;
BEGIN
    ClrScr;
    WITH coord1 DO BEGIN
        WRITE('Enter X-Y-Z coordinates of first object : ');
        READLN(X,Y,Z);
    END;
    WITH coord2 DO BEGIN
        WRITE('Enter X-Y-Z coordinates of second object : ');
        READLN(X,Y,Z);
    END;
    WRITE('Distance between objects = ',distance(coord1,coord2));
    WRITELN; WRITELN
END.
```

The translated C version is shown below:

Listing 11.7

```c
/* C program that passes a record to a function to
   calculate the distance between two space coordinates.   */
#include <stdio.h>
#include <math.h>
#include "conio.h"
struct coordinates_type {
                        double X;
                        double Y;
                        double Z;
                        };
typedef struct coordinates_type coordinates;
double distance(coordinates, coordinates);
main()
{
    coordinates coord1, coord2;
    clrscr();
    printf("Enter X-Y-Z coordinates of first object : ");
    scanf("%lf %lf %lf", &coord1.X, &coord1.Y, &coord1.Z);
    printf("Enter X-Y-Z coordinates of second object : ");
    scanf("%lf %lf %lf", &coord2.X, &coord2.Y, &coord2.Z);
    printf("\nDistance between objects = %lf\n\n\n",
            distance(coord1, coord2));
}
double distance(coordinates coord1, coordinates coord2)
{
    double delta_x, delta_y, delta_z;
    delta_x = coord1.X - coord2.X;
    delta_y = coord1.Y - coord2.Y;
    delta_z = coord1.Z - coord2.Z;
    return   sqrt(delta_x * delta_x +
                  delta_y * delta_y +
                  delta_z * delta_z);
}
```

The above C program closely resemblance its cousin Pascal version. The simplicity in translating the program stems from the fact that the **distance** function takes structured arguments, passed by value, and returns a simple-typed result. Thus, no pointers are needed in any referencing of data objects.

PASSING ARGUMENTS BY REFERENCE USING POINTERS

Sooner or later, you will need to write routines that alter the values of their arguments. These arguments may be simple data types or advanced ones, such as arrays, structures, and unions. The key player in this requirement is the pointer. Pointers provide a copy of the address of a data object, whether it is of a simple or advanced type. This permits the called routine to access and perform permanent changes on the actual data.

> **Programming Note**
>
> The bottom line for passing arguments to C functions is that all arguments are passed by value (i.e., a copy of the data objects to the function is submitted). To emulate passing variables by reference, you pass a copy of their address.

PASSING SIMPLE VARIABLES AND SIMPLE ARRAYS

The first example in this section illustrates two types of arguments passed by reference: a simple type and an array. The program creates an ordered array and puts it in reverse order, using the Shell-Metzner sorting method. The sorted array is displayed. The routines involved (in both the Pascal and C versions) are:

Routine Name	Arguments	Purpose
InitializeArray	arrays	Create ordered array.
SwapThem	single variables	Swap two integers.
ShellSort	arrays	Sort the array.
DisplayArray	arrays	Display array.

The Pascal listing is shown below:

Listing 11.8

```
Program Pass_and_Modify_Array;
Uses CRT;
{ Program will test the speed of sorting an integer array.
  The program will create a sorted array (in descending order)
  and then sort it in the reverse order.                      }
CONST ARRAY_SIZE = 1000;
TYPE numbers = ARRAY[1..ARRAY_SIZE] OF WORD;
VAR Ch : CHAR;
    A : numbers;
PROCEDURE InitializeArray(VAR A : numbers);
{ Procedure to initialize array }
VAR i : WORD;
BEGIN
    WRITELN('Initializing integer array');
    WRITELN;
    FOR i := 1 TO ARRAY_SIZE DO
        A[i] := ARRAY_SIZE - i;
END;
PROCEDURE SwapThem(VAR X, Y : WORD);
{ procedure to swap elements X and Y }
VAR temporary : WORD;
```

```
BEGIN
    temporary := X;
    X := Y;
    Y := temporary;
END;
PROCEDURE ShellSort(VAR A : numbers) ;
{ Procedure to perform a Shell-Metzner sorting }
VAR offset, i, j : WORD;
    sorted : BOOLEAN;
BEGIN
    offset := ARRAY_SIZE;
    WHILE offset > 1 DO BEGIN
        offset := offset DIV 2;
        REPEAT
            sorted := TRUE;
            FOR j := 1 TO (ARRAY_SIZE - offset) DO BEGIN
                i := j + offset;
                IF A[i] < A[j] THEN BEGIN
                    SwapThem(A[i],A[j]);
                    sorted := FALSE;
                END;
            END; { FOR j }
        UNTIL sorted;
    END; { End of while-loop }
END;
PROCEDURE DisplayArray(VAR A : numbers);
{ Display array members }
VAR i : WORD;
BEGIN
    FOR i := 1 TO ARRAY_SIZE DO
        WRITE(A[i]:4);
    WRITELN
END;
BEGIN { Main }
    InitializeArray(A);
    WRITELN('Beginning to sort press <cr>');
    Ch := ReadKey; WRITELN;
    ShellSort(A);
    WRITELN('Finished sorting!');
    DisplayArray(A);
END.
```

The C version is listed below:

Listing 11.9

```
/*
    Program will test the speed of sorting an integer array.
    The program will create a sorted array (in descending order)
    and then sort it in the reverse order.
*/
#include <stdio.h>
#include "conio.h"
enum booleans { TRUE, FALSE };
```

```c
typedef enum booleans boolean;
typedef unsigned char byte;
typedef unsigned int word;
#define ARRAY_SIZE 1000
/* define 'numbers' as an array-type identifier */
typedef word numbers[ARRAY_SIZE];
/* declare prototype of void functions used */
void initializearray(int*);
void swapthem(int*, int*);
void shellsort(int*);
void displayarray(int*);
main()
{
    numbers A;
    initializearray(A);
    printf("Beginning to sort press <cr>");
    (void) getche(); printf("\n");
    shellsort(A);
    puts("Finished sorting!");
    displayarray(A);
}
void initializearray(int *A)
/* routine to initialize array */
{
    int i;
    puts("Initializing integer array");
    for (i = 0 ; i < ARRAY_SIZE; i++)
        *(A++) = ARRAY_SIZE - i;
}
void swapthem(int *x, int *y)
/* routine that swaps elements x and y */
{
    int temporary = *x;
    *x = *y;
    *y = temporary;
}
void shellsort(int *A)
/* routine to perform a Shell-Metzner sorting */
{
    int offset, i, j;
    boolean sorted;
    offset = ARRAY_SIZE;
    while (offset > 1)   {
        offset /= 2;
        do {
            sorted = TRUE;
            for (j = 0; j < (ARRAY_SIZE - offset); j++)   {
                i = j + offset;
                if (*(A+i) < *(A+j))   {
                    swapthem((A+i),(A+j));
                    sorted = FALSE;
                }
            }
        } while (sorted == FALSE);
```

```
    }
}
void displayarray(int *A)
/* Display array members */
{
    int i;
    for (i = 0; i < ARRAY_SIZE; i++)
        printf("%4d", *(A+i));
    printf("\n");
}
```

The Pascal parameter list, which appears in three of the four routines, is (VAR A : numbers). This parameter list is translated into (int *A) in C.

The above parameter supplies a copy of the base-address of the array to the routines. This empowers the routines to access the memory location where the original arrays are stored and manipulate them. The address of the pointer in these routines need not be reset to its original value, since it is only a copy. Consider the for-loop in the routine **initializearray**:

```
for (i = 0 ; i < ARRAY_SIZE; i++)
    *(A++) = ARRAY_SIZE - i;
```

The array pointer is incremented to access the array elements sequentially. Notice that the array pointer is not reset to point to the same address it had when the routine was invoked. You could reset the address of the pointer using:

```
A -= ARRAY_SIZE;
```

but that would just be a waste of code, because a copy of the address is being passed to the functions.

The parameter list of the Pascal procedure **SwapThem**:

(VAR X, Y : WORD)

is converted into the following form in C:

(int *x, int *y)

This passes the copies of the addresses of the arguments. With this information at hand, the routine uses the following code lines to perform a swap of the original arguments:

```
{
    int temporary = *x;
    *x = *y;
    *y = temporary;
}
```

Notice that the local identifier **temporary** is declared as an integer variable and not as a pointer. It serves as a location to temporarily store the swapped data.

Examine the above listing and compare the function prototyping with the corresponding declarations:

Function Prototype	Function Declaration
`void initializearray(int*);`	`void initializearray(int *A)`
`void swapthem(int*, int*);`	`void swapthem(int *x, int *y)`
`void shellsort(int*);`	`void shellsort(int *A)`
`void displayarray(int*);`	`void displayarray(int *A)`

PASSING STRINGS

The second example is a modified version of the **uppercase** function presented earlier. In this version, the procedure **uppercase** processes as a string-typed parameter that is passed by reference. The Pascal version uses the VAR declaration to alter the string argument, while the C version uses a pointer to the string for the same purpose. The program prompts you to enter a string and displays it with lower-case characters converted into upper-case. The Pascal listing is shown below:

Listing 11.10

```
Program Pass_and_Modify_String;
{$V-}
{ Turbo Pascal program that passes a string to a procedure to
  return the uppercase version of the string. The string is
  passed by reference.                                        }
TYPE STRING80 = STRING[80];
     STRING255 = STRING[255];
VAR strng : STRING80;
PROCEDURE uppercase(VAR strng : STRING80 { in/out });
VAR i : BYTE;
BEGIN
    { loop to convert each character to uppercase }
    FOR i := 1 TO Length(strng) DO
        strng[i] := UpCase(strng[i]);
END;
BEGIN
   REPEAT
       WRITE('Enter string : ');
       READLN(strng);
       IF strng <> '' THEN BEGIN
           uppercase(strng);
           WRITELN(strng);
           WRITELN;
       END;
   UNTIL strng = '';
   WRITELN; WRITELN;
END.
```

The C version is presented below:

Listing 11.11

```c
/* C program that passes a string to a procedure to
   return the uppercase version of the string. The string is
   passed by reference.
 */
#include <stdio.h>
void uppercase(char*);
main()
{
    char dummy[81], *strng = dummy;
    do {
        printf("Enter string : ");
        gets(strng);
        if (*strng != '\0')  {
            uppercase(strng);
            puts(strng);
            printf("\n");
        }
    } while (*strng != '\0');
    printf("\n\n");
}
void uppercase(char *strng)
{
    int ascii_shift = 'A' - 'a';
    /* loop to convert each character to uppercase */
    while ( *strng != '\0')
        if (*strng >= 'a' && *strng <= 'z')
            *(strng++) += ascii_shift;
        else
            strng++;
}
```

The (VAR strng : STRING80) parameter list is translated into (char *strng). It is worthwhile to point out that the Pascal version of the procedure is general-purpose thanks only to the {$V-} directive. Otherwise, the Pascal procedure processes strings that only have the type STRING80. Compare this with the ability of C to easily create a general-purpose routine with no ifs or buts!

The above example illustrates the feature of C where copies of pointer addresses are passed. The pointer **strng** is sequentially incremented to scroll through the string characters and is not reset at the end to its original address. Yet, the puts(strng) statement that follows is able to display the converted string correctly. This would not be possible if the original pointer address was permanently altered by the routine.

PASSING STRUCTURES

The next program illustrates passing structures by reference to routines. In Pascal and C this permits routines to alter the value of the data in the

238 INTRODUCING C TO PASCAL PROGRAMMERS

structures. The program fills an array of 100 elements with random numbers and calculates the mean and standard deviation of the data in the array. The program uses a structure that has three floating-typed fields: mean, standard deviation, and degrees of freedom (= number of data points - 1). These statistical calculations are carried out in the **basic_stat** routine, to which the above structure is passed by reference. The results are returned through the fields of the structures. The Pascal program is shown below:

Listing 11.12

```
Program Basic_Statistics;
Uses CRT;
{ Turbo Pascal program that passes a structure by reference to
  alter its value. This program calculates the mean and standard
  deviation of a randomly generated array.                       }
CONST MAX = 100;
TYPE bastat = RECORD
                mean, sdev, degree_freedom : REAL;
              END;
     real_array = ARRAY [1..MAX] OF REAL;
VAR data : real_array;
    i : WORD;
    statistics : bastat;
PROCEDURE basic_stat (VAR x     : real_array; { input  }
                          count : WORD;       { input  }
                      VAR stat  : bastat      { output });
VAR sum, sumx, sumxx : REAL;
    j : WORD;
BEGIN
    { initialize statistical summations }
    sum := count;
    sumx := 0.0;
    sumxx := 0.0;
    FOR j := 1 TO MAX DO BEGIN
        sumx := sumx + x[j];
        sumxx := sumxx + x[j] * x[j];
    END;
    WITH stat DO BEGIN
        mean := sumx / sum;
        sdev := sqrt((sumxx - sumx * sumx / sum) / (sum - 1));
        degree_freedom := sum - 1.0;
    END;
END;
BEGIN
    ClrScr;
    randomize;
    FOR i := 1 TO MAX DO
        data[i] := random;
    basic_stat(data, MAX, statistics);
    WITH statistics DO BEGIN
        WRITELN;
        WRITELN('Mean = ',mean); WRITELN;
        WRITELN('Sdev = ',sdev); WRITELN;
```

ADVANCED FUNCTIONS   239

```
        WRITELN('Df = ',degree_freedom); WRITELN;
    END;
END.
```

Run the program twice. No user input is required. The following is a screen image displaying the results I obtained:

```
Mean =   5.58287928970458E-0001
Sdev =   2.95272133083472E-0001
Df   =   9.90000000000000E+0001
Mean =   4.91209929315119E-0001
Sdev =   2.86683952013391E-0001
Df   =   9.90000000000000E+0001
```

The translated C version is listed below:

Listing 11.13

```c
/* C program that passes a structure by reference to
   alter its value. This program calculates the mean and standard
   deviation of a randomly generated array.                      */
#include <stdio.h>
#include <stdlib.h>
#include "math.h"
#include "conio.h"
#define MAX 100
struct bastat_type {
                double mean;
                double sdev;
                double degree_freedom;
            };
typedef struct bastat_type bastat;
typedef unsigned int word;
void basic_stat(double*, word, bastat*);
main()
{
    double data[MAX];
    word i;
    bastat statistics;
    clrscr();
    randomize();
    for (i = 0; i < MAX; i++)
        data[i] = (double) random(100);
    basic_stat(data, MAX, &statistics);
    printf("\n");
    printf("Mean = %lf\n\n", statistics.mean);
    printf("Sdev = %lf\n\n", statistics.sdev);
    printf("Df   = %lf\n\n", statistics.degree_freedom);
}
void basic_stat(double *x, word count, bastat* stat)
{
    double sum = count, sumx = 0.0L, sumxx = 0.0L;
    word j;
    for (j = 0; j < count; j++)   {
```

```
            sumx += *x;
            sumxx += *x * *x;
            x++;
     }
     stat->mean = sumx / sum;
     stat->sdev = sqrt((sumxx - sumx * sumx / sum) / (sum - 1));
     stat->degree_freedom = sum - 1.0;
}
```

The Pascal **bastat** record:

```
bastat = RECORD
    mean, sdev, degree_freedom : REAL;
END;
```

is converted into the following C structure:

```
struct bastat_type {
            double mean;
            double sdev;
            double degree_freedom;
            };
typedef struct bastat_type bastat;
```

The Pascal **basic_stat** procedure:

```
PROCEDURE basic_stat(VAR x      : real_array;  { input  }
                         count  : WORD;        { input  }
                     VAR stat   : bastat       { output });
```

is translated into:

```
void basic_stat(double *x, word count, bastat* stat)
```

Notice that a pointer to the **double** type is utilized to pass the base-address of the array **x** in the C version. In addition, the pointer of the **bastat** type is used to pass a copy of the structure's address. Also, note that accessing the fields of the **bastat** structure is performed using the -> pointer access operator. The three assignment statements involving the fields of **bastat** enable the program to assign the results of the expressions to the address of the fields. When the **basic_stat** function exits, the changes made to the fields of the structured argument remain in effect.

Run the program twice. No user input is required. The following is a screen image displaying the results I obtained:

```
Mean  = 46.220000
Sdev  = 28.072266
Df    = 99.000000
Mean  = 51.430000
Sdev  = 29.209883
Df    = 99.000000
```

PASSING NUMERIC MATRICES

Two-dimensional arrays, or matrices, are popular data structures. Numeric matrices are used in applications that are intensive in number crunching, such as statistical programs, engineering design software and other scientific application using numerical analysis. While C is not primarily intended for number crunching (like FORTRAN is), matrices of characters are important: arrays of strings can be regarded as such. I will first discuss passing numeric matrices by reference to routines. This enables you to focus on the characteristics of handling matrices in general without worrying about some of the peculiar properties of strings in C.

The following program is based on a Pascal benchmark program that I use in reviewing different Pascal compilers. The program creates a matrix with 20 rows and 20 columns. Each nondiagonal elements is assigned a 1, while every diagonal member is assigned a 2. The matrix is inverted and its determinant is also evaluated. The program I present creates and inverts the matrix using separate routines. This dictates that the matrix-typed variable be passed by value. I have elected not to display the inverted matrix, although you can insert a few code lines to perform that task. Instead, my program displays the determinant value and compares it with the expected value of 21. The Pascal code is shown below:

Listing 11.14

```
PROGRAM MTINVERT;
{ Program to test speed of floating point matrix inversion. }
{ The program will form a matrix with ones in every member, }
{ except the diagonals, which will have values of 2.        }
CONST MAX = 20;
TYPE MATRIX = ARRAY[1..MAX,1..MAX] OF REAL;
VAR A : MATRIX;
    determinant : REAL;
    n : INTEGER;
PROCEDURE Create_Mat(VAR X : MATRIX; { output }
                     VAR n : INTEGER { in/out });
  VAR j, k : INTEGER;
  BEGIN
    IF (n < 0) OR (n > MAX) THEN n := MAX;
    { Creating test matrix }
    FOR j := 1 TO n DO BEGIN
      FOR k := 1 TO n DO
          X[j,k] := 1.0;
        X[j,j] := 2.0;
    END;
END; { Create_Mat }
PROCEDURE Invert_Mat(VAR X    : MATRIX;  { in/out }
                         n    : INTEGER; { input  }
                     VAR det  : REAL     { output });
  VAR j, k, l : INTEGER;
      pivot, tempo : REAL;
  BEGIN
    det := 1.0;
    IF (n > MAX) OR (n < 2) THEN EXIT;
    FOR j := 1 TO n DO BEGIN
        pivot := X[j,j];
        det := det * pivot;
        X[j,j] := 1.0;
```

```
        FOR k := 1 TO n DO
            X[j,k] := X[j,k] / pivot;
        FOR k := 1 TO n DO
            IF k <> j THEN BEGIN
                tempo := X[k,j];
                X[k,j] := 0.0;
                FOR l := 1 TO n DO
                    X[k,l] := X[k,l] - X[j,l] * tempo;
            END;
    END; { End of outer for-loop }
END; { Invert_Mat }
BEGIN
  WRITELN('Starting matrix inversion');
  n := MAX;
  Create_Mat(A, n);
  Invert_Mat(A, n, determinant);
  WRITELN(^G'DONE');
  WRITELN;
  WRITE('Determinant = ',determinant:3, ' ?=? ', MAX+1);
  WRITELN; WRITELN;
END.
```

The translated C program is shown below:

Listing 11.15

```c
/* Program to test speed of floating point matrix inversion. */
/* The program will form a matrix with ones in every member, */
/* except the diagonals, which will have values of 2.        */
#include <stdio.h>
#define MAX 20
typedef double varmat[][MAX];
/* define 'matrix' as an array-type identifier */
typedef double matrix[MAX][MAX];
void create_mat(double[][], int*);
void invert_mat(double[][], int, double*);
main()
{
  matrix A;
  double determinant;
  int n;
  printf("\nStarting matrix inversion\n");
  n = MAX;
  create_mat(A, &n);
  invert_mat(A, n, &determinant);
  printf("\n\007DONE");
  printf("\nDeterminant = %31f ?=? %d\n\n",determinant,MAX+1);
}
void create_mat(varmat x, int* n)
{
  int j, k;
  if (*n < 0 || *n > MAX)  *n = MAX;
  printf("Matrix size = %d\n", *n);
  /* Creating test matrix */
```

```c
    for (j = 0; j < *n; j++) {
        for (k = 0; k < *n; k++)
            *(*(x+j)+k) = 1.0;
        *(*(x+j)+j) = 2.0;
    }
} /* create_mat */
void invert_mat(varmat x, int n, double *det)
{
    int j, k, l;
    double pivot, tempo;
    *det = 1.0;
    if (n > MAX || n < 2) exit(0);
    for (j = 0; j < n; j++) {
        pivot = *(*(x+j)+j);
        *det *= pivot;
        *(*(x+j)+j) = 1.0;
        for (k = 0; k < n; k++)
            *(*(x+j)+k) /= pivot;
        for (k = 0; k < n; k++)
            if (k != j) {
                tempo = *(*(x+k)+j);
                *(*(x+k)+j) = 0.0;
                for (l = 0; l < n; l++)
                    *(*(x+k)+l) = *(*(x+k)+l) -
                                  *(*(x+j)+l) * tempo;
            }
    } /* End of outer for-loop */
} /* invert_mat */
```

In comparing the two versions, notice the following:

1. The Pascal program needs to define a type identifier for the matrix types:

   TYPE MATRIX = ARRAY[1..MAX,1..MAX] OF REAL;

   while C is able to declare the **varmat** and **matrix** types:

   typedef double varmat[][MAX];
   typedef double matrix[MAX][MAX];

   The **varmat** is an open matrix type, while **matrix** is a fixed matrix type.

2. The Pascal MATRIX type is used to declare the matrix-typed parameters:

   PROCEDURE Create_Mat(VAR X : MATRIX; { output }
                        VAR n : INTEGER { in/out });

   and

   PROCEDURE Invert_Mat(VAR X   : MATRIX; { in/out }
                        n   : INTEGER; { input }
                        VAR det : REAL   { output });

   This means that these routines work only with the MATRIX type, and do not accept matrices of different sizes or types. Compare this with the C declarations of the translated routines:

   void create_mat(varmat x, int* n)

   and,

   void invert_mat(varmat x, int n, double *det)

The above C routines use the variable matrix **varmat x** (equivalent to double **x[]MAX]**) to declare the matrix-typed parameters. The first set of brackets of **varmat** are empty, while the second set encloses a constant. If you remove the constants from the second set in the definition of **varmat** and attempt to recompile, the compiler flags an error. It informs you that it has no idea about the size of the array. Why? Much of the answer comes from looking at how pointers-to-pointers are used to access the matrix elements. For example, consider the nested for loops employed in creating the matrix:

```
for (j = 0; j < *n; j++)   {
    for (k = 0; k < *n; k++)
        *(*(x+j)+k) = 1.0;
    *(*(x+j)+j) = 2.0;
}
```

Remember that "*(x+j)" is a pointer to an array of rows, and that enclosing it in "*( )+k)" enables the program to select the k'th element, **x[j][k]**. The C program needs to have one dimension fixed to know the offset used in traversing the array of rows. This information enables pointer arithmetic to properly work with arrays of rows. For example, *x points to the first element of row 0, *(x+1) points to the first element of row 1, and so on. Thus, the size of each row must be known in order for "*(x+j)" to skip entire rows and point correctly to the j'th row.

Program Note

C enables you to write general-purpose routines that manipulate matrices less rigidly than Pascal.

3. Compare the declaration of the two C routines with their prototype declarations:

```
void create_mat(double[][], int*);
void invert_mat(double[][], int, double*);
```

The above declarations use empty brackets for all of the dimensions of the array.

PASSING POINTERS TO DYNAMIC STRUCTURES

Binary trees are among the most popular dynamic data structures. They enable you to build an ordered collection of data. The basic building block of a binary tree is a node. Each node contains one field as a sorting key, possibly some additional data fields, and two pointers to link up with other tree nodes. While binary trees can be implemented using arrays, it is seldom done (unless you are using a language like BASIC that does not support dynamic variables). Instead, dynamic memory allocation is utilized to create the space for every node and establish the links with other nodes as they are needed. For more details on binary trees consult a data structure text book.

ADVANCED FUNCTIONS   **245**

The following program contains routines to perform rather simple binary tree manipulation. The pointers to the dynamic tree structures are passed by reference. The program fills an array with random data and uses the data to build a binary tree. This places the data in the tree in an ordered fashion. By traversing the tree nodes recursively, you can display (or access) the data in an ordered fashion. This example shows some interesting differences between Pascal and C in certain aspects of tree manipulation. The code for the Pascal version is shown below:

Listing 11.16

```
PROGRAM BinTreePtr;
{
   Turbo Pascal program that creates an array of integers using
   random numbers. The array is stored in a binary tree.
   The tree is traversed to obtain an ordered list of the array
   elements.
}
Uses CRT;
CONST SIZE = 20;
TYPE BinTreePtr =  ^Node;
     Node = RECORD
               Value : WORD;
               Left, Right : BinTreePtr;
            END;
     NumArray = ARRAY [1..SIZE] OF WORD;
VAR Numbers : NumArray;
    I, Num : WORD;
    TreeRoot : BinTreePtr;
    dummy : CHAR;
PROCEDURE Create(VAR X   : NumArray;  { output }
                     Num : WORD       { in/out });
{ Create array using random numbers }
VAR J : WORD;
BEGIN
    IF (Num < 0) OR (Num > SIZE) THEN Num := SIZE;
    Randomize;
    FOR J := 1 TO Num DO
        X[J] := Trunc(Random(1000));
END;
PROCEDURE Insert(VAR Root : BinTreePtr; Item : WORD);
{ Recursive insertion of an element in the binary tree }
BEGIN
    IF Root = NIL THEN BEGIN
        NEW(Root);
        Root^.Value := Item;
        Root^.Left := NIL;
        Root^.Right := NIL
    END
    ELSE
        WITH Root^ DO
            IF Item < Value THEN Insert(Left,Item)
                            ELSE Insert(Right,Item);
END;
```

```pascal
PROCEDURE Display_Sort(VAR Root : BinTreePtr);
{ Recursively visit the binary tree nodes }
BEGIN
    IF Root^.Left <> NIL THEN Display_Sort(Root^.Left);
    WRITELN(Root^.Value);
    IF Root^.Right <> NIL THEN Display_Sort(Root^.Right);
END;
BEGIN { MAIN }
    Num := SIZE;
    Create(Numbers, Num);
    WRITE('Created array ....');
    { Building the binary tree }
    TreeRoot := NIL;
    FOR I := 1 TO SIZE DO
        Insert(TreeRoot,Numbers[I]);
    WRITELN('Created Tree');
    WRITELN('Sorted array of number is');
    Display_Sort(TreeRoot);
END.
```

The converted C version is listed below:

Listing 11.17

```c
/* C program that creates an array of integers using random
   numbers. The array is stored in a binary tree. The tree
   is traversed to obtain an ordered list of the array elements
*/
#include <stdio.h>
#include <stdlib.h>
#define ARRAY_SIZE 20
typedef unsigned int word;
typedef struct bintreeptr node;
typedef struct bintreeptr* nodeptr;
struct bintreeptr
       {
          word value;
          nodeptr left;
          nodeptr right;
       };
/* define array-type identifier */
typedef word num_array[ARRAY_SIZE];
void create(word*, word*);
nodeptr insert(nodeptr, word);
void display_sort(nodeptr);
main()
{
    num_array numbers;
    word i, num = ARRAY_SIZE;
    nodeptr treeroot = NULL;
    create(numbers, &num);
    printf("Created array ....");
    /* Building the binary tree */
    for (i = 0; i < num; i++)
```

```
        treeroot = insert(treeroot,numbers[i]);
     printf("Created Tree");
     printf("\nSorted array of number is\n");
     display_sort(treeroot);
}
void create(word* x, word *num)
/* Create array using random numbers */
{
   word j;
   if (*num < 1 || *num > ARRAY_SIZE)   *num = ARRAY_SIZE;
   randomize();
   for (j = 0; j < *num; j++)
       *(x + j) = random(1000);
}
nodeptr insert(nodeptr root, word item)
/* Recursively insert element in binary tree */
{
    if (root == NULL)  {
        root = (node *) malloc(sizeof(node));
        root->value = item;
        root->left = NULL;
        root->right = NULL;
    }
    else {
        if (item < root->value)
            root->left = insert(root->left,item);
        else
            root->right = insert(root->right,item);
    }
    return root;
}
void display_sort(nodeptr root)
/* Recursively visit the binary tree nodes */
{
    if (root->left != NULL)  display_sort(root->left);
    printf("\n %d",root->value);
    if (root->right != NULL) display_sort(root->right);
}
```

Looking at the above C listing, you notice that the **typedef** was used to define the **node** and **nodeptr** before the actual structure definition. In addition, the **nodeptr** type is used in the structure definition.

In comparing the Pascal and C code, notice the following difference in the routine declarations:

```
PROCEDURE Insert(VAR Root : BinTreePtr; Item : WORD);
 nodeptr insert(nodeptr root, word item)
```

The C version of the insertion routine is a function that returns a pointer type, while the Pascal version is merely a procedure. This is needed to update the address of the new binary tree nodes. Also, notice in the **main** function the binary tree is built using calls to function **insert**. The **treeroot** is both a function argument and the recipient of the function's result.

248 INTRODUCING C TO PASCAL PROGRAMMERS

```c
/* Building the binary tree */
for (i = 0; i < num; i++)
    treeroot = insert(treeroot,numbers[i]);
```

Run the above program and observe the output, which consists of numbers sorted in ascending order. A screen image for a sample session is shown below:

```
Created array ..Created Tree
Sorted array of number is
 44
 144
 200
 264
 320
 329
 363
 413
 488
 507
 512
 543
 751
 923
 924
 945
 947
 958
 985
 999
```

The following modification of the above program permits you to enter strings from the keyboard, store them in a binary tree, and then retrieve them sorted alphabetically. The Pascal listing is

Listing 11.18

```pascal
PROGRAM BinTreePtr2;
Uses CRT;
CONST SIZE = 20;
TYPE STRING80 = STRING[80];
     BinTreePtr =  ^Node;
     Node = RECORD
                Value : STRING80;
                Left, Right : BinTreePtr;
            END;
     StrArray = ARRAY [1..SIZE] OF STRING80;
VAR Strings : StrArray;
    I, Num : WORD;
    TreeRoot : BinTreePtr;
PROCEDURE GetData(VAR X   : StrArray; { output }
                  Num : WORD      { in/out });
{ GetData array using random numbers }
VAR J : WORD;
BEGIN
```

ADVANCED FUNCTIONS   249

```
        IF (Num < 0) OR (Num > SIZE) THEN Num := SIZE;
        FOR J := 1 TO Num DO BEGIN
            WRITE('Enter string # ',J, ' : ');
            READLN(X[J]);
        END;
END;
PROCEDURE Insert(VAR Root : BinTreePtr; Item : STRING80);
{ Insert element in binary-tree }
BEGIN
    IF Root = NIL THEN BEGIN
        NEW(Root);
        Root^.Value := Item;
        Root^.Left := NIL;
        Root^.Right := NIL
    END
    ELSE
        WITH Root^ DO
            IF Item < Value THEN Insert(Left,Item)
                            ELSE Insert(Right,Item);
END;
PROCEDURE Display_Sort(VAR Root : BinTreePtr);
{ Visit the binary tree nodes recursively }
BEGIN
    IF Root^.Left <> NIL THEN Display_Sort(Root^.Left);
    WRITELN(Root^.Value);
    IF Root^.Right <> NIL THEN Display_Sort(Root^.Right);
END;
BEGIN { MAIN }
    Num := SIZE;
    GetData(Strings, Num);
    { Building the binary tree }
    TreeRoot := NIL;
    FOR I := 1 TO SIZE DO
        Insert(TreeRoot,Strings[I]);
    WRITELN('Sorted array is');
    Display_Sort(TreeRoot);
END.
```

The corresponding C version is shown below:

Listing 11.19

```c
/* C program that sorts an array of strings using a binary
   tree structure.
*/
#include <stdio.h>
#include <stdlib.h>
#include <alloc.h>
#define ARRAY_SIZE 5
#define STRING80 81
typedef unsigned int word;
typedef struct bintreeptr node;
typedef struct bintreeptr* nodeptr;
struct bintreeptr
```

250 INTRODUCING C TO PASCAL PROGRAMMERS

```c
        {
            char* value;
            nodeptr left;
            nodeptr right;
        };
typedef char strarray[ARRAY_SIZE][STRING80];
void getdata(char[][], word*);
nodeptr insert(nodeptr, char*);
void display_sort(nodeptr);
main()
{
    strarray strings;
    word i, num = ARRAY_SIZE;
    nodeptr treeroot = NULL;
    /* get array of strings */
    getdata(strings, &num);
    /* Building the binary tree */
    for (i = 0; i < num; i++)
        treeroot = insert(treeroot,strings[i]);
    printf("\nSorted array is\n");
    display_sort(treeroot);
}
void getdata(char x[][STRING80], word *num)
/* read array of strings */
{
    word j;
    if (*num < 1 || *num > ARRAY_SIZE) *num = ARRAY_SIZE;
    for (j = 0; j < *num; j++) {
        printf("Enter string %d : ",j+1);
        gets(*(x + j));
    }
}
nodeptr insert(nodeptr root, char* item)
/* Insert element in binary-tree */
{
    if (root == NULL)   {
        root = (node *) malloc(sizeof(node));
        root->value = item;
        root->left = NULL;
        root->right = NULL;
    }
    else {
        if (strcmp(item, root->value) < 0)
            root->left = insert(root->left,item);
        else
            root->right = insert(root->right,item);
    }
    return root;
}
void display_sort(nodeptr root)
/* Visit the binary tree nodes recursively */
{
    if (root->left != NULL)  display_sort(root->left);
    printf("\n %s",root->value);
    if (root->right != NULL) display_sort(root->right);
}
```

ADVANCED FUNCTIONS

Both programs are adapted from their previous versions by converting numeric data stored in the nodes into strings. The conversion of the C program involves more work to handle strings. The **getdata** routine uses a character matrix to obtain the array of strings. They are passed as arrays with [][STRING80] subscripts, while single strings are passed using pointers to characters. The **getdata** routine obtains the array of strings from the keyboard using the following for loop:

```
for (j = 0; j < *num; j++) {
    printf("Enter string %d : ",j+1);
    gets(*(x + j)); /* read the j'th string */
```

Run the above program and enter five strings. A screen image for a sample session is shown below. The strings typed are names of American states:

```
Enter string 1 : Virginia
Enter string 2 : Maryland
Enter string 3 : California
Enter string 4 : Alabama
Enter string 5 : Alaska
Sorted array is
 Alabama
 Alaska
 California
 Maryland
 Virginia
```

MORE ARRAY SORTING

I am seizing this opportunity of dealing with the topic of sorting to present an implementation of the popular recursive QuickSort method. The next program presents an additional exercise in developing C routines for useful algorithms. The program fills an array with random numbers, sorts them using the QuickSort algorithm, and then displays the sorted array. The Pascal listing is shown below:

Listing 11.20

```
PROGRAM QSort;
{ An array is filled with random numbers and sorted using
  the recursive QuickSort method.                        }
CONST ARRAY_SIZE = 20;
TYPE Numbers = ARRAY[1..ARRAY_SIZE] OF WORD;
VAR Num : WORD;
    A : Numbers;
PROCEDURE InitializeArray(VAR X   : Numbers; { output }
                         VAR Num : WORD     { output });
{ Procedure to initialize array }
VAR I : WORD;
BEGIN
    IF (Num < 1) OR (Num > ARRAY_SIZE) THEN Num := ARRAY_SIZE;
    randomize;
```

252 INTRODUCING C TO PASCAL PROGRAMMERS

```pascal
        FOR I := 1 TO Num DO
            A[I] := Trunc(random(1000));
    END;
    PROCEDURE QuickSort(VAR X   : Numbers; { output }
                            Num : WORD     { output });
    { Procedure to perform a QuickSort }
    PROCEDURE Sort(Left, Right : WORD);
    VAR i, j : WORD;
        Data1, Data2 : WORD;
    BEGIN
        i := Left; j := Right;
        Data1 := X[(Left + Right) DIV 2];
        REPEAT
            WHILE X[i] < Data1 DO i := i + 1;
            WHILE Data1 < X[j] DO j := j - 1;
            IF i <= j THEN BEGIN
                Data2 := X[i]; X[i] := X[j]; X[j] := Data2;
                i := i + 1; j := j - 1
            END;
        UNTIL i > j;
        IF Left < j   THEN Sort(Left,j);
        IF i < Right THEN Sort(i,Right);
    END;
    BEGIN { QuickSort }
        Sort(1, Num);
    END;
    PROCEDURE DisplayArray(VAR X    : Numbers; { input }
                            Num : WORD     { input });
    { Display array members }
    VAR I : WORD;
    BEGIN
        FOR I := 1 TO Num DO BEGIN
            WRITE(X[I]:3);
            WRITE('  ');
        END; { FOR I }
        WRITELN;
    END;
    BEGIN { Main }
        Num := ARRAY_SIZE;
        InitializeArray(A, Num);
        Quicksort(A, Num);
        DisplayArray(A, Num);
        WRITELN;
        WRITELN('Finished sorting!');
    END.
```

The converted C version is shown below:

Listing 11.21

```c
/*
    An array is filled with random numbers and sorted using
    the recursive QuickSort method.
*/
#include <stdio.h>
#include <stdlib.h>
```

ADVANCED FUNCTIONS 253

```c
#define ARRAY_SIZE 20
typedef unsigned int word;
/* declare function prototypes */
void initializearray(word*, word*);
void quicksort(word*, word);
void displayarray(word*, word);
main()
{
    word num = ARRAY_SIZE;
    word A[ARRAY_SIZE];
    initializearray(A, &num);
    quicksort(A, num);
    displayarray(A, num);
    printf("\nFinished sorting!\n");
}
void initializearray(word* x, word* num)
/* routine to initialize array */
{
  word i;
  if (*num < 1 || *num > ARRAY_SIZE) *num = ARRAY_SIZE;
  randomize();
  for (i = 0; i < *num; i++)
      *(x++) = random(1000);
}
void sort(word* x, word left, word right)
/* workhorse routine for the QuickSort method */
{
    word i, j;
    word data1, data2;
    i = left; j = right;
    data1 = *( x + (left + right) / 2);
    do {
        while (*(x+i) < data1)   i++;
        while (data1 < *(x+j))   j--;
        if (i <= j) {
            data2 = *(x+i); *(x+i) = *(x+j); *(x+j) = data2;
            i++; j--;
        }
    } while (i <= j);
    if (left < j)  sort(x, left, j);
    if (i < right) sort(x, i, right);
}
void quicksort(word* x, word num)
/* routine to perform a QuickSort */
{
    sort(x, 0, num-1);
}
void displayarray(word* x, word num)
/* Display array members */
{
    word i;
    for (i = 0; i < num; i++)
        printf("%3d  ",*(x+i));
    printf("\n");
}
```

The most important difference between the Pascal and C versions is the conversion of routine **sort**. In Pascal, **sort** is a nested routine in procedure **QuickSort**. Since C does not support such overhead-consuming nested routines, the C version of **sort** must undergo the following changes:

1. The entire routine must be placed outside routine **quicksort**.
2. The parameter list must also contain the base-address of the sorted array. Otherwise, **sort** has no way of accessing the sorted array in its current implementation. If the array is made global (a no-no in the mind of many experienced C programmers), the parameter list of **sort** needs no change. The declaration of the **sort** function is written as:

```
void sort(word* x, word left, word right)
```

Consequently, the call to **sort** issued inside function **quicksort** must add the identifier **x** (the name of the array) as its first argument.

Another popular algorithm for the internal sorting of arrays is the Shell-Metzner method. The following program serves two purposes: first, its shows an implementation of the Shell method in C, and secondly, it illustrates some screen control operations. The program creates 20 strings of random lengths. Each string is between 1 and 20 characters long and is filled with the ASCII code 220. When these strings are displayed, they give the effect of a histogram plotted against the left edge of the screen. The program visually sorts the strings and offers you the choice of three visual speeds: slow, medium, and fast. During the sorting process two text indicators are displayed to point to the strings being compared. If swapping is required, it is first indicated and then visually performed. You are able to watch the Shell method at work. The Pascal code for the program is shown below:

Listing 11.22

```
PROGRAM Interactive_Sort;
{ Turbo Pascal program that sorts an array of strings using
  the Shell method.                                          }
Uses CRT;
CONST MAX_STRINGS = 20;
      MAX_SIZE = 20;
TYPE STRING20 = STRING[20];
     StrArray = ARRAY[1..MAX_STRINGS] OF STRING20;
VAR count, wait, num_strings : WORD;
    ch : CHAR;
    A : StrArray;
PROCEDURE init_array(VAR A   : StrArray; { output }
                     VAR num : WORD      { input });
{ Procedure to initialize array }
VAR I, J : WORD;
    strng : STRING20;
BEGIN
    IF (num < 0) OR (num > MAX_STRINGS) THEN num := MAX_STRINGS;
    strng := '';
    FOR I := 1 TO MAX_SIZE DO
        strng := strng + CHR(220);
```

ADVANCED FUNCTIONS 255

```pascal
    Randomize;
    FOR I := 1 TO n DO BEGIN
        Move(strng, A[I], MAX_SIZE);
        J := Trunc(20 * Random) + 1;
        IF J < 2 THEN J := 2;
        Delete(A[I], J, MAX_SIZE + 1 - J);
    END;
END;
PROCEDURE shell_sort(VAR A    : StrArray; { in/out }
                        num : WORD       { input });
{ Procedure to perform a Shell-Metzner sorting }
VAR i, j, offset : WORD;
    temporary : STRING20;
    sorted : BOOLEAN;
BEGIN
    offset := num;
    WHILE offset > 1 DO BEGIN
        offset := offset DIV 2;
        REPEAT
            sorted := TRUE;
            FOR J := 1 TO (num - offset) DO BEGIN
                I := J + offset;
                GotoXY(30,J);
                WRITE('<- comparing this element with');
                GotoXY(30,I);
                WRITE('<- this element');
                Delay(wait);
                IF A[I] < A[J] THEN BEGIN
                    temporary := A[I];
                    A[I] := A[J];
                    A[J] := temporary;
                    sorted := FALSE;
                    GotoXY(30,I);
                    ClrEol;
                    WRITE('-----> swapped ');
                    GotoXY(30,J);
                    ClrEol;
                    WRITE('-----> swapped');
                    Delay(wait);
                    GotoXY(1,I);
                    ClrEol;
                    WRITE(A[I]);
                    GotoXY(1,J);
                    ClrEol;
                    WRITE(A[J]);
                END
                ELSE BEGIN
                    GotoXY(30,I);
                    ClrEol;
                    GotoXY(30,J);
                    ClrEol;
                    Delay(wait);
                END;
            END; { FOR J }
        UNTIL sorted;
    END; { End of while-loop }
```

256   INTRODUCING C TO PASCAL PROGRAMMERS

```pascal
END; { shell_sort }
PROCEDURE DisplayArray(VAR A    : StrArray; { input }
                          num : WORD        { input });
{ Display array members }
VAR I : WORD;
BEGIN
    ClrScr;
    FOR I := 1 TO num DO
        WRITELN(A[I]);
    WRITELN
END; { display_array }
BEGIN { Main }
    ClrScr;
    WRITELN('VISUAL SORTING DEMO PROGRAM':50);
    WRITELN; WRITELN;
    WRITE('F)ast   M)oderate S)low demonstration speed ? ');
    ch := UpCase(ReadKey);
    CASE ch OF
        'F' : wait := 5;
        'M' : wait := 25;
        ELSE wait := 50;
    END;
    num_strings = MAX_STRINGS;
    DirectVideo := TRUE;
    init_array(A, num_strings);
    display_array(A, num_strings);
    shell_sort(A, num_strings);
    GotoXY(1,23);   WRITELN(^G'Finished sorting!');
END.
```

The translated C version is listed below:

Listing 11.23

```c
/* C program that sorts an array of strings using
   the Shell method.
*/
#include <stdio.h>
#include "stdlib.h"
#include "conio.h"
#define MAX_STRINGS 20
#define MAX_SIZE 20
enum BOOLEAN { FALSE, TRUE };
typedef enum BOOLEAN boolean;
typedef unsigned int word;
word wait;
void init_array(char[][], word*);
void display_array(char[][], word);
void shell_sort(char[][], word);
main()
{
    word count, num_strings = MAX_STRINGS;
    char ch;
    char A[MAX_STRINGS][MAX_SIZE+1];
    clrscr();
```

```
    printf("\t\tVISUAL SORTING DEMO PROGRAM\n\n");
    printf("F)ast M)oderate S)low demonstration speed ? ");
    ch = getche();
    if (ch >= 'a' && ch <= 'z') ch += 'A' - 'a';
    switch (ch) {
        case 'F' :
            wait = 5;
            break;
        case 'M' :
            wait = 25;
            break;
        default:
            wait = 50;
            break;
    }
    init_array(A, &num_strings);
    display_array(A, num_strings);
    shell_sort(A, num_strings);
    gotoxy(1,23);
    printf("\x007Finished sorting!");
}
void init_array(char A[][MAX_SIZE+1], word* num)
/* Procedure to initialize array */
{
    word i, j;
    char strng[MAX_SIZE+1];
    if (*num < 0 || *num > MAX_STRINGS) *num = MAX_STRINGS;
    for (i = 0; i < MAX_SIZE; i++)
        *(strng + i) = 220; /* store ASCII 220 in strng[i] */
    strng[MAX_SIZE] = '\0';
    for (i = 0; i < *num; i++)  {
        j = random(MAX_SIZE-1);
        if (j < 1) j = 1;
        strncpy(*(A+i), strng, j);
        *( *(A+i) + j ) = '\0';
    }
}
void shell_sort(char A[][MAX_SIZE+1], word num)
/* Procedure to perform a Shell-Metzner sorting */
{
    word i, j, j2, i2, offset;
    char temporary[MAX_SIZE+1];
    boolean sorted;
    void delay(word);
    offset = num;
    while (offset > 1)  {
        offset /= 2;
        do {
            sorted = TRUE;
            for (j = 0; j < num - offset; j++)  {
                i = j + offset;
                j2 = j + 1;
                i2 = i + 1;
                gotoxy(30,j2);
                printf("<- comparing this element with");
```

```c
                gotoxy(30,i2);
                printf("<- this element");
                delay(wait);
                if (strcmp(*(A+i),*(A+j)) > 0)   {
                   strcpy(temporary,*(A+i));
                   strcpy(*(A+i),*(A+j));
                   strcpy(*(A+j),temporary);
                   sorted = FALSE;
                   gotoxy(30,i2);
                   clreol();
                   printf("-----> swapped ");
                   gotoxy(30,j2);
                   clreol();
                   printf("-----> swapped");
                   delay(wait);
                   gotoxy(1,i2);
                   clreol();
                   printf("%s", *(A+i));
                   gotoxy(1,j2);
                   clreol();
                   printf("%s", *(A+j));
                 }
                 else {
                   gotoxy(30,i2);
                   clreol();
                   gotoxy(30,j2);
                   clreol();
                   delay(wait);
                  }
            }
        } while (sorted == FALSE);
    }
}
void display_array(char A[][MAX_SIZE+1], word num)
/* Display array members */
{
    word i;
    clrscr();
    for (i = 0; i < num; i++)
        puts(*(A+i));
    printf("\n");
}
void delay(word ms)
{
  double x, sum;
  int i;
  while (ms-- > 0) {
     sum = 0.0L;
     x = 0.0L;
     for (i = 0; i <= 10; i++)
         sum += x++;
  }
}
```

ACCESSING THE COMMAND LINE ARGUMENTS

A language like C that is used to develop operating systems is expected to provide a mechanism for accessing command line arguments. If you are not familiar with the last term, here is a short explanation. When you invoke a certain compiled program from the DOS prompt (typically the A> or C> prompt) you may need to supply the program with additional information. Each space-delimited word you type after the program name is a command line argument. This enables you to fine-tune the way the program works. The general format is

```
A> <program name> <argument 1> <argument 2> ... <argument n>
```

Depending on what the program does, the number of command line arguments varies.

For some Turbo Pascal programmers, accessing command line arguments is not new. Turbo Pascal supports that same feature which was inspired by C in the first place. C allows for the access of command line arguments somewhat differently from Turbo Pascal. In Turbo Pascal you use **ParamCount** to obtain the number of parameters and the string-array **ParamStr** to obtain the command line arguments themselves. In C you resort to using a special parameter list for function **main** (you probably have been wondering all this time about **main** playing the role of a function). The parameter list is shown below:

```
main(int argc, char* argv[])
```

The first parameter, **argc**, returns a count of the number of command line arguments. The **argv** is an array of character pointers that accesses the arguments.

Program Translation

In Turbo Pascal the value of **ParamCount** does not include the program name itself, while the C **argc** does. Therefore, when you translate a Turbo Pascal program, increase by 1 the value any constants used in relational comparisons with the parameter count.

The following maps the items pointed to by each element of **argv**:

i	Contents of argv[i]
0	program name
1	argument #1
2	argument #2
...	....
argc-1	argument #(argc-1)

The following program demonstrates the access of command line arguments and their use to influence its (that is, the program's) behavior. The program is a simple four-function calculator that takes its input from the DOS command line. It is used following the general syntax shown below:

CALC <operand 1> <operator> <operand 2>

When using either environments of Turbo Pascal or Turbo C you can select the Options option and enter the command line arguments before running these programs. The C command line must include the program name. The Pascal version is listed below:

Listing 11.24

```
Program Calc;
{ Turbo Pascal program that uses command line arguments to
  perform one-line calculations. Only the four basic
  operations are supported.
  For practical use make filename CALC.EXE, so that when
  you invoke it from DOS you type, for example:
        CALC  355 / 113
}
VAR ok : BOOLEAN;
    opr : CHAR;
    error1, error2, error3 : INTEGER;
    strng : STRING[80];
    result, first, second : REAL;
BEGIN
    IF ParamCount < 3 THEN BEGIN
        WRITELN('Proper usage : <number> <operation> <number>');
        WRITELN; WRITELN;
        HALT;
    END;
    Val(ParamStr(1), first, error1);
    Val(ParamStr(3), second, error3);
    strng := ParamStr(2); { must use a string as a go between
                            to avoid type mismatch }
    opr := strng[1];
    IF NOT (opr IN ['+', '-', '*', '/']) THEN
        error2 := 1
    ELSE
        error2 := 0;
    IF ((error1 + error2 + error2) > 0) THEN BEGIN
        IF error1 > 0 THEN BEGIN
            WRITELN(ParamStr(1));
            WRITELN('^':error1,'bad number');
        END;
        IF error2 > 0 THEN
            WRITELN(opr,' is an invalid operator');
        IF error3 > 0 THEN BEGIN
            WRITELN(ParamStr(3));
            WRITELN('^':error2,'bad number');
        END;
        WRITELN; WRITELN;
        HALT;
    END;
    ok := TRUE;
    CASE opr OF
```

```
        '+' : result := first + second;
        '-' : result := first - second;
        '*' : result := first * second;
        '/' : IF second <> 0.0 THEN
                 result := first / second
              ELSE BEGIN
                 ok := FALSE;
                 WRITELN('Cannot divide by zero');
              END;
     END; { CASE }
     IF ok THEN WRITELN('result = ',result);
END.
```

The translated C version is listed below:

Listing 11.25

```c
/* C program that uses command line arguments to
   perform one-line calculations. Only the four basic
   operations are supported.
   For practical use make filename CALC.EXE, so that when
   you invoke it from S you type, for example:
       CALC  355 / 113
*/
#include <stdio.h>
#include "stdlib.h"
main(int argc, char* argv[])
{
    char opr;
    int error1, error2, error3;
    char strng[81];
    double result, first, second;
    /* check for the number of arguments.
       This is a step often performed        */
    if (argc < 4) {
      /* provide simple on-line help */
      printf("Proper arguments : <number> <operation> <number>");
      printf("\n\n");
      exit(0);
    }
    /* convert operands to double */
    first  = atof(argv[1]);
    second = atof(argv[3]);
    strcpy(strng,argv[2]);
    opr = strng[0];
    if (opr != '+' && opr != '-' && opr != '*' && opr != '/')
         error2 = 1;
    else
         error2 = 0;
    if (first == 0.0 || error2 == 1 || second == 0.0) {
         printf("bad number(s) or operator\n\n");
         exit(0);
    }
    switch (opr) {
         case '+' :
```

```
            result = first + second; break;
        case '-' :
            result = first - second; break;
        case '*' :
            result = first * second; break;
        case '/' :
            result = first / second; break;
    }
    printf("result = %lf\n\n", result);
}
```

Compare the first IF statement in the Pascal program with that of the C version:

IF ParamCount < 3 THEN BEGIN   with   if (argc < 4) {

The **argc** is compared with 4 and not 3, since the name of the C program itself counts as one argument.

Notice that the way the two program versions are written enable you to have the operand argument contain multiple characters, such as:

CALC 355 /!@@#$%%^^&&** 113

which returns (355 / 113), since the characters after the '/' are ignored!

POINTERS TO FUNCTIONS

During the compilation process, variables are translated into memory addresses where data are stored and retrieved. Pointers to addresses are also able to access these addresses. This is true not only for the different kinds of variables, but also for functions. A function name is translated in the address where its compiled code resides in memory. The same philosophy implemented by the designers of C that allow you to access and manipulate variables also works with functions. While a function followed by an argument list leads to its evaluation, a bare function name is taken as a pointer to that function. Using pointers to functions, you are able to perform two basic types of tasks:

1. Assign a function to a pointer and use the pointer as an indirect reference to the function. While this sounds like it is creating more work, it can be used to reduce the code length. Consider the case of a program that has a library of similar functions (that is, they have the same parameter list and return the same data type), of which only one is needed at a time. Without using pointers to functions you must use a **switch** statement every time one of these functions is invoked. As the number of calls increase, the code length also increases rapidly. In contrast, by using pointers to functions, the code length is controlled more effectively. A **switch** statement is used once to connect the pointer to the sought function. Any reference to a library function is carried out using the pointer.

ADVANCED FUNCTIONS 263

2. Pass functions as arguments to other functions. This enables you to create an advanced function system where part of the function is another function selected from a library of routines.

I will continue discussing pointers to functions with examples. The first one is a C program that performs simple linear regression that fits the following general equation:

```
f(Y) = intercept + slope * g(X)
```

where X is the independent variable, and Y is the dependent variable or response. The values of the slope and intercept are calculated by the program, given the functions f(Y) and g(X).

The program performs the following:

1. Prompts you to enter the number of data points.
2. Queries you to enter the data points that are stored in the array x and y.
3. Prompts you to select from a menu of mathematical transformations for both the X and Y variables.
4. Displays the regression statistics. This consists of the coefficient of determination (to test the goodness of fit), the slope, and the intercept of the best fitted line.
5. Prompts you to make optional projections (that is, enter a value for X to calculate the corresponding Y for the obtained equation).
6. Queries you to try other mathematical transformations. If you select this option, resume at step (4).

I will first present the C listing and then discuss it:

Listing 11.26

```
/* C program that uses pointers to functions to implement a
   a linear regression program that supports temporary
   mathematical transformations. The program also permits
   you to perform projections.
*/
#include <stdio.h>
#include <conio.h>
#include <math.h>
#define MAX_SIZE 100
typedef unsigned int word;
typedef unsigned char byte;
enum booleans { FALSE, TRUE };
typedef enum booleans boolean;
/* defined array type */
typedef double real_array[MAX_SIZE];
/* declare function pointer */
double (*fx)();
double (*fy)();
double (*inv_fy)();
/* declare function prototypes */
```

```c
void init_array(double*, double*, word);
double linear(double);
double sqr(double);
double reciprocal(double);
main()
{
    char ok, ans;
    word count, i;
    real_array x, y;
    double sum, sumx, sumy;
    double sumxx, sumyy, sumxy;
    double xdata, ydata;
    double xx, yy;
    double meanx, meany, sdevx, sdevy;
    double slope, intercept, r_sqr;
    int trnsfx, trnsfy;
    clrscr();
    do {
        printf("Enter array size [2..%d] : ",MAX_SIZE);
        scanf("%d", &count); printf("\n");
    } while ( !(count > 1 && count <= MAX_SIZE) );
    init_array(x, y, count);
    do {
      trnsfx = select_transf("X");
      trnsfy = select_transf("Y");
      switch (trnsfx) {
       case 0 :
          fx = linear;
          break;
       case 1 :
          fx = log;
          break;
       case 2 :
          fx = sqrt;
          break;
       case 3 :
          fx = sqr;
          break;
       case 4 :
          fx = reciprocal;
          break;
       default :
          fx = linear;
          break;
      }
      switch (trnsfy) {
       case 0 :
          fy = linear;
          inv_fy = linear;
          break;
       case 1 :
          fy = log;
          inv_fy = exp;
          break;
       case 2 :
```

```
            fy = sqrt;
            inv_fy = sqr;
            break;
        case 3 :
            fy = sqr;
            inv_fy = sqr;
            break;
        case 4 :
            fy = reciprocal;
            inv_fy = reciprocal;
            break;
        default :
            fy = linear;
            break;
    }
    /* initialize statistical summations */
    sum = (double) count;
    sumx = 0L; sumxx = 0L;
    sumy = 0L; sumyy = 0L;
    sumxy = 0L;
    for (i = 0; i < count; i++) {
        xdata = (*fx)(x[i]);
        ydata = (*fy)(y[i]);
        sumx += xdata;
        sumy += ydata;
        sumxx += sqr(xdata);
        sumyy += sqr(ydata);
        sumxy += xdata * ydata;
    }
    meanx = sumx / sum;
    meany = sumy / sum;
    sdevx = sqrt((sumxx - sqr(sumx) / sum)/(sum-1.0));
    sdevy = sqrt((sumyy - sqr(sumy) / sum)/(sum-1.0));
    slope = (sumxy - meanx * meany * sum)/sqr(sdevx)/(sum-1);
    intercept = meany - slope * meanx;
    r_sqr = sqr(sdevx / sdevy * slope);
    printf("\n\n\n\n");
    printf("R-square = %lf\n\n", r_sqr);
    printf("Slope = %lf\n\n", slope);
    printf("Intercept = %lf\n\n\n", intercept);
    printf("\nWant to project more data? (Y/N) : ");
    ans = getche();
    while (ans == 'Y' || ans == 'y') {
        printf("\nEnter a value for X : ");
        scanf("%lf", &xdata);
        ydata = (*inv_fy)(intercept + slope * (*fx)(xdata));
        printf("Y = %lf\n\n", ydata);
        printf("\nWant to project more data? (Y/N) : ");
        ans = getche();
    }
    printf("\nWant to test another transformation? (Y/N) : ");
    ok = getche();
} while (ok == 'Y' || ok == 'y');
printf("\n\n");
}
```

```c
void init_array(double* x, double* y, word count)
/* read data for array from the keyboard */
{
    word i;
    for (i = 0; i < count; i++, x++, y++) {
        printf("X[%d] : ", i+1);
        scanf("%lf", x);
        printf("Y[%d] : ", i+1);
        scanf("%lf", y);
    }
}
int select_transf(char* var_name)
/* select choice of transformation */
{
    int choice = -1;
    clrscr();
    printf("select transformation for variable %s",var_name);
    printf("\n\n\n");
    printf("0) No transformation\n\n");
    printf("1) Logarithmic transformation\n\n");
    printf("2) Square root transformation\n\n");
    printf("3) Square  transformation\n\n");
    printf("4) Reciprocal transformation\n\n");
    while (choice < 0 || choice > 4) {
        printf("\nSelect choice by number : ");
        scanf("%d", &choice);
    }
    return choice;
}
double linear(double a)
{
    return a;
}
double sqr(double a)
{
    return a * a;
}
double reciprocal(double a)
{
    return 1.0L / a;
}
```

The first step in using pointers to functions is declaring them. The program employs the following declarations for the three pointers to double-typed functions:

```c
/* declare function pointer */
double (*fx)();
double (*fy)();
double (*inv_fy)();
```

The **fx** is the pointer to a function of type **double** that is used to perform mathematical transformation on the data in array **x**. Similarly, the **fy** pointer works on the array **y**. The **inv_fy** pointer is used to define a function that reverses the transformation of Y values obtained during the projections.

ADVANCED FUNCTIONS

Statistic Refresher

Linear regression does not automatically give you the slope and intercept Y vs. X all the time, but probably some function f(Y) vs. the function g(X). Thus, during projections the program should calculate

```
Y = F(intercept + slope * g(X))
```

where the mathematical function F() is the inverse of f(), or:

```
Y = F( f(Y) )
```

Therefore, the pointer **inv_fy** is used to select F().

In addition to the declaration of the above pointers, observe the list of prototyped functions:

```
/* declare function prototypes */
void init_array(double*, double*, word);
double linear(double);
double sqr(double);
double reciprocal(double);
```

The last three functions are mathematical functions that are defined in this program and use the function pointers. In addition to these functions, the program uses the logarithm (**log**) and the square root (**sqrt**) from file "math.h". Thus, this program also illustrates the use of pointers to both library and internally defined functions.

The program contains two similar **switch** statements. The first is used to assign the **fx** pointer to a function selected by the value of **trnsfx**. The second **switch** statement has each case label assign the **fy** and **inv_fy** pointers according to the value of **trnsfy**. Notice that these assignment follow a simple general format:

```
<function pointer> = <function identifier>;
```

Once the function pointers are assigned they can be ued in executing the function to which they point. The for loop that performs the update of the statistical summations uses the function pointers in its first two loop statements:

```
for (i = 0; i < count; i++) {
   xdata = (*fx)(x[i]);
   ydata = (*fy)(y[i]);
```

The general format for using a function pointer to invoke its function is

```
(*<function pointer)(<list of arguments>)
```

The function pointers **fx** and **inv_fy** are similarly used in calculating the projected Y values in:

```
ydata = (*inv_fy)(intercept + slope * (*fx)(xdata));
```

The above program with its frequent use of pointer functions is shorter than an equivalent program version that does not utilize them. Each time you use a function pointer you save yourself a **switch** statement.

C also supports the declaration of arrays of function pointers. The above program is modified to perform an automatic search for the best equation. This is carried out with a given set of mathematical transformations applied to the X and Y data. Instead of prompting you for a particular set of transformations, the program tries all of the combinations it has. First, the array of function pointers is declared as:

```
double (*ff[NUM_TRNSF])();
```

The array is then assigned the following functions:

```
/* assign array of function pointers */
ff[0] = linear;
ff[1] = log;
ff[2] = reciprocal;
ff[3] = sqrt;
```

Thus, a total of 16 equations are examined on the same data array. The program displays the results for each equation and, finally, those of the best equation obtained (that is, the one with the highest coefficient of determination). These 16 equations are processed using the following nested for loop:

```
for (iy = 0; iy < NUM_TRNSF; iy++) {
  for (ix = 0; ix < NUM_TRNSF; ix++) {
```

The first loop varies the function pointer that transforms the Y data, while the second loop varies that for the X data. The innermost for loop that performs the statistical summations is written as:

```
for (i = 0; i < count; i++) {
  xdata = (*ff[ix])(x[i]);
  ydata = (*ff[iy])(y[i]);
```

The C program is listed below:

Listing 11.27

```
/* C program that uses pointers to functions to implement a
   a linear regression program that automatically employs
   various models.
*/
#include <stdio.h>
#include <conio.h>
#include <math.h>
#define MAX_SIZE 100
#define MAX_LINES 21
#define NUM_TRNSF 4
typedef unsigned int word;
typedef unsigned char byte;
enum booleans { FALSE, TRUE };
typedef enum booleans boolean;
typedef double real_array[MAX_SIZE];
/* declare function pointer */
double (*ff[NUM_TRNSF])();
/* declare function prototypes */
void init_array(double*, double*, word);
double linear(double);
double sqr(double);
```

ADVANCED FUNCTIONS 269

```
double reciprocal(double);
main()
{
    char ok;
    word count, line, i, ix, iy;
    real_array x, y;
    double sum, sumx, sumy;
    double sumxx, sumyy, sumxy;
    double xdata, ydata;
    double xx, yy;
    double meanx, meany, sdevx, sdevy;
    double slope, intercept, r_sqr;
    double best_slope, best_intercept, best_r_sqr = -1.0L;
    word best_ix = 0, best_iy = 0;
    char* message_x[] = { "X", "log(X)", "1/X", "sqrt(X)" };
    char* message_y[] = { "Y", "log(Y)", "1/Y", "sqrt(Y)" };
    clrscr();
    do {
        printf("Enter array size [2..%d] : ",MAX_SIZE);
        scanf("%d", &count); printf("\n");
    } while ( !(count > 1 && count <= MAX_SIZE) );
    init_array(x, y, count);
    /* assign array of function pointers */
    ff[0] = linear;
    ff[1] = log;
    ff[2] = reciprocal;
    ff[3] = sqrt;
    line = 0;
    clrscr();
    for (iy = 0; iy < NUM_TRNSF; iy++) {
      for (ix = 0; ix < NUM_TRNSF; ix++) {
        /* initialize statistical summations */
        sum = (double) count;
        sumx = 0L; sumxx = 0L;
        sumy = 0L; sumyy = 0L;
        sumxy = 0L;
        for (i = 0; i < count; i++) {
          xdata = (*ff[ix])(x[i]);
          ydata = (*ff[iy])(y[i]);
          sumx += xdata;
          sumy += ydata;
          sumxx += sqr(xdata);
          sumyy += sqr(ydata);
          sumxy += xdata * ydata;
        }
        meanx = sumx / sum;
        meany = sumy / sum;
        sdevx = sqrt((sumxx - sqr(sumx) / sum)/(sum-1.0));
        sdevy = sqrt((sumyy - sqr(sumy) / sum)/(sum-1.0));
        slope = (sumxy - meanx * meany * sum) /
                    sqr(sdevx)/(sum-1);
        intercept = meany - slope * meanx;
        r_sqr = sqr(sdevx / sdevy * slope);
        line += 3;
        if (line >= MAX_LINES) {
```

```
                    printf("\npress any key to continue ...");
                    ok = getch(); printf("\n");
                    line = 0;
                }
                printf("R-square = %lf\n", r_sqr);
                printf("%s = (%lf) + (%lf) %s\n\n", message_y[iy],
                                                    intercept, slope,
                                                    message_x[ix]);
                if ( best_r_sqr < r_sqr) {
                   best_ix = ix;
                   best_iy = iy;
                   best_r_sqr = r_sqr;
                   best_slope = slope;
                   best_intercept = intercept;
                }
            }
        }
        printf("\npress any key to continue ...");
        ok = getch();
        printf("\n\n\n");
        printf("The best model is\n");
        printf("R-square = %lf\n\n", best_r_sqr);
        printf("%s = (%lf) + (%lf) %s\n\n", message_y[best_iy],
                                            best_intercept,
                                            best_slope,
                                            message_x[best_ix]);
}
void init_array(double* x, double* y, word count)
/* read data for array from the keyboard */
{
    word i;
    for (i = 0; i < count; i++, x++, y++) {
       printf("X[%d] : ", i);
       scanf("%lf", x);
       printf("Y[%d] : ", i);
       scanf("%lf", y);
    }
}
double linear(double a)
{
    return a;
}
double sqr(double a)
{
    return a * a;
}
double reciprocal(double a)
{
    return 1.0L / a;
}
```

To enhance the readability of the results, the program uses the following arrays of character pointers to select the appropriate equation to display:

```
char* message_x[] = { "X", "log(X)", "1/X", "sqrt(X)" };
char* message_y[] = { "Y", "log(Y)", "1/Y", "sqrt(Y)" };
```

ADVANCED FUNCTIONS 271

Run the above program using the following data:

X	Y
10	50
25	77
30	86
35	95
100	212

The screen image for the output is shown below:

```
R-square = 1.000000
Y = (32.000000) + (1.800000) X
R-square = 0.872953
Y = (-138.978336) + (71.116263) log(X)
R-square = 0.536191
Y = (161.069100) + (-1346.574273) 1/X
R-square = 0.974645
Y = (-41.456018) + (24.607198) sqrt(X)
R-square = 0.954831
log(Y) = (3.933905) + (0.014756) X
R-square = 0.977315
log(Y) = (2.367327) + (0.631264) log(X)
press any key to continue ...
R-square = 0.737791
log(Y) = (5.085729) + (-13.251268) 1/X
R-square = 0.997048
log(Y) = (3.289924) + (0.208794) sqrt(X)
R-square = 0.793996
1/Y = (0.017586) + (-0.000140) X
R-square = 0.988646
1/Y = (0.034598) + (-0.006623) log(X)
R-square = 0.922440
1/Y = (0.005422) + (0.154550) 1/X
R-square = 0.906180
1/Y = (0.024245) + (-0.002076) sqrt(X)
R-square = 0.990475
sqrt(Y) = (6.682145) + (0.080080) X
R-square = 0.930305
sqrt(Y) = (-1.327441) + (3.281818) log(X)
R-square = 0.631045
sqrt(Y) = (12.652908) + (-65.302329) 1/X
R-square = 0.996112
sqrt(Y) = (3.311924) + (1.112042) sqrt(X)
press any key to continue ...
The best model is
R-square = 1.000000
Y = (32.000000) + (1.800000) X
```

Function pointers provide you with the mechanism for supporting functional arguments. To illustrate this feature, I present a modified version of the first function pointer example. The new version interacts with the user in the same way the first one did. The difference is that this version isolates the statistical computations in a separate function, **calc_regression**. Since these calculations use the function pointers, **calc_regression** is coded to have the two pointers as part of its parameter list. The **calc_regression** function is declared as:

```
void calc_regression(double* x,
                     double* y,
                     word count,
                     regression* stat,
                     double (*fx)(),
                     double (*fy)())
```

and prototyped as:

```
void calc_regression(double*, double*,word,regression*,
                     double (*fx)(), double (*fy)());
```

and is called using the following statement:

```
calc_regression(x, y, count, &stat, fx, fy);
```

The C listing is shown below:

Listing 11.28

```
/* C program that uses pointers to functions to implement a
   a linear regression program that supports temporary
   mathematical transformations. The program also permits
   you to perform projections.
*/
#include <stdio.h>
#include <conio.h>
#include <math.h>
#define MAX_SIZE 100
typedef unsigned int word;
typedef unsigned char byte;
enum booleans { FALSE, TRUE };
typedef enum booleans boolean;
typedef double real_array[MAX_SIZE];
typedef struct linear_regression
        {
           double r_sqr;
           double slope;
           double intercept;
        } regression;
/* declare function pointer */
double (*fx)();
double (*fy)();
double (*inv_fy)();
/* declare function prototypes */
void init_array(double*, double*, word);
double linear(double);
double sqr(double);
double reciprocal(double);
void calc_regression(double*, double*,word,regression*,
                     double (*fx)(), double (*fy)());
main()
{
    char ok, ans;
    word count;
    double xdata, ydata;
```

ADVANCED FUNCTIONS 273

```
real_array x, y;
regression stat;
int trnsfx, trnsfy;
clrscr();
do {
    printf("Enter array size [2..%d] : ",MAX_SIZE);
    scanf("%d", &count); printf("\n");
} while ( !(count > 1 && count <= MAX_SIZE) );
init_array(x, y, count);
do {
  trnsfx = select_transf("X");
  trnsfy = select_transf("Y");
  switch (trnsfx) {
   case 0 :
       fx = linear;
       break;
   case 1 :
       fx = log;
       break;
   case 2 :
       fx = sqrt;
       break;
   case 3 :
       fx = sqr;
       break;
   case 4 :
       fx = reciprocal;
       break;
   default :
       fx = linear;
       break;
  }
  switch (trnsfy) {
   case 0 :
       fy = linear;
       inv_fy = linear;
       break;
   case 1 :
       fy = log;
       inv_fy = exp;
       break;
   case 2 :
       fy = sqrt;
       inv_fy = sqr;
       break;
   case 3 :
       fy = sqr;
       inv_fy = sqr;
       break;
   case 4 :
       fy = reciprocal;
       inv_fy = reciprocal;
       break;
   default :
       fy = linear;
       break;
```

274 INTRODUCING C TO PASCAL PROGRAMMERS

```
      }
      /*   call function with functional arguments
                                        |    |
                                        V    V    */
      calc_regression(x, y, count, &stat, fx, fy);
      printf("\n\n\n\n");
      printf("R-square = %lf\n\n", stat.r_sqr);
      printf("Slope = %lf\n\n", stat.slope);
      printf("Intercept = %lf\n\n\n", stat.intercept);
      printf("\nWant to project more data? (Y/N) : ");
      ans = getche();
      while (ans == 'Y' || ans == 'y') {
         printf("\nEnter a value for X : ");
         scanf("%lf", &xdata);
         ydata = (*inv_fy)(stat.intercept +
                         stat.slope * (*fx)(xdata));
         printf("Y = %lf\n\n", ydata);
         printf("\nWant to project more data? (Y/N) : ");
         ans = getche();
      }
      printf("\nWant to test another transformation? (Y/N) : ");
      ok = getche();
   } while (ok == 'Y' || ok == 'y');
   printf("\n\n");
}
void init_array(double* x, double* y, word count)
/* read data for array from the keyboard */
{
   word i;
   for (i = 0; i < count; i++, x++, y++) {
      printf("X[%d] : ", i);
      scanf("%lf", x);
      printf("Y[%d] : ", i);
      scanf("%lf", y);
   }
}
int select_transf(char* var_name)
/* select choice of transformation */
{
   int choice = -1;
   clrscr();
   printf("select transformation for variable %s",var_name);
   printf("\n\n\n");
   printf("0) No transformation\n\n");
   printf("1) Logarithmic transformation\n\n");
   printf("2) Square root transformation\n\n");
   printf("3) Square   transformation\n\n");
   printf("4) Reciprocal transformation\n\n");
   while (choice < 0 || choice > 4) {
      printf("\nSelect choice by number : ");
      scanf("%d", &choice);
   }
   return choice;
}
double linear(double a)
{
```

```
    return a;
}
double sqr(double a)
{
    return a * a;
}
double reciprocal(double a)
{
    return 1.0L / a;
}
void calc_regression(double* x,
                     double* y,
                     word count,
                     regression* stat,
                     double (*fx)(),
                     double (*fy)())
{
    double meanx, meany, sdevx, sdevy;
    double sum, sumx, sumy;
    double sumxx, sumyy, sumxy;
    double xdata, ydata;
    word i;
    /* initialize statistical summations */
    sum = (double) count;
    sumx = 0L; sumxx = 0L;
    sumy = 0L; sumyy = 0L;
    sumxy = 0L;
    for (i = 0; i < count; i++) {
        xdata = (*fx)(*(x+i));
        ydata = (*fy)(*(y+i));
        sumx += xdata;
        sumy += ydata;
        sumxx += sqr(xdata);
        sumyy += sqr(ydata);
        sumxy += xdata * ydata;
    }
    meanx = sumx / sum;
    meany = sumy / sum;
    sdevx = sqrt((sumxx - sqr(sumx) / sum)/(sum-1.0));
    sdevy = sqrt((sumyy - sqr(sumy) / sum)/(sum-1.0));
    stat->slope = (sumxy - meanx * meany * sum) /
                  sqr(sdevx)/(sum-1);
    stat->intercept = meany - stat->slope * meanx;
    stat->r_sqr = sqr(sdevx / sdevy * stat->slope);
}
```

FUNCTIONS WITH A VARIABLE NUMBER OF ARGUMENTS

As a Pascal programmer you have learned the discipline and conciseness of Pascal's routine definitions and calls. Pascal procedures and functions have a fixed number of arguments. All calls must match the arguments in number and in the majority cases, the data types. C permits you to write functions that accept a variable number of arguments. For example, if you write somewhat specialized console output routines in Pascal you are limited by the number of arguments displayed. The following routine heading shows multiple versions of a routine to accommodate a varying number of argument:

```
{ Display integers }
PROCEDURE Put_One_Int(X,Y : BYTE; I : INTEGER);
PROCEDURE Put_Two_Int(X,Y : BYTE; I, J : INTEGER);
PROCEDURE Put_Three_Int(X,Y : BYTE; I, J, K : INTEGER);
```

In C, similar routines are consolidated into one:

```
int put_int(int x, int y, ...)
```

The **put_int** function is able single-handedly to display a varying number of arguments. The same feature in C enables you to write your own versions of **printf** with its variable number of arguments. By contrast, you cannot write a procedure that works like WRITE or WRITELN in Pascal.

Since the concept is new to Pascal programmers, I will begin with an example and then explain the components required in writing variable-argument functions.

The following C program uses a function with a variable number of arguments to detect the largest number in a numeric list. The list is the variable-sized argument list. The code is shown below:

Listing 11.29

```
/* C program that illustrates functions with a variable
   number of arguments
*/
#include <stdio.h>
#include <stdarg.h>
#define EOL -1
void vmax(int*, char*, ...);
main()
{
   int big;
   vmax(&big, "The largest of 55, 67, 41 and 28 is ",
                          55, 67, 41, 28, EOL);
   printf("%d\n",big);
}
void vmax(int* large, char* message, ...)
{
   int num;
   va_list num_ptr;
   va_start(num_ptr, message);
   printf("%s",message);
   *(large) = -1;
   while ((num = va_arg(num_ptr, int)) != EOL) {
         /* printf("%d\n", num); */
         if (num > *(large))
             *(large) = num;
   }
   va_end(num_ptr);
}
```

The components you need in writing functions with a variable number of arguments include data objects and routines defined in library "stdarg.h". The following general steps must be followed:

1. Include file "stdarg.h" in your C code.
2. If the variable-argument function is not of type **int**, you prototype it using:
   ```
   <type> <function>(<list for the type of fixed arguments>,...);
   ```
   Notice that there must be at least one fixed argument in the function.
3. The function is declared:
   ```
   <type> <function>(<list of fixed parameters>,...);
   ```
4. The **va_list** pointer-type, defined in "stdarg.h" is used to declare a pointer to the variable argument list:
   ```
   va_list <list pointer>;
   ```
5. The variable-list pointer is initialized by calling **va_start** (also declared in "stdarg.h"), using the following syntax:
   ```
   va_start(<list pointer>,<name of last fixed parameter>);
   ```
   This enables the list pointer to point to the first variable-argument.
6. Accessing the variable-arguments is carried out using the **var_arg** function, which takes two arguments. The first is the list pointer, previously initialized. The second is the name of the data type of the variable-argument. The result returned by the **va_arg** is the same as the latter data-type argument:
   ```
   <variable> = va_arg(<list pointer, <type casted>);
   ```
   To stop reading the variable-argument list, place an end-of-list element at the end of the list and check for its value. A while loop is well suited for that purpose, as shown in the above example.

CHAPTER SUMMARY

- Declaring one-dimensional arrays as function arguments passed by value requires that you state the array name followed by empty brackets, as shown in the following example:
  ```
  double average(double data_array[], int count)
  ```
  The prototype of such functions is declared by using a pointer-type to match the array-typed parameters, as in:
  ```
  double average(double*, int);
  ```
- Using strings as function arguments follows the same rules as passing arrays by value. However, since many string-manipulating functions return strings, the function type in these cases should be a character-pointer. An example is the following function:
  ```
  char* leftstr(char strng[], int numchar)
  ```
  with this prototype:
  ```
  char* leftstr(char*, int);
  ```

- Passing structures by value to functions that return simple (or no) types is very straightforward. No pointers are involved in the functions' arguments. An example is the following function declared using:

  ```
  double abs_complex(complex_struct c)
  ```

  and prototyped using:

  ```
  double abs_complex(complex_struct);
  ```

- Passing addresses of arguments to C functions enables you to access the arguments by reference. C functions pass a copy of the address to the function, but that is enough to perform lasting changes on the referenced arguments. Thus, to write functions that alter their array-typed arguments you must utilize a pointer, such as the one used in the following example:

  ```
  void create_array(double data_array*, int num_data)
  ```

- Command line arguments can be access by C program . You employ a special parameter list for function **main**. The parameter list is shown below:

  ```
  main(int argc, char* argv[])
  ```

  The first parameter, **argc**, returns a count of the number of command line arguments. The **argv** is an array of character pointers that accesses the arguments. The following maps the items pointed to by each element of :

i	Contents of argv[i]
0	program name
1	argument #1
2	argument #2
...	....
argc-1	argument #(argc-1)

- Passing a variable number of arguments is supported by C. This requires the a number of data objects and routines defined in library "stdarg.h". Variable-argument functions must have at least one fixed parameter, and the arguments in variable-list are treated as having the same data type.

CHAPTER

12

Basic File I/O

CHAPTER GOALS

This chapter looks at the basics of file I/O in C and covers the following:
- Modes of file I/O.
- Character file I/O.
- String file I/O.
- Writing and reading numeric data using sequential files.
- Using structures to write and read numeric data in sequential binary files.
- Using unions in random-access of numeric data from files.
- Basic Low-level file I/O.

First, it must be pointed out that C itself has no predefined I/O routines. Instead, C depends on libraries to provide this vital aspect of program interaction. Thus, theoretically, you can write your own I/O library that suit`s your needs. However, C has a number of standard libraries that are commonly used to develop portable code. The "stdio.h" provides all of the I/O routines that are discussed in this chapter. All further references to I/O in C actually refer to the library "stdio.h", for the sake of brevity.

MODES OF FILE I/O IN C

C promotes the abstract concept of streams to unify treatment of data flow to various devices, such as disk drives, printers, communication ports, and the console.

The "stdio.h" supports two types of streams, text and binary, as well as low-level system I/O. Since text streams are involved with the I/O of text, the related I/O functions perform character translation on the text-line delimiters. The newline characters used to delimit text-lines in text streams are translated into pairs of carriage-return and line feed characters when reading text streams. The reverse translation occurs when writing to text streams. By contrast, binary streams are handled without any such character translation.

As with most other languages, file I/O requires you to open a stream to specify the data file involved, the file handle, and the I/O mode. C employs the function **fopen** to accomplish this. The general syntax for using **fopen** is:

```
file_ptr = fopen(filename,"<I/O mode>");
```

The file pointer, **file_ptr**, is the file handle and is declared as:

```
FILE *file_ptr;
```

All further references to the stream are made through the file pointer. If opening the stream fails, a NULL value is assigned to the file pointer. Comparing the file pointer with NULL should be used to verify that the stream has been successfully opened. The filename is a string constant, variable, or expression that specifies the name of the DOS file involved. The I/O mode is specified by using one of the following:

I/O Mode	Implication
r	Open an existing file for input.
w	Open a file for output. If the file already exists, its contents are overwritten. If the file does not exist, it is created.
a	Open a file to append data. If the file does not exist, it is created.
r+	Open an existing file for input and output.
w+	Open a file for input and output. If the file already exists, its contents are overwritten.
a+	Open a file to append and read data. If the file does not exist, it is created.

In addition to the above I/O mode specifiers, you can append the letter "t" to indicate that the file should be opened as a text stream. Similarly, you may use "b" to specify that the file be opened as a binary stream. The default is determined by the setting of a global variable, **_fmode**. If it is set to O_BINARY, streams are opened by default in binary mode. If **_fmode** is assigned O_TEXT, streams are opened by default in text mode. The O_TEXT and O_BINARY are found in file "fnctl.h".

If the program prompts the end-user for a filename, then I suggest using the following do-while loop (or a variation of it) to ensure that a correct filename is provided:

```
char filename[65];
   FILE *file_ptr;
do {
   printf("Enter filename : ");
   gets(filename);
```

```
       if ((file_ptr = fopen(filename,"<mode>")) == NULL)
           printf("Cannot open file %s\n\n",filename);
   } while (file_ptr == NULL);
```

The above error handling is equivalent to the following in Turbo Pascal:

```
VAR filename : STRING[64];
    file_ptr : TEXT;
    OK : BOOLEAN:
REPEAT
  WRITE('Enter filename : ');
  READLN(filename);
                Assign(file_ptr,filename)
                {$I-} Reset(file_ptr); {$I+}
  OK := IOResult = 0;
  IF NOT OK THEN BEGIN
     WRITELN('Cannot open file ',filename);
     WRITELN;
  END;
UNTIL OK;
```

Like most other languages, C provides the a routine, **fclose**, to close the stream, flush its buffer, and reclaim the buffer space. The general syntax for **fclose** is

```
fclose(file_ptr);
```

Compared to Pascal, C offers more I/O routines, each specialized with a specific I/O mode, data format, and type. Thus, you can view I/O using "stdio.h" divided into the categories described below:

Text Streams

- Character I/O.
- String I/O.
- Formatted I/O: to perform file I/O that involves integers, floating point numbers, and characters. This subcategory is noted for storing numbers in a text image and thus utilizing more file space, since each digit occupies a byte of storage.

Binary Streams

These streams generally store their data in a more compact form than text streams, especially with numeric data; the binary coded contents of the data in the memory are copied onto the stream.

- Structure and union file I/O. This involves storing data structures in a more compact and efficient method.
- Block file I/O.
    The above categories of file I/O are explained with examples in the next sections.

CHARACTER I/O

A number of applications require that you read a file character-by-character. Examples are word counting programs and text-file format converters.

To write characters to a text stream, utilize the following steps:
1. Declare a file pointer using the predefined **FILE** type. This data type is declared in the "stdio.h" header file.
2. Open the stream using an appropriate mode and check the file pointer for a NULL value.
3. Write characters to the text stream using **putchar**, as shown below:
   ```
   putchar(ch, file_ptr);
   ```
   The source for the characters may be the console, the contents of a string, or another text stream.
4. Close the stream.

Program Translation

Pascal:
```
      VAR fileptr : TEXT;
          filename : STRING[64];
          mychar : CHAR;
      Assign(fileptr, filename);
      Rewrite(fileptr);
      Write(fileptr,mychar);
      Close(fileptr);
```
C:
```
      #include <stdio.h>
      FILE *fileptr;
      char filename[65];
      char mychar;
      fileptr = fopen(filename,"w");
      putchar(mychar,fileptr);
      fclose(fileptr);
```

To read characters from a text stream, employ the following steps:
1. Declare a file pointer using the predefined **FILE** type. The variable used to read the characters should be typed as an **int**.
2. Open the stream using an appropriate mode and check the file pointer for a NULL value.
3. Read characters from the text stream using **getc**. To read to the end of the stream, you may use one of two methods:
   - The **foef** function, that works in a manner similar to Pascal's EOF, as shown below:
     ```
     while (!feof(file_ptr)) {
        ch = getc(file_ptr);
        /* other statements */
     }
     ```

- The C **EOF** constant, against which an input character is compared, as shown below:
  ```
  while ((ch = getc(infile)) != EOF) {
      /* loop body */
  }
  ```
  The above method reads a character and also tests the end-of-file in the while loop condition statement. The value of **EOF** is either -1 or 0, depending on the implementation.
4. Close the stream.

Program Translation

```
Pascal: VAR fileptr : TEXT;
            filename : STRING[64];
            mychar : CHAR;
        Assign(fileptr, filename);
        Reset(fileptr);
        Read(fileptr,mychar);
        Close(fileptr);
C:
        FILE *fileptr;
        char filename[65];
        int mychar;
        fileptr = fopen(filename,"r");
        mychar = getc(fileptr);
        fclose(fileptr);
```

The following program converts WordStar text files into pure ASCII text. Each WordStar® paragraph that includes soft-carriage returns is converted into one long line of ASCII text with no special control characters. The program prompts you to enter the name of the input and output files. It then verifies that you are not using the same filename for the both the input and output text files. Once it has finished processing a file, it asks you whether or not you wish to handle more WordStar files. The Pascal listing is shown below:

Listing 12.1

```
PROGRAM WordStar_to_ASCII;
{ Turbo Pascal program that strips soft carriage returns
    from WordStar text files. This turns each paragraph
    into one long line.                                  }
Uses CRT;
TYPE STRING64 = STRING[64];
VAR Ch : CHAR;
    OK : BOOLEAN;
    Source, Target : STRING64;
    InFile, OutFile : TEXT;
PROCEDURE UpCaseStr(VAR Strng : STRING64);
VAR i, n : BYTE;
BEGIN
    n := Length(Strng);
```

```pascal
        FOR i := 1 TO n DO
            Strng[i] := UpCase(Strng[i]);
END;
BEGIN
  ClrScr;
  REPEAT
    REPEAT
        WRITE('Enter Source Filename -> ');
        READLN(Source); WRITELN;
        Assign(InFile, Source);
        {$I-} Reset(InFile); {$I+}
        OK := IOResult = 0;
        IF NOT OK THEN BEGIN
            WRITELN('Error: Cannot open ',Source);
            WRITELN;
        END;
    UNTIL OK;
    REPEAT
        WRITE('Enter Target Filename -> ');
        READLN(Target); WRITELN;
        Assign(OutFile, Target);
        {$I-} Rewrite(OutFile); {$I+}
        OK := (IOResult = 0);
        IF NOT OK THEN BEGIN
            WRITELN('Error: Cannot open ',Target);
            WRITELN;
        END;
        UpCaseStr(Source);
        UpCaseStr(Target);
        OK := OK AND (Source <> Target);
        IF NOT OK THEN BEGIN
            WRITE('Sorry! Source and target filenames ');
            WRITELN('must be different');
            WRITELN;
        END;
    UNTIL OK;
    WHILE NOT EOF(InFile) DO BEGIN
            READ(InFile,Ch);
            IF ORD(Ch) = $8d THEN
               READ(InFile,Ch) {Get rid of LF too}
            ELSE BEGIN
               Ch := CHAR(ORD(Ch) AND $7F); {Get rid of high bit}
               IF Ch = ^O THEN Ch := ' ';   {Hard space convert}
               IF (Ch >= ' ') OR
                  (Ch = ^I)    OR
                  (Ch = ^J)    OR
                  (Ch = ^M) THEN
                     WRITE(OutFile,Ch);
            END;
    END;
    WRITE(OutFile,^Z);
    Close(InFile);
    Close(OutFile);
    WRITELN;
    WRITE('Process another file? (Y/N) ');
```

```
      Ch := ReadKey; WRITELN(Ch);
   UNTIL NOT (Ch IN ['Y','y']);
END.
```

The translated C version is shown below:

Listing 12.2

```c
/* C program that strips soft carriage returns from WordStar
   text files. This turns each paragraph into one long line.
*/
#include <stdio.h>
#include "conio.h"
#include <string.h>
enum booleans { FALSE, TRUE };
typedef enum booleans boolean;
main()
{
     int ch; /* declare ch variable as int instead of char */
     boolean ok;
     char source[65], target[65];
     FILE *infile, *outfile;
     clrscr();
     do {
      do {
         printf("Enter source Filename -> ");
         gets(source); printf("\n");
         if ((infile = fopen(source,"r")) == NULL)
             printf("\nError: Cannot open %s\n\n",source);
      } while (infile == NULL);
      do {
         printf("Enter target Filename -> ");
         gets(target); printf("\n");
         ok = TRUE;
         if ((outfile = fopen(target,"w")) == NULL) {
             printf("\nError: Cannot open %s\n\n",target);
             ok = FALSE;
         }
         if (stricmp(source,target) == 0) {
             printf("Sorry! source and target filenames ");
             printf("must be different\n\n");
             ok = FALSE;
         };
     } while (ok == FALSE);
     while ((ch = getc(infile)) != EOF)   {
             if (ch == 0x8D)
                 ch = getc(infile); /*Get rid of LF too*/
             else {
                 ch &= 0x7F;   /*Get rid of high bit*/
                 if (ch == 15) ch = ' ';  /* Hard space convert */
                 if (ch >= ' ' ||
                     ch == 9  ||
                     ch == 10 ||
                     ch == 13)
```

```
                    putc(ch,outfile);
            }
    }
    putc(-1,outfile);  /* send end-of-file */
    fclose(infile);
    fclose(outfile);
    printf("\nProcess another file? (Y/N) ");
    ch = getche(); printf("\n\n");
  } while (ch == 'Y' || ch == 'y');
}
```

A comparison of the two listings reveals the following differences:

1. With C you can test the file pointer for a NULL value. The outcome of the test determines whether or not the stream was successfully opened for the specified mode. This is a bit cleaner than in Turbo Pascal, where the predefined **IOResult** is instead used to detect the successful establishment of a stream buffer.
2. The character variable **ch** is declared as **int** in the C version. Declaring it as **char** causes the program to work improperly (don't worry, it won't crash) by merely failing to convert WordStar paragraphs into long lines.
3. Most of the characters in the C version are read using **getc** placed in the while loop, which also tests for the end-of-file:

   ```
   while ((ch = getc(infile)) != EOF)  {
   ```

   This is different from the Pascal WHILE loop, that tests for the end-of-file only:

   ```
   WHILE NOT EOF(InFile) DO BEGIN
   ```

   This is yet another example that demonstrates the terseness of C.
4. Each character read is ANDed with hex 7F (decimal 127) to turn off its high bit. Compare the Pascal statement:

   ```
   Ch := CHAR(ORD(Ch) AND $7F);
   ```

   with the much simpler C form:

   ```
   ch &= 0x7F;   /*Get rid of high bit*/
   ```
5. The EOF character in C is -1, not the ^Z character which PC/MS-DOS uses.
6. The **(stricmp(source,target) == 0)** test is used to compare the filenames without having to convert them into upper-case forms. The **stricmp** is a library function declared in the "string.h" file.

STRING I/O

While performing character I/O may suit certain applications, the majority of programs run more efficiently by handling strings of characters. The following should be noted when handling text lines in C:

> **Programming Note**
>
> Each text file line created by C ends with the newline (also known as line feed) character (ASCII code 10), while under PC-/MS-DOS two characters [the carriage return (ASCII 13) and the line feed] are used. Turbo C translates the newline characters into the carriage return and line feed when writing to a DOS text file. The reverse translation is carried out by Turbo C when reading a text file.

To write strings to a text stream, the following steps are employed:

1. Declare a file pointer using the predefined **FILE** type.
2. Open the stream using an appropriate mode and check the file pointer for a NULL value.
3. Write strings to the text stream using **fputs**, as shown below:
   ```
   fputs(string, file_ptr);
   fputs("\n", file_ptr);
   ```
   The second **fputs** ensures that your strings are delimited by newlines. This is needed so that you can correctly read back the strings later.

   You can instead use **fprintf**, which is a file output version of the popular **printf**, to output strings:
   ```
   fprintf(file_ptr,"%s\n",string);
   ```
4. Close the stream.

> **Program Translation**
>
> Pascal:
> ```
>         VAR fileptr : TEXT;
>             filename : STRING[64];
>             line : STRING[80];
>         Assign(fileptr, filename);
>         Rewrite(fileptr);
>         Write(fileptr,line);
>         Close(fileptr);
> ```
> C:
> ```
>         FILE *fileptr;
>         char filename[65];
>         char line[81];
>         fileptr = fopen(filename,"w");
>         fputs(line, fileptr);
>         fputs("\n", fileptr);
>         /* ── or ── */
>         fprintf(fileptr,"%s\n", line);
>
>         fclose(fileptr);
> ```

To read strings from a text stream, use the following steps:
1. Declare a file pointer using the predefined **FILE** type.
2. Open the stream using an appropriate mode and check the file pointer for a NULL value.
3. Read the strings from the text stream using **fgets**. To read to the end of the file, use one of the following methods:
   - The **feof** function, that works in a manner similar to Pascal's EOF, as shown below:
     ```
     while (!feof(file_ptr)) {
         fgets(string, num_chars, file_ptr);
         /* other statements */
     }
     ```
   - The C **EOF** constant, as shown below:
     ```
     while (fgets(string, num_chars, file_ptr) != EOF) {
         /* loop body */
     }
     ```
   The above method reads a string and also tests for the end-of-file in the while loop test.

   The **fgets** takes three arguments: the string variable, the maximum number of characters to be read, and the file pointer.

   You can also use the **fscanf** function, which is the formatted file input version of **scanf**, to read strings:
   ```
   while (fscanf(filestring, "%s", file_ptr) != EOF) {
       /* loop body */
   }
   ```

> **Programming Hint**
>
> Do not alternate between the **fgets** and **fscanf** functions. Use either of them consistently. In addition, **fscanf** stops reading characters when it encounters a space character or a newline.

4. Close the stream.

Turbo C enables you to access a number of devices as streams. The following are the predefined standard files:

File Name	Device
aux	Standard auxiliary device (the serial port)
err	Standard output device (the screen)
in	Standard input device (the keyboard)
out	Standard output device (the screen)
prn	Standard printer (the parallel printer)

Program Translation

Pascal:
```
      VAR fileptr : TEXT;
          filename : STRING[64];
          line : STRING[80];
      Assign(fileptr, filename);
      Reset(fileptr);
      Read(fileptr,line);
      Close(fileptr);
```
C:
```
      FILE *fileptr;
      char filename[65];
      char line[81];
      fileptr = fopen(filename,"r");
      fgets(line, 80, fileptr);
      /* —— or —— */
      fscanf(fileptr, "%s", line);
      fclose(fileptr);
```

I present two examples for using text streams. The first is a simple file lister that sends the source code to a line printer. The program demonstrates the string file input and output, and sending text to the printer.

The program assumes that the page width is 80 characters and prints 60 lines of source code per page. Each page has the filename printed at the top.

Listing 12.3

```
PROGRAM File_Printer;
{ Turbo Pascal 4 program that prints programs. }
Uses CRT, PRINTER;
CONST MAX_LINES = 60;
      LINE_WIDTH = 80;
TYPE STRING255 = STRING[255];
VAR Filename : STRING[64];
    FileVar : TEXT;
    Line : STRING255;
    N, Page : INTEGER;
    Ch : CHAR;
    OK : BOOLEAN;
BEGIN
  REPEAT
    ClrScr;
    WRITELN('PROGRAM LISTER':40);
    WRITELN('_____':40);
    WRITELN; WRITELN;
    REPEAT
        WRITE('Enter filename -> ');
        READLN(Filename); WRITELN;
        Assign(FileVar, Filename);
        {$I-} Reset(FileVar); {$I+}
        OK := IOResult = 0;
        IF NOT OK THEN BEGIN
```

```
            WRITELN;
            WRITELN('Cannot open file ',Filename);
            WRITELN;
        END;
    UNTIL OK;
    N := 0;
    Page = 1;
    WRITELN;
    WRITE('Reading ');
    WRITELN(LST,Filename:-70,'Page ',Page));
    WRITELN(LST); WRITELN(LST);
    WHILE NOT EOF(FileVar) DO BEGIN
        READLN(FileVar, Line);
        INC(N, (Length(Line) div LINE_WIDTH) + 1);
        IF N >= MAX_LINES THEN BEGIN
            N = 0;
            INC(Page);
            GotoXY(1,20);
            WRITE('Printing page ',Page);
            WRITELN(LST,^L);
            WRITELN(LST,Filename:-70,'Page ',Page);
            WRITELN(LST); WRITELN(LST);
        END;
        WRITELN(LST,Line)
    END;
    GotoXY(1,20); ClrEol;
    Close(FileVar);
    WRITELN; WRITELN;
    WRITE('Print another file? (Y/N)');
    Ch := ReadKey; WRITELN(Ch);
  UNTIL NOT (Ch IN ['Y','y']);
END.
```

The translated C version of the program code lister is

Listing 12.4

```
/* C program that prints programs. */
#include <stdio.h>
#include "conio.h"
#include "string.h"
#define MAX_LINES 60
#define MAX_WIDTH 80
#define MAX_STR 255
typedef char STRING[MAX_STR+1];
main()
{
    char filename[65];
    FILE *filevar, *lister;
    STRING line;
    int n, page;
    char ch;
  do {
    clrscr();
    printf("\t\t\tPROGRAM LISTER\n");
```

```
        printf("\t\t\t_____\n\n\n");
        do {
            printf("Enter filename -> ");
            gets(filename); printf("\n");
            if ((filevar = fopen(filename, "r")) == NULL) {
                printf("\n\nCannot open file %s\n",filename);
            }
        } while (filevar == NULL);
        lister = fopen("prn","w"); /* open printer */
        n = 0;
        page = 1;
        printf("\n");
        printf("Reading ");
        fprintf(lister,"%70s Page 1\n\n", filename);
        while (fgets(line,MAX_STR,filevar) != EOF)   {
            n += strlen(line) / MAX_WIDTH + 1;
            if (n >= MAX_LINES)   {
                n = 0;
                page++;
                gotoxy(1,20);
                printf("Printing page %d", page);
                fprintf(lister,"%c %70s Page %d\n\n", '\014',
                                filename, page);
            }
            fprintf(lister,"%s\n",line);
        }
        gotoxy(1,20); clreol();
        fclose(filevar);
        fclose(lister);
        printf("\n\nPrint another file? (Y/N) ");
        ch = getche();
    } while (ch == 'Y' || ch == 'y');
}
```

Compare the two versions and you will notice the following:

1. Turbo Pascal 4 (and later) uses the PRINTER library unit to provide access to **LST** (the file that represents the standard line printer) such that you need not explicitly assign, open, and close the device. In Turbo C, you employ **fopen** with the predefined **prn** filename and treat the printer in a manner very similar to an output file. This includes using **fclose** to close the printer file handle.

2. Detecting bad filenames in the C version involves testing the file pointer for a NULL address. Compare this with using the **$I** compiler directive and the **IOResult** function in Turbo Pascal.

The second program is a screen file lister. It is able to read up to 750 lines of a source code file (the extra lines are ignored). The program allows you to use the up and down arrow cursors keys, as well as the [PgUp], [PgDn], [Home], and [End] keys. The program shows you how to read an array of strings from a text file. I will take this opportunity to also illustrate cursor and screen control in C. The Pascal code is shown on the following page:

Listing 12.5

```pascal
PROGRAM File_Lister;
{ Turbo Pascal program that lists small programs. The cursor
  and screen control keys are used to navigate in the listing.
  The listings are protected from any modification.           }
{$R+,S+}
Uses CRT;
CONST MAX_LINES = 750;
      LINES_PER_SCREEN = 23;
TYPE STRING80 = STRING[80];
     LineType = ARRAY [1..MAX_LINES] OF STRING80;
VAR Filename : STRING[64];
    FileVar : TEXT;
    Line : LineType;
    N, M, Count : INTEGER;
    Ch : CHAR;
    OK : BOOLEAN;
BEGIN
  REPEAT
    ClrScr;
    WRITELN('PROGRAM LISTER':40);
    WRITELN('_____':40);
    WRITELN; WRITELN;
    REPEAT
        WRITE('Enter filename -> ');
        READLN(Filename); WRITELN;
        Assign(FileVar, Filename);
        {$I-} Reset(FileVar); {$I+}
        OK := IOResult = 0;
        IF NOT OK THEN BEGIN
            WRITELN;
            WRITELN('Cannot open file ',Filename);
            WRITELN;
        END;
    UNTIL OK;
    N := 0;
    WRITELN;
    WRITE('Reading ');
    WHILE (N <= MAX_LINES) AND (NOT EOF(FileVar)) DO BEGIN
        IF (N MOD 50) = 0 THEN WRITE('.');
        INC(N);
        READLN(FileVar, Line[N]);
    END;
    Close(FileVar);
    M := 0;
    DirectVideo := TRUE;
    REPEAT
        ClrScr;
        FOR Count := 1 TO LINES_PER_SCREEN DO
            WRITELN(Line[M+Count]);
        WRITELN;
        WRITE('use cursor/page control keys, [Q] to quit');
        Ch := ReadKey;
        IF (Ch = #0) AND KeyPressed THEN BEGIN
```

```
                Ch := ReadKey;
                CASE Ord(Ch) OF
                    71 : M := 0; { Home}
                    79 : M := N - LINES_PER_SCREEN; { End }
                    73 : BEGIN { PageUp }
                            IF M > 1 THEN DEC(M,LINES_PER_SCREEN);
                            IF M < 0 THEN M := 0;
                         END;
                    81 : BEGIN { PageDown }
                            IF M < N THEN INC(M,LINES_PER_SCREEN);
                            IF M >= (N - LINES_PER_SCREEN) THEN
                                 M := N - LINES_PER_SCREEN;
                         END;
                    72 : { Arrow Up }
                            IF M > 0 THEN DEC(M);
                    80 : BEGIN { Arrow Down }
                            IF M < N THEN INC(M);
                            IF M >= (N - LINES_PER_SCREEN) THEN
                                 M := N - LINES_PER_SCREEN;
                         END;
                END; { CASE }
                Ch := ' ';
            END; { IF }
        UNTIL Ch IN ['Q','q'];
        GotoXY(1,25); ClrEol;
        WRITE('View another file ? (Y/N) ');
        Ch := UpCase(ReadKey); WRITELN(Ch);
        WRITELN; WRITELN;
    UNTIL Ch <> 'Y';
    ClrScr;
END.
```

The translated C program is listed below:

Listing 12.6

```
/* C program that lists small programs. The cursor
   and screen control keys are used to navigate in the listing.
   The listings are protected from any modification.          */
#include <stdio.h>
#include "conio.h"
enum booleans { FALSE, TRUE };
typedef enum booleans boolean;
#define MAX_LINES 750
#define LINES_PER_SCREEN 23
main()
{
    char filename[65];
    FILE *filevar;
    char line[MAX_LINES][81];
    int n = 0, m = 0, count;
    char ch;
  do {
    clrscr();
```

```c
gotoxy(33,1);
printf("PROGRAM LISTER");
gotoxy(33,2);
printf("_____\n\n\n");
do {
    printf("Enter filename -> ");
    gets(filename); printf("\n");
    if ( (filevar = fopen(filename,"rt")) == NULL)
        printf("\nCannot open file %s\n\n",filename);
} while (filevar == NULL);
printf("\n");
printf("Reading ");
while (n < MAX_LINES && !feof(filevar))  {
    if ((n % 50) == 0) putch('.');
    fgets(line[n], 80, filevar);
    n++;
}
fclose(filevar);
n--;
do {
    clrscr();
    for (count = 0; count < LINES_PER_SCREEN; count++)
        printf(line[m+count]);
    gotoxy(1,25);
    printf("use cursor/page control keys, [Q] to quit");
    ch = getche();
    if (ch == 0) {
        ch = getche(); /* get second byte */
        switch (ch) {
            case 71 :
                    m = 0; /* Home */
                    break;
            case 79 :
                    m = n - LINES_PER_SCREEN; /*End*/
                    break;
            case 73 :   /* PageUp */
                    if (m > 1)  m -= LINES_PER_SCREEN;
                    if (m < 0)  m = 0;
                    break;
            case 81 :   /* PageDown */
                    if (m < n)  m += LINES_PER_SCREEN;
                    if (m >= (n - LINES_PER_SCREEN))
                        m = n - LINES_PER_SCREEN;
                    break;
            case 72 :   /* Arrow Up */
                    if (m > 0)   m--;
                    break;
            case 80 :   /* Arrow Down */
                    if (m < n)   m++;
                    if (m >= (n - LINES_PER_SCREEN))
                        m = n - LINES_PER_SCREEN;
                    break;
        } /* switch */
        ch = ' ';
    }
```

```
        } while ( !(ch == 'Q' || ch == 'q') );
        gotoxy(1,25); clreol();
        printf("View another file ? (Y/N) ");
        ch = getche();
        if (ch >= 'a' || ch <= 'z') ch += 'A' - 'a';
        printf("\n\n");
    } while (ch == 'Y');
    clrscr();
}
```

Concerning the aspects of file I/O, the C version uses the **feof** function to detect the end-of-file. The **fgets** is used to read strings into the array **line** using:

`fgets(line[n], 80, filevar);`

The two versions are very similar regarding the detection of cursor and screen control keys. Both display a number of lines (the Turbo Pascal is faster since it writes directly to the screen) and prompt the user to press the [Q] key to exit, or a cursor/screen control key. To detect the latter, each program reads a character and tests whether its value is an ASCII 0. If this is so, a second character is read from the keyboard buffer and processed in a CASE or switch statement. The different case labels identify the key pressed. If it is one of the *valid* keys, the statements in the corresponding case label are executed, resulting in the sought action.

WRITING AND READING NUMERIC DATA USING SEQUENTIAL FILES

Many applications, especially those involving number-crunching, require that numerical data be stored on file to be read in future sessions. This section looks at employing sequential text files for the task of storing numbers. Keep in mind that text files merely offer one alternative that has certain advantages as well as disadvantages. On the positive side, storing numbers (possibly with text) has the following appeal:

1. The contents of the text file can be examined with a text editor. You may also edit the data directly without resorting to a separate application employed for this purpose. This, of course, gives you greater freedom to carry out quick fixes. At the same time, it puts the responsibility on your shoulders that you know what you are doing.

2. Using text files, you can set up the data in a certain format so that it can be read by other major commercial applications.

   On the negative side, the same numeric data occupies more text file space than memory space. Numbers are stored coded within a fixed number of bytes. All the variables of the same numeric type occupy the same number of bytes, regardless of the amount of significant digits they have. However, when you send a string image to a text file, each digit, sign, decimal, and exponent occupies a single byte of disk storage. Compare this with storing numeric data in binary files where the memory image of numbers are stored. As the data size and the number of digits increase, the disk space wasted by text files becomes significant.

The major vehicle for storing numeric data in C text files is **fprintf**. Using the power of output formatting of this function, you can store multiple data objects on one line. Thus, you can place numbers, characters, and strings on the same line in a text file.

The following program writes a small numeric database in a sequential text file. The data file contains the following items:

1. A "DATA0" file type identifier.
2. A string-typed title.
3. The number of variables (that is, columns) and data points (that is, rows).
4. The data variable names, each not exceeding 15 characters.
5. The numeric data is copied from a matrix variable. The data is stored such that each line contains the row number, column number, and corresponding matrix element. This enables you to perform efficient editing and data insertion using your text editor. In addition, you can make the text file contain matrix elements that are not contiguous (that is, create a sparse matrix) or write data in no particular order. You can insert a new matrix element anywhere in the text file. Since you include the row and column numbers of each element, the programs that read this type of file will be able to store the matrix elements correctly: they look at the row/column numbers, not the order in which they read the data.

The program prompts you for the title, number of variables, number of data, names of variables, and the numeric matrix. You are given an opportunity to edit specific elements before you store them on file. Even if you miss correcting a number you typed, you can always utilize your text editor for that purpose. The Pascal listing is shown below:

Listing 12.7

```
PROGRAM Write_Sequential_Data;
{ Turbo Pascal program that saves a numeric matrix
  in a sequential file. The data format is:
  "DATA0"
    Title
    number of variables
    number of data points
    variable names
    numeric matrix
}
Uses CRT;
CONST MAX_COL = 3;
      MAX_ROW = 5;
      VAR_NAME_LEN = 15;
      DATA_ID = 'DATA0';
TYPE STRING80 = STRING[80];
     STRING15 = STRING[VAR_NAME_LEN];
```

BASIC FILE I/O

```
    Matrix = ARRAY [1..MAX_ROW,1..MAX_COL] OF REAL;
    NameArray = ARRAY [1..MAX_COL] OF STRING15;
VAR OK : BOOLEAN;
    ch, ans : CHAR;
    i, j, nvar, ndata : WORD;
    x : Matrix;
    varname : NameArray;
    filename, strng, title : STRING80;
    filevar : TEXT;
BEGIN
    clrscr;
    REPEAT
        WRITE('Enter filename : ');
        READLN(filename); WRITELN;
        Assign(filevar, filename);
        {$I-} Rewrite(filevar); {$I+}
        OK := IOResult = 0;
        IF NOT OK THEN BEGIN
            WRITELN('Cannot open ',filename);
            WRITELN; WRITELN;
        END;
    UNTIL OK;
    WRITE('Enter title : '); READLN(title); WRITELN;
    REPEAT
        WRITE('Enter number of variables [1..',MAX_COL,'] : ');
        READLN(nvar); WRITELN;
    UNTIL nvar IN [1..MAX_COL];
    REPEAT
        WRITE('Enter number of data points [1..',MAX_ROW,'] : ');
        READLN(ndata); WRITELN;
    UNTIL ndata IN [1..MAX_ROW];
    FOR i := 1 TO nvar DO BEGIN
        REPEAT
            WRITE('Enter name for variable # ',i);
            WRITE(' [15 chars max] : ');
            READLN(strng);
        UNTIL Length(strng) IN [1..VAR_NAME_LEN];
        varname[i] := strng
    END;
    WRITELN;
    FOR i := 1 TO ndata DO BEGIN
        FOR j := 1 TO nvar DO BEGIN
            WRITE(varname[j],'[',i,'] : ');
            READLN(x[i,j]);
        END;
        WRITELN;
    END;
    REPEAT
        WRITELN;
        REPEAT
            WRITE('Want to alter data? (Y/N) ');
            ch := UpCase(ReadKey); WRITELN(ch);
        UNTIL ch IN ['Y','N'];
        WRITELN;
        IF ch = 'Y' THEN BEGIN
```

298   INTRODUCING C TO PASCAL PROGRAMMERS

```
                WRITE('Enter row and column numbers : ');
                READLN(i,j);
                WRITELN('You seek X[',i,',',j,'] = ',x[i,j]);
                WRITE('Enter new value? (Y/N) ');
                ans := UpCase(ReadKey); WRITELN(ans);
                IF ans = 'Y' THEN BEGIN
                    WRITE('Enter new value : ');
                    READLN(x[i,j]); WRITELN;
                END;
            END;
    UNTIL ch = 'N';
    WRITELN(filevar,DATA_ID);
    WRITELN(filevar,title);
    WRITELN(filevar,nvar);
    WRITELN(filevar,ndata);
    FOR j := 1 TO nvar DO
        WRITELN(filevar,varname[j]);
    FOR i := 1 TO ndata DO
        FOR j := 1 TO nvar DO
            WRITELN(filevar,i,' ',j,' ',x[i,j]);
    Close(filevar);
    WRITELN('Data saved in file ',filename);
END.
```

The translated C version is listed below:

Listing 12.8

```
/* C program that saves a numeric matrix in a text stream.
   The data format is:
   "DATA0"
   Title
   number of variables
   number of data points
   variable names
   numeric matrix
*/
#include <stdio.h>
#include <stdlib.h>
#include <string.h>
#include "conio.h"
#define MAX_COL 3
#define MAX_ROW 5
#define VAR_NAME_LEN 15
#define DATA_ID "DATA0"
#define STRING80 81
#define STRING15 16
enum booleans { FALSE, TRUE };
typedef enum booleans boolean;
typedef unsigned char byte;
typedef unsigned int word;
char readkey(void);
main()
{
```

```
boolean ok;
char ch, ans;
word i, j, nvar, ndata, strnglen;
double x[MAX_ROW][MAX_COL];
char varname[MAX_COL][STRING15];
char filename[STRING80], strng[STRING80], title[STRING80];
FILE *filevar;
clrscr();
do {
    printf("Enter filename -> ");
    gets(filename); printf("\n");
    if ((filevar = fopen(filename, "w")) == NULL)
        printf("\nCannot open %s\n\n",filename);
} while (filevar == NULL);
printf("Enter title : "); gets(title); printf("\n");
do {
    printf("Enter number of variables [1..%d] : ",MAX_COL);
    scanf("%d", &nvar); printf("\n");
} while (nvar < 1 || nvar > MAX_COL);
do {
    printf("Enter number of data points [1..%d] : ",MAX_ROW);
    scanf("%d", &ndata); printf("\n");
} while (ndata < 1 || ndata > MAX_ROW);
for (i = 0; i < nvar; i++)   {
    do {
        printf("Enter name for variable # %d ",i+1);
        printf(" [15 chars max] : ");
        scanf("%s", &strng);
        strnglen = strlen(strng);
    } while (strnglen < 1 || strnglen > STRING15);
    strcpy(varname[i],strng);
}
printf("\n");
for (i = 0; i < ndata; i++)   {
    for (j = 0 ; j < nvar; j++)   {
        printf("%s[%d] : ",varname[j],i+1);
        scanf("%lf",&x[i][j]);
    }
    printf("\n");
}
do {
    printf("\n");
    do {
        printf("Want to alter data? (Y/N) ");
        ch = readkey();
    } while (ch != 'Y' && ch != 'N');
    printf("\n");
    if (ch == 'Y')   {
        printf("Enter row and column numbers : ");
        scanf("%d %d", &i, &j);
        i--; j--;
        printf("\nYou seek X[%d,%d] = %lf\n",i+1,j+1,x[i][j]);
        printf("Enter new value? (Y/N) ");
        ans = readkey();
        if (ans == 'Y')   {
```

```
              printf("Enter new value : ");
              scanf("%lf", &x[i][j]); printf("\n");
           }
        }
    } while (ch != 'N');
    fprintf(filevar,"%s\n",DATA_ID);
    fprintf(filevar,"%s\n",title);
    fprintf(filevar,"%d \n",nvar);
    fprintf(filevar,"%d \n",ndata);
    for (j = 0; j < nvar; j++)
        fprintf(filevar,"%s\n",varname[j]);
    for (i = 0; i < ndata; i++)
        for (j = 0; j < nvar; j++)
            fprintf(filevar,"%d %d %lg\n",i,j,x[i][j]);
    fclose(filevar);
    printf("Data saved in file %s\n",filename);
}
char readkey(void)
{
   char c;
   c = getche();
   if (c >= 'a' && c <= 'z') c += 'A' - 'a';
   return c;
}
```

Notice that the following nested Pascal loop is used to store the row and column numbers, along with the matrix elements:

```
FOR i := 1 TO ndata DO
    FOR j := 1 TO nvar DO
        WRITELN(filevar,i,' ',j,' ',x[i,j]);
```

A space is inserted between the row, column, and matrix elements. This ensures that the multidata line can be read properly by the next application. Compare it with the **fprintf** which also inserts spaces between the data, but as part of the format string:

```
for (i = 0; i < ndata; i++)
    for (j = 0; j < nvar; j++)
        fprintf(filevar,"%d %d %lg\n",i,j,x[i][j]);
```

While the Pascal program employs WRITELN statements to write to the text file, the C version resorts to **fprintf** to carry out this task. Keep in mind that the text files created by each version differ in the way the floating numbers are stored: Pascal uses scientific notation, while C employs either a fixed or scientific notation, depending on the number.

Since the two versions perform the same task, I present here a sample run with the C version. The following sample session writes to the file MAT.DAT, given the following tabulated data:

Test_C_Data

X	Y
1	1
2	2
3	3

Looking at the above data title "Test_C_Data", you may wonder why I did not write "Test C Data" instead. The reason is that the title must be a string of characters void of space characters (remember that **fscanf** stops reading a string if it encounters a space). This enables the **fscanf** in the next program to read it properly. In general, you can use **fgets** to read strings containing spaces, BUT YOU CAN'T MIX **fgets** AND **fscanf**! Since I need the **fscanf** to read the numbers, I have to use it consistently.

The screen image of the sample session is shown below:

```
Enter filename -> MAT.DAT
Enter title : Test_C_Data
Enter number of variables [1..3] : 2
Enter number of data points [1..5] : 3
Enter name for variable # 1   [15 chars max] : X
Enter name for variable # 2   [15 chars max] : Y
X[1] : 1
Y[1] : 1
X[2] : 2
Y[2] : 2
X[3] : 3
Y[3] : 3
Want to alter data? (Y/N) n
Data saved in file MAT.DAT
```

The contents of the MAT.DAT file are shown below:

```
DATA0
Test_C_Data
2
3
X
Y
0 0 1
0 1 1
1 0 2
1 1 2
2 0 3
2 1 3
```

The next program reads the numeric database created by the last one. The application verifies two facts about the contents of the text-based data file:

1. The first record must be the string "DATA0", which is the file type identifier.
2. The number of data and variables of the numeric matrix are within the current dimension limits.

The above conditions are assumed (with reasonable limits) to suffice for verifying the readability of the text file. The program proceeds with reading all of the data according to the preset file format structure. The program displays the title, number of data points, number of variables, and the data itself. Each datum is shown using the variable names read from the text file. The Pascal listing is presented on the following page:

Listing 12.9

```pascal
PROGRAM Read_Sequential_Files;
{ Turbo Pascal program that reads a numeric matrix
  from a sequential file. The data format is:
  "DATA0"
   Title
   number of variables
   number of data points
   variable names
   numeric matrix
}
Uses CRT;
CONST MAX_COL = 3;
      MAX_ROW = 5;
      MAX_LINES = 22;
      VAR_NAME_LEN = 15;
      DATA_ID = 'DATA0';
      MISSING = -1.0E+30;
TYPE STRING80 = STRING[80];
     STRING15 = STRING[VAR_NAME_LEN];
     Matrix = ARRAY [1..MAX_ROW,1..MAX_COL] OF REAL;
     NameArray = ARRAY [1..MAX_COL] OF STRING15;
VAR OK : BOOLEAN;
    ch, ans : CHAR;
    i, j, nvar, ndata, count : WORD;
    x : Matrix;
    varname : NameArray;
    filename, strng, title : STRING80;
    filevar : TEXT;
BEGIN
    clrscr;
    REPEAT
        WRITE('Enter filename : ');
        READLN(filename); WRITELN;
        Assign(filevar, filename);
        {$I-} Reset(filevar); {$I+}
        OK := IOResult = 0;
        IF NOT OK THEN BEGIN
            WRITELN('Cannot open ',filename);
            WRITELN; WRITELN;
        END;
    UNTIL OK;
    READLN(filevar,strng);
    IF strng = DATA_ID THEN BEGIN
        READLN(filevar,title);
        READLN(filevar,nvar);
        READLN(filevar,ndata);
        IF NOT ( (nvar IN [1..MAX_COL]) AND
                 (ndata IN [1..MAX_ROW])) THEN BEGIN
            WRITELN('Size of rows or columns is out of bounds');
            WRITELN('Number of variables = ',nvar);
            WRITELN('Number of data points = ',ndata);
            Close(filevar);
            HALT;
```

```
        END;
        FOR j := 1 TO nvar DO
            READLN(filevar,varname[j]);
        { initialize matrix with numeric code for missing data }
        FOR i := 1 TO MAX_ROW DO
            FOR j := 1 TO MAX_COL DO
                x[i,j] = MISSING;
        { this loop is able to store data at random, since the
          row and column indices are also read.                }
        FOR count := 1 TO ndata * nvar DO
                READLN(filevar,i,ch,j,ch,x[i,j]);
        clrscr;
        WRITELN('Title : ',title); WRITELN;
        WRITE('File has ',nvar,' variables and ');
        WRITELN(ndata,' data points'); WRITELN;
        count := 5;
        FOR i := 1 TO ndata DO BEGIN
            FOR j := 1 TO nvar DO BEGIN
                INC(count);
                IF count > MAX_LINES THEN BEGIN
                    count := 0;
                    WRITE('press any key to continue ');
                    ch := ReadKey;
                END;
                WRITELN(varname[j],'[',i,'] = ',x[i,j]);
            END;
            WRITE('press any key to continue ');
            ch := ReadKey; WRITELN; WRITELN;
        END;
    END
    ELSE
      WRITELN('File is not a recognized data file');
    Close (filevar);
END.
```

The C version is shown below:

Listing 12.10

```c
/* C program that reads a numeric matrix from a text stream.
   The data format is:
  "DATA0"
   Title
   number of variables
   number of data points
   variable names
   numeric matrix
*/
#include <stdio.h>
#include <stdlib.h>
#include <string.h>
#include "conio.h"
#define DATA_ID "DATA0"
#define MAX_COL 3
```

304 INTRODUCING C TO PASCAL PROGRAMMERS

```c
#define MAX_ROW 5
#define VAR_NAME_LEN 15
#define STRING80 81
#define STRING15 16
#define MISSING -1.0e+30
#define MAX_LINES 22
enum booleans { FALSE, TRUE };
typedef enum booleans boolean;
typedef unsigned char byte;
typedef unsigned int word;
char readkey(void);
main()
{
    boolean ok;
    char ch, ans;
    word i, j, count, nvar, ndata, strnglen;
    double x[MAX_ROW][MAX_COL], *ptr = x;
    char varname[MAX_COL][STRING15];
    char filename[STRING80], strng[STRING80], title[STRING80];
    FILE *filevar;
    clrscr();
    do {
        printf("Enter filename -> ");
        gets(filename); printf("\n");
        if ((filevar = fopen(filename, "r")) == NULL)
            printf("\nCannot open %s\n\n",filename);
    } while (filevar == NULL);
    fscanf(filevar,"%s",strng);
    if (strcmp(strng,DATA_ID) == 0)  {
        fscanf(filevar,"%s",title);
        fscanf(filevar,"%d",&nvar);
        fscanf(filevar,"%d",&ndata);
        if ( ndata < 1 || ndata > MAX_ROW ||
             nvar  < 1 || nvar  > MAX_COL )  {
            printf("Size of rows or columns is out of bounds\n");
            printf("Number of variables = %d\n",nvar);
            printf("Number of data points = %d\n",ndata);
            exit(0);
        }
        for (j = 0; j < nvar; j++)
            fscanf(filevar,"%s",&varname[j]);
        /* initialize matrix with numeric code for missing data */
        for (i = 0; i < MAX_ROW; i++)
              for (j = 0; j < MAX_COL; j++)
                  *(ptr++) = MISSING;
        /* this loop is able to store data at random, since the
           row and column indices are also read.           */
        for (count = 0; count < (nvar * ndata); count++) {
           fscanf(filevar,"%d %d ",&i, &j);
           /* the break in statements is needed for 'i' and 'j'
              to be assigned their correct values.          */
           fscanf(filevar,"%lg", (*(x+i)+j));
        }
        clrscr();
        printf("Title : %s\n",title);
```

```
            printf("File has %d variables and ",nvar);
            printf("%d data points\n\n",ndata);
            count = 5;
            for (i = 0; i < ndata; i++)   {
                for (j = 0; j < nvar; j++)   {
                    count++;
                    if (count > MAX_LINES)   {
                        count = 0;
                        printf("press any key to continue ");
                        ch = getche();
                    }
                    printf("%s[%d] = %lg\n",varname[j],i+1,x[i][j]);
                }
                printf("press any key to continue ");
                ch = getche(); printf("\n\n");
            }
        }
        else
            printf("File is not a recognized data file\n\n");
        fclose(filevar);
}
```

Unlike the Pascal READLN statements, the **fscanf** requires you to employ a format string to specify the exact data format. Using the **fscanf** function, the C version is able to read the data file. As with the console version, **scanf**, you need to supply a pointer to the variable receiving the data. String variables need only their bare names to act as the required pointers, while numeric variables need to use the ampersand operator or pointer variables, as shown below:

```
fscanf(filevar,"%s",title);    <- bare name is a pointer
fscanf(filevar,"%d",&nvar);    <- uses &
fscanf(filevar,"%d",&ndata);   <- uses &
```

In reading the array elements and their row and column numbers, compare the Pascal code that uses a dummy character **ch**:

```
FOR count := 1 TO ndata * nvar DO
        READLN(filevar,i,ch,j,ch,x[i,j]);
```

with the C version that does away with the dummy character and instead employs the format string for tight control of the input:

```
for (count = 0; count < (nvar * ndata); count++)   {
   fscanf(filevar,"%d %d ",&i, &j);
   /* the break in statements is needed for 'i' and 'j'
      to be assigned their correct values.             */
   fscanf(filevar,"%lg", (*(x+i)+j));
}
```

While writing the above program I was using:

```
fscanf(filevar,"%d %d lg",&i, &j, (*(x+i)+j));
```

but was getting displayed results. Breaking the above **fscanf** call into two statements, I was able to correctly read the data. This seems to be a bug in the version of Turbo C that I use.

Looking at the loops used to read the numeric matrix, notice that no end-of-file test is used. This assumes that an uncorrupted file contains (ndata * nvar) elements (any extra lines are ignored).

Running the C version and reading the contents of file MAT.DAT results in the following screen image:

```
Title : Test_C_Data
File has 2 variables and 3 data points
X[1] = 1
Y[1] = 1
press any key to continue
X[2] = 2
Y[2] = 2
press any key to continue
X[3] = 3
Y[3] = 3
press any key to continue
```

BINARY STREAM I/O

Binary files are able to store numeric data in a form that is more compact than text files. In addition, they are able to store structures and unions that text files cannot store without converting everything into strings. Binary files are also available in Pascal. They are declared as FILE OF <type identifier>.

Binary file I/O is divided into two main categories: the first is related to writing structures and unions in either sequential or random-access files. The second category of binary file I/O is engaged in low-level block I/O.

USING STRUCTURES TO WRITE AND READ NUMERIC DATA IN BINARY STREAMS

As stated earlier, a better approach for storing numeric data and structures involves binary files. To write structures to a binary file, employ the following steps:

1. Declare a file pointer using the predefined **FILE** type.
2. Open the stream using an appropriate mode and check the file pointer for a NULL value.
3. Write the structure to the binary stream using **fwrite**, as shown below:

   ```
   fwrite(struct_ptr, size, num_items, file_ptr);
   ```

   The **fwrite** routine takes four parameters. The first is the pointer to the structure. The second is the size of the data object or structure. The third parameter is the number of data items read. The last one is the file pointer. The **fwrite** function returns an integer that represents the number of bytes written.

   To write an array of items using **fwrite**, you have two routes:

- Use the **size** argument to indicate the size of the entire array, and make the number of data items equal to 1. This is shown in the code below:
    ```
    #include <stdio.h>
    main()
    {
        double numbers[3] = { 1.0, 2.0, 3.0 };
        FILE *fileptr;
        fileptr = fopen("sample.dat", "wb");

        fwrite(numbers, sizeof(numbers), 1, fileptr);
        fclose(fileptr);
    }
    ```
- Use the **size** argument to indicate the size of a single array element and make the number of data items equal to the size of the array. This is shown in the code below:
    ```
    #include <stdio.h>
    main()
    {
        double numbers[3] = { 1.0, 2.0, 3.0 };
        FILE *fileptr;
        fileptr = fopen("sample.dat", "wb");

        fwrite(numbers, sizeof(double), 3, fileptr);
        fclose(fileptr);
    }
    ```

The above method enables you to write part of an array. This is done by pointing to the first element sending data and the number of items to write, as shown below:

```
fwrite(&numbers[1], sizeof(double), 2, fileptr);
```

The above writes two data items starting with numbers[1].

4. Close the stream.

Program Translation

Pascal:
```
VAR fileptr : FILE OF <record>
    filename : STRING[64];
    data : <record>;
Assign(fileptr, filename);
Rewrite(fileptr);
Write(fileptr, data);
Close(fileptr);
```
C:
```
#include <stdio.h>
FILE *fileptr;
char filename[65];
```

```
            struct <structure name> data;
            fileptr = fopen(filename,"wb");
            fwrite(&data, sizeof(data), 1, fileptr);

            fclose(fileptr);
```

The next program is a modified version of the previous one that writes a numeric database. Instead of using a text stream, this program version defines a record structure that contains the database title, number of variables, number of data points, names of variables, and numeric matrix. The record structure that stores the entire numeric database is written to a binary file using one call to **fwrite**. Likewise, the Pascal version uses one Write statement to output the record structure to the binary file. This version does not store the row and column numbers of each numeric matrix element. Instead, the memory image of the matrix is stored on file. The Pascal listing is presented below:

Listing 12.11

```
PROGRAM Write_Sequential_Records;
{ Turbo Pascal program that saves a numeric matrix and its
  related data as a single record.
}
Uses CRT;
CONST MAX_COL = 3;
      MAX_ROW = 5;
      VAR_NAME_LEN = 15;
TYPE STRING80 = STRING[80];
     STRING15 = STRING[VAR_NAME_LEN];
     Matrix = ARRAY [1..MAX_ROW,1..MAX_COL] OF REAL;
     NameArray = ARRAY [1..MAX_COL] OF STRING15;
     DataBase = RECORD
                  title    : STRING80;
                  nvar,
                  ndata    : WORD;
                  varname  : NameArray;
                  x        : Matrix;
        END;
VAR OK : BOOLEAN;
    ch, ans : CHAR;
    i, j : WORD;
    filename, strng : STRING80;
    data : DataBase;
    filevar : FILE OF DataBase;
BEGIN
 clrscr;
  WITH data DO BEGIN
    REPEAT
        WRITE('Enter filename -> ');
        READLN(filename); WRITELN;
        Assign(filevar, filename);
        {$I-} Rewrite(filevar); {$I+}
        OK := IOResult = 0;
```

```
            IF NOT OK THEN BEGIN
                WRITELN('Cannot open ',filename);
                WRITELN; WRITELN;
            END;
        UNTIL OK;
        WRITE('Enter title : '); READLN(title); WRITELN;
        REPEAT
            WRITE('Enter number of variables [1..',MAX_COL,'] : ');
            READLN(nvar); WRITELN;
        UNTIL nvar IN [1..MAX_COL];
        REPEAT
            WRITE('Enter number of data points [1..',MAX_ROW,'] : ');
            READLN(ndata); WRITELN;
        UNTIL ndata IN [1..MAX_ROW];
        FOR i := 1 TO nvar DO BEGIN
            REPEAT
                WRITE('Enter name for variable # ',i);
                WRITE(' [15 chars max] : ');
                READLN(strng);
            UNTIL Length(strng) IN [1..VAR_NAME_LEN];
            varname[i] := strng
        END;
        WRITELN;
        FOR i := 1 TO ndata DO BEGIN
            FOR j := 1 TO nvar DO BEGIN
                WRITE(varname[j],'[',i,'] : ');
                READLN(x[i,j]);
            END;
            WRITELN;
        END;
        REPEAT
            WRITELN;
            REPEAT
                WRITE('Want to alter data? (Y/N) ');
                ch := UpCase(ReadKey); WRITELN(ch);
            UNTIL ch IN ['Y','N'];
            WRITELN;
            IF ch = 'Y' THEN BEGIN
                WRITE('Enter row and column numbers : ');
                READLN(i,j);
                WRITELN('You seek X[',i,',',j,'] = ',x[i,j]);
                WRITE('Enter new value? (Y/N) ');
                ans := UpCase(ReadKey); WRITELN(ans);
                IF ans = 'Y' THEN BEGIN
                    WRITE('Enter new value : ');
                    READLN(x[i,j]); WRITELN;
                END;
            END;
        UNTIL ch = 'N';
        WRITE(filevar, data);
        Close(filevar);
        WRITELN('Data saved in binary file ',filename);
    END; { WITH data }
END.
```

The translated C version is listed below:

Listing 12.12

```
/* C program that saves a numeric matrix and its related
   data structure in a binary sequential file.
   The data format is:
  "DATA0"
  Title
  number of variables
  number of data points
  variable names
  numeric matrix
*/
#include <stdio.h>
#include <stdlib.h>
#include <string.h>
#include "conio.h"
#define MAX_COL 3
#define MAX_ROW 5
#define VAR_NAME_LEN 15
#define DATA_ID "DATA0"
#define STRING80 81
#define STRING15 16
enum booleans { FALSE, TRUE };
typedef enum booleans boolean;
typedef unsigned char byte;
typedef unsigned int word;
typedef struct database_rec {
        char title[STRING80];
        word nvar;
        word ndata;
        char varname[MAX_COL][STRING15];
        double x[MAX_ROW][MAX_COL];
     } database;
char readkey(void);
main()
{
    boolean ok;
    char ch, ans;
    word i, j, strnglen;
    database data;
    char filename[STRING80], strng[STRING80];
    FILE *filevar;
    clrscr();
    do {
        printf("Enter filename -> ");
        gets(filename); printf("\n");
        if ((filevar = fopen(filename, "wb")) == NULL)
            printf("\nCannot open %s\n\n",filename);
    } while (filevar == NULL);
    printf("Enter title : "); gets(data.title); printf("\n");
    do {
        printf("Enter number of variables [1..%d] : ",MAX_COL);
```

BASIC FILE I/O

```c
            scanf("%d", &data.nvar); printf("\n");
    } while (data.nvar < 1 || data.nvar > MAX_COL);
    do {
        printf("Enter number of data points [1..%d] : ",MAX_ROW);
        scanf("%d", &data.ndata); printf("\n");
    } while (data.ndata < 1 || data.ndata > MAX_ROW);
    for (i = 0; i < data.nvar; i++)   {
        do {
            printf("Enter name for variable # %d ",i);
            printf(" [15 chars max] : ");
            scanf("%s", &strng);
            strnglen = strlen(strng);
        } while (strnglen < 1 || strnglen > STRING15);
        strcpy(data.varname[i],strng);
    }
    printf("\n");
    for (i = 0; i < data.ndata; i++)   {
        for (j = 0 ; j < data.nvar; j++)   {
            printf("%s[%d] : ",data.varname[j],i);
            scanf("%lf",&data.x[i][j]);
        }
        printf("\n");
    }
    do {
        printf("\n");
        do {
            printf("Want to alter data? (Y/N) ");
            ch = readkey();
        } while (ch != 'Y' && ch != 'N');
        printf("\n");
        if (ch == 'Y')   {
            printf("Enter row and column numbers : ");
            scanf("%d %d", &i, &j);
            i--; j--;
            printf("\nYou seek X[%d,%d] = %lf\n",
                                     i, j, data.x[i][j]);
            printf("Enter new value? (Y/N) ");
            ans = readkey();
            if (ans == 'Y')   {
                printf("Enter new value : ");
                scanf("%lf", &data.x[i][j]); printf("\n");
            }
        }
    } while (ch != 'N');
    fwrite(&data, sizeof(database), 1, filevar);
    fclose(filevar);
    printf("Data saved in binary file %s\n",filename);
}
char readkey(void)
{
    char c;
    c = getche();
    if (c >= 'a' && c <= 'z') c += 'A' - 'a';
    return c;
}
```

The Pascal version utilizes the following record type:

```
DataBase = RECORD
            title   : STRING80;
            nvar,
            ndata   : WORD;
            varname : NameArray;
            x       : Matrix;
END;
```

which is translated into the following C structure:

```
typedef struct database_rec
   {
      char title[STRING80];
      word nvar;
      word ndata;
      char varname[MAX_COL][STRING15];
      double x[MAX_ROW][MAX_COL];
   } database;
```

Notice that the above data structure does not include a field for the "DATA0" file identification. This is due to the fact that the entire database is written (and likewise, read) with one I/O statement. Consequently, the structure stored on file read must match the one in the program. Error handling must rely on routines provided by each language.

The Pascal version makes use of the "WITH data DO" statement to enable you to directly reference the fields of **data** as ordinary variables. The C version uses **data.** with all of the structure fields.

Both the Pascal and C versions write the entire database with single WRITE and **fwrite** statements, respectively:

```
WRITE(filevar, data); { Pascal }
fwrite(&data, sizeof(database), 1, filevar); /* C */
```

To read structures from a binary stream, use the following steps:

1. Declare a file pointer using the predefined **FILE** type.
2. Open the stream using an appropriate mode and check the file pointer for a NULL value.
3. Write the structure to the binary stream using **fread**, as shown below:

   ```
   fread(struct_ptr, size, num_items, file_ptr);
   ```

The **fread** routine takes four parameters. The first is the pointer to the structure. The second is the size of the data object or structure. The third parameter is the number of data items read. The last one is the file pointer. The **fread** function returns the number of items that were actually read. The **fread** function returns an integer that represents the number of bytes read.

To read an array of items using **fread**, you have two choices:

- Use the **size** argument to indicate the size of the entire array, and make the number of data items equal to 1. This is shown in the code below:

```
#include <stdio.h>
main()
{
    double numbers[3];
    FILE *fileptr;
    fileptr = fopen("sample.dat", "rb");

    fread(numbers, sizeof(numbers), 1, fileptr);
    fclose(fileptr);
}
```

- Use the **size** argument to indicate the size of a single array element and make the number of data items equal to the size of the array. This is shown in the code below:
```
#include <stdio.h>
main()
{
    double numbers[3];
    FILE *fileptr;
    fileptr = fopen("sample.dat", "rb");

    fread(numbers, sizeof(double), 3, fileptr);
    fclose(fileptr);
}
```

The above method enables you to read part of an array. This is done by pointing to the first element receiving data and the number of items to be read, as shown below:

```
fread(&numbers[1], sizeof(double), 2, fileptr);
```

The above reads two data items starting with numbers[1].

4. Close the stream.

Program Translation

Pascal:
```
VAR fileptr : FILE OF <record>
    filename : STRING[64];
    data : <record>;
Assign(fileptr, filename);
Reset(fileptr);
Read(fileptr, data);
Close(fileptr);
```
C:
```
#include <stdio.h>
FILE *fileptr;
char filename[65];
int bytes_read
struct <structure name> data;
fileptr = fopen(filename,"rb");
bytes_read = fread(&data, sizeof(data), 1, fileptr);

fclose(fileptr);
```

To accompany the above program that writes data to a binary stream, I present the counterpart application: programs to read the data structure from binary files. The previous Pascal record and C structure are also used with the data input programs. The Pascal listing is shown below:

Listing 12.13

```
PROGRAM Read_Sequential_Record;
{ Turbo Pascal program that reads the record structure
  containing a numeric matrix from a binary file.
}
Uses CRT;
CONST MAX_COL = 3;
      MAX_ROW = 5;
      VAR_NAME_LEN = 15;
      MAX_LINES = 22;
TYPE STRING80 = STRING[80];
     STRING15 = STRING[VAR_NAME_LEN];
     Matrix = ARRAY [1..MAX_ROW,1..MAX_COL] OF REAL;
     NameArray = ARRAY [1..MAX_COL] OF STRING15;
     DataBase = RECORD
                  title   : STRING80;
                  nvar,
                  ndata   : WORD;
                  varname : NameArray;
                  x       : Matrix;
                END;
VAR OK : BOOLEAN;
    ch, ans : CHAR;
    i, j, count : WORD;
    filename, strng : STRING80;
    filevar : FILE OF DataBase;
    data : DataBase;
BEGIN
    clrscr;
    REPEAT
        WRITE('Enter filename -> ');
        READLN(filename); WRITELN;
        Assign(filevar, filename);
        {$I-} Reset(filevar); {$I+}
        OK := IOResult = 0;
        IF NOT OK THEN BEGIN
            WRITELN('Cannot open ',filename);
            WRITELN; WRITELN;
        END;
    UNTIL OK;
    READ(filevar,data);
    WITH data DO BEGIN
        clrscr;
        WRITELN('Title : ',title); WRITELN;
        WRITE('File has ',nvar,' variables and ');
        WRITELN(ndata,' data points'); WRITELN;
        count := 5;
        FOR i := 1 TO ndata DO BEGIN
            FOR j := 1 TO nvar DO BEGIN
```

```
                INC(count);
                IF count > MAX_LINES THEN BEGIN
                    count := 0;
                    WRITE('press any key to continue ');
                    ch := ReadKey;
                END;
                WRITELN(varname[j],'[',i,'] = ',x[i,j]);
            END;
            WRITE('press any key to continue ');
            ch := ReadKey; WRITELN; WRITELN;
        END;
    END; { WITH data }
    Close(filevar);
END.
```

The translated C program is shown below:

Listing 12.14

```
/* C program that reads the structure of numeric matrix
   and its related data from a binary stream.
*/
#include <stdio.h>
#include <stdlib.h>
#include <string.h>
#include "conio.h"
#define MAX_COL 3
#define MAX_ROW 5
#define VAR_NAME_LEN 15
#define STRING80 81
#define STRING15 16
#define MAX_LINES 22
enum booleans { FALSE, TRUE };
typedef enum booleans boolean;
typedef unsigned char byte;
typedef unsigned int word;
typedef struct database_rec
   {
       char title[STRING80];
       word nvar;
       word ndata;
       char varname[MAX_COL][STRING15];
       double x[MAX_ROW][MAX_COL];
   } database;
char readkey(void);
main()
{
    boolean ok;
    char ch, ans;
    word i, j, count, strnglen;
    char filename[STRING80], strng[STRING80];
    database data;
    FILE *filevar;
    clrscr();
```

```
    do {
        printf("Enter filename -> ");
        gets(filename); printf("\n");
        if ((filevar = fopen(filename, "rb")) == NULL)
            printf("\nCannot open %s\n\n",filename);
    } while (filevar == NULL);
    /* read data structure */
    fread(&data, sizeof(data), 1, filevar);
    clrscr();
    printf("Title : %s\n",data.title);
    printf("File has %d variables and ",data.nvar);
    printf("%d data points\n\n",data.ndata);
    count = 5;
    for (i = 0; i < data.ndata; i++)  {
        for (j = 0; j < data.nvar; j++)  {
            count++;
            if (count > MAX_LINES)  {
                count = 0;
                printf("press any key to continue ");
                ch = getche();
            }
            printf("%s[%d] = %lf\n",
                                data.varname[j],i,data.x[i][j]);
        }
        printf("press any key to continue ");
        ch = getche(); printf("\n\n");
    }
    fclose(filevar);
}
```

Both programs invoke one call to a binary file input routine to obtain the entire numeric database:

```
READ(filevar, data);
fread(&data, sizeof(data), 1, filevar);
```

USING UNIONS WITH RANDOM-ACCESS BINARY STREAMS

Binary streams may be accessed either sequentially or at random. Random-access files are popular in database applications. Depending on the nature of an application, either fixed or variant record structures are utilized. In general, variant record structures enable you to store records with heterogeneous structures. This is important for databases, since the first few records may contain information such as file size statistics, passwords, date of creation, and last update. The rest of the random-access records in the file contain the data structures.

Use these steps to write structures or unions to a random-access binary file:

1. Declare a file pointer using the predefined **FILE** type.
2. Open the stream using an appropriate mode and check the file pointer for a NULL value.

3. Write the structure to the binary stream using **fwrite**, as shown below:

    ```
    fwrite(struct_ptr, size, num_items, file_ptr);
    ```

    This is the same **fwrite** function used in writing data to binary files. So what is the difference? The **fseek** function may be used to zoom in on a particular record:

    ```
    fseek(file_ptr, offset, integer_reference_point);
    ```

    The **fseek** has three parameters. The first is the file pointer. The second is a long integer offset value, which determines the the distance, in bytes, from the reference point. The third parameter is an integer-typed reference point or anchor. The **fseek** function returns 0 if the pointer moved successfully and a nonzero interger if the pointer movement has failed. Turbo C predefines three symbolic constants:

Reference Point	Value	File Location
SEEK_SET	0	File beginning.
SEEK_CUR	1	Current location.
SEEK_END	2	End of the file.

    If you do not employ **fseek** before every data I/O, the file pointer moves to the next location in the stream. This enables you to employ both sequential and random access schemes in accessing data using binary streams.

4. Close the stream.

Program Translation

Pascal:
```
VAR fileptr : FILE OF <record>
    filename : STRING[64];
    data : <record>;
    offset : LONGINT;
Assign(fileptr, filename);
Rewrite(fileptr);
Seek(fileptr, offset);
Write(fileptr, data);
Close(fileptr);
```
C:
```
#include <stdio.h>
FILE *fileptr;
char filename[65];
struct <structure name> data;
/* ──── or ──── */
union <union name> data;
long offset;
fileptr = fopen(filename,"wb");
fseek(fileptr, offset, {0|1|2});
fwrite(&data, sizeof(data), 1, fileptr);

fclose(fileptr);
```

318 INTRODUCING C TO PASCAL PROGRAMMERS

The next applications present another modification of the original numeric database program set. Actually, they resemble more closely the text stream version than the ones using structures. The first few records include the following information found in the text-based data file:

1. "DATA0" string used as a file type identifier.
2. The title.
3. The number of variables and data points.
4. The variable names, each stored in a separate random-access record.

These records are followed by the data from the numeric matrix, stored by rows (each row is stored in one random-access record). The application programs interact just as the version using text files does. The Pascal listing is shown below:

Listing 12.15

```
PROGRAM Write_Random_Data;
{ Turbo Pascal program that saves a numeric matrix
  in a random-access file. The data format is:
  "DATA0"
   Title
   number of variables
   number of data points
   variable names
   numeric matrix
}
Uses CRT;
CONST MAX_COL = 3;
      MAX_ROW = 5;

      VAR_NAME_LEN = 15;

      DATA_ID = 'DATA0';
TYPE STRING80 = STRING[80];
     STRING15 = STRING[VAR_NAME_LEN];
     Matrix = ARRAY [1..MAX_ROW,1..MAX_COL] OF REAL;
     Vector = ARRAY [1..MAX_ROW] OF REAL;
     DataRec = RECORD
         Dummy_field : WORD;
         CASE INTEGER OF
             0 : (str_field : STRING80);
             1 : (int_field : WORD);
             2 : (name_field : STRING15);
             3 : (vect_field : Vector);
     END;
     DataFileRec = FILE OF DataRec;
     NameArray = ARRAY [1..MAX_COL] OF STRING15;
VAR OK : BOOLEAN;
    ch, ans : CHAR;
    i, j, k, nvar, ndata : WORD;
    x : Matrix;
    varname : NameArray;
```

```
        Buffer : DataRec;
        filename, strng, title : STRING80;
        filevar : DataFileRec;
BEGIN
    clrscr;
    REPEAT
        WRITE('Enter filename : ');
        READLN(filename); WRITELN;
        Assign(filevar, filename);
        {$I-} Rewrite(filevar); {$I+}
        OK := IOResult = 0;
        IF NOT OK THEN BEGIN
            WRITELN('Cannot open ',filename);
            WRITELN; WRITELN;
        END;
    UNTIL OK;
    WRITE('Enter title : '); READLN(title); WRITELN;
    REPEAT
        WRITE('Enter number of variables [1..',MAX_COL,'] : ');
        READLN(nvar); WRITELN;
    UNTIL nvar IN [1..MAX_COL];
    REPEAT
        WRITE('Enter number of data points [1..',MAX_ROW,'] : ');
        READLN(ndata); WRITELN;
    UNTIL ndata IN [1..MAX_ROW];
    FOR i :=  1 TO nvar DO BEGIN
        REPEAT
            WRITE('Enter name for variable # ',i);
            WRITE(' [15 chars max] : ');
            READLN(strng);
        UNTIL Length(strng) IN [1..VAR_NAME_LEN];
        varname[i] := strng
    END;
    WRITELN;
    FOR i := 1 TO ndata DO BEGIN
        FOR j := 1 TO nvar DO BEGIN
            WRITE(varname[j],'[',i,'] : ');
            READLN(x[i,j]);
        END;
      WRITELN;
    END;
    REPEAT
        WRITELN;
        REPEAT
            WRITE('Want to alter data? (Y/N) ');
            ch := UpCase(ReadKey); WRITELN(ch);
        UNTIL ch IN ['Y','N'];
        WRITELN;
        IF ch = 'Y' THEN BEGIN
            WRITE('Enter row and column numbers : ');
            READLN(i,j);
            WRITELN('You seek X[',i,',',j,'] = ',x[i,j]);
            WRITE('Enter new value? (Y/N) ');
            ans := UpCase(ReadKey); WRITELN(ans);
            IF ans = 'Y' THEN BEGIN
                WRITE('Enter new value : ');
```

```
            READLN(x[i,j]); WRITELN;
        END;
    END;
UNTIL ch = 'N';
SEEK(filevar,0);
Buffer.str_field := DATA_ID;
WRITE(filevar,Buffer);
SEEK(filevar,1);
Buffer.str_field := title;
WRITE(filevar,Buffer);
SEEK(filevar,2);
Buffer.int_field := nvar;
WRITE(filevar,Buffer);
SEEK(filevar,3);
Buffer.int_field := ndata;
WRITE(filevar,Buffer);

FOR j := 1 TO nvar DO BEGIN
    SEEK(filevar,3+j);
    Buffer.name_field := varname[j];
    WRITE(filevar,Buffer);
END;
k := 3 + nvar;
FOR i := 1 TO ndata DO BEGIN
    FOR j := 1 TO nvar DO
        Buffer.vect_field[j] := x[i,j];
    INC(k);
    SEEK(filevar,k);
    WRITE(filevar,Buffer);
END;
Close(filevar);
WRITELN('Data saved in file ',filename);
END.
```

The translated C program is shown below:

Listing 12.16

```c
/* C program that saves a numeric matrix
   in a random-access binary stream. The data format is:
   "DATA0"
   Title
   number of variables
   number of data points
   variable names
   numeric matrix
*/
#include <stdio.h>
#include <stdlib.h>
#include <string.h>
#include "conio.h"
#define MAX_COL 3
#define MAX_ROW 5
#define VAR_NAME_LEN 15
#define DATA_ID "DATA0"
```

BASIC FILE I/O

```c
#define STRING80 81
#define STRING15 16
enum booleans { FALSE, TRUE };
typedef enum booleans boolean;
typedef unsigned char byte;
typedef unsigned int word;
typedef union datarec_type
    {
      char str_field[STRING80];
      word int_field;
      char name_field[STRING15];
      double vect_field[MAX_COL];
      } datarec;
char readkey(void);
main()
{
    boolean OK;
    char ch, ans;
    word i, j, k, nvar, ndata, strnglen;
    word datalen = sizeof(datarec);
    double x[MAX_ROW][MAX_COL];
    char varname[MAX_COL][STRING15];
    datarec buffer;
    char filename[STRING80], strng[STRING80], title[STRING80];
    FILE *filevar;
    clrscr();
    do {
        printf("Enter filename -> ");
        gets(filename); printf("\n");
        if ((filevar = fopen(filename,"wb")) == NULL)
            printf("Cannot open %s\n\n",filename);
    } while (filevar == NULL);
    printf("Enter title : "); gets(title); printf("\n");
    do {
        printf("Enter number of variables [1..%d] : ",MAX_COL);
        scanf("%d", &nvar); printf("\n");
    } while (nvar < 1 || nvar > MAX_COL);
    do {
        printf("Enter number of data points [1..%d] : ",MAX_ROW);
        scanf("%d", &ndata); printf("\n");
    } while (ndata < 1 || ndata > MAX_ROW);
    for (i = 0; i < nvar; i++)   {
        do {
            printf("Enter name for variable # %d ",i);
            printf(" [15 chars max] : ");
            scanf("%s", &strng);
            strnglen = strlen(strng);
        } while (strnglen < 1 || strnglen > STRING15);
        strcpy(varname[i],strng);
    }
    printf("\n");
    for (i = 0; i < ndata; i++)   {
        for (j = 0 ; j < nvar; j++)   {
            printf("%s[%d] : ",varname[j],i);
            scanf("%lf",&x[i][j]);
        }
```

322 INTRODUCING C TO PASCAL PROGRAMMERS

```c
            printf("\n");
        }
        do {
            printf("\n");
            do {
                printf("Want to alter data? (Y/N) ");
                ch = readkey();
            } while (ch != 'Y' && ch != 'N');
            printf("\n");
            if (ch == 'Y')  {
                printf("Enter row and column numbers : ");
                scanf("%d %d", &i, &j);
                i--; j--;
                printf("\nYou seek X[%d,%d] = %lf\n",
                                                i, j, x[i][j]);
                printf("Enter new value? (Y/N) ");
                ans = readkey();
                if (ans == 'Y')  {
                    printf("Enter new value : ");
                    scanf("%lf", &x[i][j]); printf("\n");
                }
            }
        } while (ch != 'N');
        fseek(filevar, 0, SEEK_SET);
        strcpy(buffer.str_field,DATA_ID);
        fwrite(&buffer, datalen, 1, filevar);
        strcpy(buffer.str_field,title);
        fseek(filevar, datalen, SEEK_SET);
        fwrite(&buffer, sizeof(datarec), 1, filevar);
        buffer.int_field = nvar;
        fseek(filevar, 2 * datalen, SEEK_SET);
        fwrite(&buffer, sizeof(datarec), 1, filevar);
        buffer.int_field = ndata;
        fseek(filevar, 3 * datalen, SEEK_SET);
        fwrite(&buffer, sizeof(datarec), 1, filevar);
        k = 3;
        for (j = 0; j < nvar; j++)  {
            strcpy(buffer.name_field,varname[j]);
            k++;
            fseek(filevar, k*datalen, SEEK_SET);
            fwrite(&buffer, sizeof(datarec), 1, filevar);
        }
        for (i = 0; i < ndata; i++)  {
            for (j = 0; j < nvar; j++)
                buffer.vect_field[j] = x[i][j];
            k++;
            fseek(filevar, k * datalen, SEEK_SET);
            fwrite(&buffer, sizeof(datarec), 1, filevar);
        }
        fclose(filevar);
        printf("Data saved in binary random-access file ",filename);
}
char readkey(void)
{
    char c;
```

BASIC FILE I/O   323

```
    c = getche();
    if (c >= 'a' && c <= 'z') c += 'A' - 'a';
    return c;
}
```

The variant Pascal record:

```
DataRec = RECORD
    Dummy_field : WORD;
    CASE INTEGER OF
        0 : (str_field : STRING80);
        1 : (int_field : WORD);
        2 : (name_field : STRING15);
        3 : (vect_field : Vector);
END;
```

is translated into the C union:

```
typedef union datarec_type
    {
        char str_field[STRING80];
        word int_field;
        char name_field[STRING15];
        double vect_field[MAX_COL];
    } datarec;
```

I deliberately chose to use a file seek before every file output operation. The Pascal version SEEK requires only a record number, while **fseek** needs both a byte offset and a reference point. This reflects the flexibility and superiority of I/O in C over Pascal, using the "stdio.h" library.

Both the Pascal and C versions copy data from variables to different structure fields before sending the copied information to the binary stream.

To read structures or unions from a random-access binary stream, employ the following steps:

1. Declare a file pointer using the predefined **FILE** type.
2. Open the stream using an appropriate mode and check the file pointer for a NULL value.
3. Read the structure to the binary stream using **fread**, as shown below:

    ```
    fread(struct_ptr, size, num_items, file_ptr);
    ```

    As with the **fwrite** function, the **fseek** function may be used to zoom in on a particular record.
4. Close the stream.

Program Translation

Pascal:
```
    VAR fileptr : FILE OF <record>
        filename : STRING[64];
        data : <record>;
        offset : LONGINT;
    Assign(fileptr, filename);
```

```
        Reset(fileptr);
        Seek(fileptr, offset);
        Read(fileptr, data);
        Close(fileptr);
    C:
      FILE *fileptr;
      char filename[65];
      struct <structure name> data;
      /* ―――― or ―――― */
      union <union name> data;
      long offset;
      fileptr = fopen(filename,"rb");
      fseek(fileptr, offset, {0|1|2});
      fread(&data, sizeof(data), 1, fileptr);

      fclose(fileptr);
```

The last numeric database program reads the random-access records. It verifies that "DATA0" is found in the first record. In addition, it checks to see whether the program's matrix variable has enough space to accommodate the matrix read from the binary file. The Pascal source code is listed below:

Listing 12.17

```
PROGRAM Read_Random_Data;
{ Turbo Pascal program that reads a numeric matrix
  from a random-access file. The data format is:
  "DATA0"
    Title
    number of variables
    number of data points
    variable names
    numeric matrix
}
Uses CRT;
CONST MAX_COL = 3;
      MAX_ROW = 5;
      VAR_NAME_LEN = 15;
      DATA_ID = 'DATA0';
      MAX_LINES = 22;
TYPE STRING80 = STRING[80];
     STRING15 = STRING[VAR_NAME_LEN];
     Matrix = ARRAY [1..MAX_ROW,1..MAX_COL] OF REAL;
     Vector = ARRAY [1..MAX_ROW] OF REAL;
     DataRec = RECORD
         Dummy_field : WORD;
         CASE INTEGER OF
             0 : (str_field : STRING80);
             1 : (int_field : WORD);
             2 : (name_field : STRING15);
             3 : (vect_field : Vector);
     END;
     DataFileRec = FILE OF DataRec;
     NameArray = ARRAY [1..MAX_COL] OF STRING15;
```

BASIC FILE I/O 325

```
VAR OK : BOOLEAN;
    ch, ans : CHAR;
    i, j, k, count, nvar, ndata : WORD;
    x : Matrix;
    varname : NameArray;
    Buffer : DataRec;
    filename, strng, title : STRING80;
    filevar : DataFileRec;
BEGIN
    clrscr;
    REPEAT
        WRITE('Enter filename : ');
        READLN(filename); WRITELN;
        Assign(filevar, filename);
        {$I-} Reset(filevar); {$I+}
        OK := IOResult = 0;
        IF NOT OK THEN BEGIN
            WRITELN('Cannot open ',filename);
            WRITELN; WRITELN;
        END;
    UNTIL OK;
    SEEK(filevar, 0);
    READ(filevar,Buffer);
    strng := Buffer.str_field;
    IF strng = DATA_ID THEN BEGIN
        SEEK(filevar, 1);
        READ(filevar,Buffer);
        title := Buffer.str_field;
        SEEK(filevar, 2);
        READ(filevar,Buffer);
        nvar := Buffer.int_field;
        SEEK(filevar, 3);
        READ(filevar,Buffer);
        ndata := Buffer.int_field;
        IF (NOT (ndata IN [1..MAX_ROW])) OR
           (NOT (nvar IN [1..MAX_COL])) THEN HALT;
        k = 3;
        FOR j := 1 TO nvar DO BEGIN
            INC(k);
            SEEK(filevar, k);
            READ(filevar, Buffer);
            varname[j] := Buffer.name_field;
        END;
        FOR i := 1 TO ndata DO BEGIN
            INC(k);
            SEEK(filevar, k);
            READ(filevar,Buffer);
            FOR j := 1 TO nvar DO
                x[i,j] := Buffer.vect_field[j];
        END;
        clrscr;
        WRITELN('Title : ',title); WRITELN;
        WRITE('File has ',nvar,' variables and ');
        WRITELN(ndata,' data points'); WRITELN;
        count := 5;
        FOR i := 1 TO ndata DO BEGIN
```

326   INTRODUCING C TO PASCAL PROGRAMMERS

```
            FOR j := 1 TO nvar DO BEGIN
                INC(count);
                IF count > MAX_LINES THEN BEGIN
                    count := 0;
                    WRITE('press any key to continue ');
                    ch := ReadKey;
                END;
                WRITELN(varname[j],'[',i,'] = ',x[i,j]);
            END;
            WRITE('press any key to continue ');
            ch := ReadKey; WRITELN; WRITELN;
        END;
    END
    ELSE
        WRITELN('File is not a recognized data file');
    Close(filevar);
END.
```

The translated C version is shown below:

Listing 12.18

```
/* C program that reads a numeric matrix
   from a random-access file. The data format is:
   "DATA0"
   Title
   number of variables
   number of data points
   variable names
   numeric matrix
*/
#include <stdio.h>
#include <stdlib.h>
#include <string.h>
#include "conio.h"
#define MAX_COL 3
#define MAX_ROW 5
#define VAR_NAME_LEN 15
#define DATA_ID "DATA0"
#define STRING80 81
#define STRING15 16
#define MAX_LINES 22
enum booleans { FALSE, TRUE };
typedef enum booleans boolean;
typedef unsigned char byte;
typedef unsigned int word;
typedef union datarec_type
    {
        char str_field[STRING80];
        word int_field;
        char name_field[STRING15];
        double vect_field[MAX_COL];
    } datarec;
main()
{
```

BASIC FILE I/O   327

```c
boolean OK;
char ch, ans;
word i, j, k, nvar, ndata, count;
word datalen = sizeof(datarec);
double x[MAX_ROW][MAX_COL];
char varname[MAX_COL][STRING15];
datarec buffer;
char filename[STRING80], strng[STRING80], title[STRING80];
FILE *filevar;
clrscr();
do {
    printf("Enter filename -> ");
    gets(filename); printf("\n");
    if ((filevar = fopen(filename,"rb")) == NULL)
        printf("Cannot open %s\n\n",filename);
} while (filevar == NULL);
fseek(filevar, 0, SEEK_SET);
fread(&buffer, sizeof(datarec), 1, filevar);
strcpy(strng,buffer.str_field);
if (strcmp(strng,DATA_ID) == 0)  {
    fseek(filevar, datalen, SEEK_SET);
    fread(&buffer, sizeof(datarec), 1, filevar);
    strcpy(title,buffer.str_field);
    fseek(filevar, 2*datalen, SEEK_SET);
    fread(&buffer, sizeof(datarec), 1, filevar);
    nvar = buffer.int_field;
    fseek(filevar, 3*datalen, SEEK_SET);
    fread(&buffer, sizeof(datarec), 1, filevar);
    ndata = buffer.int_field;
    if ( ndata < 1 || ndata > MAX_ROW ||
         nvar  < 1 || nvar  > MAX_COL)   {
        printf("Size of rows or columns is out of bounds\n");
        printf("Number of variables = %d\n",nvar);
        printf("Number of data points = %d\n",ndata);
        exit(0);
    }
    k = 3;
    for (j = 0; j < nvar; j++)   {
        k++;
        fseek(filevar, k*datalen, SEEK_SET);
        fread(&buffer, sizeof(datarec), 1, filevar);
        strcpy(varname[j],buffer.name_field);
    }
    for (i = 0; i < ndata; i++)   {
        k++;
        fseek(filevar, k*datalen, SEEK_SET);
        fread(&buffer, sizeof(datarec), 1, filevar);
        for (j = 0; j < nvar; j++)
            x[i][j] = buffer.vect_field[j];
    }
    clrscr();
    printf("Title : %s\n",title);
    printf("File has %d variables and ",nvar);
    printf("%d data points\n\n",ndata);
    count = 5;
    for (i = 0; i < ndata; i++)   {
```

```
            for (j = 0; j < nvar; j++)  {
                count++;
                if (count > MAX_LINES)  {
                    count = 0;
                    printf("press any key to continue ");
                    ch = getche();
                }
                printf("%s[%d] = %lf\n",varname[j],i+1,x[i][j]);
            }
            printf("press any key to continue ");
            ch = getche(); printf("\n\n");
        }
    }
    else
        printf("File is not a recognized data file\n\n");
    fclose(filevar);
}
```

The above Pascal and C versions use the same data structures declared in their sister programs that write the data to files. The same comments on using the seek operation I made (regarding the output program) also apply to the above versions.

STREAM I/O ERROR

All of the programs presented so far tackled one type of system-based file error, namely, detecting bad-filename errors. The above programs assumed that once a file is opened everything proceeds smoothly. This approach is extremely optimistic and does not consider the case of errors that emerge as the file I/O is in progress. The "stdio.h" library provides two routines that permit you to handle such errors. They are **ferror** and **perror**. The **ferror** function takes one argument, the file pointer, and returns a numeric value that indicates the file I/O error status associated with the file pointer. A zero value indicates that the last file I/O operation was error-free. Conversely, a nonzero value indicates an error. The **perror** routine is a void-typed function that displays its string-typed argument. You may employ **perror** to display an error message of your choice.

To illustrate how the **ferror** and **perror** routines work, I will present a rewrite of the last C program. A new void-type function **check_input_error** is added to use **ferror** and **perror**. The **check_input_error** routine is inserted after every **fread** call to detect any error in data input. If there are any, you get the message "Bad read operation" and the program halts.

Listing 12.19

```
/* C program that reads a numeric matrix
   from a random-access file. The data format is:
   "DATA0"
     Title
     number of variables
```

```
       number of data points
       variable names
       numeric matrix
*/
#include <stdio.h>
#include <stdlib.h>
#include <string.h>
#include "conio.h"
#define MAX_COL 3
#define MAX_ROW 5
#define VAR_NAME_LEN 15
#define DATA_ID "DATA0"
#define STRING80 81
#define STRING15 16
#define MAX_LINES 22
enum booleans { FALSE, TRUE };
typedef enum booleans boolean;
typedef unsigned char byte;
typedef unsigned int word;
typedef union datarec_type
    {
       char str_field[STRING80];
       word int_field;
       char name_field[STRING15];
       double vect_field[MAX_COL];
    } datarec;
void check_input_error(FILE*);
main()
{
    boolean OK;
    char ch, ans;
    word i, j, k, nvar, ndata, count;
    word datalen = sizeof(datarec);
    double x[MAX_ROW][MAX_COL];
    char varname[MAX_COL][STRING15];
    datarec buffer;
    char filename[STRING80], strng[STRING80], title[STRING80];
    FILE *filevar;
    clrscr();
    do {
        printf("Enter filename -> ");
        gets(filename); printf("\n");
        if ((filevar = fopen(filename,"rb")) == NULL)
            printf("Cannot open %s\n\n",filename);
    } while (filevar == NULL);
    fseek(filevar, 0, SEEK_SET);
    fread(&buffer, sizeof(datarec), 1, filevar);
    strcpy(strng,buffer.str_field);
    if (strcmp(strng,DATA_ID) == 0)   {
        fseek(filevar, datalen, SEEK_SET);
        fread(&buffer, sizeof(datarec), 1, filevar);
        check_input_error(filevar);
        strcpy(title,buffer.str_field);
        fseek(filevar, 2*datalen, SEEK_SET);
        fread(&buffer, sizeof(datarec), 1, filevar);
        check_input_error(filevar);
```

```c
            nvar = buffer.int_field;
            fseek(filevar, 3*datalen, SEEK_SET);
            fread(&buffer, sizeof(datarec), 1, filevar);
            check_input_error(filevar);
            ndata = buffer.int_field;
            if ( ndata < 1 || ndata > MAX_ROW ||
                 nvar  < 1 || nvar  > MAX_COL)    {
                printf("Size of rows or columns is out of bounds\n");
                printf("Number of variables = %d\n",nvar);
                printf("Number of data points = %d\n",ndata);
                exit(0);
            }
            k = 3;
            for (j = 0; j < nvar; j++)   {
                k++;
                fseek(filevar, k*datalen, SEEK_SET);
                fread(&buffer, sizeof(datarec), 1, filevar);
                check_input_error(filevar);
                strcpy(varname[j],buffer.name_field);
            }
            for (i = 0; i < ndata; i++)   {
                k++;
                fseek(filevar, k*datalen, SEEK_SET);
                fread(&buffer, sizeof(datarec), 1, filevar);
                check_input_error(filevar);
                for (j = 0; j < nvar; j++)
                    x[i][j] = buffer.vect_field[j];
            }
            clrscr();
            printf("Title : %s\n",title);
            printf("File has %d variables and ",nvar);
            printf("%d data points\n\n",ndata);
            count = 5;
            for (i = 0; i < ndata; i++)   {
                for (j = 0; j < nvar; j++)   {
                    count++;
                    if (count > MAX_LINES)   {
                        count = 0;
                        printf("press any key to continue ");
                        ch = getche();
                    }
                    printf("%s[%d] = %lf\n",varname[j],i+1,x[i][j]);
                }
                printf("press any key to continue ");
                ch = getche(); printf("\n\n");
            }
        }
    else
        printf("File is not a recognized data file\n\n");
    fclose(filevar);
}
void check_input_error(FILE* fileptr)
{
    if (ferror(fileptr))   {
        perror("Bad read operation");
```

```
        fclose(fileptr);
        exit(0);
    }
}
```

BASIC LOW-LEVEL FILE I/O

In Turbo Pascal the **BlockRead** and **BlockWrite** procedures are used for low-level I/O. Untyped Pascal files and untyped variables are used to move blocks of bytes from a source file to a destination file. C has very similar routines that also perform low-level block I/O.

To read blocks of bytes from a binary file, use the following steps:

1. Declare a file handle as an **int** type instead of the FILE type.
2. Open the file using the **open** function, that utilizes the following general syntax:
   ```
   file_handle = open(filename, access_mode);
   ```
   If the file is successfully opened, the **open** function returns a nonnegative value. A value of -1 is returned if a bad filename or directory path is supplied. The **access_mode** defines the type of access allowed. Turbo C offers two sets of predefined flags, found in file "fcntl.h", that can be logically ORed. The first list is:

Flag	Meaning
O_RDONLY	Open for input only.
O_WRONLY	Open for output only.
O_RDWR	Open for both reading and writing.

Flags of the above set cannot be Ored with one another. This restriction is lifted for the second set:

Flag	Meaning
O_NDELAY	Not used. Available for UNIX compatibility.
O_APPEND	Open to append.
O_CREAT	Create the output file, if it does not exist.
O_TRUNC	Clear the file by truncating its length to 0.
O_EXCL	Not used. Available for UNIX compatibility.
O_BINARY	Open as a binary file.
O_TEXT	Open as a text file.

3. Read the blocks of bytes from the binary file using **read**, as shown below:
   ```
   num_read = read(file_handle, buffer_ptr, num_bytes);
   ```
   The **buffer_ptr** is the pointer to an array of characters acting as a buffer.

   The **num_bytes** is the requested number of bytes to read into the buffer. The **num_read** is the actual number of bytes read, a result returned by the **read** I/O function.

4. Close the file using **close(file_handle);**.

> **Program Translation**
>
> Pascal:
> ```
> CONST BUFFER = 1024;
> VAR file_handle : FILE;
>     filename : STRING[64];
>     data : ARRAY [1..BUFFER] OF CHAR;
>     num_read : WORD;
> Assign(file_handle, filename);
> Reset(file_handle,1);
> BlockRead(file_handle, data, BUFFER, num_read);
> Close(file_handle);
> ```
> C:
> ```
> #include <fcntl.h>
> #define BUFFER 1024
> int file_handle;
> char filename[65];
> char data[BUFFER];
> int num_read;
> file_handle = open(filename,
>                    <access mode depends on application>);
> numread = read(file_handle, data, BUFFER);
>
> close(file_handle);
> ```

To write blocks of bytes to a binary file, use the following steps:

1. Declare a file handle as an **int** type instead of the FILE type.
2. Open the file using the **open** function, just as in reading blocks of bytes.
3. Write the blocks of bytes from the binary file using **read**, as shown below:
   ```
   write(file_handle, buffer_ptr, num_bytes);
   ```
   The **buffer_ptr** is the pointer to an array of characters acting as a buffer. The **num_bytes** is the requested number of bytes to be copied from the buffer. The **write** function returns an integer that represents the number of bytes written, or -1 in the case of I/O error.
4. Close the file using **close(file_handle);**.

> **Program Translation**
>
> Pascal:
> ```
> CONST BUFFER = 1024;
> VAR file_handle : FILE;
>     filename : STRING[64];
>     data : ARRAY [1..BUFFER] OF CHAR;
>     num_read : WORD;
> Assign(file_handle, filename);
> Rewrite(file_handle,1);
> ```

BASIC FILE I/O

```
      BlockWrite(file_handle,data,num_write,num_actual_write);
      Close(file_handle);
```
C:
```
   #define BUFFER 1024
   int file_handle;
   char filename[65];
   char data[BUFFER];
   int num_read;
   file_handle = open(filename,
                      <access mode depends on application>);
   write(file_handle, data, num_write);

   close(file_handle);
```

The low-level block I/O is illustrated using the next program. The Pascal and C versions copy files from the current directory to another one. The general syntax for using the compiled program, call it "copyto", is

A> copyto <destination path> <filename1> <filename2>...

The destination path must end with a backslash. No wildcard filenames are allowed. The Pascal listing is shown below:

Listing 12.20

```
PROGRAM CopyTo;
{ Turbo Pascal program that copies files from the current
  directory to another directory.                        }
CONST BUFFER = 1024;
TYPE STRING80 = STRING[80];
VAR target : STRING80;
    buff_array : ARRAY [1..BUFFER] OF CHAR;
    i, num_read, num_write : WORD;
    in_handle, out_handle : FILE;
    in_ok, out_ok : BOOLEAN;
BEGIN
   IF ParamCount < 2 THEN BEGIN
      WRITE('Proper usage: copyto <destination dir> ');
      WRITELN('<list of filenames>');
      WRITELN('No wildcards are allowed');
      WRITELN; WRITELN;
      HALT;
   END;
   FOR i := 2 TO ParamCount DO BEGIN
      target := ParamStr(1) + ParamStr(i);
      Assign(in_handle,ParamStr(i));
      {$I-} Reset(in_handle, 1 { 1 byte is the record size});
      {$I+}
      in_ok := IOResult = 0;
      Assign(out_handle, target);
      {$I-} Rewrite(out_handle, 1 { 1 byte is the record size});
      {$I+}
      out_ok := IOResult = 0;
      IF in_ok AND out_ok THEN BEGIN
         WRITELN('Copying file ',ParamStr(i),' to ',target);
```

```
        REPEAT
            BlockRead(in_handle, buff_array,
                        SizeOf(buff_array), num_read);
            BlockWrite(out_handle, buff_array,
                        num_read, num_write);
        UNTIL (num_read = 0) OR (num_read <> num_write);
        Close(in_handle);
        Close(out_handle);
      END
      ELSE BEGIN
        IF NOT in_ok THEN
            WRITELN('Cannot open file ', ParamStr(i));
        IF NOT out_ok THEN
            WRITELN('Cannot open file ',target);
      END;
    END; { FOR }
END.
```

The C version is shown below:

Listing 12.21

```
/* C program that copies files from the current directory
   to another directory.
*/
#include <stdio.h>
#include "fcntl.h"
#define BUFFER 1024
main(int argc, char* argv[])
{
   char target[81];
   char buff_array[BUFFER];
   int i, in_handle, out_handle, num_read;
   if (argc < 2) {
      printf("Proper usage: copyto <destination dir> ");
      printf("<list of filenames>\n\n");
      printf("No wildcards are allowed\n\n");
      exit(0);
   }
   for (i = 2; i < argc; i++) {
      strcpy(target, argv[1]);
      strcat(target, argv[i]);
      in_handle = open(argv[i], O_RDONLY | O_BINARY | O_TEXT);
      out_handle = open(target, O_WRONLY | O_BINARY |
                                 O_TEXT    | O_CREAT   );
      if (in_handle && out_handle) {
         printf("Copying file %s tp %s\n", argv[i], target);
         while ((num_read = read(in_handle, buff_array, BUFFER)) > 0)
            write(out_handle, buff_array, num_read);
         close(in_handle);
         close(out_handle);
      }
      else {
         if (!in_handle)
            printf("Cannot open file %s\n\n", argv[i]);
```

```
        if (!out_handle)
            printf("Cannot open file %s\n\n",target);
    }
  }
}
```

In comparing the Pascal and C versions, notice the following:

1. The C version is able to use the integer-typed file handles as error flags. The Pascal version resorts to the boolean variables **in_ok** and **out_ok**.
2. The input file is opened with an access mode made up of the ORed values of the read-only, binary file, and text file flags:

   ```
   in_handle = open(argv[i], O_RDONLY | O_BINARY | O_TEXT);
   ```

   The access mode of the output file is made up of ORing the write-only, binary file, text file, and create-if-nonexistent flags:

   ```
   out_handle = open(target, O_WRONLY | O_BINARY |
                             O_TEXT    | O_CREAT   );
   ```
3. Low-level block copying in the Pascal version is carried out using the following REPEAT-UNTIL loop:

   ```
   REPEAT
       BlockRead(in_handle, buff_array,
                   SizeOf(buff_array), num_read);
       BlockWrite(out_handle, buff_array,
                   num_read, num_write);
   UNTIL (num_read = 0) OR (num_read <> num_write);
   ```

   while the C version uses a more compact while-loop:

   ```
   while ((num_read = read(in_handle,buff_array,BUFFER))>0)
       write(out_handle, buff_array, num_read);
   ```

   The while loop test is a form of **while not eof** and thus needs only to test the **num_read** for positive values. By contrast, the Pascal code needs an additional test in the UNTIL clause: the (**num_read <> num_write**) to detect whether or not the last portion of a copied file was accessed.

CHAPTER SUMMARY

C relies completely on external libraries for all I/O operations. The "stdio.h" contains popular file I/O functions that provide the programmer with much flexibility. C promotes the abstract concept of streams to unify treatment of data flow to various devices, such as disk drives, printers, communication ports, and the console. The "stdio.h" supports two types of streams, text and binary, as well as low-level system I/O. Since text streams are involved with the I/O of text, the related I/O functions perform character translation on the text-line delimiters. This translation is performed when reading and writing text streams. By contrast, binary streams are handled without any similar character translation.

- Opening and closing text and binary streams use the **fopen** and **fclose** functions. The general syntax for using **fopen** is

```
file_ptr = fopen(filename,"<I/O mode>");
```
The file pointer, **file_ptr,** is the file handle and is declared as:
```
FILE *file_ptr;
```
All further references to the file are made through the file pointer. If opening the file fails, a NULL value is assigned to the file pointer. A comparison of the file pointer with NULL should be used to verify that the file has been successfully opened. The filename is a string constant, variable, or expression that specifies the name of the DOS file involved. The I/O mode is specified by using one of the following:

I/O Mode	Implication
r	Open an existing file for input.
w	Open a file for output. If the file already exists, its contents are overwritten. If the file does not exist, it is created.
a	Open a file to append data. If the file does not exist, it is created.
r+	Open an existing file for input and output.
w+	Open a file for input and output. If the file already exists, its contents are overwritten.
a+	Open a file to append and read data. If the file does not exist, it is created.

In addition to the above I/O mode specifiers, you append the letter "t" to indicate that the file should be opened as a text file. Similarly, you may use "b" to specify that the file be opened as a binary file. The default is set by the predefined global variable **_fmode**.

- The general syntax for fclose is
  ```
  fclose(file_ptr);
  ```
- Character output in text stream is carried out using the **putchar** functions:
  ```
  putchar(ch, file_ptr);
  ```
- Read characters from the text stream using **getc**. To read to the end of the file, you may use one of two methods:
  1. The **foef** function, which works in a manner similar to Pascal's EOF, as shown below:
     ```
     while (!feof(file_ptr)) {
        ch = getc(file_ptr);
        /* other statements */
     }
     ```
  2. The C **EOF** constant as shown below:
     ```
     while ((ch = getc(infile)) != EOF) {
        /* loop body */
     }
     ```

The above method reads a character and also tests for the end-of-file marker in the while loop test.
- Write strings to a text stream using **fputs**, as shown below:
    ```
    fputs(string, file_ptr);
    fputs("\n", file_ptr);
    ```
    The second **fputs** ensures that your strings are delimited by newlines. You can also use **fprintf** to output strings:
    ```
    fprintf(file_ptr,"%s\n",string);
    ```
- Read the strings from a text stream using **fgets**. To read to the end of the file, use one of the following methods:
1. The **feof** function, as shown below:
    ```
    while (!feof(file_ptr)) {
        fgets(string, num_chars, file_ptr);
        /* other statements */
    }
    ```
2. The C **EOF** constant, as shown below:
    ```
    while (fgets(string, num_chars, file_ptr) != EOF) {
        /* loop body */
    }
    ```
- Writing variables, structures, unions, and arrays to a binary file uses **fwrite**, as shown below:
    ```
    fwrite(struct_ptr, size, num_items, file_ptr);
    ```
    The **fwrite** routine takes four parameters. The first is the pointer to the structure. The second is the size of the data object or structure. The third parameter is the number of data items read. The last one is the file pointer.
- Reading variables, structures, unions, and arrays to a binary file uses **fread**, as shown below:
    ```
    fread(struct_ptr, size, num_items, file_ptr);
    ```
    The **fread** routine takes four parameters. The first is the pointer to the structure. The second is the size of the data object or structure. The third parameter is the number of data items read. The last one is the file pointer. The **fread** function returns the number of items that were actually read.
- The **fseek** function may be used with binary streams to zoom in on a particular file location:
    ```
    fseek(file_ptr, offset, integer_reference_point);
    ```
    The **fseek** has three parameters. The first is the file pointer. The second is a long integer offset value which determines the distance, in bytes, from the reference point. The third parameter is an integer-typed reference point or anchor. Turbo C predefines three symbolic constants:

Reference Point	Value	File Location
SEEK_SET	0	File beginning.
SEEK_CUR	1	Current location.
SEEK_END	2	End of the file.

If you do not employ **fseek** before every data I/O, the file pointer moves to the next location in the file. This enables you to employ both sequential and random access schemes in accessing data using binary files.

- Low-level system I/O employs the **open, close, read, write,** and **seek** functions. These functions use integer-typed file handles instead of file pointers and delegate the task of managing the I/O buffer to the C application.

APPENDIX A

C Escape Sequences

Sequence	As Hex Value	Decimal Value	Task of Sequence
\a	0x07	7	Bell.
\b	0x08	8	Backspace.
\f	0x0C	12	Formfeed.
\n	0x0A	10	New line.
\r	0x0D	13	Carriage return.
\t	0x09	9	Horizontal tab.
\v	0x0B	1	Vertical Tab.
\\	0x5C	92	Backslash.
\'	0x2C	44	Single quote.
\"	0x22	34	Double quote.
\?	0x3F	63	Question Mark.
\OOO			1 to 3 digits for an octal value.
\XHHH and \xHHH	0xHHH		1 to 3 digits for a hexadecimal value.

339

APPENDIX B

Formatted I/O String Control

% [flags] [width] [.precision] [F|N|h|l] <type character>

Flag Character	Effect
-	Justify to the left within the designated field. The right side is padded with blanks.
+	Display the plus or minus sign of value.
blank	Display a leading blank if value is positive. If output is negative a minus sign is used.
#	Display a leading zero for octals. Display a leading 0X or 0x for hexadecimals. Display the decimal point for reals. No effect on integers.

Category	Type Character	Output Format
character	c	single character
integer	d	signed decimal int
	i	signed decimal int
	o	unsigned octal int
	u	unsigned decimal int
	x	unsigned hexadecimal int. The numeric character set used is [01234567890abcdef]
	X	unsigned hexadecimal int. The numeric character set used is [01234567890ABCDEF]
pointer	p	prints only offset of near pointers as AAAA and far pointers as SSSS:OOOO
pointer to int	n	
real	f	signed value in the form [-]dddd.dddd
	e	signed scientific format using [-]d.dddd e[+|-]ddd
	E	signed scientific format using [-]d.dddd E[+|-]ddd
	g	signed value using either 'e' or 'f' formats, depending on value and specified precision.
	G	signed value using either 'E' or 'f' formats, depending on value and specified precision.
string pointer	s	emits characters until a null-terminator or precision is attained.

APPENDIX C

Predefined Data Types in Turbo C

Simple Data Type	Byte Size	Value Range	Sample Constant(s)
char	1	-128 to 127	-5, 'a'
signed char	1	-128 to 127	5, 'b'
unsigned char	1	0 to 255	5, 'x'
int	2	-32768 to 32767	-234
signed int	2	-32768 to 32767	-344
unsigned int	2	0 to 65535	65000
short int	2	-32768 to 32767	1230
signed short int	2	-32768 to 32767	345
unsigned short int	2	0 to 65535	40000
long int	4	-2147483648 to 2147483647	1000000
signed long int	4	-2147483648 to 2147483647	-2000000
unsigned long int	4	0 to 4294967295	300000000
float	4	3.4E-38 to 3.4E+38 and -3.4E-38 to -3.4E+38	-1.23e-02
long float	8	1.7E-308 to 1.7E+308 and -1.7E-308 to -1.7E+308	2.3e+100
double	8	1.7E-308 to 1.7E+308 and -1.7E-308 to -1.7E+308	-4.32e-100
long double	8	1.7E-308 to 1.7E+308 and -1.7E-308 to -1.7E+308	12.34e+100

APPENDIX D

Operators in C

Arithmetic Operators

C Operator	Function
+	Unary Plus
-	Unary Minus
+	Add
-	Subtract
*	Multiply
/	Divide
%	Modulus

Relational Operators

C Operator	Pascal Operator
&&	AND
||	OR
!	NOT
N/A	XOR
<	<
<=	<=
>	>
>=	>=
==	=
!=	<>
? :	N/A

Arithmetic Assignment Operators

Assignment Operator	Equivalent Long Form
x += y	x = x + y
x -= y	x = x - y
x *= y	x = x * y
x /= y	x = x / y
x %= y	x = x % y

Bit-manipulating Operators

C Operator	Pascal Operator
&	AND
|	OR
^	XOR
~	NOT
<<	SHL
>>	SHR

Bit-manipulating Assignment Operators

C Operator	Long Form
x &= y	x = x & y
x |= y	x = x | y
x ^= y	x = x ^ y
x <<= y	x = x << y
x >>= y	x = x >> y

Operators in C with their precedence and evaluation direction

Category	Name	Symbol	Eval. Direction	Precedence
Selection	Parentheses	()	left to right	1
	Array indexing	[]	left to right	1
	Field reference	.	left to right	1
		->	left to right	1
Monadic	Post-increment	++	left to right	2
	Post-decrement	−	left to right	2
	Address	&	right to left	2
	Bitwise NOT	~	right to left	2
	Type cast	(type)	right to left	2
	Logical NOT	!	right to left	2
	Negation	−	right to left	2
	Plus sign	+	right to left	2
	Pre-increment	++	right to left	2
	Pre-decrement	−	right to left	2
	Type cast	(type)	right to left	2
	Size of data	sizeof	right to left	2
Multiplicative	Modulus	%	left to right	3
	Multiply	*	left to right	3
	Divide	/	left to right	3
Additive	Add	+	left to right	4
	Subtract	−	left to right	4
Bitwise Shift	Shift left	<<	left to right	5
	Shift right	>>	left to right	5
Relational	Less than	<	left to right	6
	Less or equal	<=	left to right	6
	Greater than	>	left to right	6
	Greater or equal	>=	left to right	6
	Equal to	==	left to right	7
	Not equal to	!=	left to right	7
Bitwise	AND	&	left to right	8
	XOR	^	left to right	9
	OR	|	left to right	10
Logical	AND	&&	left to right	11
	OR	||	left to right	12
Ternary	Cond. Express.	? :	right to left	13
Assignment	Arithmetic	=	right to left	14
		+=	right to left	14
		−=	right to left	14
		*=	right to left	14
		/=	right to left	14
		%=	right to left	14
Shift		>>=	right to left	14
		<<=	right to left	14
Bitwise		&=	right to left	14
		|=	right to left	14
		^=	right to left	14
Comma		,	left to right	15

APPENDIX E

Memory Models for Turbo C

	Pointer Reference		Number of 64K Segments for			
Model	to code	to data	data	code	total	one data object
tiny	near	near	[share 1]		1	1
small	near	near	1	1	2	1
medium	far	near	1	> 1	> 1	1
compact	near	far	> 1	1	> 1	1
llarge	far	far	> 1	> 1	> 1	1
huge	far	far	> 1	> 1	> 1	> 1

INDEX

Note: Bold page numbers indicate main discussion of a topic.

#define, **62-70**
#elif, 71
#else, 71
#endif, 71
#error, 71
#if, 71
#include, 71
#line, 72
#pragma, 72-73
#undef, **63**

A
advanced functions, 223
arrays, 11, 153
   multidimensional, 157-158
      storage of, 158
   one-dimensional, 153-154
   pointer access of, 161-162, 167-169
automatic variables, 140

B
basic console I/O, 7, **27-29**
break, 102, **104**

C
C program components, 4
calloc, 149
character escape sequences, 26
character I/O, 282-283
character input, 32
   getche, 32
   getch, 32
   getchar, 32
close, 332
clreol
   macro for, 70
   function for, 132, 135
clrscr
   macro for, 70
   function for, 132, 135
command line arguments, 259
comments in, C 4, 19
compiler directives, 71
   #elif, 71
   #else, 71
   #endif, 71
   #error, 71
   #if, 71
   #include, 71
   #line, 72
   #pragma, 72-73
conditional expression, **51-52**
constants, 7, **24**
continue, 102, **104**

345

D
decision-making, 7, **75**
  if-else, 9, **78-79**
    nested, 80-81
  if, 7, **75-76**
  switch, 9, **85-87**
    case label, 9, **85-87**
  do-while loop, 10, **105**

E
enumerated, 13, **187-189**
exit, 102, **104**
exiting functions, 137
extern variable, 143

F
fclose, 281
fclose, 281
feof, 282, 288
ferror, 328
fgets, 288
file I/O, 15
  modes, 279-280
  streams, 15, 32
    binary, 281, 306
    character, I/O 282-283
    feof, 282, 288
    ferror, 328
    fgets, 288
    fopen, 280
    fprintf, 300
    fputs, 287
    fread, 312-313, 323
    fscan,f 301, 305
    fseek, 317, 323
    fwrite, 306-308, 323
    getc, 282-283
    I/O error, 328
    perror, 328
    putchar, 282
    string I/O, 286-289
    text, 281, 295-296, 301-302
fopen, 280

for loop, 10, **96**
  nested, 99
fprintf, 300
fputs, 287
fread, 312-313, 323
free, 149
fscanf, 301, 305
fseek, 317, 323
function arguments
  using arrays as, 223-224, 240-241
  using strings as, 227, 236
  using struct as, 229-230, 237-238, 244-245
  using addresses as, 231-232
  variable number of, 275-277
functions, 14
fwrite, 306-308, 323

G
getc, 282-283
getch, 32
getchar, 32
getche, 32
goto, 102
gotoxy
  macro for, 70
  function for, 132, 135

I
if, 7, **75-76**
if-else, 9, **78-79**
  nested, 80-81

L
library of string functions, 176-182
loops, 10, **95**
  do-while loop, 10, **105**
  for loop, 10, **96**
    nested, 99
  while loop, 11, **111**
low-level I/O, 331-333
  close, 332
  open, 331
  read, 331

write, 332-333

M
main function, 4, 19
malloc, 149

O
open, 331
operators, 6, 36
    arithemtic, 36
        table of, 39
    assignment, 39
        table of, 41
    bitwise, **55-56**
        table of, 55-56
    character, **43-44**
    comma, 58
    decrement, 39
    increment, 39
    pointer, 148-149
    precedence of, 58-59
    relational **51-52**
        table of, 51
    sizeof, 45
    table of, 58-59

P
perror, 328
pointers, 148
    to simple types, 148-149
    to functions, 262, 266-268
    dynamic allocation with, 149-150
    dynamic deallocation of, 149-150
    far, 218-219
    malloc, 149
    calloc, 149
    free, 149
predefined macros, 71
preprocessors, 62
    #define, **62-70**
    #undef, **63**
printf, **26-29**
    format options, 27, 28-29
putchar, 282

R
random-access file, I/O
    using unions for output with, 316-318
    using unions for input with, 323-324
read, 331
recursive functions, 135-136
register variable, 144

S
scanf, **29**
scope of variables, 144
sequential file, I/O
    numeric data output using, 295-296
    numeric data input using, 301-302
    structured data output using, 306-308
    structured data input using, 312-313
simple C functions, 120-122
    parameter list
        ANSI, 122-123
        K&R, 122-123
    void functions, 131-132
    recursive functions, 135-136
    exiting functions, 137
simple data types, 5, **20-21**
    type modifier, 20
standard I/O devices, 289
static variables, 140
storage classes, 139-144
    automatic variables, 140
    extern variable, 143
    register variable, 144
    static variables, 140
streams, 15, 32
    binary, 281, 306
    character I/O, 282-283
    feof, 282, 288
    ferror, 328
    fgets, 288
    fopen, 280
    fprintf, 300
    fputs, 287
    fread, 312-313, 323
    fscanf, 301, 305
    fseek, 317, 323

fwrite, 306-308, 323
getc, 282-283
I/O error, 328
perror, 328
putchar, 282
string I/O, 286-289
text, 281, 295-296, 301-302
string I/O, 286-289
strings, 12, **169**
struct, 13, **193-195**
   arrays of, 196
   accessing arrays of, 196
   bitfields, 203-204
   using pointer to, 205-206
structure, *see struct*
switch, 9, **85-87**
   case label, 9, **85-87**

T
type casting, **47-48**
typedef, 185-186

U
unions, 211-212
   pointer to, 212
user-defined types, 13

V
void functions, 131-132

W
while loop, 11, **111**
write, 332-333

If you hate typing, read this!

Many programmers dislike typing source code that is already available in electronic form. They find it a complete waste of time to key in listings and spend even more time hunting for typos.

This offer provides you instant access to the code in this book. It enables you to begin utilizing the book's programs. You may select one of two disk formats made available for your convenience: Two 5.25" DSDD, or one 5.25" HD.

Send your order to:

Namir C. Shammas
P.O. Box 1297
Glen Allen, VA 23060
Attention: Pascal to C Disk Offer

Please send me copies of the Pascal to C disk. Enclosed is a check or money order for $24.95 (shipping & handling included).

Disk format available:

    5.25" DSDD _____ (Default Choice)

    5.25" HD   _____ (Need AT drive)

Please type or print the information below:

Name _____

Company (for Business Address) _____

Address _____

City _____ State _____ Zip Code _____

Daytime Phone (_____) _____ - _____